POLICE-COMMUNITY RELATIONSHIPS

AN INTRODUCTORY
UNDERGRADUATE READER

POLICE-COMMUNITY RELATIONSHIPS

Edited by

WILLIAM J. BOPP

Assistant Professor of Law Enforcement
Florida Technological University
Orlando, Florida

Formerly with
Dade County, Florida, Public Safety Department
Oakland, California, Police Department
Central Piedmont Community College

HV
7936
.P8
B65

CHARLES C THOMAS • PUBLISHER
Springfield • Illinois • U.S.A.

Published and Distributed Throughout the World by
CHARLES C THOMAS • PUBLISHER
BANNERSTONE HOUSE
301–327 East Lawrence Avenue, Springfield, Illinois, U.S.A.

This book is protected by copyright. No part of it may be reproduced in any manner without written permission from the publisher.

© 1972, by CHARLES C THOMAS • PUBLISHER

ISBN 0-398-02461-8

Library of Congress Catalog Card Number: 70-187645

With THOMAS BOOKS *careful attention is given to all details of manufacturing and design. It is the Publisher's desire to present books that are satisfactory as to their physical qualities and artistic possibilities and appropriate for their particular use.* THOMAS BOOKS *will be true to those laws of quality that assure a good name and good will.*

Printed in the United States of America
BB-14

CONTRIBUTORS

Thomas J. Aaron

Jean Anderton

Carter Barber
Star News
Pasadena, California

Harold Barney
International Association
of Chiefs of Police

George Berkley
Tufts University
Medford, Massachusetts

David A. Booth
Department of Government
University of Massachusetts
Amherst, Massachusetts

William J. Bopp
Assistant Professor
of Law Enforcement
Florida Technological University
Orlando, Florida

Lee P. Brown
Department of Law Enforcement
Portland State University
Portland, Oregon

Louis Cobarruviaz
Prevention and Control Division
San Jose Police Department
San Jose, California

J. Colling
Detroit Police Department
Detroit, Michigan

J.E. Curry
Chief of Police
Dallas Police Department
Dallas, Texas

Edgar Davis
Human Relations Section
Chicago Police Department

Robert L. Derbyshire

J. Ross Donald
Deputy Chief
San Jose Police Department
San Jose, California

Edward Doyle
New York Police Department
New York, New York

Howard H. Earle
Office of the Sheriff
Los Angeles County, California

Fred Ferguson

G. Thomas Gitchoff
Director, Criminal Justice Program
San Diego State College
San Diego, California

Solomon Gross
Law Enforcement Program
Northwestern Connecticut
  Community College
Winsted, Connecticut

Jack Harpster

Everett F. Holladay
Chief of Police
Monterey Park, California

Leroy C. Jenkins
Police Chief
Racine, Wisconsin

James P. Kelley
Athol-Royalston School District
Athol, Massachusetts

Keith Kellogg
Student
University of Minnesota
Minneapolis, Minnesota

Henry Kennedy
Department of Political Science
Florida Technological University
Orlando, Florida

Glen D. King
Information Services Division
International Association of
  Chiefs of Police

M.R. Kopmeyer

Jack L. Kuykendall
Department of Administration
  of Justice
San Jose State College
San Jose, California

Lee E. Lawder
Editor Emeritus
Law and Order

William McGarry
New York Police Department
New York, New York

Louis W. McHardy
Circuit Court Judge
St. Louis, Missouri

Geraldine Michael
Independence, Missouri

Clement S. Mihanovich
St. Louis University
St. Louis, Missouri

Raymond M. Momboisse
Attorney General's Office
State of California
Sacramento, California

J. Morche
Detroit Police Department
Detroit, Michigan

George D. Olivet
New York Police Department
New York, New York

Louis A. Radelet
School of Criminal Justice
Michigan State University
East Lansing, Michigan

Roger Ricklefs
Wall Street Journal

Donald O. Schultz
Department of Police Science
Broward Community College
Ft. Lauderdale, Florida

Heber Taylor
Public Relations
Memphis State University
Memphis, Tennessee

Contributors

Bruce J. Terris
Attorney at Law
Washington, D. C.

Robert Y. Thornton

Sterling Tucker
National Urban League, Inc.

L.G. Tyler
William Temple College
Rugby, England

Piet J. Van der Walt
University of South Africa
  in Pretoria
Pretoria, South Africa

Walter Varnes
Monterey Park
  Police Department
Monterey Park, California

Roy A. Wilson
Commissioner of Police
Canberra City, Australia

T.T. Winant
Illinois State University
Normal, Illinois

Donald Wrightington
Harwich Police Department
Harwich (Massachusetts)

PREFACE

In this technological age, the primary objectives of the police—to protect life and property and to prevent crime and maintain order—have not changed one whit from when colonial constables walked America's cobblestone streets shouting out the time and loudly informing all of the state of the settlement. But although the goals of law enforcement have remained relatively intact, the relationship of the police to the general community has, over the years, undergone dramatic changes, motivated in no small measure by the fluid social structure of a nation constantly (it seems) in transition. Unfortunately, police-community relations have deteriorated to the point that in some communities, outright hatred and violent action have been aimed at police officers, an outpouring that has achieved a degree of mutuality from the ranks of the men in blue. What has transpired during the past several centuries to bring on this sad state of affairs? The theories are numerous, but one only needs to read the daily newspaper to determine that the police, especially those working in urban settings, are facing an uphill fight in their battle to win the public's confidence.

The dilemma that historically aware police administrators find themselves facing is this: How do you on the one hand *professionalize* your police department, and on the other improve its relationship with the community, in light of almost overpowering historical data which clearly indicates that as law enforcement has become more professional, the social distance between police and the public has increased, though not necessarily in direct proportion.

A century ago, American law enforcement was characterized by corruption, collusive involvement with criminals, brutality, and political domination. However, policing in the "old days" was characterized by something else, an element that may aptly be termed *social consciousness*, for aside from their traditional enforcement duties, police forces functioned as a kind of social service agency, performing charitable and humanitarian services which would otherwise have gone undischarged. Drunks and indigents were lodged in jail in lieu of arrest. Hundreds of gallons of soup and tons of bread were dispensed to the needy, who twice daily lined up in the rear of the station houses. Christmas food baskets were given to deprived families. Policemen served as parole officers, social workers and youth counselors. In fact, the country's first probation officer was a former Boston police chief, Edward H. Savage.

In addition, policemen were physically closer to the community. They walked beats singularly and in pairs, often in the very neighborhoods in which they lived. Each identifiable city neighborhood had a precinct station, easily accessible to most residents. Interested citizens formed police reserves to assist their neighbors, the police. Then came progress, the age of specialization, technology and the technician, whose emphasis was on managerial efficiency, seemingly to the exclusion of humane practice. Social welfare services were grasped from the police and assigned to specialized agencies. Officers were relieved of walking duty and assigned to patrol cars.* Precincts were closed and police operations were centralized. Police budgets became cold instruments that reflected the end result of cost-benefit analysis, bereft of the human factor.

Yet, to even infer that the crisis in police-community relations is solely the result of police professionalization is to perpetrate a fraud. The issue is too complex to lend itself easily to single explanations and simplistic solutions. As government's most visible representatives, the police have been consistently thrust stopgap into situations not of their making—labor disputes, racial disorders, student revolts, protest demonstrations. They have been ordered to enforce the unenforceable, to partially and selectively regulate public morality, and to solve, through traditional means, massive social issues that have been classified as "crimes"—narcotics abuse, drunkenness, traffic accidents.

* Changing the national description of an approaching law enforcement officer from "here comes a *policeman*" to "here comes a *police car*," grim testimony to encroaching isolationism and depersonalization.

Preface

Recognizing the critical importance of improving the relationship between the police and the community, experts in the field have produced a wealth of written material on the subject, an outpouring which is aimed at attacking foresquare an issue of overwhelming social significance. This book brings together a number of varied perspectives, collected, arranged and introduced in a way calculated to make the work both interesting and meaningful. The purpose of the book is to present facts and concepts essential for an understanding of the relationship between law enforcement and citizens. It is designed primarily for undergraduate criminal-justice students, and is divided into seven main parts, each of which offers an intensive view of a police-community relation's subfield or crisis area. Each of the main divisions is designed to develop more limited objectives which, in turn, contribute to the overall objective of developing an understanding of this critical issue.

The purpose of Part I is to provide an understanding of the nature of the role(s) of the police in the community; to gain an insight, through a number of perspectives, into the philosophical nature of the police task. In Parts II, III and IV, the intent is to lead the student to an understanding of the relationship between the police and three components of the total community—minority groups, young people and the press.

Part V is designed to acquaint students with the foreign police experience, with selected readings on police administration and community relations in other lands. Part VI introduces the *concepts* of police-community relations, while Part VII presents a field-oriented view of the concepts as workable elements of a total P-CR system.

CONTENTS

                       Page

Contributors v

Preface ix

PART I
PERSPECTIVES ON THE ROLE OF THE POLICE IN THE COMMUNITY

Introduction 5

Chapter

1. THE POLICE—*William J. Bopp and Donald O. Schultz* 7
2. A POLICEMAN'S JOB IS TO . . . HELP!—*M.R. Kopmeyer* 10
3. THE ROLE OF THE POLICE—*Bruce J. Terris* 22
4. THE SOCIAL-CONTROL OF THE POLICE IN CHANGING URBAN COMMUNITIES—*Robert L. Derbyshire* 39
5. POLICE-COMMUNITY RELATIONS: THE ROLE OF THE FIRST-LINE PEACE OFFICER—*Howard H. Earle* 46
6. THE POLICE GO TO WAR—*William J. Bopp and Donald O. Schultz* 58
7. "LAW AND ORDER" GAINS WHERE LEAST LIKELY—GREENWICH VILLAGE—*Roger Ricklefs* 61
8. SOCIAL SCIENCE EDUCATION FOR POLICE OFFICERS—*Geraldine Michael* 65
9. A DYING ART?—*William J. Bopp* 78

PART II
MINORITY GROUPS AND THE POLICE

	Page
Introduction	85

Chapter

10. THE EFFECT OF PREJUDICE ON MINORITIES—*J.E. Curry and Glen D. King* 86

11. POLICE AND MINORITY GROUPS: TOWARD A THEORY OF NEGATIVE CONTACTS—*Jack L. Kuykendall* 91

12. SOCIAL CHANGE AND THE POLICE—*Louis A. Radelet* 113

13. THE NEGRO COMMUNITY—*President's Commission on Law Enforcement and Administration of Justice* 125

14. THE POLICE AND THE COMMUNITY—*National Advisory Commission on Civil Disorders* 133

15. THE GHETTO, THE GHETTOIZED AND CRIME—*Sterling Tucker* .. 144

PART III
YOUTH AND THE POLICE

Introduction 159

16. POLICE RESPONSE TO JUVENILE HOSTILITY IN SUBURBIA—*G. Thomas Gitchoff* 160

17. SCHOOL VS. COPS—*James P. Kelley* 173

18. THE COURT, THE POLICE AND THE SCHOOL—*Louis W. McHardy* 177

19. COP ON CAMPUS—*Walter Varnes* 184

20. MARYLAND STATE POLICE'S STUDENT TRAINING PROGRAM—*Lee E. Lawder* 188

21. CAMPUS CONFRONTATION—NORTHWESTERN STYLE—*Solomon Gross* 190

PART IV
THE PRESS AND THE PEOPLE

Introduction 197

Chapter

22. IMPORTANCE OF THE NEWS MEDIA—*Raymond M. Momboisse* . 199

23. A MAGNA CARTA FOR MEDIA-POLICE RELATIONS—*Carter Barber* 205

24. WINNING AN IMPORTANT ALLY—*Jack Harpster* 215

25. CAMPUS TO SQUAD ROOM—*Heber Taylor* 220

PART V
THE FOREIGN EXPERIENCE

Introduction 229

26. THE EUROPEAN POLICE: CHALLENGE AND CHANGE—
    George Berkley 231

27. LAW ENFORCEMENT IN GREAT BRITAIN—*David A. Booth* 245

28. THE POLICE AND SOCIAL TENSION—*L.G. Tyler* 256

29. THE ROYAL ULSTER CONSTABULARY: ITS FUNCTION AND CHANGING ROLE—*Henry Kennedy* 261

30. POLICE ADMINISTRATION IN AUSTRALIA—*Roy A. Wilson* 276

31. THE DANISH POLICE: FUNCTION, ORGANIZATION AND ADMINISTRATION—*Thomas J. Aaron* 292

32. THE POLICE OF TOKYO—*T.T. Winant* 304

33. THE KIDOTAI—*Robert Y. Thornton* 312

PART VI
AN INTRODUCTION TO THE POLICE-COMMUNITY RELATIONS CONCEPT

Introduction 339

34. POLICE-COMMUNITY RELATIONS—*William J. Bopp and Donald O. Schultz* 340

Chapter	Page
35. TYPOLOGY—*Lee P. Brown*	343
36. PROGRAMMING FOR CITIZEN PARTICIPATION IN POLICE ACTION PROGRAMS—*Clement S. Mihanovich*	354
37. COMMUNITY RELATIONS—*Harold Barney*	366
38. POLICE AND PUBLIC—*Piet J. Van der Walt*	371
39. A METHOD OF APPROACH TO THE TASKS OF A HUMAN RELATIONS OFFICER—*Edgar Davis*	380
40. PUBLIC RELATIONS FOR A SMALL DEPARTMENT—*Donald Wrightington*	388
41. OBSTACLES TO GOOD POLICE-COMMUNITY RELATIONS—*William J. Bopp*	392

PART VII
OPERATIONALIZING THE POLICE-COMMUNITY RELATIONS CONCEPT

Introduction	399
42. STOREFRONT CENTERS—*Glen D. King*	401
43. UNIFORMS AND THE DEPARTMENT IMAGE—*Keith Kellog*	409
44. DETROIT'S NEW "COMMUNITY-ORIENTED PATROL"—*J. Morche and J. Colling*	413
45. POLICE-COMMUNITY RELATIONS COFFEE KLATCH PROGRAM—*Jean Anderton and Fred Ferguson*	417
46. FOOTBRIDGES FOR LAW ENFORCEMENT—*Everett F. Holladay*	425
47. AN INVITATION TO UNDERSTANDING—*William McGarry, Edward Doyle and George D. Olivet*	428
48. ELIMINATING THE LANGUAGE BARRIER—*J. Ross Donald and Louis Cobarruviaz*	442
49. "IT DOESN'T LOOK LIKE A POLICE STATION"—*Leroy C. Jenkins*	445

POLICE-COMMUNITY RELATIONSHIPS

PART I

PERSPECTIVES ON THE ROLE OF THE POLICE IN THE COMMUNITY

INTRODUCTION

To the citizen, a policeman's job is to "handle" calls in as expeditious a manner as possible, to capture robbers and burglars and to maintain "law and order." However, simplistic definitions of the police task do not allow for the fact that the vast majority of law enforcements activities are noncriminal in nature. Many police calls are, in fact, service-related, with the responding patrolman acting more as a social service officer than a policeman. In addition, police work is becoming increasingly *situational*. That is, the rapidly unfolding events in a community make it essential that officers be able to adapt to fluid situations. Pragmatically and philosophically, policemen are required to fill a variety of roles, to wear a number of hats, some simultaneously. The eight readings in this section address themselves to the question of just what types of attitudinal attributes and role models the police should adopt in American society.

Chapter 1, "The Police," by William Bopp and Donald Schultz, gives the sterile textbook definition of the role of the police. Chapter 2, M.R. Kopmeyer's "A Policeman's Job Is to Help!" defines the police job in terms of helpfulness, community service and an ability to demonstrate and sell to the public an image that is based on the service ideal. Bruce J. Terris', "The Role of the Police," is based on the assumption that problems in police-community relations are in reality problems in police-minority relations, a difficulty which will not be lessened by conventional police professionalization, such as higher education, human relations training and minority recruitment. Instead, Terris recommends that, due to the delicate nature of the police task, people skilled in interpersonal relations—teachers, recreation workers, social workers—should be encouraged to seek police careers and that the concept of lateral entry should be expanded so that these professionals will not have to start at the bottom, a somewhat confusing thesis, since the battle for good community relations is being fought at the bottom.

In Chapter 4, Robert L. Derbyshire presents a discourse on "The Social Control Role of the Police in Changing Urban Communities" and offers a number of suggestions for improving crime-prevention techniques during periods of rapid social change.

In "Police-Community Relations: The Role of the Firstline Peace Officer," P-CR expert Howard H. Earle contends, rather realistically, that it is the individual police officer, not community relations specialists, who most encounters ciitzens, so it is he who must be reached and persuaded to accept his social responsibilities in the community as a solemn public trust.

Chapter 6, "The Police Go to War," by Bopp and Schultz, is a brief historical excerpt that describes law enforcement during World War II, a time of international strife and domestic peace, when citizen involvement with *their* police, and vice versa, may very well have represented law enforcement's finest hour in terms of mutual trust, respect and admiration.

Roger Ricklefs' "Law and Order Gains Where Least Likely—Greenwich Village" recounts the struggle of a group of residents in New York City's bohemian community to secure their persons and property in the wake of rampant drug abuse and violent crime. Like the previous article, it illustrates how, during times of crisis, personal animosity, political ideology and mutual hostility are pushed aside when abstract issues become bitter flesh-and-blood realities.

Chapters 8 and 9, "Social Science Education for Police Officers," and "(Police Administration) A Dying Art?" present mildly competitive philosophies regarding the way in which police officers should be educated, an important factor in police role definition. In the first, Geraldine Michael reveals the findings of a study which indicates the necessity for broad social science education, while in the second, Bopp recognizes the need for a "liberal" broad-based education, but not to the exclusion of technical coursework that will help patrolmen to someday ascend to leadership position their agencies.

Chapter 1

THE POLICE

WILLIAM J. BOPP and DONALD O. SCHULTZ

Over the years, law enforcement has become increasingly complex. A century ago, police officers communicated with one another by rapping their nightsticks on the cobblestone streets; today computerized radio systems do the job. Sophisticated hardware has replaced the crude devices of old; extended periods of training have replaced the early apprenticeship system; helicopters and automobiles have replaced fixed-post sentries and horse-drawn patrol wagons. Yet, contemporary policemen have the same general objectives as did their counterparts of old:

1. To protect life and property and safeguard the individual liberties guaranteed by the Constitution.
2. To prevent crime and disorder and preserve the peace.

Policemen are given certain limited powers to pursue these objectives. Those powers are either derived from or limited by six sources:

1. The United States Constitution.
2. Legislation of the United States Congress.
3. Legislative enactments of the various states.
4. Local and county ordinances.
5. Court decisions interpreting the constitutions and the statutes.
6. Court precedents.

THE POLICE MISSION[1]

The police mission, succinctly stated, is maintenance of social order within carefully prescribed ethical and constitutional restrictions. The mission, as currently defined, involves:

NOTE: From Bopp, W.J. and Schultz, D.O.: *Principles of American Law Enforcement and Criminal Justice*. Springfield, Thomas, 1972.
[1] Reprinted with permission from the International City Management Association's *Municipal Police Administration*, Washington, The International City Management Association, 1969, pp. 3–4.

1. *The prevention of criminality.* This activity views the police role in constructive terms and involves taking the police into sectors of the community where criminal tendencies are bred and individuals motivated to indulge in antisocial behavior, and includes seeking to reduce causes of crime.
2. *Repression of crime.* This activity stresses adequate patrol plus a continuing effort toward eliminating or reducing hazards as the principal means of reducing the opportunities for criminal actions.
3. *Apprehension of offenders.* This activity views quick apprehension as the means to discourage the would-be offender. The certainty of arrest and prosecution has a deterrent quality which is intended to make crime seem less worthwhile. Additionally, apprehension enables society to punish offenders, lessens the prospect of repetition by causing suspects to be incarcerated and provides an opportunity for rehabilitation of those convicted.
4. *Recovery of property.* This activity seeks to reduce the monetary cost of crime, as well as to restrain those who, though not active criminals, might benefit from the gains of crime.
5. *Regulation of noncriminal conduct.* This aspect of the police mission involves sundry activities that are only incidentally concerned with criminal behavior, such as the enforcement of traffic and sanitary code provisions. The main purpose is regulation, and apprehension and punishment of offenders are means of securing compliance. Other methods used to obtain compliance are education (e.g. observance of laws) and the use of warnings, either oral or written, to inform citizens of the violations without taking punitive actions.
6. *Performance of miscellaneous services.* This involves many service activities peripheral to basic police duties and includes, for example, the operation of detention facilities, search-and-rescue operations, licensing, supervising elections, staffing courts with administrative and security personnel, and even such completely extraneous things as chauffeuring officials.

While these six general responsibilities may be accepted by the police and the community at large as the police mission, there is often sharp disagreement on the appropriateness of specific methods and operations used to fulfill them. Various groups may staunchly defend different points of view or values and seemingly or actually work against one another; the resulting conflict may cause the police to fall short in reaching the common objective—superior law enforcement protection for the community.

Chapter 2

A POLICEMAN'S JOB IS TO . . . HELP!

M. R. KOPMEYER

REPLACE "POLICE BRUTALITY" WITH "POLICE HELPFULNESS"

Police brutality is a wrong impression which antagonizes and alienates people. A recent survey of a cross-section of public opinion showed that more than 70 per cent strongly believe that police brutality exists and should be eliminated. Public belief in the continued existence of police brutality is harmful to law enforcement because, among many other reasons, it causes public resentment and ill will toward the police. A police department cannot operate effectively and efficiently without the willing cooperation, support and good will of the public which it serves and with which it constantly deals. A police department which does not have the respect, admiration, willing cooperation and support of the public is in deep trouble.

It is not enough to say that the public impression of "police brutality" is undeserved, unfair and untrue. It is not enough to say that the public does not realize nor understand the deliberate provocations, the abusive language and actions, the unseen as well as seen physical dangers to which the police are so frequently exposed.

It is sufficient to say that the hated image of police brutality must be eliminated and replaced with the contrasting impression of police helpfulness.

Neither the individual mind nor the public mind can hold two opposite thoughts (images) at the same time. So if the police establish a new public image of helpfulness, the old public image of police brutality will soon disappear.

Police rightly claim that they already are helpful. Of course

NOTE: From *Police*, July-August, 1970, pp. 68–72.

they are! People call on the police for help in almost every kind of emergency, and in many nonemergencies. Unfortunately, the kind of help which the police provide with routine efficiency is taken for granted. People expect it as a matter of course. It is the kind of help for which police are paid. So to provide the kind of help which will replace the public image of police brutality, the police need to provide additional help in a way which is the complete opposite of force. Force, even if it is not brutal, implies the real potential of brutality.

Police must do more than protect the community. The police must assist the community for two reasons:

1. The police have the manpower, organization, equipment, training, skills, communications, and mobility to provide a massive 24-hour-a-day, 7-days-a-week community assistance service to greatly supplement and implement the existing social and welfare services.
2. Police must become involved in this type of police helpfulness to replace the image of police brutality.

The police department is the only service which can—and already does—provide 24-hour, 7-days-a-week total community coverage with instant mobility and two-way communication. Thus, the police already have the manpower, organization, and constant mobile community coverage with the opportunity to observe and know individuals and groups, to appraise conditions, note apparent needs and inquire concerning less-apparent needs. This is an unequalled community asset which should become an integral part of the total community-assistance program. It would in no way replace or duplicate the services and value of any present social service or community-welfare agency. It would immeasurably assist, supplement and implement them.

The assistance, cooperation and coordination of the police department, with its manpower, organization, fast mobility, continuity of coverage and communications, is the only way to provide a total community-assistance program. The obvious lack of total community assistance is the result of not fully utilizing the resources of the police in new and imaginative ways in greater cooperation and coordination with more specialized social service and welfare agencies.

It is undeniable that there is need for more massive and more efficient community assistance, group assistance and individual assistance, in impoverished, underprivileged and "trouble" neighborhoods and communities. The overworked, understaffed, underfinanced social-service agencies need police help. By providing community assistance in the manner suggested later, police will increase their efficiency and effectiveness in maintaining law and order, because of the following:

1. Police community assistance will replace public resentment of police brutality (real or imagined) and will replace ill will which exists toward some policemen, with friendship and goodwill at the community level.

2. Friendship and goodwill toward all policemen will provide acceptance, cooperation, confidential information and actual assistance by individuals, groups and the community—all of which make the policemen's jobs easier and more effective. It is very, very difficult, as well as much more dangerous, to police a hostile community.

3. Police community assistance permits police involvement in community activities and problems which usually are in some way related to impending trouble. Thus the police often can stop trouble before it starts or, with group or individual cooperation, keep minor disturbances from escalating.

4. Police community assistance pays for itself because it makes law enforcement easier. It requires no appreciable increase in personnel unless and until results prove that increases are desirable and feasible. The same men are in the same place, and the first priority is, of course, law enforcement. Since most police time is spent patrolling, community assistance should be an organized part of patrolling and surveillance.

ORGANIZING YOUR OWN COMMUNITY ASSISTANCE DIVISION

First, you simply announce that your police department has established a Community-Assistance Division, which will include every member of your own Police Department. Your community-assistance division will be your entire Police Department, exactly as is. You do not actually change anything except its attitude and community involvement. No personnel changes are made. No changes are made in rank, position, law-enforcement duties or anything which would in any way disrupt or complicate your present law-enforcement procedures.

You do change the attitude of your entire department and instruct your total personnel in becoming personally involved in the interests, activities and problems of the areas they patrol. Specific suggestions will be made later in this chapter. Basically, you draw up a list of all the ways in which your policemen can be friendly and helpful. Then you instruct and train your men to do those things, some of which will be beyond routine duties.

Make a personnel inventory of the skills which each man in your police department has which are not necessarily associated with routine police work. These might include taking movies; projecting movies and slides; speaking to small groups or to large groups; supervising groups of children, teen-agers and adults on tours and trips; coaching athletic teams; obtaining merchandise, equipment and materials; enlisting volunteers, etc.

SELLING THE IDEA TO THE PUBLIC

The following are a few suggestions on how to "sell" your police department as a community-assistance service.

1. Announce that your Police Department now has a Community-Assistance Division. Announce it through every available advertising, publicity and public relations media. Depending upon the size of your city, you can obtain—free—from thousands to millions of dollars worth of very favorable publicity by announcing and actually conducting vital, interesting, exciting, newsworthy community-assistance programs.

2. Instruct all of your personnel to tell everybody about it. They should simply say, "Our Police Department now has a Community-Assistance Division. How can we help you?" Or, if the person addressed obviously does not need help, change the question to: "Do you know of someone who needs help?" You can change the question to suit the occasion, just so it em-

phasizes that your police department and every individual policeman wants to help.

3. Put focus on your community-assistance division by having letterheads, envelopes, personal cards, even ID cards, which conspicuously display in the most prominent type: "Community Assistance Division" and then under it in much smaller type: "(Your City) Police Department."

4. Except when performing actual law-enforcement duties, instruct all of your men to introduce themselves and to refer to themselves as being with: "The Community Assistance Division of the (Your City) Police Department.

COOPERATE WITH OTHER AGENCIES— DON'T REPLACE THEM

Following are some suggestions in winning the cooperation and goodwill of present social and welfare agencies already engaged in community assistance.

Be sure—be *very* sure—that all present social and welfare agencies, including city recreation and other departments, clearly understand that your police department's community assistance division is *not* going to *compete* with them or in any way replace them but that you will use your vast manpower and facilities to *help* them in whatever ways you can. Constantly and emphatically reassure all others engaged in community assistance that you do not have the intention, the desire or the funds to do more than help them but that you are placing at their service, *when and as available,* your 24-hour 7-day, community-wide, mobile manpower and communications resources for quickly providing highly trained emergency help fast. Also explain to all those now engaged in social and welfare services that because your community assistance division already provides complete, continuous coverage of all areas, with detailed knowledge of the conditions in each area, that you will be in constant communication with all appropriate agencies and that you will be able to provide them with cooperation and help not available from any other source. Do not do or say anything which implies a threat to the existence, future, or public regard for present social and welfare agencies or government departments. Your community assistance efforts are not to replace existing services, but to implement and expand them.

DEMONSTRATING HELPFULNESS

There are thousands of ideas which police can use to demonstrate friendliness, helpfulness and community assistance, and we will discuss a few of them. But first, remember it is *not* your job to provide financial welfare aid, family support or any continuing service normally provided by social-welfare agencies. You can help by putting the needy in the care of such agencies. You can communicate. You can coordinate. Every policeman should be provided with a directory of the names, addresses, phone numbers and listings of all services rendered by every welfare, social service and assistance agency in his city and surrounding area. Calls for help for which those agencies are financed, staffed, equipped and responsible for handling, should immediately be communicated to those agencies, with the police providing only the coordinating and communicating function in all cases brought first to their attention.

Police, of course, should continue to provide emergency and interim help, and should seek to expand the scope of those services. However, welfare and social cases should be promptly channeled to the proper agency.

It is highly desirable that police follow up on cases which come to them for help, even after such cases are directed to other agencies. Persons asking the police first for help continue to feel that the police have some responsibility in the matter and will blame the police if needed help is not provided. Also follow-up calls demonstrate police interest in, and concern for, the needy. This is one of the best ways to build a police reputation for helpfulness, friendliness, kindness—the opposite of police brutality.

Some of the thousands of other things police can do to build a police reputation for helpfulness, friendliness, kindness are the following:

1. Make a constant effort to maintain continuous clean-up,

fix-up, paint-up campaigns in the neighborhoods you patrol. Pitch in and help, yourself. Arrange with your police community-assistance division to obtain (by methods described herein) the necessary lumber, nails, tools, paint, brushes, etc. Be a leader! Organize each neighborhood. Get help from civic, social and labor organizations. Instill neighborhood pride.

2. Be sure the neighborhoods are all adequately supplied with closed garbage and trash containers. Carry a litter container in your police cruiser. Do not be too proud or too lazy to get out and pick up unsightly litter yourself. That is an easy and impressive way to demonstrate police helpfulness.

3. Report excessively littered neighborhoods to your City Sanitation Department. Arrange with them to have small litter clean-up trucks, manned by the hard-core unemployed, to make special runs to clean up littered neighborhoods. Be often conspicuously present yourself. Talk to the neighborhood leaders. Urge them to keep it clean. Police work? Yes indeed! Littered neighborhoods breed trouble. Your job is to prevent trouble, and one way of doing this is to remove litter.

4. Declare all-out war on rats. Do not be satisfied as long as there is even one rat in the entire area you patrol. Ask the residents if they know where there are any rats. Let them know that you will not tolerate rats on your beat. Track down rats as you would criminals—because they are. Then insist that your City Health and City Sanitation Departments exterminate all rats. Follow up. Ask the residents. Get a reputation for police helpfulness in getting rid of all rats.

5. Beautify! Yes, even the most rundown neighborhoods can be beautified to some extent. At least the residents will notice it and give you credit for police helpfulness. Of course clean-up, fix-up, paint-up campaigns come first. Then plant flowers, shrubs, even trees. Yes, you can, too! Even a drab tenement will be brighter with cans and jars, gaily painted and planted with pretty, inexpensive plants (which you can get free, or almost free from sympathetic florists, nurseries or gardeners). Where there is earth, there should be a shrub or tree.

6. People who would lift up the spirits of underprivileged and poverty neighborhoods often do not take advantage of the

fact that vast quantities of almost every kind of product become slightly imperfect for one reason or another and therefore unsalable to the affluent who demand perfection, so they are often discarded, given away to anyone who will take them (especially for charity) or sold for much less than cost. Yet these often slightly imperfect products and articles are welcomed by the poor who have too little of everything to require or even need perfection. This enables your police community-assistance division—through a persistent, friendly Procurement Department—to continuously acquire vast quantities of quite usable products, supplies and merchandise free or far below cost.

This applies to flowers, shrubs and trees. Florists, nurserymen and landscape gardeners all have flowers, shrubs or trees which are not perfect for their regular customers, so they will give or cheaply sell them to you, especially to help your police community-assistance division. You can help plant them to greatly improve the appearance of ugly, barren neighborhoods and instill pride.

Also, it is increasingly popular for the public to buy "living" Christmas trees, complete with roots, to be replanted after Christmas. Conduct a campaign to pick up these "living" trees after Christmas and plant them in underprivileged neighborhoods.

The procurement department of your police community-assistance division can acquire free, or at negligible cost, toys, balls, playground equipment and all kinds of merchandise which has become slightly soiled, shopworn, damaged or otherwise unsalable as perfect, but which is fixable and usable for your distribution where it will help. Then when you see a group of boys with nothing to do but look for trouble, do not harass them; give them a free basketball.

7. And, on the subject of giving to children, every policeman should have a supply of candy and chewing gum to make friends with all the children in the area he patrols. Being liked by children is excellent police public relations. And being liked by everybody is better—better than "police brutality."

8. Very big problems in large city ghettos and smaller underprivileged communities are transportation and change. People,

especially children and teenagers, who are constantly crowded in ghettos and poverty areas need different situations and changed environments which can only be provided by supervised free transportation and free admissions. These should be provided by the police, and this can be accomplished by getting a bus. In large cities, get a lot of buses, depending on the size of the city and the scope of the projects. Beg, borrow, rent or buy buses, new or used. Paint them in gay colors with your name (or the name of a public-spirited "sponsor" who pays for the bus).

9. One of the best way for police to win goodwill—and continuous, favorable, unlimited publicity in all news media—is to gather together a group of happy, excited children (teenagers and adults, too!) and take them in your bus or buses away from their depressing surroundings to a circus, ballgame, picnic, zoo, tour, boat ride, train ride, museum, fair, exhibit or sporting event—Anywhere, just so it is out of their depressing environment and so it is fun—always escorted by friendly, good-humored, fun-loving policemen!

Police, just by asking and explaining the need, can get free admission tickets to almost every amusement and sporting event. Promoters want a full house! Vacant seats provide no income and are bad advertising. Police can get them free for the underprivileged—if the police will provide transportation and supervision. Also, get civic clubs to "sponsor" underprivileged groups by paying for admission tickets at cut-rates.

COMMUNITY ASSISTANCE FUNDS, MATERIALS AND SERVICE

The following are a few suggestions about how and where to get the needed money:

1. "Charity begins at home." Every policeman should contribute at least a dollar out of every pay check to the police community-assistance fund. Officers should contribute more. Authorized deductions will make these collections easy, painless and automatic. Sure, I know that the police are underpaid. But this small amount contributed regularly by every policeman will enable them to say, "We are putting our own money into this."

2. Almost all police organizations have some money. Many have a lot. The Detroit Police Officers' Association recently spent 250,000 dollars to oppose a city amendment. Police organizations in Boston, Philadelphia and New York have huge sums. The New York Patrolmens' Benevolent Association has more than four million dollars which it uses for lobbying and police benefits. Local police organizations could contribute a "nest egg" to help get the police community-assistance fund off to a good start.

3. Get local individuals, businesses and civic clubs to chip in. Making your appeal tangible will be easiest: "Will you give ten basketballs to poor kids?"

4. Your own city treasury should help.

5. The federal government has so much assistance money in so many bureaus that all states and most larger cities have a man or department working full time to find where the money is and how to get it. Ask for their help. Also ask your senator and congressmen. And be sure to keep in constant contact with: Law Enforcement Assistance Administration, U.S. Department of Justice, Washington, D.C. 20530. The Law Enforcement Assistance Administration of the U.S. Department of Justice was created by the Omnibus Crime Control and Safe Streets Act of 1968. This agency recently has provided 63 million dollars to police at state levels; 300 million more was authorized beginning July 1, 1969.

6. Most Federal money will be distributed through state (regional) crime commissions, so be sure to keep in contact with them.

Needed materials and donated services can be obtained from many sources, such as the following:

1. Local businesses will give—or sell to you at or below cost—almost everything you will need. For example, if you are helping repair a riot-damaged church, you can get much of the material from building-material suppliers. And you can get skilled help donated by local building unions. (Be sure to take photos, get them published and give credit. The more credit, gratitude and publicity you give, the more help you will get.)

2. Ask for specific things. Ask the local Rotary Club to sponsor one or more bus tours for poor kids. Ask the Kiwanis

Club for circus tickets. Ask the local Carpenter's Union for 100 man-hours of free help in fencing play areas or installing playground equipment. Ask sporting goods and toy stores to give you shop-worn sports equipment and toys after Christmas. (A FREE TOY AFTER Christmas is better than no toy at all.)

3. Organize the entire population to help you help others. Make everybody a police associate: businesses, labor unions, civic clubs, social clubs, groups, schools, churches, individuals, everybody!

"IT PAYS TO ADVERTISE"

Obtaining continuous (often daily) publicity in all news media praising daily acts of police helpfulness will promote needed recognition by the public of police community assistance. The following are some suggestions:

1. Note the emphasis on "daily" acts of police helpfulness to obtain daily publicity. Police community assistance is an everyday job and each day's acts of help must be worthy of publicity.
2. Publicity obtained must be publicity deserved. Do not expect to obtain newspaper, radio, television or other publicity on any "Support Your Local Police" plea. You won't get news media publicity unless you make news and do what is newsworthy.
3. You must make favorable news! Pleas for publicity and support just because you are the police will get you exactly nowhere! But take 200 poor kids to the circus and you'll get publicity everywhere—with pictures (if you notify all news media in advance).
4. The police are now so famous for their "brutality" that any act of kindness and helpfulness is news. Keep all news media informed daily.
5. Get at least 20 friends to write favorable letters to the "Point of View" column of your local newspaper. Also encourage people you have helped to write "thank you" letters to the "Point of View" column of your local paper.

6. Organize a "Speakers' Program" to provide capable speakers to all clubs and organizations.
7. Employ—free if possible, but paid if necessary—professional publicity and public relations counsel.
8. Publicize and advertise: "When you need HELP—call the POLICE!"

Chapter 3

THE ROLE OF THE POLICE

BRUCE J. TERRIS

American policemen today are faced with two overriding problems. First, crimes of violence or threatened violence—murder, rape, robbery, serious assault, and burglary—appear to be rising steadily. The statistical rise can be explained, in part, by factors such as more accurate and complete police reporting of crimes to the Federal Bureau of Investigation and increases in population, particularly among juveniles and young adults, who commit most crimes. Nonetheless, violent crime does seem to be increasing, even though probably not nearly so quickly or menacing as the statistics suggest.

Whether or not there is, in actuality, a precipitous increase, most Americans believe this to be the fact. This belief, this perception of lack of safety on the streets, is affecting the character of urban life. People who can do so move to safer areas, often to the suburbs, thereby affecting the tax base and availability of leadership in the central city. Other people are afraid to venture out at night, to take advantage of the parks and the cultural and social life of the city. And citizens throughout the country are demanding from all levels of government, and especially from the courts and police, that they take immediate and effective action to reduce violent crime, often even if this means the sacrifice of other important values such as the right of privacy.

THE PROBLEM

The problem of violent crime is, in large part, a problem of crimes committed by Negroes against other Negroes in the ghetto.

NOTE: *The Annals of the American Academy of Political and Social Science* (Nov. 67), pp. 58–69. Reprinted with permission.

The Presidents Commission on Crime in the District of Columbia found that 85 per cent of the murders, 79 per cent of the rapes, and 84 per cent of serious assaults in Washington were committed by Negroes against Negroes.[1] The percentage for robbery in Washington would be substantially less, but a great many of the robberies, as well as other crimes, committed by Negroes against whites are committed against storekeepers or other whites while they are in the Negro ghetto. While the proportions of crimes committed by Negroes against Negroes would be lower in cities with smaller Negro populations than Washington, it is still clear that most of the high-crime areas of our large cities are the Negro ghettos.

Furthermore, it is a reasonable assumption that most of the crimes committed by Negroes against whites are the acts of Negroes who have previously committed either crimes against Negroes or crimes such as disorderly conduct which occurred in the ghetto but by their nature have no victim. If these crimes in the ghetto had been detected and if the offenders had been dealt with in a manner which would have either deterred or rehabilitated them (a critical problem which this article does not consider) crime throughout the city would be substantially lessened. In short, if violent crime in our large cities is to be met squarely, it is certain that major steps must be taken to reduce crime where it most often occurs, in the ghettos where Negroes, as well as Spanish-speaking Americans, live.

The second major problem involves the relationship between the police, on the one hand, and Negroes and Spanish-speaking Americans, including Puerto Ricans and Mexican-Americans, on the other. The extent of the split between Negroes and the police can be quickly seen from the results of a few surveys. A poll in Washington, done for the National Crime Commission, found that 49 per cent of Negro men responding believed that at least half of the police force would have to be replaced to get a really good department; 59 per cent thought that "many police enjoy giving Negroes a hard time;" and 62 per cent thought that the

---

[1] President's Commission on Crime in the District of Columbia, *Report*. Washington, D.C., U.S. Government Printing Office, 1966, pp. 42, 44, 54, 78.

police discriminated.² A survey of junior high school students in Cincinnati found that 59 per cent of Negro boys believed that "the police are mean," and 70 per cent thought that the police tried to get smart with you when asked a question.³

Another survey in the general area of Watts, conducted after the riot by a research group from the University of California at Los Angeles, found the Negro beliefs which are expressed on page 25 in tabular form.⁴

These remarkable figures include all adults. For males below the age of 35—those most likely to be involved in crime, to know of crimes committed by others and to participate in disturbances—the hostility is even greater. Over 90 per cent of them believed that each of these kinds of incidents occurred in the area. Fifty-three per cent said that they had themselves been subjected to insulting language; 44 per cent, to search without reason; 22 per cent, to unnecessary force in being arrested; and 10 per cent, to being beaten up while in custody.⁵

Such surveys generally understate the degree of hostility to the police. Interviewers generally find that many members of minority groups start by indicating little antagonism toward the police or other parts of the "Establishment" but that after extended informal conversation, their deeper feelings often come forth. It is just these pent-up feelings of hostility, feelings that may not even be verbalized to themselves, which frequently are revealed in moments of crisis, such as the arrest of a friend or the start of a disturbance.

It should hardly need saying that the opinions of Negroes—

---

[2] Biderman, Albert D., Johnson, Louise A., McIntyre, Jennie, and Weir, Adrianne W.: *Report on a Pilot Study in the District of Columbia on Victimization and Attitudes toward Law Enforcement.* President's Commission on Law Enforcement and Administration of Justice Field Survey I. Washington, D.C., U.S. Government Printing Office, 1967, pp. 137, 144. On the other hand, 84 per cent of the Negro males responding believed that police officers 'deserve a lot more thanks and respect than they get from the public."

[3] Portune, Robert G.: "Attitudes of Junior High Pupils toward Police Officers." Cincinnati: University of Cincinnati, unpublished, 1966, p. 2.

[4] Paine, Walter J.: "Los Angeles Riot Study: The Perception of Police Brutality in South Central Los Angeles Following the Revolt of August 1965." Los Angeles: University of California at Los Angeles, unpublished, Figure 1.

[5] *Ibid.*, Figures 6, 7, 8.

TABLE 1
LOS ANGELES RIOT STUDY: SOME SURVEY RESULTS

Police	Happened in Area	Saw It Happen	Happened to Someone You Know	Happened to You
Lack respect or use insulting language	85	49	52	28
Roust, frisk, or search cars for no good reason	83	51	49	25
Roust, frisk, or search people for no good reason	85	52	48	25
Search homes for no good reason	63	22	30	7
Use unnecessary force in making arrests	86	47	43	9
Beat up people in custody	85	27	46	5

and, to a lesser extent, of Spanish-speaking citizens—concerning police misconduct do not themselves prove how often such misconduct actually occurs. Nevertheless, the perceptions of minority groups that such misconduct is frequent is a fact just as much as the widespread attitude that crime is rampant and increasing. And this fact vitally affects the actions of minority citizens with relation to the police and the white community.

All too often, police-community relations are seen only as an issue in the struggle of minority groups for equal rights and full opportunity to take their place in American society. It is, of course, properly such an issue. Just as members of minority groups are entitled to good jobs at fair wages, excellent education and decent housing, they are also entitled to receive police protection as good as that received by their white fellow citizens and to be treated by police officers courteously, humanely and legally.

But improved police-community relations are essential not only to minority groups, but to the police and to the entire community. The police simply cannot operate effectively as long as they are viewed with skepticism or hostility by much of the population in large sections of the city. Such attitudes mean that crimes are often not reported, that witnesses often refuse to identify themselves or to testify in court and that suspects resist arrests with the tacit or even physical support of bystanders.

Police officers do their work with the consciousness that they are distrusted or hated by many of the people they see or talk to; they are frequently taunted or cursed; they are sometimes physically attacked. Even though statistics show that police work is less dangerous than occupations in mining, agriculture, construction, and transportation,[6] many police officers worry constantly about the danger to their lives and limbs. In turn, this hostility has a marked effect on the morale of police departments and therefore on their effectiveness as organizations, their efforts to recruit new officers and their ability to retain existing officers.

Finally, hostility between the police and minority groups is increasingly having a serious impact on the stability of our larger cities. Virtually every major disturbance in the last three years has been triggered, in the immediate sense, by an incident involving the police and a Negro or Puerto Rican. Sometimes the police officers have been acting properly; in other instances, they have acted illegally, or at least unwisely. Even when the police officer was acting correctly, the minority community has been quick to see improper police conduct because of the long-accumulated distrust and hostility toward the police, which is the tinder in all of our cities waiting for a match to light it.

We have now come full circle. The problem of violent crime must be met in our ghettos where it principally occurs. Yet, the state of police-community relations in these areas now makes it almost impossible for the police to deal with crime there. At the same time, both the prevalence of violent crime and the threat of disorders compound the already serious problems in our cities. Consequently, relations between the police and minority groups must be drastically and immediately improved if our cities are to reduce crime and to have the reasonable degree of stability necessary to solve their other problems.

PROFESSIONALIZATION OF THE POLICE

Since World War II, leading police officials and authors have talked increasingly about "professionalization" of the police. The objective has been to make policing as respectable, and perhaps

[6] As of 1955, the rate of police fatalities while on duty (including accidents) was 33 per 100,000 officers in comparison to 94 in mining, 76 in construction, 55 in agriculture, and 44 in transportation. Robin, Gerald D.: Justifiable homicide by police officers. *Journal of Criminal Law, Criminology and Police Science*, 54:228–229. Since 1955, the rate for police officers has slightly declined.

as well paid, as the more traditional professions, such as medicine and law. The methods employed have generally been to raise educational standards for recruits, to lengthen the period of police training and particularly to increase the efficiency of police departments by improving their management, organization and operations.

Leading police departments are requiring higher educational levels for recruits to police work. Twenty-four per cent of police departments surveyed in 1961 had no educational requirements; only 30 per cent of police officers polled in 1964 had taken even one college course, and only 7 per cent had a college degree.[7] On the other hand, only 22 police departments, including 21 in California, had requirements ranging from one semester of college to a four-year degree.[8]

The trend to more police officers having college degrees, or at least some college work, is certain to grow as more departments impose requirements each year, more Americans attend college and colleges increasingly add programs in police science. The National Crime Commission has simply recognized and supported this movement in recommending that police departments require immediately that all administrators and supervisors have a baccalaureate degree and that all sworn personnel ultimately have such degrees.[9]

The second major change in American policing is the increased length and improved content of police training. In 1931, the Wickersham Commission (the National Crime Commission of the 1930's) found that only 20 per cent of the 383 cities surveyed conducted any formal training at all.[10] In other words, officers

[7] O'Connor, George W.: *Survey of Selection Methods.* Washington, D.C.: International Association of Chiefs of Police, 1962. O'Connor, George W. and Watson, Nelson A.: *Juvenile Delinquency and Youth Crimes: The Police Role.* Washington, D.C.; International Association of Chiefs of Police, 1964. p. 79.

[8] President's Commission on Law Enforcement and Administration of Justice: *Task Force Report: The Police.* Washington, D.C., U.S. Government Printing Office, 1967, p. 126.

[9] President's Commission on Law Enforcement and Administration of Justice: *The Challenge of Crime in a Free Society.* Washington, D.C.: U.S. Government Printing Office, 1967, p. 126.

[10] National Commission on Law Observance and Enforcement: *Report on the Police.* Washington, D.C. U.S. Government Printing Office, 1931, p. 71.

were recruited and placed directly on the street. Today, while police training, both in length and quality, leaves much to be desired, a majority of police departments in cities of over 250,000 population have over eight weeks of training.[11] And most departments are continuing to improve both recruit and in-service training of their officers.

While American business and other areas of government have been analyzing and attempting to rationalize their operations, police departments have largely been operating on the basis of common sense. Traditional methods have been generally continued, with only slight and gradual modifications. Police departments on the Pacific Coast and the Chicago Police Department under Orlando Wilson, however, have pioneered in mitigating the appallingly low efficiency of police departments. The efforts have included improving the organization of the department so that commanders can better control the officers under them; developing planning units to formulate and carry out long-range objectives; using computers to allocate field personnel on the basis of need; improving crime laboratories to obtain stronger evidence; forming internal investigation units to ferret out police corruption; analyzing report forms and providing clerical staff to reduce the time spent in report preparation; and improving police communications so that police officers can respond more rapidly to crime reports. These efforts constitute, essentially, the application of modern business methods and technology to policing.

There can be little doubt that improved efficiency, better training and more qualified police officers will result in greater prevention of crime and detection of criminals than would occur if these changes had not been made. It might also appear that some of these changes, such as better-educated police officers and longer and higher-quality training, should result in improved police-minority relations. Unfortunately, the available evidence suggests that this has not been the case.

Los Angeles, Oakland, Chicago, Cincinnati and St. Louis would rank at or close to the top in any list of professional police departments. Yet, these cities have generally at least as serious

[11] President's Commission on Law Enforcement and Administration of Justice: *Task Force Report: The Police, op. cit.,* p. 138.

problems with police-community relations as less-professional departments. The reason appears to be because professional departments have emphasized efficiency over closer relations with the people they are policing.

For example, traditionally, police officers have patrolled on foot until they saw or were notified of a crime or other occurrence needing their services. Such officers would talk to residents, and human relationships would naturally develop. Professional police departments, in contrast, have almost entirely replaced foot with motorized patrols, as the latter can cover much more area. They have tended to discourage or even to forbid idle conversation with residents as, at best, a waste of time or, worse, because it might lead to friendships which make it difficult for officers to enforce the law or to resist corruption. They have ordered officers to engage in "aggressive patrol" that is, if they have nothing else to do at the moment to stop suspicious-looking citizens, to question and often to search them. And they have instructed their officers to treat citizens civilly when making an arrest or even when talking to a victim or witness, instead of showing any human emotion, such as sympathy or friendship.

These methods plainly reduce the opportunity for friendly relationships to develop. "Aggressive patrol" means that thousands of citizens, approximately 40,000 in one year in San Diego,[12] are stopped on the basis of little or no evidence. Since this practice usually discriminates against Negroes and youths and is all too often conducted discourteously, it has become one of the principal causes of poor police-minority relations in the cities in which it is employed.[13] A survey for the National Crime Commission found that, since citizens generally seek respect and courtesy from the police, the civil and correct manner which police officers are trained to adopt tends to be seen as disrespect or a desire to establish superiority.[14]

[12] *Ibid.*, p. 184.
[13] *Ibid.*, pp. 184–185.
[14] Black, Donald J. and Reiss, Albert J., Jr.: Patterns of Behavior in police and citizen transactions. In Reiss, Albert J., Jr. (ed.): *Studies in Crime and Law Enforcement in Major Metropolitan Areas.* President's Commission on Law Enforcement and Administration of Justice, Field Survey III. Washington, D.C.: U.S. Government Printing Office, 1967, pp. 57–58.

This is not to suggest that traditional police departments are beloved in minority communities. They are not. But the efficient methods of professional departments have tended to reinforce the view of ghetto residents, which is so often expressed, that the police are an "army of occupation" imposed upon them by the white man. Consequently, police methods, adopted in order to fight crime more efficiently, have often seriously interfered with police-minority relations, which must be improved if this objective is to be reached.

There is, of course, no inherent reason why professional police departments must automatically adopt procedures which interfere with improved police-minority relations. On the contrary, more education and longer training can produce police officers better able to deal with citizens. Field interrogations can be restricted to situations where there is factual basis for suspicion. Officers can be instructed to get out of patrol cars and talk informally with citizens as often as possible. As we will discuss in more detail below, true professionalism will result in combining efficiency with better police-minority relations.

PROGRAMS FOR POLICE-COMMUNITY RELATIONS

Police experts, civil rights leaders and crime commissions have been recommending to police departments a variety of reforms designed to improve police-minority relations. The most frequent recommendations include:[15]

1. Extending human-relations training of recruits and officers.
2. Creating or enlarging police-community relations units within police departments.
3. Starting precinct and city-wide citizen advisory committees, including minority leaders, to meet with the police.
4. Developing programs to educate the public about the police, such as visits of school children to precinct stations. lectures by police officers to adults or youth groups and school courses concerning police work.

[15] President's Commission on Law Enforcement and Administration of Justice: *Task Force Report: The Police, op. cit.*, pp. 144–207.

5. Running recruitment campaigns aimed at members of minority groups.
6. Ending discrimination within police departments, such as that relating to promotions and integration of patrols.
7. Issuing orders banning use of abusive words or excessive force by police officers.
8. Developing procedures to handle citizen complaints within the police department which are fair and designed to impose real discipline.

Many of these ideas are being adopted in different urban police departments with a fair degree of rapidity. Nonetheless, there seems to be little, if any, improvement in police-minority relations; instead, relations between the police and Negroes may be worse than they have ever been before.

First, in this field, as in others, the aspirations of minority groups are outrunning the ability of our society to meet them. Consequently, while police departments have been making some progress, minority groups are demanding more and demanding it immediately—that they be treated with dignity, that the police department reflect their numbers, that it be responsive to their culture and desires, and the like. While these demands are hardly radical—they are no more than what middle-class white Americans already have—they are far from being satisfied.

Second, the reforms being adopted by police departments often look better on paper than in practice. The National Crime Commission found that police-community relations personnel usually had little support from the chief of police or other ranking officers, were disliked by line officers and had little authority.[16] For example, perhaps the country's best community-relations unit was not even allowed on the street by its chief of police in order to attempt to calm tensions during a recent riot. The Commission studies also found that citizen advisory committees and other police-citizen programs generally are designed only for middle-class and "responsible" citizens, not to reach the young and hostile, whose relations with the police are most im-

---

[16] *Ibid.*, pp. 151–156.

portant.[17] A few hours or days of community-relations training are rarely effective when the officers sense that what they are being taught is inconsistent with the basic ethic of the department. New disciplinary procedures cannot change the habits of police officers in treating citizens on the street when policemen know that officers are not severely disciplined, if at all, for physical or verbal abuse, in contrast to discipline for corruption or even tardiness.

Third, police departments generally misconceive the real problems of police-community relations. They see the problem as a lack of communication with the "responsible" minority leadership. They therefore usually consider police-community relations as educating the public about police work and operations through public relations, speeches before civic groups and school programs.

In fact, minority groups know a great deal about the police. Since both crime rates and the concentration of police officers are high in the ghetto, minority citizens see or hear about police operations constantly. Youths, in particular, often become students of police activity. The problem is that knowledge of the police, not ignorance, has generally caused the hostility which is so prevalent in minority communities.

Minority leaders have long made serious allegations about police conduct. These allegations have generally been discounted not only by the police, but by most white Americans. The commonly held view is that police misconduct against citizens has declined sharply, even though occasional lapses still occur. The best available evidence, however, suggests that the allegations of minority leaders usually understate the problem substantially.

Studies sponsored by the National Crime Commission were conducted in Chicago, Washington and Boston, in eight largely low-income precincts, by placing neutral observers in police cars. The observers found that police officers initiated 14 per cent of their contacts involving suspected crimes with some abusive language.[18] These contacts were not only with suspects but also included victims, witnesses and bystanders.

[17] *Ibid.*, pp. 156–159.
[18] Black and Reiss, *op. cit.*, p. 98.

The same study found that a clear case of physical abuse occurred on an average of once for every 42 eight-hour patrols. This ratio does not include cases of physical force involving any doubt that the officer's actions might be improper. While the abuse seemed directed as much against low-income whites as low-income Negroes, the effect, since Negroes in our cities have much lower incomes, is to support the view of Negroes that they are victimized much more often than whites.

The study suggests that in a city like Washington, with approximately 2,800 officers, clear physical abuse occurs thousands of times a year, and verbal abuse, tens of thousands of times.[19] There is no reason to believe that the study exaggerated the occurrence of these events, as it is a reasonable assumption that police officers are more careful when accompanied by a neutral observer. And there is no reason to believe that police officers in these three cities treat citizens better or worse than officers in other medium and large cities throughout the country.

Individual police misconduct is contrary to police regulations, whether or not these regulations are effectively enforced. On the other hand, most police departments have policies governing street operations which also seriously interfere with police-minority relations. We have already mentioned the use of aggressive patrols to stop, question and often search citizens, with little or no evidence of wrongdoing. In addition, tactical units are increasingly being employed in routine patrols, even though they know little of the neighborhood and tend toward overenforcement of statutes relating to minor crimes. Dogs are used on ordinary patrols despite the fear and hostility which they commonly arouse in Negroes. Minor crime statutes are enforced without consideration for the mores or wishes of the neighborhood. Regulations generally permit police officers to shoot at fleeing felons even if the suspected crime has not involved violence (such as auto theft) and the suspect is not an immediate danger to anyone.

The traditional remedies for police misconduct have been better training, supervision and discipline. But these methods, as

[19] President's Commission on Law Enforcement and Administration of Justice: *Task Force Report: The Police, op. cit.,* p. 182.

we have noted, have not been effective in view of the inconsistency between them and the attitudes of police officers, from patrolmen to the chief of police. As long as most police officers are prejudiced against minority groups (the study for the National Crime Commission in Chicago, Washington, and Boston found that 72 per cent of the white officers who were accompanied on patrol expressed prejudiced remarks to the observer, including 38 per cent who expressed highly prejudiced, extremely anti-Negro remarks[20]); as long as police supervisors are often as prejudiced as the men they supervise; as long as police promotions are based more on arrests made than on ability to improve police-minority relations; as long as police officers who themselves would not engage in physical and verbal abuse invariably refuse to report their colleagues; as long as police internal-investigations units spend virtually all their time investigating corruption, rather than abuse of citizens; as long as severe discipline is rarely meted out for abuse of citizens, it is not likely that police misconduct against citizens will be controlled.

The remedy for police policies which produce resentment is obvious—modification of the policy by civilian officials or the chief of police. However, in practice, this often means a difficult choice between more efficient law enforcement and better community relations. For example, aggressive patrol may both catch some additional criminals and raise police-community tensions. On the other hand, as we have stressed above, since efficient law enforcement would be substantially improved if the police had the full support of the public in minority neighborhoods, compromises in favor of improved relations would likely bear fruit manyfold in the long run.

ROLE OF THE POLICE

The thesis of this article is that the serious problems of police-minority relations, and therefore the equally serious prob-

[20] Black and Reiss, *op. cit.*, p. 135. Of the 28 per cent of white officers who did not make prejudiced remarks, 11 per cent made neutral statements; 1 per cent made pro-Negro statements; and 16 per cent made no relevant statements at all.

lem of violent crime on the streets, cannot be remedied by merely adopting the litany of recommendations generally made in order to improve police-minority relations. Instead, improved police-minority relations require a radical change in the conception of both the police and community of what police work is all about.

Basing their opinions, perhaps, on the western, the detective story and the "cops and robbers" saga, Americans tend to see police officers as spending most of their time in investigating felons and arresting them, often after a gun battle. In fact, most officers can serve for years without using their guns except for practice, and their arrests of felons, or even serious misdemeanants are not very frequent. Except for detectives, who usually constitute only a small proportion of an urban police department, most officers do not even spend a substantial portion of their time in investigation.

Most officers spend their time doing routine patrol. This patrol is interrupted frequently or occasionally, depending on the character of the area, by events requiring their presence. These events are likely to consist of a fight, which may include use of a knife or other weapon, between spouses, relatives, or friends; a party which is noisy and disturbing the neighborhood; a group of youngsters congregating on a street corner and bothering passers-by; a drunk lying on the sidewalk; or a person who is lost.

These situations require delicate judgments about how the officer should handle the situation. He has a variety of possible methods from which to choose. For example, after a fight, the officer can often make an arrest for assault as a felony or misdemeanor—the line between the two is extremely imprecise; order one or both persons to leave the scene on threat of being arrested; refer one or both persons to a social agency for help; or himself attempt to settle the matter. Similarly, a group of youngsters who are congregating can be arrested for loitering or another minor crime; warned to move on upon threat of arrest; or influenced to leave or behave themselves by friendly advice from an officer who has previously earned their respect.

The point is that the situations in which police officers most frequently find themselves do not require the expert aim of a marksman, the cunningness of a private eye, or the toughness of a stereotyped Irish policeman. Instead, they demand knowledge of human beings and the personal, as opposed to official, authority to influence people without the use or even threat of force.

These characteristics are not commonly found in police officers because police departments do not consider these values as paramount. As a result, persons with these abilities are not attracted to police work nor rewarded by promotion or other incentive if they happen to enter a department.

The image of police officers must be radically changed to consider them as a part of the broad category of occupations which deal with people who are sometimes difficult to handle. Others with similar problems include teachers, gang workers, recreation workers and parole, probation and correctional officers. If police work were seen in this light, individuals who were more sympathetic to human beings and less prejudiced on racial or other grounds would enter police work because they wanted to help human beings, instead of young men who are looking for excitement and the opportunity to exercise authority. However, just as gang work generally requires persons with above-average physical abilities in order to deal with delinquents, so police officers must have the physical bearing needed to deal with delinquents and other hostile persons without constantly using force.

One method for changing the image of the police would be through public relations techniques. Television could present police officers handling human situations rather than engaging in violent conflict. Police publicity officers could emphasize the same kind of activity.

While such public relations work can be important, it is not likely that it will be effective as long as police attitudes are so inconsistent with it. It is more important that police departments change their internal policies to further their development as one of several government agencies dealing with human problems and attempting to serve human beings.

For example, qualified teachers, gang and recreation workers, parole officers and others should be not only allowed, but actively recruited, to enter police work after brief specialized police training. They should not be forced to start at the bottom. Instead, their expertise should be recognized by allowing them to transfer laterally at the same or higher pay. Pension systems should be changed so that persons can enter, or later leave, police work without penalty; recruits should be sought with educational backgrounds in psychology, sociology or social work and rewarded with higher pay; officers should be paid to go back to school to study there subjects; police science colleges should emphasize these academic fields rather than police organization or patrol methods; recruitment standards should screen out persons whose personalities will interfere with their dealing properly and intelligently with all kinds of citizens; promotion criteria should stress the officer's abilities in relating with people and improving community relations rather than the number of arrests he has made; police recruit and in-service training should be devoted largely to such subjects as psychology, urban problems, alcoholism, mental illness and the culture and history of the Negroes and Spanish-speaking Americans, even though it would still include subjects relating to traditional police work; and officers should be instructed to work closely with social agencies such as the schools, recreation department, hospitals and family services, virtually as in-take workers.

These changes would not apply to officers who do detective work, conduct tests in the laboratory, or do filing. But staff specialists are common in any complex organization. The heart of police work would be seen as consisting in work with difficult human problems by the majority of officers who would be recruited, trained and promoted largely for this purpose.

In short, police departments should be run on the basis that they must attract and use highly trained men who have the ability to make delicate judgments concerning complex human behavior. Such a department would almost automatically have improved police-community relations. The community-relations unit would be seen as having a highly respected staff function at the very core of the department's mission. Police training in human relations would not be immediately forgotten while the law of arrest and evidence remained firmly embedded in the recruit's mind. Physical or verbal abuse would be an aberration which, if detected, would be severely punished. And police departments would not be so prone to adopt policies sacrificing good minority relations to more immediately effective law enforcement.

Few institutions, and especially few institutions as conservative as police departments, are influenced by exhortation. However, police agencies are beginning to move in these directions. In Honolulu, the police department has a social worker available to assist when a juvenile is brought to the station. The San Francisco police community-relations unit has assigned six full-time officers to help youths with police records to obtain jobs, and the Atlanta department is likewise working with the local antipoverty agency. More generally, police departments are increasingly seeking recruits with college degrees, including fields other than police science, and police officers are returning to school.

Under the pressure of extreme tension and serious disturbances, many departments are beginning to comprehend the complexity of police work and particularly the complexity of police work in minority neighborhoods. Many officers are becoming open to more radical changes in the basic concept of police work. The time is therefore right for political scientists, psychologists and other civilians to assist police departments to a broader understanding of their service role and to take the consequent actions which are essential to make our cities safe for all citizens.

Chapter 4

THE SOCIAL-CONTROL ROLE OF THE POLICE IN CHANGING URBAN COMMUNITIES

ROBERT L. DERBYSHIRE

Public criticism of police and their tactics is a favorite Amercan pastime. The validity of most police criticism is analogous to reprimanding a physician for not saving the life of one whose heart has been punctured by a bullet. In the case of the physician, there are biological and physiological forces determining the patient's expiration, over which the physician has little or no control. Similarly, policemen are exposed, in their battle against deviancy, to cultural, social and psychological forces over which they have little or no control. Generally, these social forces are the political structure of the community, including the efficiency and reliability of elected and appointed officials; the patterns of coercion, leadership and responsibility of and between police officials and political leaders; the capabilities, training and experience of policemen; the attitudes and behavior of citizens toward the police; and the particular conditions or set of circumstances under which these forces interact.

The urban condition is complex. Reciprocal relations between community and police present myriad problems. Police systems operate at an efficiency level commensurate with their ability and training, their status and salary and the community's attitude toward its own responsibility for social control. More recent problems illustrated by urban conflict in Northern cities during the summer of 1964 require a reevaluation and reexamination of the social-control role of police systems in these centers of culturally excluded citizens.

NOTE: from *Excerpta Criminologica*, May-June, 1966, pp. 315-331. Reprinted with permission.

Social control among *Homo sapiens* is based upon custom. The system of social control consists of those mechanisms and techniques used to regulate the behavior of persons to meet societal goals and needs. All cultures provide adequate control over behavior. Controls are initiated either formally or informally. Informal controls usually start in the family and consist of orders, rebukes, criticisms, reprimands, ridicule, blame, gossip, praise, rewards, etc. How an individual responds to informal and formal social control in the community frequently depends upon the consistency and certainty of these controls in his family experience while growing up. Most frequently, informal controls are used by primary groups. Primary affiliations require emotional reciprocity; therefore they are more subject to informal control.

Formal controls are those sanctions instituted by the body politic and its agencies. Since emotional attachment is seldom a part of secondary associations, laws, sanctions and punishments are explicitly stated and theoretically apply to everyone, no matter what his position in the social structure. Schools, hospitals, welfare agencies and the police are examples of secondary socializing agencies who use formal social-control methods.

Social-control systems operate most effectively and efficiently, the police notwithstanding, where there is constant and unified, both overt and covert, cultural and social support from all social-control agencies. This support must be unambiguously stated in the value systems of families, community and the greater society of which the individual is a functional part.

Urban centers, particularly inner-city areas, are the most difficult places to maintain overt behavior at a level acceptable to middle-class standards. Frontier and farm towns need a sheriff more because of the transients than the town-folk. Sheriffs had the most trouble with the out-of-towners who lacked integration with the local community and who, with their anonymity, used Friday and Saturday nights as moral holidays. As towns became larger and centers for attracting transients, segments of the community became notorious for harboring persons with little integration in community life. Although most of the nation's population is essentially urban, the urban attitude is most pronounced in the inner city. The inner city or slum areas exemplify excessive amounts of personal, social, political, religious, family and economic instability. A disproportionate amount of time is spent policing inner city areas.

Summer riots in Northern cities were not led by communists or any other organization, nor were they racial in nature, states the Federal Bureau of Investigation. Although these riots predominantly involved Negroes they were a product of conflicts in values and norms. The ghettoized lower-class Negro exists in a contraculture, prone to deviancy from middle-class values. Absent father households with matrifocal structures, insufficient skills for adequate employment opportunities, overrepresentation as welfare recipients, overcrowded and deteriorated inner city ghettos, education significantly lower and crime rates significantly higher than comparable white populations, ten times more out-of-wedlock births than whites and twice the Caucasian infant mortality rate are social facts related to being a lower-class Negro in the urban United States. There is a reciprocal relationship between these social facts, urban conflict and problems of the United States Negro's acceptance and assimilation into American culture.

Lack of social cohesion and integration is a major problem in areas of high mobility. Cohesion and integration are major social-control devices. Secondary socializing agencies are most effective when cohesion and integration have existed but for some reason have suddenly broken down. Evidence supports the fact that the police, social workers, courts and other secondary socializing agencies do their most effective work with persons who temporarily lack integration with the prevailing society, while they help the least those individuals who have rarely or never experienced cohesive and integrated community life.

Norm and social role conflicts are rampant in the inner city. Next door to a law-abiding citizen who maintains conventional sexual and moral behavior may live a sexually promiscuous person who has little respect for law, officials, property or others. Tremendous variation exist in religious beliefs, family systems and means of achieving and satisfying human relationships.

The increased impersonality of city life fosters individual freedom. This individualism is a peculiar type. Most inner-city or slum persons pay lip service to their own individuality while simultaneously conforming to the expected behavior of those persons or segments of their associations applying the most pressure at any particular time. With these persons frequently there is a lack of intimacy yet a need to conform to perceived wishes; this type of man has been termed by David Riesman as "other-directed."

Primary socializing agencies are the immediate family, relatives by blood and marriage, age and sex peers, neighbors and others who aid persons, usually on a long term, face-to-face basis, with intimate contact, to learn culturally approved ways of controlling one's behavior. On the basis of present knowledge, it appears that social control is most effective when it is practiced at this level. Secondary socializing agencies are those whose specific purpose is to aid in socialization or to resocialize individuals whose primary agencies have, for some reason, become ineffective. The presently established secondary agents of social control are most effective as reintegrators and are less effective as substitutes for primary agents of social control.

The police, particularly for the inner-city urban community, is the most important agency of social control. Historically, police systems have been primarily concerned with coercive control. Coercive control which emanates from law and government agencies is accomplished by force or threat of force.

Power and authority are vested in the symbols of the uniform and badge and, if that is not enough, the spontoon, side arm and handcuffs take on functional elements of legal authority. Pillars of the middle-class community feel safe with the knowledge that this type of control protects their neighborhoods, while lower-class persons more frequently view the coercive powers of the police as a threat. There is every reason to believe that the coercive powers of the police are most effective with persons who have internalized controls over their behavior.

In other words, coercive control is most effective with those who need it the least.

Coercive control is a necessary function for all police systems, but more important, particularly in urban centers, is the need for persuasive control functions of the police. Middle-class youth who have the advantage of intact homes and adequate supervision seldom see a policeman except possibly directing traffic. Middle-class citizens learn in school that "we should obey the laws" and "the policeman is our friend," but direct contact with him is seldom encountered. Little firsthand knowledge of behavior patterns associated with the police role exists in middle-class culture.

On the other hand, in the inner city, many youngsters observe the police more frequently than their own fathers or other important relatives. These same children lack much of the informal social controls taught by and expected of the middle class. Young persons in lower-class communities see policemen breaking up family fights, taking drunks and derelicts off the street, raiding a prostitute's flat or a gambling house, picking up some of the local boys for interrogation, knocking on the door because a disturbance had been reported, breaking up a game of pitching coins or shooting dice on the street, checking locked doors of merchant neighbors, evicting slum residents, asking questions pertaining to rat control, transporting patients to mental hospitals, beating others and being beaten, taking bribes and arresting bribers, and numerous other behaviors associated with most police systems. It is within this context that the growing lower-class child forms his impressions and develops attitudes toward the police. These attitudes are then transferred toward the larger adult world and its system of social control. Within this environment, he gains his most purposive information about law, rights, duties, privileges, loyalties and many other items necessary for adulthood. Many of these are developed from impressions received from the policeman, one of the few representatives of the social-control system with whom he has had direct contact.

In the lower-class community, the function of the police is integrated into the child's knowledge before he knows the role of teachers. More important for the policeman in inner-city crime control is the role of persuasive control. Lower-class youngsters need a stable, steady, friendly person with whom to identify, to help them understand that controlling their behavior is most effective and appropriate when it is controlled because one wants to do what significant persons in his life wish him to do and not because he is afraid of force if he does not control his behavior.

Effective persuasive control emanates from a particular type of policeman who has the personality, motivation, interest, time, training and fortitude to work closely with slum families and other human beings. He should be specifically and adequately trained for this role and commensurately rewarded. An emulative image must be presented consistently so that children, adolescents and young and old adults alike will look to him for guidance in areas other than crime control.

Cities and states must pay adequate salaries, extend fringe benefits and provide professional pride and status to the degree that police departments can hire the type of men and women necessary to fulfill the role of future policemen. This new role should place greater emphasis upon crime prevention. Excellent persuasive control is good crime prevention. Certainly, knowledge of riot control and police tactics is essential to stopping riots and criminal activity after they start; this is a necessary coercive function of the policeman's social role. But more important than stopping a crime is its prevention.

A number of suggestions for more effective social control over urban conflict during a period of rapid social change are the following. (a) More important than placing Negro policemen in Negro communities is to rid the police hiring procedures of discrimination. Hiring a man on the basis of his ability to meet specific criteria does more to increase the social status and image of the police in all Negro areas than "tokenism" as it has been practiced in the past. (b) The most highly educated and motivated, and those persons whose character is beyond reproach, should be placed in inner-city areas. These persons should seek out and identify indigenous leadership. Also, they should learn to communicate effectively with persons in the community. Knowledge of potential ignitors of tension and conflict is a necessary part of the police role. After identification of such persons, the policeman's duty is to seek a change in attitudes, to call in appropriate resocializing aid when necessary or at least to see that those persons who are potential agitators are immobilized during periods of high tension. In an area where stability is seldom evident, the policeman should be emotionally stable and a pattern of social stability must exist, in that turnover of men on these assignments must be minimized. Inner-city dwellers need some source of a stable predictable relationship; this the police can provide. (c) Raise the social status of the police by increasing the quality of men hired and requesting improvement programs for those who are already on the force. Education programs sponsored and promoted by law-enforcement agencies in collaboration with behavioral scientists in universities are indispensable. State and local officials and police organizations must stop paying lip service to the need for responsible, educated policemen. Responsible, emotionally stable, well-educated policemen will make more lasting contributions to crime prevention and control than many other measures already requested by responsible politicians. (d) The police image must be changed to such a degree that middle-class mothers will say with pride, "my son, the policeman." (e) Each policeman involved in learning this role must be aided to live with himself. That is, the dichotomy between persuasion and coercion is great and frequently appears incompatible, therefore, each law-enforcement officer must learn to integrate both roles with as little discomfort as possible. (f) Discrimination toward Negroes and other minorities in areas of employment, housing, in fact in all areas, must cease. As long as it exists institutionally or socially, the American lower-class ghettoized Negro is a potential for urban conflict. He is in this conflict-producing situation partly because he is Negro but more because he has the same American aspirations for achievement and success, but the social structure restricts this American's ability to obtain his goal.

Chapter 5

POLICE-COMMUNITY RELATIONS: THE ROLE OF THE FIRST-LINE PEACE OFFICER

HOWARD H. EARLE

Police-community relations is a field as rife with social dissension as any endeavor in the history of man. And whether they know it or not—or like it or not—peace officers spend a lot more time engaged in police-community-relations activities than they suppose.

To begin with, what is police-community relations? Many people will define it with the polite-sounding cliche, "the relationship the police have with the community." This is fine, but a more substantive definition is needed. Doctor Louis A. Radelet, Professor at Michigan State University, writes that "it is the sum total of the many and varied ways in which it may be emphasized that the police are a part of, not apart from, the communities they serve."[1]

Raymond M. Momboisse, Deputy Attorney General of California, put it another way. He said, "Police-community relations means exactly what the term implies—the relationship between members of the police force and the community as a whole. This includes human, race, public, and press relations. In other words, it is broader than just the terms, police and community. This relationship can be bad, indifferent, or good. It depends upon the attitude and demeanor of every member of the force, both individually and collectively."[2]

The President's Crime Commission defines what police-community relations is not:

NOTE: From *Police*, September-October, 1969, pp. 23–28.
[1] Radelet, Louis A.: Police and community relations. *The Police Chief*, September, 1964, p. 41.
[2] Momboisse, Raymond M.: *Community Relations and Riot Prevention*. Springfield, Thomas, 1967, p. 97.

It is not a public relations program to sell police ethics to the people. It is not a set of expedients. Its purpose is not to tranquilize, for a time, an angry neighborhood by, for example, suddenly promoting a few Negro officers in the wake of a racial disturbance. It is a long-range, full-scale effort to acquaint the police and the community with each other's problems and to stimulate action aimed at solving these problems.[3]

These definitions present a long-range point of view, almost ethereal in some ways because they are so broad. Another useful conceptual definition might be that police-community relations is an art; it is concerned with the ability of the police within a given jurisdiction to understand and deal appropriately with that community's problems; it involves an idea of community awareness of the role and difficulties faced by the police and the honest effort of both the police and the community to share in the common goal of understanding the problems of both, with conscientious effort for harmony and cooperation.

Police-community relations is not new. In a letter to the Corinthians, Saint Paul wrote that "evil communications corrupt good manners." He went on to relate how government officials can be responsible for creating their own problems with the public.

John Milton put it a bit differently, although he said about the same thing: "Good, the more communicated—the more abundant grows;" and that brings it up to more modern times.

Rhett Butler expressed it quite differently with a viewpoint which is probably descriptive of many community-relations programs today. What he said was, "Quite frankly, Scarlett, I don't give a damn!"

Before the Watts riot, police-community relations could not have been sold to many peace officers with a shotgun! They might concede that it was needed but felt there was too much talk about all the things police had to do and not enough thought and action about stopping the crime problem. After the Watts riot, an amazing transformation started across this

---

[3] President's Commission on Law Enforcement and Administration of Justice: *The Challenge of Crime in a Free Society.* Washington, D.C., United States Government Printing Office, 1967, p. 100.

country. People everywhere—citizen and lawmen alike began asking themselves, in retrospect, "What happened to that great city that couldn't have a riot? It just couldn't happen in Los Angeles!"

But it did. And the tragic consequences of it, in terms of social trauma and problems which we live with today, are awesome indeed. It did have one beneficial result, if such a thing is possible: Law enforcement began looking at itself more intensely than ever before, in terms of "How can we perform our functions better?"

Peace officers perform a complex type of activity—some people have called it the "most difficult job in the world today." The work is viewed and reviewed by thousands of people. And if they expect to be clothed in love, universally wanted and liked, the best thing to do right away is—forget it! All we can hope to do is to improve our level of being liked through good police-community relations, so that we can accomplish our purposes.

It is my opinion that until recently, our efforts to improve this level have been inadequate; we have a lot of correcting to do. Why? One reason is that we became "hung up" on saying what was not our job and what was not our role, and we started eliminating every activity which constituted a positive public contact. We tried to get out of juvenile activities; we tried to get out of going into the schools; we tried to get out of giving speeches; and when some holocaust occurred, we sat back and said, "Why doesn't anybody understand the role of the police?" Who is going to tell the public about the role of the police if it isn't the police? No one else is going to go out and tell it the way it is! This means that every peace officer has more at stake than he realizes.

Let's look at another example, the police-review boards. Few officers are in favor of them. But if police-review boards are thrust upon us, it will be our fault—yours and mine. We have not bothered to tell the public what excellent procedures we have for dealing with the problem of citizen complaints. We have not really made them aware that we would rather clean our own house and that we do, in fact, clean our own house. If we fail ourselves, let us not turn around and talk about a public that fails to understand what our function is and what our role is. If anybody is to tell our story, we have to do it.

California is often referred to as a leader in progressive police methods and rightfully so. And yet it was only in 1959 that California finally adopted a formalized minimum recommended training program for its peace officers. Before that date, many agencies failed to provide even token training for a job which had already become highly sophisticated and extremely sensitive.

The current time is labeled as the most educationally oriented and sophisticated era of mankind. And peace officers must remember the words of Henry Baron Brougham: "Education makes a people easy to lead but difficult to drive; easy to govern but impossible to enslave." The truth of this statement is being etched in our consciousness by daily events, and law enforcement has no alternative but to involve itself in this age of scholasticism.

Law enforcement must upgrade itself both internally and externally. For example, we have all worked for someone who unquestioningly adhered to the *status quo*—where "don't make waves" was the watchword. Take the case of a patrolman asking the sergeant, "Why have we been making up this form in four copies? The secretary types them up and she brings them in to you, and you sign them, and then she takes them back, tears off the three copies underneath and throws them away?" And the sergeant replies testily, "We've always done it that way. Now why don't you get on with doing your job?" This kind of attitude is too prevalent in law enforcement.

To upgrade ourselves by educational involvement means something more than textbooks and training sessions. It also means a broadening of our professional perspectives and operational procedures to include better communication with, and understanding of, the public we serve.

Perhaps the biggest social problem we face today is communication—we talk *at* each other rather than *with* each other. To communicate involves the concept that we have a two-way problem, and its solution can only be found through a two-way exchange of ideas. I think this is what many of the minority groups are saying today. They are talking. They are not just talking at us . . . they want us to listen. They want us to hear what they have to say. Do we listen??? Think about it.

Another vital question is, "Do we know what our communities think?" Even more important, do we understand the reasons they think that way? We have a pressing need for greater contact with people. For example, should we hold in-depth meetings with militant groups? I am not saying we should or should not, but we do need to consider this in terms of knowing what these groups are thinking. Many times we could possibly deal with them more appropriately if we knew what was, in fact, their motivating force.

Groups—militant and otherwise—frequently do not grasp the various facets of police problems. Is this matched by a sincere effort on our part to explain our position so they will understand? No! We communicate—but *at* them, and they *at* us. This is not communicating, but rather "verbal handcuffing." The point is that we must give more thought to this idea we call "dealing with groups." Whatever their opinions or backgrounds, they represent a part of the community. And we must deal with attitudes which actually exist rather than those we think should exist.

All too often when communicating with groups, we listen for awhile and then tune them out because their views conflict with our own. It really does not matter whether we like their views—or whether we agree; if members of the public are thinking a certain way, we had better listen.

A great king once ruled the entire world. The king had seven sons, and as each of the sons became of age he was sent out to rule one-seventh of the earth. In a very private conference with each son, the father asked each—as the son was to leave the family home—what was the one possession of the father that the son wished to have when the father passed on. Each of the seven sons indicated privately that the one possession he wanted more than anything else was the ring which the father wore.

Finally the father died. Shortly thereafter, messengers came seeking the seven sons—now located in seven corners of the earth—and delivered the rings. Obviously, six of them had to be fraudulent. But they were enough like the real thing so they appeared to be real. What does this mean in terms of communication patterns and systems of response? We have to understand that what looks like a cold hard case of right or wrong to us may also look like the precise opposite to someone else. There are many different people, and they have different viewpoints. And we must tune them in, just as we would expect them to tune us in. Because if we all tune out on one another, I will guarantee you one thing: police-community relations is lost and it could not possibly survive!

About 90 per cent of a peace officer's time is spent in nonpunitive activities. In other words, for 90 per cent of their time, they can be "good guys." And, yet, a recent highly sophisticated survey conducted by the National League of Cities revealed four basic complaints that the public has against peace officers. Surprisingly, the number-one complaint was discourtesy. They are talking about the "ten-pound lip" and the "twenty-pound badge!" The other three complaints are equally surprising. Number two was traffic-citation issuance. Note that there is a subtle difference between just receiving the citation and the manner in which it is issued. Third—clear down in third place—was police brutality; and the fourth was response time—getting to the location where there is some kind of trouble.

The main theme of this survey is not so much whether these problems do, in fact, exist but that the public believes the problems exist. Our job must now be to correct, in the eyes of the public—this belief system. If their beliefs are not in tune with the way things are, we must bring them in tune. We must search continually for answers and for better ways to deal with our problems. We just cannot live with the world the way it should be. It is not going to be the way it should be; it is going to be the way it is, and we are going to have to live with it that way. And to hope for a changing world with no overt action on our part to improve our lot is ridiculous. The role of the police is changing and we, the police, are the leading engineers in designing our future role.

In 1929, the two-way radio car was put into operation; and, with rare exception, we have not changed our patrolling patterns and techniques since that time. The sirens are louder, the lights are brighter and redder, the cars go faster and the tires are safer, but the basic procedures have not changed. This resistance to change or, perhaps, satisfaction with the *status quo* obstructs progressive police work.

On the other hand, improvements have been implemented. In 1926, a book was written on police interrogation. The fourth paragraph of the first chapter contained this classic statement: "The judicious use of corporal punishment will elicit an admission from even the most hardened of criminals." In other words, beat somebody long enough and he will say something! How times have changed! Today, we fire and prosecute peace officers for such criminal conduct.

While the great majority of complaints against police are unfounded, circumstances do occur where we must all realize that brutality, for example, still happens; and if it happens at all, it is wrong. What we must do is to firm up our policies, procedures and supervision so derelictions happen as rarely as possible.

This is especially true of overreaction. Today, as never before, the police just cannot afford to overreact. We know how easy and normal it is to meet aggression with aggression. When a part of the public acts aggressively toward the police, the natural tendency for the police is to respond in like manner. We cannot do it! Overreaction has been talked about and dealt with extensively. The consensus is that we must react and perform in a manner which we can live with afterward.

Another deplorable activity is for police to strike or "pseudo-strike." The shame and sham of so-called mass sickness in certain areas of our country is something law enforcement can do without.

Law enforcement needs help, but we have surely advanced

to a status that would not consider jeopardizing the public safety to gain this help. There are better ways to do this, with more benefits in the long run, such as selling and educating the public to our needs.

Along with this education, we might be able to resolve another two-way problem which hampers police-community relations—"generalizations" or "role defamation," as it is currently called. Examples of role defamation would include sweeping statements like "All students are liberal" or "All policemen are conservative." Also included would be statements where a particular group, usually a minority, is classified into one restricted category.

Peace officers frequently complain that people stereotype them in a specific category, such as, all policemen do this or all policemen do that. Yet, which is the worse group to stereotype, says the taxpayer—policemen! For example, while on duty, we stop someone and a first impression is formed. Psychologists and most sociologists warn that first impressions are usually false—and lasting. Yet we frequently judge the goodness or evil of a person with no more evidence than an impression that is likely false. A great American, Oliver Wendell Holmes, put this in a far better manner when he said, "Generalizations aren't worth a damn;" and he quickly added, "and that's generalization."

Peace officers have been "typed" as a very conservative group. Indeed, quite a few people believe that police comprise one of the few groups that would classify the John Birch Society as left-wing radicals. This may or may not be true, but one truth is that there is greater social pressure today for change than ever existed before. And for better or for worse, police are going to participate in this process of change.

Change happens so fast that today's roles and occupations cannot be well defined because they are in a constant state of alteration. In fact, some authors have suggested striking the word "change" from our language and substituting the word "changing" in its place. J. Robert Oppenheimer characterized the essence of the modern world: "One thing that is new is the prevalence of newness, the changing scale and scope of change itself, so that the world alters as we walk on it . . . not some small growth or rearrangement or moderation . . . but great upheaval."[4]

How do these changing, confusing times affect police-community relations? The McCone Commission, the National Commission on Civil Disorders, and the President's Crime Commission all point to four major sociological problems which police have to be concerned with because they are the root causes of civil disobedience: unemployment, undereducation, and substandard housing. These three can be considered "casual" as compared to the fourth problem: police-community relations.

Police-community relations is perhaps the most visible adjunct of government because it is out in front. Yes, we are out front, and we receive the brunt of all the social evils created by unemployment, poor housing, and undereducation, which have built up for years. Also, we cannot say that these are not our problems. They are not ours to solve, but they are major sociological problems which every working policeman should be aware of as he does his job. Also, we should inform the public that these problems affect law enforcement in a manner which cannot be corrected by policemen being "good guys."

A current example of these sociological problems is seen in commodity riots of Washington, D.C. People form bands for the purpose of breaking store windows and stealing merchandise. This was their way of obtaining goods which they could not have otherwise. A sad commentary on our society today, and who falls heir to this dilemma? The police.

The term *anomie* was developed many years ago in France; it means "normlessness.' All of us at one time have been either homesick or felt that the world was against us. Anyone who has not had this feeling is rare indeed. How does *anomie* apply to police-community relations?

Think about a person being educated with the concept that

[4] Bennis, Warren G.: *Changing Organizations.* New York, McGraw-Hill, 1966, p. 19.

he is going to have two jobs and get all sorts of good things—role expectation, preparing for something and then it never happens. Look at him a little later, especially a youngster, since the peak age of criminality in this country is now fifteen. What he probably wants most is a car. He sees one he cannot afford, and he begins to wonder why he fails to fit in that part of an "in group." And he thinks about the parents he seldom sees, and then he sees an "in group" that says burglaries are viewed as socially acceptable within that group. He goes from normlessness to a norm which is contrary to the norms of society. He becomes a criminal by our standards when he becomes a member of this "in group," and their standards become his new standards.

How do the police deal with these subcultures of criminal structure? Cultures spawned by the squalor and hopelessness of the ghetto proliferate police problems. What is the police role in this sociological morass . . . in society today? Is it to maintain the social order; to protect life and property? What about that funny word "service" which today has a broader connotation than ever before in police work?

Perhaps we expect too much if we want a complete definition of the police role. The concept of changing certainly applies here, and a narrowing of parameters of police definition—if it could be done—may not be beneficial. It is safe to assume that our changing role of the past reflects the future, and thus we must be committed to a philosophy of greater and greater open-mindedness; and perhaps more important is to learn from our past mistakes.

We all know of many instances of good police action, and we know of too many instances of poor police action. One recent instance involved an officer eating his lunch at a drive-in restaurant. A young student of police science ran up to him and said, "Officer, there is a woman over in the vacant lot across the street and she's screaming and laying on the ground." The officer looked back and said, "Let her scream. I'm eating a sandwich."

This instance illustrates an important concept about the police role. It is fine for police administrators to talk about police-community relations programs; and often, the working police officers say of it, "Well, here comes another P-CR program and a lot of chit-chat about what we have to do!"

But if the individual officer does a good job in his role, first-line police work, this so-called need for redefining our role will become a minimal thing. The public will not need definitions because good police officers do not put us in a position of having the public criticize. An illustration: a bad arrest occurs, and the case goes through the court system and a *Miranda* comes down to haunt us. But never forget—we are living with problems created by a few officers who did not really believe in this thing called police-community relations. It takes something as terrible as a riot to convince all parties concerned that we do have a problem.

Jerome Skolnick, Associate Professor of Sociology at the University of Chicago, has written several articles on police and their future role in society. He visualizes the peace officer, just a few years from now, as being more qualified than the police agent recommended by the Crime Commission . . . possibly a kind of "street-corner ombudsman." If the officer sees a health problem, he reports it to the proper people in the health field; he makes sure the problem is being solved. If he sees a fire hazard, he does the same thing; a water hazard; food hazard; any type of hazard—and he is still out there to handle the police role. Skolnick is saying that even though we have already expanded the concept of what we do, it is expanding and changing even more drastically and thus is requiring much more expertise and ability on the part of each individual officer.

I believe we shall eventually progress to a stage in this country when we will hire people for police work right out of high school; but they will not see police work "per se" as regulars until they have spent about four years in a program that (hopefully) will be as prestigious as the military in terms of West Point and Annapolis; and as educationally sound as any criminology, police science or public administration program existing today. If peace officers are going to have to be more qualified in the future, we must upgrade their abilities to cope with the problems with which they must deal.

Peace officers today are not in the same role as they were yesterday; yet many agencies still give them just a few weeks of training. In other agencies, they receive eight or ten or twelve or sixteen or twenty weeks of training; all of which are totally inadequate to adapt to the new role being pressed on the police.

People outside police work declare that police have more responsibilities and more problems than ever before. This may be true. If it is, then law enforcement must demand that the public accept, along with this philosophy of requiring more of a peace officer, the philosophy that they, the public, must be responsible for assisting in preparing *their* officers before they are sent out to handle "the most difficult job in the world today."

John F. Kennedy once said, "A man does what he must in spite of personal consequences, in spite of obstacles and dangers and pressures, and that is the basis of all human morality." This is exactly what must be done in terms of the police role definition. If individual officers think about it and are willing to try to do something, then police-community relations will progress. But we must define our role in our own minds, individually, if we are going to accept it.

In the final analysis, is it not the individual officer that gets us into trouble, and is it not individual officers that can get us out of all this trouble?

Chapter 6

THE POLICE GO TO WAR

WILLIAM J. BOPP and DONALD O. SCHULTZ

During World War II, the ranks of local and state police agencies were seriously depleted as tens of thousands of officers went off to war. The war may well have been law enforcement's finest hour to date. Policemen abroad distinguished themselves in battle, but they paid a heavy price. More than a few police stations contain plaques honoring the department's war dead. At home, the shortage in qualified manpower created the need for extraordinary measures.

A Civilian Defense Corps was established to perform work created by the war. Air raid drills became a constant part of American life, and civilian air raid wardens were assigned to see that citizens complied with the rather strict blackout procedures that had been specified by government. Meetings and awareness lectures were also conducted by these dedicated people, who served on a volunteer basis.

Most police departments found it necessary to mobilize auxiliary police units to fill the vacancies created by the war. Auxiliary policemen were individuals who for one reason or another— advanced age, a phsyical infirmity, etc.—could not serve in the military. The auxiliary units were often activated by special legislation which stipulated that they would be disbanded when the war ended and the troops returned home. Auxiliary officers were generally full-time policemen, with limited police training, who acted as replacements for regular officers in the service. Auxiliary policemen performed admirably during their tours of duty and some gallantly forfeited their lives in defense of their communities. Some auxiliary police units, especially those in coastal cities

NOTE: From *A Short History of American Law Enforcement.* Springfield, Thomas, 1972. Reprinted with editorial adaptation from Covell, Howard V.: *A Brief History of the Metropolitan Police Department:* Washington, 1946, pp. 7–9.

where an enemy attack was considered a possibility, were trained in first aid, chemical warfare and bomb-dismantling procedures in case of invasion.

Reserve (part-time) police units were established in many communities. Reserve officers, who generally worked without pay, were put to work performing routine duties such as traffic direction, guard duty, clerical work, etc. Reserve officers also rode with policemen to maintain two-man patrol cars.

Most major law-enforcement agencies were subjected to basically the same war-related pressures; however, one department, the Metropolitan Police Department in the District of Columbia, found itself faced with a crisis, for obvious reasons. Although the exigencies that the men of the Metropolitan Police Department encountered were in many ways unique, their sacrifice and dedication in the face of adversity was typical of that made by their brothers nationwide.

With the declaration of war on December 7, 1941, the call upon the services of the Metropolitan Police Department increased rapidly. Some members of the department were immediately detailed to augment the White House police force, while others were dispatched to guard embassies, power plants, bridges, and other vital installations against sabotage. The Board of Commissioners afforded the department some relief when, on March 5, 1942, it permitted the hiring of fifty special policemen, who were known as defense guards. These defense guards were strategically deployed so that policemen could be relieved for patrol duty. The department was fast losing its experienced manpower to the Armed Services. No fewer than 341 had either enlisted or been drafted. Civilian augmentation of the police department began, and 6,000 volunteers were processed for an auxiliary police force. The Washington Police Academy was founded to train the recruits. Citizens from every walk of life generously offered their sevices as clerks, instructors, even laborers. Regular police personnel, after completing their tours of duty, often came back for another eight or ten hours of work with the volunteers. Precinct captains virtually worked 24 hours per day, and dozens of volunteers worked in the precinct stations registering more auxiliary policemen. This grand force of Washington citizens, armed with a badge, an overseas cap, a raincoat, a web belt, whistle, baton, armband and helmet, was a great deterrent to the commission of crime, not only during blackouts, but at other times. When the war ended, the *ad hoc* bodies of civilian volunteers disbanded after long and honorable service.

Chapter 7

"LAW AND ORDER" GAINS WHERE LEAST LIKELY—GREENWICH VILLAGE

Roger Ricklefs

A young man wearing nothing but blue jeans and hair hawks Maoist literature on the corner. A nearby store features burlap drapes printed with giant peace symbols. Another shop pushes Mick Jagger posters, tomato-scented organic bath salts and Day-Glo paints. It is clearly about the last place on earth to start a J. Edgar Hoover fan club. But permissive Greenwich Village, while still a center of left-wing, antipolice sentiment, is turning into a surprisingly fertile field for the law-and-order movement. The reason is quite simple. Crime in the area has risen sharply, and most Village residents clearly put safety above ideology.

Villagers now are heatedly demanding increased police protection, forming committees to fight crime, helping police catch dope pushers and talking a new line. "Crime is definitely changing my point of view," says a mod-dressed young real estate agent. "Ten years ago, I was an extreme leftist; today I'd favor the death penalty for dope pushers." Deputy Inspector Salvatore Matteis, commander of the 6th Police Precinct, which serves the area, says: "Attitudes toward the police are changing fast. People here have always been permissive—but now they're getting robbed."

SOARING CRIME RATE

The number of robberies (thefts involving violence or threat of violence) reported in the 6th Precinct soared to 896 last year, one per 96 residents and a staggering 89 per cent rise from two years earlier. Some sections of the Village have become major dope-peddling centers that attract addicts and criminals from the

Note: From *The Wall Street Journal*, July 9, 1971. Reprinted with permission.

whole city. Residents say they still consider parts of the Village relatively safe at any hour. But studies show that in terms of violent crimes per 1,000 citizens, Greenwich Village as a whole now is only about average for the city. It used to be considered one of New York's safest places.

So there is a whole new scene in the Village now. Last March, the area's volunteer, city-sponsored Planning Board established a Joint Emergency Committee to Fight Crime. Besides campaigning for improved police protection, the Committee has participated directly in catching criminals. In several incidents, members have observed signs of dope peddling in their neighborhoods and tipped off the police. This has produced numerous arrests so far, Inspector Matteis says.

Near one hotel, drug trading was so common that committee members were able to gather up and bring to the police hypodermic needles and other paraphernalia of addicts, says Mrs. Rachele Wall, Chairman of the Planning Board. The police then sent in a narcotics squad, which arrested pushers living in the hotel.

INVITING THE COPS

Other citizens are acting, too. "We're getting two or three times as much information from citizens as we got last year," says Inspector Matteis. "People who once wouldn't talk to a policeman are inviting us to address their block association meetings," he adds.

Recurring incidents of New York police corruption and abusiveness still feed widespread "anti-pig" sentiment in the Village. But the change in climate is still enough to make a policeman gloat. In this area's famous liberal newspaper, *The Village Voice*, reporter Clark Whelton writes: "Anti-police politics in the Village is rapidly losing its appeal. You can't have your cops and hate them, too." As Mr. Whelton noted in a crusading anticrime series, many Villagers now blame the area's crime rise partly on their own permissiveness, hostility toward police and resistance toward taking a "tough" line on crime. Today, Mr. Whelton contends, "the masochism quotient among Village liberals is almost down to zero. . . . There's nothing like getting knocked on the head by a mugger or coming home to a ransacked apartment to make you feel your dues are paid."

While acceptance of the police is rising, so is pressure for increased police protection. This pressure is a major reason the Police Department recently started an experimental project that will sharply increase the number of foot patrolmen in parts of the Village, police officials say.

This public pressure to fight crime increasingly comes from block associations, which are proliferating. "In the last two or three months alone, at least a dozen block associations have been formed in the Village, and the main impetus has been the rise in crime," says Inspector Matteis. Typically, the newly formed West 10th Street Block Association has attracted overflow audiences at its meetings. "To a man and woman, crime is the rallying point," says Mollie Allen, a book editor and one of the group's founders. "You have your own isolated incident and then you find you're one of many," she adds. Among other activities, the group has pressed homeowners to improve their outdoor lighting and has compaigned for increased police protection on the street.

Many Villagers are worried enough to change their own individual ways of life. Five years ago, Harold Silversmith kept his Food-O-Mart delicatessen on Seventh Avenue open until 1 A.M. and "never really thought about crime." Today he closes at 9:30 "to improve my chances. . . ." Mary Perot Nichols, city editor of *The Village Voice*, says: "I always used to feel this was the safest area in town. But now if it's late at night, I get into a cab just to go a few blocks."

A few individuals are even turning to vigilante activity. For many decades, residents of the South Village, a conservative enclave in Greenwich Village, have occasionally beaten up "undesirables." This activity now is on the rise, residents say. "Greenwich Village is on the brink of a serious vigilante problem," contends Art D'Lugoff, bearded owner of the area's Village Gate, a nightclub and theater. "People I would consider liberal are condoning vigilante activity now," he says.

As many of the area's criminals and addicts are black, the

crime wave is generating racism in the traditionally colorblind Village. "This is the best integrated area in the whole city, but some of the storekeepers are definitely turning racists," says Mr. D'Lugoff. "I just wouldn't have expected this ten years ago." To be sure, the Village's strong reaction to crime has its limits. "Most people here increasingly want police protection, but they wouldn't for one moment tolerate a breach of civil liberties," contends Mrs. Wall, the Planning Board chairman.

Perhaps surprisingly, the crime rise has not noticeably diminished the demand to live in the area. Though one-bedroom apartments sometimes rent for more than $400 a month, the Village is still one of the hardest places in the city to find an apartment. Many New Yorkers say they wouldn't live anywhere else.

Mrs. Wall, who lives in a house built in 1830 that still has its original rough plank floors, says: "I like the relaxed but lively life-style. It's interesting just to walk on the streets. I wouldn't move." Last year, every house on the block but hers was burglarized.

Chapter 8

SOCIAL SCIENCE EDUCATION FOR POLICE OFFICERS

GERALDINE MICHAEL

As society attempts to solve problems of criminal justice and law enforcement, police education and training becomes a top priority. In the absence of clear standards for recruitment and training, police departments have followed independent practices and policies which evolved through the years. Police training tended to focus almost exclusively on the technical aspects of police work and a gap between stated police philosophy and actual work practices developed.

Investigations to determine specific educational needs of police officers and studies such as the *Task Force Report: The Police* (1967), *Kerner Report* (1967) and the *Commission on Violence, Staff Report* (1969) found that police recruits tend to consider knowledge of firearms, un-armed defense and knowledge of the laws of the state and city sufficient information to be a good officer. Often officers, as well as recruits, appear to be unaware of (or at least to disregard) social explanations of human behavior. That is, they do not respond to events as though they were aware of the effects of poverty, discrimination, environment and the wide range of individual differences in our pluralistic society as causal factors in social unrest.

Thus to continue to train police officers in programs that emphasize technical training alone does not provide the officer with the kinds of information necessary for performance of his role in contemporary society. Furthermore, assuming that the officer will learn the other aspects of his job role performance "on the job" is an obvious fallacy.

NOTE: From *The Police Chief*, June, 1971, pp. 56–61. Reprinted with permission.

The influence on attitudes and performance of members of work groups has been noted in much of the investigations dealing with occupations and professions. While practically all investigations report that members of work groups are influenced to a greater or lesser degree, it would appear that influence on members of police officer work groups is more significant. Several studies (Dempsey, 1966; Kerner Report, 1967; Task Force, 1967) have found evidence of a police subcultural work group. Some groups are comprised of officers hostile towards persons and groups not in the subculture and are characterized by clannish, prejudicial attitudes. Such work groups' affiliations tend to exert great influence on attitudes and performance of officers, contributing to the tensions existing between officers and members of the public. When officers are sent into the field and subjected to the attitudes of the subculture, they tend to adopt this group's norms and values, thus perpetuating undesirable work attitudes and practices.

Attempts to reduce the friction thus created between police and the community as well as to reduce general tension and misunderstanding have utilized sensitivity training. However, there has been an alarming increase in negative criticism concerning sensitivity training and emotional confrontation. This criticism leads to serious doubts about sensitivity training as a part of police officer training programs.

That which follows is a report of the development of a general education social science program, presented at a Police Training Unit, which was created to meet the criticisms of existing training programs. This program was formulated by modifying an existing program which had focused on the technical aspects of law enforcement. The new program preserved technical features and added material dealing with social science principles and theories. The thrust of the program was threefold—technical training, 12 weeks; classroom instruction in social science, 40 hours; and situational training, 80 hours.

Situational training, a modification and combination of sociopsychodrama, situation testing and role playing was seen as a method to teach and/or modify behavior, to modify attitudes and cognitions and also as an opportunity for the officer-trainee to learn his expected behavior in a specific situation as well as behavior of others in related positions. Alternative modes of behavior could be perceived by the officer as he interacted with others in face-to-face encounters in controlled situations. The trainee's expectations of various roles could enable him to adjust his behavior in accordance with a presented situation in light of new information received in the "social awareness" education program. The trainee could use previously learned skills of communication to verbalize the problem and could receive immediate feedback as to the effectiveness of his solutions.

Operating on the principle that participation of those involved was prerequisite for success and effectiveness, systematic trials and variations of subject material and teaching techniques were undertaken. Individual differences, assignment, methods of classroom instruction, course content, the use of visual aids and various techniques to increase trainee participation, involvement and commitment to the problem at hand were considered. The officers themselves were continually involved in the decision-making processes in what finally constituted the program.

The trainees were officers and recruits attending classes at a police training unit. The classes were divided into four groups. Group 1 received only 12 weeks technical training. Groups 2, 3 and 4 received 12 weeks technical training, 40 hours social science, and 80 hours situational training. I was the instructor for Group 2. The instructors for Groups 3 and 4 were two police officers with over ten years of service, experience as an instructor at the training unit and more than two years of college work toward a degree in law enforcement. I trained them.

A multipurpose classroom was used which permitted not only lecture and discussion but also the use of films and other visual aids. Lectures were held to a minimum. Pamphlets on each topic, written by this investigator especially for use in this program, were handed out a day or two before that topic was to be discussed in class. Methods of instruction included discussion groups, guest speakers, small-group projects, individual research and question-and-answer sessions.

Topics discussed in the classroom included introduction to social science and methods of research; development of the individual, including perception, attitudes, stereotyping and behavioral patterns; man and society including the work ethic, change in the United States and resistance to change; urbanization, including trends in cities, poverty, welfare, economic systems, and economic equality. Race and minority groups, Black leaders and Negro history; civil disorders including student protest, riots and violence; crime deviant behavior, criminals, juveniles and Supreme Court decisions; and role of the police officer today and professionalism.

A city park and an unused apartment building were used as settings for situational training. This city park was used as a setting to simulate situations involving vehicular accidents, crowd control and other outdoor activities. The apartment building was used as a setting for a variety of situations. Actors were volunteers from various police units and occasionally from outside the department. Situations were designed to illustrate both technical and sociopsychological aspects of police work. For example, situations were designed to show how effectively the trainees handled a potentially dangerous situation; trainees' attitude toward various ethnic or minority groups; trainees' ability to follow direction; and trainees' ability to handle a situation in which they are accused of cowardliness, of prejudice or of theft. Other situations illustrated what is reasonable cause to stop and search; in a situation of mutual accusations, who to search and who to arrest; legal aspects of intoxication; attempts to evade arrest; complaints involving teenagers; socioeconomic stereotyping; detection techniques; community relations situations; psychiatric incidents; use of force to stop a fight; and domestic problems.

In any situation, it was possible to have any desired combination of race and sex, either of the actors or the trainees. In all situations, evaluations proceeded on the basis of the trainee's performance. Trainees were given the opportunity to reconstruct the situations and try out alternative solutions.

ASSESSMENT OF THE PROGRAM

Classroom performance was evaluated by a preliminary test and a final test. Item content of the two tests was identical. Response to the preliminary test items indicated that 68 per cent of the trainees held opinions similar to those reported as "typical" by the *Kerner Report* and the *Commission on Violence, Staff Report*. Views stated were generally contrary to the findings of social scientists.

A comparison of the responses to the two written tests showed that trainees in the social science program stated different opinions and responses on the final test. Of the responses of groups 2, 3 and 4, 95 per cent were congruent with the discussion and/or demonstrations provided in the classroom and in situational training. Apparently the trainees in the social science program could and did provide explanations which were not typical of expressions provided by other police officer groups.

A significant difference was found between Group 1 (technical training only) and Groups 2, 3, and 4 (social science program) in overall performance and by item in situational training. The data indicated that those trainees taking part in the program were rated as more respectful, courteous, pleasant and sincere than those not receiving the training. They were also rated as having available to them more ways of handling situations than those who had not taken part in the program.

No difference between groups was found relative to items concerned with skills acquired in technical training such as use of correct search techniques, knowledge of weapons, knowledge of radio, control of situations; or in ratings on neatness of appearance.

UTILIZATION OF PUBLIC RESPONSE

Letters of commendation and complaints by the public are routinely used as a method of evaluation of officer performance and are made a part of the officer's permanent record. As part of the evaluative aspects of this report, only complaints data were analyzed. Some commendation data are presented but these data are not to be viewed as complete, exact or precise.

Complaints are filed under categories of brutality, missing property, harassment, procedure, conduct and service. The accompanying table reflects complaints received by the four study groups during the first six months after leaving the training unit.

COMPLAINTS

Complaint	Group 1 N = 60	Groups 2, 3, 4 N = 154
Brutality	5	0
Missing Property	0	0
Harassment	0	0
Procedure	2	5
Conduct	12	5
Service	2	2

More complaints were received for Group 1 than for the combined complaints received for Groups 2, 3 and 4. It is recognized that these results could be due to many complex and interacting factors. Nevertheless, some of the difference can indeed be attributed to the experiences of the trainees in the social science program herein described. No complaints of verbal abuse were made against any trainee in the social science education program.

The following data are presented with reservations due to the inaccessibility of some records. As mentioned previously, a clannish, prejudicial work group was identified which was composed primarily of officers with three to ten years of service. Available data indicate that less than one-third of the officers received one-half the complaints. Seventy-five percent of the letters of commendation were received by officers with less than three or more than ten years of service:

Length of Service: Years	Commendations %	Complaints %	Percent of Force
1 to 3, inclusive and 10 or more	75	50	71
4 to 10, inclusive	25	50	29

All percentages are approximate.

Approximately 66 per cent of those officers with less than four years of service have taken part in the social science program. It is assumed that as these officers enter the four-to-ten-years-of-service group, the influence of the subcultural work group will decline. This is based primarily on the generally accepted thesis that the best psychological protection against unwarranted influence is "individual and collective awareness which could forestall insidious manipulation by dominant leaders or conformist tyranny by a group." This, theoretically, can also reduce the differences between stated philosophy of police departments and actual practice of officers. As stated previously, these data and discussion are presented with reservations.

PREDICTING PERFORMANCE

Relying primarily on observations of performance of trainees during situational training, predictions were made of posttraining performance for 24 trainees. These predictions were made for performance categories of brutality, procedure and conduct, resignation and injury. Predictions refer to specific individuals.

PREDICTIONS FOR FIRST SIX MONTHS
POSTTRAINING PERFORMANCE

Category	No. of Trainees N = 24	Performance
Brutality	2	2 complaints
Injury	2	2 killed
Resignation	2	2 resigned
Procedure or conduct	18	18 complaints

Based on such a small number, the data are considered inconclusive. However, the instructors at the training unit have continued to make predictions of posttraining performance with a 95 per cent accuracy. It is therefore assumed that some of the behavior of officers in actual working conditions can be predicted from test results and observations during situational training. All predictions reported in this study related to inappropriate behavior. It is recommended that future research investigate the possibility of developing predictive criteria for both appropriate and inappropriate behavior.

PERFORMANCE EVALUATION BY FIELD SUPERVISOR

As a trainee completed training, he was assigned to a field supervisor. Analysis of the supervisor's reports for the study groups indicated that the reports do not discriminate between performance or allow one to determine with any degree of precision what the performance is. This data appears to produce the doubtful data. That which in theory should have produced the most useful data failed to provide anything of analytical utility.

Since this method of evaluation is the most common evaluation used by police departments throughout the country, it is recommended that future research be concerned with field-supervisor qualifications and training with regard to personnel evaluation. Also, in view of the above, a recommendation is made for instituting an evaluating procedure that is continuous and constant and which does not depend upon traditional field-supervisor evaluation.

TRAINING OFFICERS AS INSTRUCTORS

Task Force Report, The Police (1967) emphasized that when officers with expertise in social science are available, they should be used as instructors. Outside instructors lack credibility and the information they present is therefore often rejected. The officers working at the training unit cooperated at all times in an effort to eliminate any credibility gap between a civilian instructor and the trainees.

A sergeant and a patrolman requested that they be given the opportunity to serve as social science instructors in the program. They observed the classroom setting with one as instructor. They were trained in classroom presentation and preparing material. Both officers were familiar with instruction techniques and evaluation of situational training as applied to technical skills. They had previously worked as evaluator and actor in the technical situations. They served as instructor for Groups 3 and 4.

An attempt was made to determine if a difference between instructors was evident. A comparison of scores on a multiple-choice test over content of classroom instruction indicated no significant difference between groups in ability to answer questions.

A difference was found in situational training evaluation, notably on the item "listen to what others say." Also a higher percentage of responses rated "needs improvement" and "unsatisfactory" were recorded for Group 3 (10%) and Group 4 (8.8%) compared to 7 per cent for Group 2. Data provides both affirming and disaffirming evidence, and is therefor inconclusive. Given the fact that colleges which offer police training and also police-training units tend to utilize instructors with law enforcement experience rather than academic credentials, the procedure becomes questionable. The question, "Are the most appropriate instructors being used?" remains unresolved. The extent and implications of this practice needs to be systematically investigated. Furthermore, police training units often use personnel from other law-enforcement agencies as instructors. It is recommended therefore, that (a) studies be made of the relationship of police departments to other agencies and (b) the relationship of officer education to related persons and agencies.

Three questions which served as a frame of reference for the study remain to be answered. Some findings could be considered as providing partial answers to each of the questions. Each question is restated below and findings are discussed.

1. *Can the traditional norms and values of police officers as reflected in various reports and public complaints be modified by an overall program of classroom instruction and situational training?*

Analysis of the data indicates changes in performance that may reflect changes in traditional norms and values. These changes are attributable in part to the impact of exposure to the social science program. Differential responses to evaluative items indicated that Group 2, 3 and 4 were characterized by different attitudes and norms than Group 1 which was not involved in the program. The data are relevant for making statements about short-term or immediate effects of exposure to social science content. Nothing can be said about persistence of effects until longitudinal investigations of police-officer attitudes and performance are undertaken to determine relationships over time between attitudes and performance, attitudes and time factors, and attitudes and work-group characteristics.

2. *Does participation in the program help reduce the difference between stated police philosophy and actual police-officer behavior?*

In part, this study represents an attempt to reduce this gap by utilizing role theory. Comparing the performance of trainees in the modified program and the previous program indicates there are discernible differences in performances. The trainees who participated in the modified program displayed modalities of performance that more closely approximated that stated philosophic prescriptions for police-officer performance.

3. *Can one obtain effective criteria for assessing the efficiency of a police officer?*

It would appear that effective criteria for assessing an officer can be obtained. A major issue focuses on the fact that both private citizens and government agencies have not established guidelines for recruitment, training and placement of officers. A recommendation is made that future research deal with the problem of establishing guidelines and standards for recruitment, training and placement.

GENERAL IMPLICATIONS

On the basis of this study, the quality, character and impact of technical training cannot be evaluated. However, logically, all aspects of a program—technical training, social science education and situational training—should be integrated. Future studies should focus on the relationships between the components of the program and the effect on the total program.

Situations designed for situational training for this program were based in part on the complaints received from the public. Some situations incorporated into the program allowed trainees to demonstrate ability to improve police-community relationships. Complaints, however, continued to indicate that members of the general public lack an understanding of the nature of the role of the police officer. Improved police-community relations may result from a public cognizant of the rights, obligations and limitations of the police officer role. It is recommended that research involving evaluation of existing police-community relation programs be instituted.

It has also been noted that theoretically the police officer could function effectively as a change agent within the department as well as with the public. Social science education may make the officer more aware of the problems of those he polices and therefore may be a factor in improving police-community relations.

No attempt was made to place trainees according to individual abilities, attributes or performance during training. Yet, it is obvious that some individuals would be more suited in one area, or unit, over another. People who come into police work reflect varying degrees of aptitudes and specializations. Trainees need not be hired into the department at the same grade, nor do all trainees require a perfectly homogeneous training exposure. Police departments might profit by doing selective as well as general recruitment. Also, training units should offer training especially tailored to the individual.

Regardless of the effectiveness of social science programs in general, unless accepted by police departments, social training will not become part of police education. Even if social science programs are included in training programs, unless those in authority are convinced, accept the premises and convey to the trainees the meaningfulness of such training, the trainees may view the training as purely useless exercises.

In general, emphasis in training focuses on traditional technical skills rather than social science information or understanding the individuals or groups the officer will serve. "The place to learn about people is on the job," is an answer given by law-enforcement personnel generally. This might be effective if one could establish a practice of assigning new police officers to "effective" officers for "on-the-job" training. This does not occur, and situation training assures some exposure to setting-situations which approximate actual work experiences.

Thus it would appear that a most urgent need (among many) in police-officer training and education today is to convince those in authority of the necessity of an educated officer. Sufficient economic support must be provided for training and education.

SUMMARY

This report of a social science education program for police officers utilized six questions as a frame of reference.

1. Do police officers make the most appropriate instructors for police training units?

2. Can the behavior of police officers in actual working conditions be predicted during training?
3. Are field supervisor's evaluations of officer performance of any utility?
4. Can the traditional norms and values of police officers as reflected in various reports and public complaints be modified by an overall program of classroom instruction and situational training?
5. Can a training program help reduce the widely noted difference between stated police philosophy and actual police officer behavior?
6. Can one obtain effective criteria for assessing a good officer?

Findings indicated that programs can be designed to achieve specific goals but also indicated the need for future investigation. Therefore the following recommendations were made:

1. Establish criteria for appropriate and inappropriate behavior of police officers.
2. Institute evaluating procedures that are continuous and constant and which do not depend upon traditional field supervisor evaluations.
3. It is necessary to have systematic investigation of extent and implications of using only police officers as instructors in training units.
4. Establish guidelines and standards for recruitment, training, and placement.
5. Evaluate existing police-community relations programs.
6. Begin selective as well as general recruitment.

The study points to the desirability of modifying officer training and education. It would also imply convincing those in authority of the necessity of producing educated police officers.

In retrospect, there is great promise in involving social scientists in studies such as this which use social science theories and principles. Many programs utilized for policy making and decision making which affect the general public are based on non-social science perspectives. There appears to be a real gap between utilization of social science information and planning and policy making in the general community. Therefore, in this sense, this kind of an effort should encourage others to apply social science information to generation of programs in other areas of criminal justice and law enforcement.

OTHER REFERENCES

Commission on Violence, Staff Report. Government Printing Office, 1969.

Dempsey, Jack: Nation-wide survey of selected police departments. *Interoffice Communication,* Kansas City, Mo., Police Department, 1967.

Lakin, M.: Some ethical issues in sensitivity training. *Am. Psychol.* 24: 10, October, 1969. pp. 923–928.

Michael, Geraldine: Social Science Education for Police Officers.—Ph.D. Dissertation, University of Missouri, Kansas City, 1970.

Moreno, S.L.: *Psychodrama.* New York, Beacon House, 1946.

Sikes, M.P. and Cleveland, S.E.: Human relations training for police and community. *Am. Psychol.,* October, 1968, pp. 766–769.

Chapter 9

A DYING ART?

WILLIAM J. BOPP

The past decade has seen a great profusion of writings—some scholarly, some not—on the police and their role in society. Although the scope and direction differed in each work, the conclusions seemed to carry the same message: the police were ill-equipped to handle the broad range of social issues that were surfacing, often violently, in the country. When, in 1967, the President's Commission on Law Enforcement and Administration of Justice released its task-force report on the police, it reached the same conclusion, stating that "The quality of police service will not significantly improve until higher educational requirements are established for its personnel."[1]

Yet, education per se was not enough, said the President's Commission, for too many of the existing police science programs offered curricula so vocational in nature as to be unworthy of a college discipline. Many programs emphasized the technical skills needed in police work, to the exclusion of almost everything else, notably instruction in a policeman's social responsibilities. The Commission, probably the most influential body of its type in the history of American law enforcement, had a dramatic impact upon all phases of the profession, especially police education. A virtual revolution has occurred in colleges and universities which offers programs in police science. As a result, "nuts and bolts" programs have been discredited, criminal justice as a concept and a professional discipline has come into prominence, the role of social science in police instruction has become paramount, and the word "technical" has fallen into disrepute among academicians.

NOTE: From *The Police Chief*, April, 1970, pp. 42–47. Reprinted with permission.

[1] President's Commission on Law Enforcement and Administration of Justice: *Task Force Report: The Police*. Washington: U.S. Government Printing Office, 1967, p. 126.

College programs—be they police science, law enforcement, criminology or criminal justice—now seek to fulfill both a short-range and a long-range goal: (a) to provide officers and prospective officers with an education which will assist them in meeting their social responsibilities and (b) to prepare officers to assume leadership positions in their respective police departments. These goals are being reached, say the professors, through a "liberal education" which emphasizes a "software" (as opposed to "hardware") approach to the profession. To oversimplify, community and interagency relations are in; "how-to-handcuff" is out. No attempt will be made here to discredit the approach, for my undergraduate degree is in social science, and anyway such an attack would be akin to attacking motherhood. Yet, regardless of the value of the approach—and it must be stated unequivocally that it has enormous value—a certain bothersome side effect is occurring.

Professors readily acknowledge the immediate and the long-range aims of higher education, but they differ on the ways in which these aims should be reached. Too many academicians seem to be saying that if you emphasize the short-term goal (the officer's social responsibilities), the long-term goal (the officer's ascension to leadership roles) will take care of itself. Expose the patrolman to a good liberal arts education, they say, and someday you'll have a good chief of police. Unfortunately, this is not the case.

Police executives are not, nor should they be, sociologists. They must certainly have knowledge of the social sciences and humanities, but it should be remembered that they are first and foremost *administrators*. Any discipline which has as one of its primary goals the training of future administrators, is a professional, not an academic discipline. And, regardless of how police educators abhor the "technical" aspects of police work, technical courses do have a place in the college curriculum, especially executive-development courses.

If some are uncomfortable with this assertion, let them consider several factors. First, administration (not just police administration, but administration in the broad concept) is, in every sense of the term, "an art." An eminent professor once defined administration as "cooperative rational action,"[2] a definition which is in no way incompatible with contemporary educational programs for policemen. Second, other disciplines have been able to integrate within their curricula both the academic and technical branches of their respective programs. Public administration, education, business administration and industrial management are but a few fields which have achieved an acceptable blend of technical and academic offerings. Third, the words "technical" and "vocational" are often used interchangeably, as if they were synonyms. They are not! Vocational education, most would agree, has no place in a college program for policemen. Technical education does have a place, as any professor of business administration will tell you.

Most programs offer a course or two in police administration; however, one or two courses serve only to introduce one to the subject. It is a rare program indeed which has as many as three or four administration courses within the major, and those that do still do not give the student a real grasp of administration as an art.

Two points are clear. Police administration needs to be lifted dramatically from its position of subordination, and this upgrading need not be done at the expense of the social science approach. Recall, if you will, that, of the eight chapters (excluding the introduction) in *Task Force Report: The Police*, five were devoted to administrative subjects. One full chapter was on the police executive's role in policymaking; yet how many police policymaking courses exist in police curricula? Unfortunately, when meaningful administrative courses are offered by colleges, they are often placed in noncredit workshops, scheduled for short periods of time, with enrollment limited to high-ranking officers. We have a good deal to learn from other professional disciplines in this regard. By all means we should present workshops; and we should schedule seminars on selected topics and use in-service training whenever possible; but we should use such techniques as an adjunct to, rather than a substitute for, college-level courses.

[2] Waldo, Dwight: *The Study of Public Administration.* New York, Random House, 1967, p. 5.

There are reasons to believe that the externally oriented police chief of the 60's will be more inward looking in the 70's; that because of the fledgling "blue power" phenomenon, he will be unable to devote his time to outside community problems as much as he may like because of internal activities in his department. It is not only desirable but imperative that future police executives be exposed to the same type of education that business executives have had for years. Courses in policy making, budgeting, decision making, employee relations and the like are no longer luxuries which college students can take as electives outside the major. They are necessities which must be offered within the major.

This article will probably be construed by some as a polemic against the social science approach to law enforcement. Not so! Social science has a place in the college law-enforcement curriculum but not to the exclusion of police administration. The pendulum, as followers of the Supreme Court are fond of saying, has swung too far in one direction. It is time, once again, for a reevaluation of priorities. It is time to begin integrating the social aspects of police work with the technical elements of administration. The two are not incompatible!

PART II
MINORITY GROUPS AND THE POLICE

INTRODUCTION

It has often been said that the P-CR problem is, in reality, a problem of P-MR—police-minority relations. Indeed, some of the bloodiest and most costly riots have been racial explosions triggered by police action. In fairness to law enforcement, almost all of the conditions that breed poor police-minority relations are not of police making and not within their power to solve, though there are those who constantly decry police failures in this matter. Be that as it may, the police still have a responsibility to understand minority problems and to act in a way calculated to improve their rapport with society's deprived groups.

In Chapter 10, J.E. Curry and Glen D. King chronicle "The Effect of Prejudice on Minorities." In Chapter 11, Jack L. Kuykendall asserts that both minority groups and the police have, over the years, been involved in a series of unpleasant encounters that has led to mutual hostility and negative perceptions. He states that repetitive and frequent negative contacts will continue to lead to individual and collective confrontation and violence.

In "Social Change and the Police," Louis A. Radelet says that the two major problems at the root of Negro antagonism toward the police are permissive law enforcement and discriminatory field practices, a contention that is reinforced in Chapter 13, "The Negro Community," and Chapter 14, "The Police and the Community," both products of presidential-commission studies.

Sterling Tucker's "The Ghetto, the Ghettoized, and Crime" points up the self-defeating and often purposeless life of innercity dwellers, which historically has led to a higher crime rate for residents of deprived areas.

Chapter 10

THE EFFECT OF PREJUDICE ON MINORITIES

J.E. Curry and Glen D. King

Police officers have frequently commented on certain distinctive behavior traits of the Negroes as a group. Other minority groups also seem to have fallen into behavior patterns which are dissimilar from the culture of society as a whole. It is important that the real reasons for such behavior be understood.

Most minority groups live in an atmosphere where prejudice, discrimination and scapegoating are prevalent. This affects the people's behavior in significant ways. Because of the prejudice and discrimination so frequently directed against them, members of minority groups are more than usually sensitive and defensive. This is not too difficult to understand, for when people are made to feel from childhood that they are different from other people, they are bound to be affected in some way.

Because minority-group individuals sometimes feel that other persons are prejudiced against them, they are continually fearful of assault, insult or discrimination. They live in an atmosphere of constant apprehensiveness. Because of the conditions under which they are forced to live, they frequently develop strong self-protective reactions. When a person is constantly treated as if he were inferior, he must eventually begin to feel that this inferiority actually exists. He may then develop aggressiveness as a compensation for his feelings of inferiority, or he may develop an overpowering shyness which causes him to retreat from the cause of his condition.

While this occurs frequently in minority groups, it is by no means restricted to them but is a universal human reaction. Any-

Note: From Curry, J.E. and King, G.D.: *Race Tensions and the Police.* Springfield, Thomas, 1962, pp. 39–43.

one who feels insecure or inferior must eventually develop some defense mechanism. Psychologists realize that arrogance is very frequently only a cover for inferiority complexes.

Many privileges which members of the majority group generally take for granted are denied to members of minority groups. In many areas, the privilege on unlimited use of hotels, restaurants and theaters, free choice of residence and free competition for jobs are included in this classification. Because of the frustration which must invariably accompany such denial, many persons within minority groups react either by aggression or by withdrawal and an attempt to avoid further frustration.

This might be a partial explanation of the fact that some members of minority groups seem to be more inclined to commit crimes of violence. Others are generally withdrawn from contacts with whites, which would expose them to discrimination. Still others respond by aggression of a competitive nature. They compete vigorously and try had to excel in finance or the arts.

It should not be difficult for the police officer to understand what minority-group members have to contend with and why they react defensively as they do. In many ways, the police are themselves a minority group. An exaggerated illustration used in training programs for new officers is, "You may have been beating your wife for years before you joined the police department but then you were just a man up the street who beat his wife. Now you are that policeman who beats his wife." or "You were that idiotic driver who drove like wild on a quiet residential street but now you are that policeman who drives recklessly." It is almost impossible for a police officer to become involved in any activity either on or off duty in which his occupation does not enter. This is proven time and time again in social functions when members of the public feel constrained to tell the police officer about a traffic citation they received. Almost invariably the explanation will begin with, "I know that your men are normally right but on this occasion . . ."

Minority groups face much the same problem. We are inclined to think of their transgressions in terms of their race rather than in terms of the individuals involved. Many newspaper accounts relate the race of offenders when such information is not actually relevant to the story.

Carrying a bit further the parallel between police officers and other minority groups, let us look at some of the generalizations made about a policeman. We all resent the portrayal of policemen so frequently found in motion pictures and in the press. Cartoons frequently show the officer as having a small head, huge stomach and big feet. If the cartoonist really wants to show the police officer at his best, he usually shows him reaching back to get an apple or a banana off a fruit stand. Law-enforcement officers who are consciously striving to improve the level of service provided and professionalize the vocation find that this constant stereotyping crucifies them. Because of the public attitude such caricatures foster, police officers find it extremely difficult to develop a code of ethics which will demand for them recognition as professionals.

Discrimination bred by such generalizations has a direct bearing on the number of offenses committed by the groups against whom the discrimination is directed. If for no other reason, the police officer should seek to avoid discriminatory practices because of this. The realization that a lessening of discrimination tends to result in a lowering of the crime rate should be incentive enough for the police officer to avoid discriminatory practices.

It is frequently pointed out that members of minority groups are responsible for a percentage of crime far out of proportion with the percentage they constitute of the total population. This is pointed to as an indication that by nature, the members of the group are more than usually lawless. It must, however, be realized that because of discrimination, a great majority of the minority groups are forced to live under conditions conducive to crime. Regardless of the race of the person involved, slum conditions and a vicious environment breed criminal offenses. Practically always, the highest crime rate occurs in the poorest districts.

Because of discrimination, the economic status of many minority groups is very low. Due partly to poverty and partly to the fact they are not permitted residence in other sections, they live mainly in the slum areas of the city. Their housing is generally poor and overcrowded. The neighborhoods in which they live usually have few recreational facilities and what do exist are normally of inferior quality. The areas in which they live are frequently centers of prostitution, gambling and other vicious activities.

The environment to which they are exposed means that the people living in these areas are more exposed to conditions conducive to crime than are other members of the public. This has been frequently cited as a part of the reason for the high delinquency and crime rates in these groups.

Restriction of the normal activities of a minority group often brings about exaggerated behavior in other directions. Minority groups suffer from restrictions in many types of activities that other people take for granted, such as the enjoyment of restaurants, hotels, bowling alleys, swimming pools and others. Discrimination results in the narrowing of the minority group member's field of opportunities and activities. It should not be surprising that many people so restricted intensify their activities in fields where they are not the subjects of discrimination.

One aspect of the sensitiveness and defensiveness of minority groups which should be of special concern to all police officers is to distrust and fear of the police which these groups frequently have. This attitude obviously makes more difficult the officer's role in dealing with racial prejudices and tensions. In many parts of the country the members of minority groups believe that if they are arrested, they will be physically abused and that they will not be given the same sort of treatment normally afforded persons in a like condition. There is too great a resentment on the part of many members of minority groups toward the police in general. This resentment is not always justified, but unfortunately in many instances there is ample justification.

There have been many instances when the police authorities were law-enforcement officials, in the usually accepted meaning of the term, only so far as the majority group was concerned. Occasionally the police have made no pretense of impartiality so far as the minority groups were concerned. They seemed to feel that it was their job not only to enforce the law but also to enforce white supremacy and to keep other groups in their places.

A serious problem in public relations exists when the police are feared and distrusted by the minority group. In order to do a good job of law enforcement, officers must have the confidence and support of the public. In the field of race relations, police can accomplish little unless they have the confidence of both the majority and minority groups.

If minority groups are uncooperative and antagonistic toward the police, it is only human for police officers to respond in the same manner, especially if they have had bad experiences with that group in the past. The situation then becomes a vicious circle, with neither the police nor the minority group taking the first steps which could lead to a better understanding. When a condition of mutual antagonism exists, it is almost impossible for the police to do a fair and effective job of law enforcement. A situation is created which is very damaging to the public peace. For this reason, it is extremely important that every police officer makes sure that in his contacts with members of a minority group his conduct is above reproach.

Chapter 11

POLICE AND MINORITY GROUPS: TOWARD A THEORY OF NEGATIVE CONTACTS

Jack L. Kuykendall

INTRODUCTION

The police in the United States are a focal point of conflict during periods of social change. As the state's instrument of legitimatized force, they are representatives of the existing social system. Yet in a democratic society which emphasizes the "rule of law," the police must act as a governing mechanism for the processes of social change: "To maintain a balance between conflict and consensus necessary to a democratic society, the police hold to the old value system and, simultaneously, protect legitimate social change resulting from society's structural strain." (Fox, 1966.)

A major source of "structural strain" in society results from the aspirations of minority groups as they press for equity in the distribution of social, economic and political rewards. Challenges to the "system" and strategies utilized to effectuate change continually place police and some minority groups in confrontation. The pervasive hostility and danger inherent in these conflicts has caused a proliferation of anxiety, distrust and hatred. The police and some minority groups often view each other as enemies—each group representing an obstacle to what the other is trying to achieve. The National Advisory Commission on Civil Disorders (1968, p. 299) says that ". . . abrasive relationships between police and Negroes and other minority groups have been a major source of grievance, tension and, ultimately, disorder."

These "abrasive relationships" are viewed as an immediate consequence of a continuing series of negative contacts between

Note: From *Police*, September-October, 1970, pp. 47–54.

police officers and members of minority groups. Negative contacts are defined as those situations in which minority-group members perceive they have been treated inequitably by police. Such contacts have the possible implicit dimension of initiating or reinforcing negative stereotyping of one group by the other. The purpose of this paper is to move toward development of a theory of the negative contact situations.

In analyzing police behavior, five factors will be considered: selective recruitment; socialization process of the organization; dual responsiveness of the police system to a "legal" and "order" orientation; the institutionalization of the police as a power group, and the conflicting and discretionary aspects of the police role.

The minority groups, that is, Indian-Americans, Oriental-Americans, Spanish-speaking-Americans and Black-Americans, are evaluated in terms of factors that will bring them into contact with police. These include their spatial location, the cultural norms which conflict with implicit and explicit values of the police, the degree to which a minority is pressing for change in status and the strategies utilized to effectuate such change, police perception of the minority as a "problem" and specific complaints of inequitable police treatment.

After a discussion of the police and each minority group, a section on the dynamics of the negative-contact situations is presented. The final section suggests propositions that may be useful in theory building.

THE POLICE
Selective Recruitment

There has long been a concern about the possibility of "undesirables" being attracted to the police profession (Blum, 1964). Supposedly, the role provides the opportunity for individuals with personality, emotional or character disorders to act out aggressive or inappropriate behavior in a societally sanctioned capacity. Such behavior could include dominance drive, sado-masochism, a desire to control one's antisocial tendencies or to legitimatize criminal impulses, compensatory reactions for inferiority feelings, displaced aggression, authoritarianism, immorality and dishonesty (Chwast, 1965; Wilson, 1953). Under the guise of legitimate justification, individuals can indulge in behavioral excesses without explicit condemnation. The number of such "types" actually recruited into law enforcement is not known; however, there is important information available concerning the individuals who do become police officers.

Lohman and Misner (1966, pp. 192–193) have assumed that a great majority of police officers are recruited from the lower socioeconomic or "working" classes. Studies by Niederhoffer (1967, p. 37) and Bayley and Mendelsohn (1969, pp. 4–6) confirm the predominance of police recruits with "working-class" backgrounds. Vander Zanden (1966, p. 105) points to several studies which indicate that prejudice is more likely in lower-class whites than in members of higher socioeconomic groups because of the threat blacks (and other minority groups) pose in social and economic competition.

The individual from the "working class" also brings to the police role a "preoccupation with maintaining self-respect, proving one's masculinity, 'not taking any crap,' and not being 'taken in'" (Wilson, 1968, p. 34). The emphasis upon masculinity among police has been substantiated in the studies of Matarazzo et al. (1964), and Dillman (1964). The results of the Edwards Personal Preference Schedule given to 81 successful police applicants by Matarazzo indicate that ". . . [they] describe themselves as having strong needs to excell or achieve, be the center of attention, understand and dominate others, stick to a job until it is done, and to be 'one of the boys' among men." Similar findings were derived from Minnesota Multiphasic Personality Inventories completed by 35 applicants: ". . . [These aspiring police officers were found to be] typical of the enlisted man one often encounters in the military service; blustery, sociable, exhibitionistic, active, manipulating others to gain their own ends, opportunistic, unable to delay gratification, impulsive, and showing some tendencies toward overindulgence in sex and drinking. In a word, fitting the lower socioeconomic groups' stereotype of the 'man's man.'" (Matarazzo et al., 1964)[1] Dillman also an-

[1] Examinations administered to 243 successful police (116) and fireman applicants in Portland, Oregon, were the Wechsler Adult Intelligence Scale,

alyzed police recruit responses to the Michigan Sentence Completion Test and concluded that among other factors there was an "idealized and highly masculine" relationship with the male parent.

There are indications that some police departments intentionally recruit from the "working-class" strata of society because of the type of skills developed during socialization. These individuals have stood the test of a "street-corner" or "gang" society and have the ability to better understand and cope with the element of the community the police must frequently contact (Niederhoffer, 1966, pp. 37–39; Frost, 1955).

The prevalence of explicit recruitment from the "working classes" is not known. The social and economic characteristics of law enforcement may attract a predominance of such individuals to police ranks. Regardless of the causes, individuals with "working-class" backgrounds bring to their jobs attitudes and experiences which have important implications for the police system.

The Police Organization[2]

The police organization is an agency of social control whose function is to minimize criminal activity and maintain order through the enforcement of laws. Criminal law is both substantive and procedural—substantive laws define the elements of a crime, and procedural laws, in part, determine behavioral guidelines for police tactics. Within the existing legal framework, the maintenance of order does not always follow the enforcement of laws. Consequently, the organizational response becomes a function of not only a legalistic perspective but also police per-

---

Rorschach Inkblot Test, Miale-Holsopole Sentence Completion Test, Taylor Manifest Anxiety Scale, Saslow Psychomatic Inventory, Cornell Medical Index, California and Adorno Authoritarian F Scales, and the Edwards Personal Preference Schedule or Minnesota Personality Inventory. This study also found that most of the applicants were from lower socioeconomic backgrounds. The general result was that of intelligent, emotionally stable young men.

[2] Numerous writings have provided substantially to this section's evaluation. See Fox (1966), Chwast (1965), Lohman and Misner (1966), Niederhoffer (1967), Bayley and Mendelsohn (1969), Wilson (1968), Skolnick (1967 and 1969), Black and Reiss (1966), Reiss and Boruda (1967), Stoddard (1968), Lundstedt (1965), Levy (1968), and Goldstein (1968).

ceptions of minimal acceptable levels of order and the degree to which an organization is responsive to public demands to suppress disruptive elements in society.

The police organization is a dual structure—manifest and latent—fluctuating between the "legalistic" and the "order" orientation. Each structure has its own goals, normative standards, customs and socialization process. Although these are intricately intermixed, they are discernible and provide support and a rationale for behavior as either a "legal actor" or as an "agent of order" or both.

The manifest, or legal function, is the idealized organizational role. Collectively, the police function in this capacity during periods of social stability. Individually, they may invoke the latent, or order, structure for support during situational crises. It is possible to have collective observance of the legalistic perspective and individual and subgroup observance of the order perspective.

During periods of social stress, it is possible for the police, collectively, to assume a posture which emphasizes order. However, the "rule of law" (legalistic perspective) is sufficiently internalized among the police and in some segments of society to preclude the police from acting indiscriminately. Therefore, they revert to a traditional means of exercising influence—politics. They assert a philosophy of order which posits restrictive conformity to accepted standards and suppression of deviations from those standards. The instrument for order becomes a viable political force, competing as a strategy to determine the extent and direction of social change rather than as an overseer to its legitimate processes.

The police can become institutionalized as a power group in society, responsive neither to law nor the public but instead to their own philosophy which has evolved from role requirements, perceptions of how behavior is controlled (punishment) and a capitalistically cultivated ideal to compete successfully.

This latter factor has resulted in a formal internal reward structure in police departments which encourages managerial efficiency and a "production" orientation. Success is measured quantitatively in terms of arrests, contacts, crime rate, etc. The reward system is identical for both latent and manifest structures. Both determine success in terms of "counting." However, each structure has separate "means"—order or legal. In a given situation, the officer can shift from one structure to the other, depending upon which means provides the greater support for behavior; and as noted previously, there can be collective reliance upon the order structure during periods of social stress.

The police system also provides the officer with values which emphasize conforming patterns of behavior that are akin to those of the middle-class. The officer develops a "control" orientation in behavior from the socialization processes—for example, training and customs—in the department. He becomes conditioned to seek out "disruptive" or nonconforming clues as indicators of criminal activity. This results in the development of stereotypes of "trigger cues" that activate action.[3]

In summary, the organization provides the police officer with personal values emphasizing conformity, reinforces his desire to compete quantitatively for success, provides reference group support for legalistic or order-oriented behavior, or both, and socializes the officer to be sensitized to stereotyped "cues" which portend of disruptive or criminal activity. When the policeman goes into the streets to perform the police role, his perceptions are shaped by his experiences in the organization and the characteristics of his personal background.

The Police Role

Police work requires that the officer have both the willingness and capacity to use force. Westley (1953) says that violence is an occupational prerogative of the police. Danger necessitates the use of force (violence), and the role demands assertion of authority in many situations. However, the danger/authority trait of the police role results in conflicting demands on behavior. Skolnick (1967, p. 67) has commented most aptly in this regard:

> The combination of danger and authority found in the task of the policeman unavoidably combine to frustrate procedural regu-

[3] For a discussion of the concept of "law and order" see Skolnick (1967, pp. 6–22).

larity. If it were possible to structure social roles with specific qualities, it would be wise to propose that these two should never, for the sake of the rule of law, be permitted to coexist. Danger typically yields self-defensive conduct, conduct that must strain to be impulsive because danger arouses fear and anxiety so easily. Authority under such conditions becomes a resource to reduce perceived threats rather than a series of reflective judgments arrived at calmly.

Danger can result in potentially disruptive social situations which the officer must attempt to structure in a manner acceptable to the authority dimension of his role. The reactive nature of the police response limits the officer's ability to predetermine a choice of tactics which can be successfully employed. Since all situations cannot be precisely defined, guidelines for behavior are often vague or sufficiently abstract to be subject to a variety of interpretations.

Consequently, the officer must develop an interpersonal role style in "handling" the various contacts that are made. This results in a wide range of approaches to situational problems (McNamara, 1967, pp. 163–252; Reiss and Bordua, 1967, pp. 25–55; Wilson, 1968, pp. 57–82). As a result of this, the police have traditionally had implicit discretionary powers.[4] This provides a latitude in responding to calls but can also result in insufficient control over the response employed by the officer. In many situations, the role gives the officer the opportunity to do exactly what his personal values dictate: He becomes the sole arbiter of guilt or innocence—he becomes the "law."

MINORITY GROUPS[5]

Indian-Americans

During westward expansion in the United States Indians were dominated through treaty or by violence and finally placed on

[4] Failure to provide guidelines for the discretion of the officer can also result from managerial inadequacies in the police department. (President's Commission on Law Enforcement and Administration of Justice, 1967, pp. 13–41.)

[5] Robin M. Williams, Jr., (1964, p. 304) defines minority groups as ". . . any culturally or physically distinctive and self-conscious social aggregates, with hereditary membership and a high degree of endogamy, which are subject to political, or economic, or social discrimination by a dominant segment of an environing political society."

reservations under control of the federal government. The Indians have remained a depressed minority and many of them still reside on reservations where they have their own tribal laws, police and judicial system (Rose, 1964, pp. 20–24; U.S. Commission on Civil Rights, 1961, pp. 144–148).

In growing numbers, Indians are now leaving the reservation and settling in urban areas. Often they have become "ghettoized" as the result of discrimination (Rose, 1964, pp. 20–24), and tribal kinship and cultural traits. Kuttner and Lorinez (1967), in their study of Omaha, Nebraska, found that Indians had been assimilated but into the "skid row" community. This was the result of patterns of alcohol consumption—the Indians failed to adapt to the more demanding social roles. Perhaps this is the consequence of the indirect effects of historic discrimination.

One study (Hayner, 1942) indicates that police perceptions of Indians as a "problem" involve drinking and sex crimes; however, this study does not apply to urban areas. Kuttner and Lorinez (1967) found high crime and delinquency rates among Indians in Omaha and there are indications that crime is one means employed to support alcohol and drug usage. If Indians reside primarily in "slums" or ghetto areas, they are probably heavily policed, but there is no evidence that Indians are presently viewed as a crime problem.

Violation of treaty rights of Indians has led to open confrontation with law-enforcement officers in rural areas. During a "fish-in" to protest laws limiting fishing in Washington, Indians accused police of beating women and children without provocation. "Fish-ins" are an indication of the rapidly increasing organized efforts of Indians to effectuate a change in status. Reliance on "red power" and a swing toward harsh militancy is becoming apparent (*New York Times*, October 12, 1969; Binus, 1967; Washburn, 1969; *Time*, February 9, 1970).

Indian complaints against police concern the lack of maintenance of "law and order" in Indian sections of towns and cities; a tendency of officials to "throw the book" more at Indian violators in comparison to whites; the ignoring of Indian violations against Indians, but a severe response when Indians become involved with whites; the use of excessive force in making arrests; and the "rolling" of intoxicated Indians (U.S. Commission on Civil Rights, 1961, pp. 144–148). The relationship between reservation police and Indians is not known. There are indications of a greater latitude in criminal proceedings, but any implication for police behavior is speculative (Cohen and Mause, 1968).

Oriental-Americans

Japanese and Chinese constitute almost the entire Oriental population in the United States. Although dispersed throughout the nation, they are primarily located in rural and urban areas in the western states and Hawaii. Initially "ghettoized" in Chinatown, succeeding generations of Chinese-Americans have become increasingly integrated into the white community. Japanese-Americans have been assertive in obtaining integration, and are even more assimilated than the Chinese. In large measure, this is the result of the acquisition of economic skills and strong cultural and family institutions which have led to an enhanced socioeconomic status. As a group, the Oriental-Americans are not economically deprived, and there is presently no evidence of militant efforts to alter their status (Rose, 1965, pp. 39–42; Vander Zanden, 1966, pp. 255–262; Kitano, 1969; Lee, 1960).

Historically, the Chinese have had "tong" wars (gang activity), and there have been perceptions of licentious, corrupt and exotic behavior in the "yellow ghetto," but in recent years this has apparently subsided. Generally, rates of criminal activity among Orientals have been low, but there are indications that among Chinese there is "hidden" crime and delinquency. Reasons given for the success of Orientals in maintaining effective social control and minimizing proliferation of marginal groups are the strength of community and family institutions. However, as the Orientals have become increasingly acculturated, there is evidence of rising rates of delinquent activity (Lee, 1960, pp. 325–353; Kitano, 1969, pp. 116–148; U.S. Commission on Civil Rights, 1967, p. 207).

One aspect of Oriental culture that has led to conflict with the police is the Chinese interest in gambling. This is the basis for the only complaint of Orientals against the police that could be found. Chinese believe that they are disproportionately arrested for a gambling game that is almost exclusive to their culture. Japanese-Americans have indicated that there is little, if any, discrimination against them (U.S. Commission on Civil Rights, 1960a, pp. 746–762; U.S. Commission on Civil Rights, 1960b, pp. 111–115).

Police do not perceive that Orientals present any "problem" other than a proclivity of the Chinese towards gambling and believe the social-control mechanisms of the Oriental family to be the reason for low crime rates.

Spanish-Speaking Americans

The Spanish-speaking minorities consist of Puerto Rican, Hispano-Americans and Mexican-Americans. Puerto Ricans are scattered throughout the United States but are primarily concentrated in New York City. Hispanos are of Spanish-Indian ancestry and reside primarily in the urban and rural areas in Arizona, New Mexico, Texas, and California. Mexican-Americans are immigrants from Mexico and their descendants. Many of the Mexican-Americans are seasonal farm workers and are a transient population for part of each year. While the majority of Mexican-Americans reside in the southwest (including California), there are sizeable populations in some midwestern and western urban areas (Rose, 1964, pp. 42–43; Vander Zanden, 1966, pp. 242–254).

In New York City, Puerto Ricans are concentrated in a ghetto area called Spanish Harlem. The Hispanos are predominantly an agricultural people and reside in rural slums. They face less discrimination than blacks, but in urban areas they generally live in segregated areas. Mexican-Americans, when present in large numbers, are segregated into "Mexican Colonies" in southwestern urban areas (Rose, 1964, pp. 42–44; Vander Zanden, 1966, pp. 242–254). Although generally segregated, the Spanish-speaking minorities have made some progress in integrating white communities. Puerto Ricans with "fair" skin are able to leave Spanish Harlem. Hispano-Americans and Mexican-Americans in the higher socioeconomic strata of society are considered "Spanish" and therefore acceptable. In southern California, where they are the single largest minority, the Spanish-speaking Americans have gradually become more integrated since World War II (Vander Zanden, 1966, pp. 242–254; Penolosa, 1967).

An important aspect of this minority's culture is the language. Breakdowns in communication have led to complaints of police nonresponsiveness in protection and services (U.S. Commission on Civil Rights, 1962, pp. 445–461). A popular cultural pattern of the Puerto Ricans is "street corner" gathering for recreational and social activities (U.S. Commission on Civil Rights, 1962, pp. 445–461). Migrant Mexican-Americans often gather in cities and towns during nonworking hours and generally concentrate in one area for recreational and social reasons. Undoubtedly, inadequate recreational facilities and housing, and perhaps unemployment, have resulted in ghetto minorities developing cultural patterns of activity that place them on the street more frequently than dominant groups.

Spanish-speaking minorities, to the extent that they live in identifiable ethnic communities, are viewed as a police problem. These segregated areas are typically disadvantaged; they present the most ambiguous law-enforcement encounters and a greater perceived danger for the officer (Bayley and Mendelsohn, 1969, pp. 87–108). Police have a tendency to view high–crime-rate areas, which is a trait of most lower socioeconomic urban areas, as enemy territory (Black and Labes, 1967). The general police perception of the Spanish-speaking minorities as being "racially" criminal is not known. However, from my experiences and observations, Mexican-Americans in the southwest are seen by some police as "sneaky, dishonest, and immoral," with a proclivity towards use of drugs and intoxicants. When migrant farm workers are present in these communities, the police often show a marked concern about the possibility of increased crime and personal danger.

The depressed socioeconomic status of the Spanish-speaking minorities is resulting in rapidly increasing and militantly organized efforts to effectuate change. In Spanish Harlem, indications are that Puerto Ricans believe legalistic strategies have failed. They are beginning to adopt aggressive action which has already led to a confrontation with the police (Rendon, 1968; Hammer, 1966, pp. 324–330). "Brown power" is becoming an outcry for Mexican-Americans and Hispanos in the southwest. This is illustrated by the recent marches, strikes and violent confrontations in New Mexico, Texas and California (*Time,* July 4, 1969, pp. 16–21; *Newsweek,* March 25, 1968, p. 37).

Complaints against the police involve the emphasis placed on property rights to the exclusion of individual rights and liberties; verbal harassment, that is, use of derogatory words such as "pancho," "muchacho" and "amigo"; excessive patrolling of minority neighborhoods; use of excessive force; unnecessary interrogations and searches; and in general, violation of constitutional rights. Two recent landmark Supreme Court cases—*Escobedo v. Illinois* and *Miranda v. Arizona*—which limit police interrogation of suspects, involved Spanish-speaking minorities.

Mexican-Americans are particularly fearful of the Immigration Service and Border Patrol, whom they view as the "Gestapo." A major problem of these agencies is the use of Mexican bracero (legal entrants) and "wetback" (illegal entrants) as seasonal farm workers. Officers are authorized to question and search within one hundred miles of the border, without warrant, anyone suspected of being an alien. With the influx of "wetbacks," this undoubtedly leads to harassment of many lawful Mexican-Americans (U.S. Commission on Civil Rights, 1968, pp. 15–21; U.S. Commission on Civil Rights, 1967, pp. 25–252; U.S. Commission on Civil Rights, 1960b, pp. 300–301; Hammer, 1966, pp. 324–330; Rendon, 1968).

Black Americans

Evolving from a heritage of slavery, black Americans in this century, and particularly in the last three decades, have steadily moved from rural to urban areas—and from the south to the north and west. Approximately 70 per cent of the black population now resides in metropolitan areas. In all parts of the United States, blacks are racially segregated and have suffered extensive discrimination (National Advisory Commission on Civil Disorders, 1968, pp. 203–247).

The black culture is often characterized by personal and social disorganization. Black ghettoes typically have high crime rates that are disproportionate to white, lower socioeconomic areas. Unemployment, lack of adequate recreational facilities, inadequate housing and masculine gang activities frequently place blacks on the streets. There exists among black Americans a subculture that has high aspirations but limited available opportunities, sees the "power structure" as remote and impersonal and sanctions violence (National Advisory Commission on Civil Disorders, 1968. Lang and Lang, 1968, pp. 1–28, 266–267). These factors create potentially challenging and disruptive situations for the police.

Blacks are militantly, even violently, organized to pressure for changes in status. From the legalistic strategies of the National Association for the Advancement of Colored People to the nonviolent acts of the Southern Christian Leadership Council, to the aggressively violent tactics of the Black Panthers, blacks are demanding a change in the distribution of power. They want to determine their own future—they want "Black Power" (Vander Zanden, 1966, pp. 220–228, 356–375; National Advisory Commission on Civil Disorders, 1968, pp. 224–236; Cleaver, 1968; Skolnick, 1969, pp. 125–176).

Police, collectively and individually, believe that blacks represent a serious law-enforcement problem. Black ghettoes are the most dangerous areas to work in, and civil disturbances have, at times, led to open "warfare" (Bayley and Mendelsohn, 1969, pp. 46–108; National Advisory Commission on Civil Disorders, 1968, pp. 299–339; Skolnick, 1969, pp. 241–292; Lohman and Misner, 1966). Police resources are usually assigned on the basis of criminal incidents and potentially disorderly areas. From the police perspective, these traits characterize black communities.

Black complaints against police include the following: police are viewed as representatives of an inequitable "system" and as an army of occupation; police do not respond to complaints and have inadequate grievance mechanisms; they are either oppressive or fail to provide sufficient protection; exclusively black incidents are underenforced while black-white incidents are overenforced; police are either too impersonal or too personal, that is, paternalistic or condescending; verbal and physical harassment and abuse is believed a common practice; police patrolling tactics are seen as suppressive; constitutional rights are consistently violated, and blacks in white neighborhoods are harassed, as are black men in the company of white women (National Advisory Commission on Civil Disorders, 1968, pp. 299–322; Lohman and Misner, 1966, pp. 53–103; Michigan State University, 1967, pp. 13–18; Bayley and Mendelsohn, 1969, pp. 137–138; Fogelson, 1968; Skolnick, 1969, pp. 211–288; Edwards, 1968, pp. 28–31).

DYNAMICS OF NEGATIVE-CONTACT SITUATIONS

Macro-Level Analysis[6]

Police–minority-group negative-contact situations can be analyzed from the "power-maintenance" function of police and the overt threats posed by a minority group in power challenges. Minority-group segregation is a consequence of dominant-group rejection and ingroup solidarity of minorities, and represents distinct boundaries of separation. Dominant groups also possess the power—economic, social, and political resources—often sought by the minority group.

Denial of equitable distribution of power is based on the threat minorities pose in being permitted access and control of resources. In one sense, a minority can be viewed as a resource by which certain power is maintained. For example, they provide cheap labor; they are an acceptable outgroup for scapegoating; they enhance the status of lower strata dominants by providing an inferior hierarchial group, and minorities can often be manipulated to alter the success of competing political dominants.

Minorities are dominated through an intricate network of overt and covert, informal and formal techniques. The extent to which they continue to accept dominance is a function of their own resources—possessed upon coming into contact with the

[6] Concepts used in this analysis are taken from authorities previously cited: Blalock (1967), and Cloward and Ohlin (1960). In addition, the author's own ideas are incorporated.

dominant group, or that are subsequently acquired. Minority resources for consideration here are their adaptive capacity, visible concentration and organized pressure tactics for status change.

Oriental-Americans have demonstrated a high adaptive capacity with strong community and family institutions, and the acquisition of economic skills which have led to enhanced acceptance by the dominant group. Initially, the possession of economic skills and concentrated visibility posed a serious threat, but the availability of adequate resources and the general rapid acculturation of essential skills has led to increasing assimilation.

Indian-Americans, to date, have not manifested any meaningful adaptive capacity in assimilation. Not only have they faced de facto segregation but they have been visibly segregated (isolated). With increased movement to cities and a recent "red" awareness, Indians may rapidly become more visible. Use of militant tactics for status changes, plus visible ghettoization, may lead to conflict with police. There are recent indications of this in Minneapolis where an "Indian Patrol" has been developed to prevent "harassment by police" (*Time*, February 9, 1970).

Spanish-speaking Americans have manifested a limited adaptive capacity. In part, this is due to some higher socioeconomic positions which can be related to a "Spanish" heritage and varying degrees of visibility of physical identification. In the main, however, they represent a concentrated and visible minority which is increasingly employing militant tactics to obtain equity in distribution of resources. They are a perceived threat to power and therefore a police problem.

Blacks are more threatening than the Spanish-speaking minorities because they are intensely visible and concentrated, and they are the principal power-challenge group in society. Their use of pressure tactics has resulted in rewards being administered by the dominant group. Blacks have institutionalized militancy through white recognition, and other minorities are emulating black successes. However, the blacks' adaptive capacity is limited and has not correspondingly increased with the success of pressure tactics. Therefore blacks become even a greater threat because power is redistributed only on the basis of institutionalized aggression.

An important aspect of a minority's adaptive capacity is cultural strengths and weaknesses. Discrimination can influence cultural characteristics of minority groups. Important considerations here are cultural influences on behavior of minority members and the implications for relationships with police—as a law-enforcing institution of the dominant group.

Law represents a formal mechanism by which power contests and individual behavior are regulated. As laws can represent the dominant group interest, they can also be equitable in evaluating individual deviance reprehensible to both dominant and minority groups. However, dominant-influenced power laws coupled with informal and interpersonal acts of discrimination often lead to extensive personal and social disorganization in minority-group cultures. With denial of resources, legitimate opportunities are limited, and a deviant or illegitimate opportunity structure develops. This often leads to extensive violation of equitable substantive laws governing personal conduct which, in turn, provides perceptions of a collective minority deviancy. Negative stereotyping ensues and reinforces the dominant groups' rationale for continued discrimination and resource denial.

Police, as a "power-maintenance" agency, are involved in enforcing both dominant influenced and equitable laws. Cast in this role, they have an institutionalized self-conception as a moral and just power group. The police and some minority groups are traditionally in conflict by virtue of extensive and visible minority deviancy and perceptions of minorities as distorted by ongoing experiences, and when trying to maintain the power distribution desired by the dominant group, they are, in effect, fighting a "holy war."

Police have a vested interest in their own power, the existing distribution of power, and are in large measure responsible for its maintenance. If the minority becomes collectively disruptive and highly visible, anxiety pervades the dominant group, and police responsiveness leads to an invoking of the order posture. The police, to the degree they have the resources, will be required to suppress civil disturbances. If minority activity does not become collectively violent, some officers indulge in situational suppression, supported by the latent order structure of the organization. The police role is personalized and institutionalized; the police are arbiters of dominant values and not objective and responsive regulators of human conduct. Not only are they a symbol of an inequitable society, but they are, in fact, frequently and perhaps unavoidably inequitable.

Micro-Level Analysis[7]

In negative-contact situations, the minority-group member perceives he has been treated inequitably by police. The police officer brings to these situations an ethnocentric background, a need to maintain his masculinity, values which emphasize conforming patterns of behavior, a sensitivity to disruptive or criminal activity as identified by stereotyped cues, wide discretionary powers in enforcement encounters, reference-group support and emphasis upon "order"-oriented or "tough" responses. If he is bigoted as well, he is very close to inappropriate responses whenever he enters the minority-group culture. Moreover, the challenges to the various dimensions of his role are unusually high in the environment. In fact, they are so numerous that it is not only the individual minority-group member but the collective, visible and segregated minority that becomes a threat. Collective minority violence is met with collective police violence; individual minority violence is met with individual police violence; the anticipation of either is met by police suppression.

The police and minorities are sensitized to each other—the police officer, as an individual and a representative of the "system," controls the life of minority citizens; members of the minority are a threat to the police, both to the individual policeman doing his job and to the organization as a whole. As the police anticipation of situational and organizational threats fluctuate, so will their response. When the officer enters a threatening situation, he is likely to employ some form of abuse, especially if the

[7] Concepts used in this analysis are taken from sources previously cited and those developed from the author's experiences and observations.

actor(s) is a minority-group member. The power-maintenance role of police and the extensive social disorganization in the minority culture create numerous stressful situations. When a policeman enters this kind of situation and it is not quickly structured to minimize personal danger, he will employ the strategies needed to control the situation. These strategies may be in accord with the officer's personal values and not those of the law. Often his response is perceived as inequitable, and frequently that perception is justified. If the police organization lacks sufficient control mechanisms, the officer's response will often be indiscriminate without regard to precipitous situations.[8]

The police represent a readily available target for outlets to minority dissatisfactions. The minority individual often expresses his frustration in challenging those he thinks are suppressing him—he gets the "pigs."

The police-minority contact situation often becomes a vicious circle perpetuating negative reinforcement of each group by the other. The police, by their power position, *are* oppressive, and when minorities begin to exert pressure for redistribution of power, conflict results. This conflict becomes personalized in the interaction of the minority-group member and police officer. When either can be "read" as manifesting what the other already believes, the situation becomes negative and enhances the possibility of negativism in future contacts. Repeated situations may preclude positive contacts of any nature between police and minorities.

TOWARD A THEORY OF NEGATIVE CONTACTS

1. The police "power maintenance" function in society establishes dual organizational structures in police departments that are responsive to "legalistic" and "order" perspectives. Legalistic behavior is emphasized during periods of social stability in society. Order, or suppressive behavior, is emphasized in periods of social stress and acceptable during situational stress for the individual officer.

[8] See Kuykendall (1969) for an analysis of a response hierarchy of police power strategies used in controlling various types of situations which police officers encounter.

2. Police negative perceptions of minority groups are a function of (a) concentrated visibility; (b) extent of personal and social disorganization of the minority culture which is determined by the police on the basis of the prevalence of perceived minority criminal deviance, and prevalence of perceived threatening and challenging situations; and (c) pressure strategies utilized for effectuating changes in status.

3. Police negative perceptions of minority groups are perpetuated by (a) selective recruitment from working classes of dominants, (b) inadequate control mechanisms in the organization, (c) reward (quantitative evaluations) structure of the organization, (d) implicit and explicit socialization in the use of stereotyping as a skill requisite, (e) danger-authority conflict of the police role, (f) dominant group support and encouragement for the use of suppressive tactics, and (g) latent order structure which tolerates and reinforces situational order-oriented behavior by police officers.

4. Minority-group negative perceptions of police are a function of (a) the "power maintenance" function of police, (b) non-responsiveness of police to minority needs and grievances, and (c) the perceived, and actual, verbal and physical abuse and harassment resulting from factors in hypotheses 2 and 3, and which create negative contact situations.

5. Minority-group negative perceptions of police are perpetuated by negative contact situations which reinforce factor c in proposition 4.

6. Police negative perceptions of minority groups are also perpetuated by negative contacts which reinforce factor b in proposition 2, and factors c and d in proposition 3.

7. Repetitive and frequent negative-contact situations lead to individual and collective polarization of police and minority groups, and individual and collective confrontation and violence.

REFERENCES

Bayley, David H. and Mendelsohn, Harold: *Minorities and the Police: Confrontation in America.* New York, Free Press, 1969.

Binis, Hamilton: Indian uprising for civil rights. *Ebony,* 22:64–72, February, 1967.

Black, Donald J. and Reiss, Albert J., Jr.: Patterns of behavior in police and citizen transactions. *Studies of Crime and Law Enforcement in Major Metropolitan Areas: Field Surveys III, II, Section I.* Report to the President's Commission on Law Enforcement and Administration of Justice, Washington, D.C., U.S. Government Printing Office, 1966.

Black, Harold and Labes, Marvin J.: An analogy to police-criminal interaction. *Am. J. Orthopsychiatr.*, 37:123–129, July, 1967.

Blalock, Hubert M., Jr.: *Toward a Theory of Minority-Group Relations.* New York, Wiley, 1967.

Blum, Richard: Psychological testing. In Blum, Richard (Ed.): *Police Selection.* Springfield, Thomas, 1964, pp. 85–139.

Chwast, Jacob: Value conflicts in law enforcement. *Crime Delinquency*, 11:151–161, April, 1965.

Cleaver, Eldridge: *Soul on Ice.* New York, Delta Books, 1968.

Cloward, Richard A., and Ohlin, Lloyd B.: *Delinquency and Opportunity: A Theory of Delinquent Gangs.* Glencoe Free Press, 1960.

Cohen, Warren H. and Mause, Philip J.: The Indian: The forgotten American. *Harvard Law Rev.*, 81:1818–1858, June, 1968.

Dillman, Everett G.: Analyzing police recruitment and retention problems. *Police*, 8:22–26, May-June, 1964.

Edwards, George: *The Police on the Urban Frontier.* New York, American Jewish Committee, 1968.

Fogelson, Robert M.: From resentment to confrontation: The police, the Negroes, and the outbreak of the nineteen sixties riots. *Political Sci. Quart.*, 83:217–247, June, 1968.

Fox, Vernon: Sociological and political aspects of police administration. *Sociol. Soc. Res.*, October, 1966, (Reprint).

Frost, Thomas M.: Selection methods for police recruits. *J. Crim. Law, Criminol. Police Sci.*, 46:135–145, May-June, 1955.

Goldstein, Herman: Police response to urban crises. *Public Admin. Rev.*, 27:417–423, June, 1968.

Hammer, Richard: Report from a Spanish Harlem "Fortress." In Segal, Bernard E. (Ed.): *Racial and Ethnic Relations.* New York, Crowell, 1966, pp. 324–330.

Hayner, Norman S.: Variability in the criminal behavior of American Indians. *Am. J. Sociol.*, 47:602–613, January, 1942.

Kitano, Harry H.L.: *Japanese Americans: The Evolution of A Subculture.* Englewood Cliffs, Prentice-Hall, 1969.

Kullner, Robert and Lorinez, Albert B.: Alcoholism and addiction in urbanized Sioux Indians. *Ment. Hyg.*, 51:530–542, October, 1967.

Kuykendall, Jack L.: *Police Deviancy in the Enforcement Role: Situational Cooperation/Compliance—Responsive Hierarchy of Deviant and Non-Deviant Power Strategies.* Submitted for publication, 1969.

Lang, Kurt and Lang, Gladys Engel: Racial disturbances as collective behavior. *Am. Behav. Sci.*, 4:11–13, March-April, 1968.

Lee, Rose Hum: *The Chinese in the United States of America.* Hong Kong, University Press, 1960.

Levy, Burton: Cops in the ghetto: A problem of the police system. In Massotta, Louis H. and Bowen, Don R. (Eds.): *Riots and Rebellion: Civil Violence in the Urban Community.* Beverly Hills, Sage Publications, 1968.

Lohman, Joseph and Misner, Gordon: *The Police and the Community: The Dynamics of Their Relationship in a Changing Society: Field Survey IV.* Report for the President's Commission on Law Enforcement and Administration of Justice. Washington, D.C., U.S. Government Printing Office, 1966.

Lundstedt, Sven: Social psychological contributions to the management of law enforcement agencies. *J. Crim. Law, Criminol. Police Sci., 56:* 375–381, September, 1965.

Matarazzo, Joseph D. et al.: Characteristics of successful policemen and firemen applicants. *J. Appl. Psychol.,* 48:123–133, 1964.

McNamama, John H.: *Uncertainties in police work: The relevance of police recruits background and training.* In Bordua, David J. (Ed.): *The Police: Six Sociological Essays.* New York, Wiley, 1967, pp. 163–252.

Michigan State University: *A National Survey of Police and Community Relations: Field Survey V.* Report for the President's Commission on Law Enforcement and Administration of Justice. Washington, D.C., U.S. Government Printing Office, 1967.

National Advisory Commission on Civil Disorders: *Report.* Washington, D.C., U.S. Government Printing Office, 1968.

New York Times, October 12, 1969.

Newsweek, March 25, 1968, p. 37.

Niederhoffer, Arthur: *Behind the Shield: The Police on the Urban Frontier.* Garden City, Doubleday, 1967.

Penolosa, Fernado: *The Changing Mexican-American in Southern California. Sociol. Soc. Res.,* 51:405–417, July, 1967.

President's Commission on Law Enforcement and Administration of Justice Task Force Report: *The Police.* Washington, D.C., U.S. Government Printing Office, 1967.

Reiss, Albert J. and Bordua, David J.: Environment and organization: A perspective on the police. In Bordua, David J. (Ed.): *The Police: Six Sociological Essays.* New York, Wiley, 1967, pp. 25–55.

Rendon, Armando: El Puertorriqueno: No more, no less. *Civil Rights Digest,* 1:27–35, Fall, 1968.

Rose, Peter I.: *They and We: Racial and Ethnic Relations in the United States.* New York, Random, 1964.

Skolnick, Jerome H.: *Justice Without Trial: Law Enforcement in a Democratic Society.* New York, Wiley, 1967.

Skolnick, Jerome H.: *The Politics of Protest.* Report to the National Commission on the Causes and Prevention of Violence. New York, Ballantine, 1969.

Stoddard, Ellwyn R.: The informal 'code' of police deviancy: A group approach to blue coat crime. *J. Crim. Law, Criminol. Police Sci.*, 59. 201–213, June, 1968.

Time, July 4, 1969, pp. 16–21; February 2, 1970, pp. 14–20.

U.S. Commission on Civil Rights: *Hearings in San Francisco: January 27-28.* Washington, D.C., U.S. Government Printing Office, 1960a.

U.S. Commission on Civil Rights: *Hearings in Los Angeles: January 25–26.* Washington, D.C., U.S. Government Printing Office, 1960b.

U.S. Commission on Civil Rights: *Justice.* Washington, D.C., U.S. Government Printing Office, 1961.

U.S. Commission on Civil Rights: *Hearings in Newark, New Jersey: September 11–12.* Washington, D.C., U.S. Government Printing Office, 1962.

U.S. Commission on Civil Rights: *Hearings in Cleveland, Ohio: April 1–7.* Washington, D.C., U.S. Government Printing Office, 1966.

U.S. Commission on Civil Rights: *Hearings in San Francisco: May 1–3.* Washington, D.C., U.S. Government Printing Office, 1967.

U.S. Commission on Civil Rights: *The Mexicans.* Washington, D.C., U.S. Government Printing Office, 1968.

Vander Zanden, James W.: *American Minority Relations: The Sociology of Race and Ethnic Groups,* 2nd ed. New York, Ronald, 1966.

Washburn, Wilcomb E.: Red power: *Am. West,* 6:52–53, January, 1969.

Westley, William A.: Violence and the police. *Am. J. Sociol.,* 59:34–41, July, 1953.

Williams, Robin M., Jr.: *Strangers Next Door.* Englewood Cliffs, Prentice-Hall, 1964.

Wilson, James Q.: *Varieties of Police Behavior.* Cambridge, Harvard, 1968.

Wilson, O.W.: Problems in Police Personnel Administration. *J. Crim. Law, Criminol. Police Sci.,* 43:840–847, March-April, 1953.

Chapter 12

SOCIAL CHANGE AND THE POLICE

Louis A. Radelet

It has been noted that police–community-relations programs tend to deal predominantly with the police and racial tensions. There should be no surprise in the discovery that the police and community relationship cannot be understood apart from some of the more vexing social issues of our time. It is at the heart of such questions as civil rights and crime, and clearly related also to the problems of urbanization and poverty.

There is little question that social control is vastly more difficult and demanding in today's rapidly changing, mobile, heterogeneous society than was the case in the relatively simple community of yesteryear. Banton suggests that no social changes occur without costs, and one of the costs of economic development is a decline in social integration. One index of this can be seen in the crime rate.[1] There is undoubtedly a close relationship between the changing nature of social controls and changing attitudes toward authority and authority symbols, e.g. the police. It has become far more difficult in our modern society to achieve consensus on human values. The maintenance of social control so that social cooperation is possible has become increasingly complex.

Basically the shift has been from a predominantly rural, agricultural, stable folk society, to an urban, industrial, highly mobile bureaucratic society. Yesterday, it was a family-centered society; today, the metropolis has become the major social unit. Yesterday, work was a moral calling and a way of life, a means of self-identity; today, work is done through impersonalized, bureaucratic systems involving ever-increasing specialization.

NOTE: From *Municipal Police Administration*, 6th ed. Washington, International City Management Association, 1969, pp. 226–231. Reprinted with permission.

[1] Banton, Michael: The *Policeman in the Community*. New York, Basic Books, 1964, pp. 1–11.

Yesterday, government was a local affair and the citizen had a voice and a sense of meaningful participation in political processes; today, decisions in the arena of public affairs are made remotely, and the communication gap is wide between the citizen and the decision-making "expert." Yesterday, education beyond the early grades was regarded as the privilege of a few, rather than the expectation of the masses, as it is today.

In our metropolitan centers, where approximately 70 per cent of the population is concentrated, the mix of people is such as to make commonplace what the sociologists call "contra-cultural conflict." The potential for social disorder is further heightened by the qualitative nature of the population decentralization process within these metropolitan complexes. The movement, generally outward from central city to suburbia, has created the conditions referred to as "social dynamite" by James Conant, by its pattern of differentialism and discrimination by race, sometimes religion or national origin, sometimes language or cultural ways, and always in terms of socioeconomic class, based largely upon relative ability to compete for more desirable housing.

The shifting population pattern has posed special problems for the Negro migrant:

> As recently as 1910, only 27 per cent of the Negroes in this country lived in cities. . . . By 1956 as a result of migration, 90 per cent of Negroes in the North and West lived in cities. In the South, Negro urbanization had increased 48 per cent. These figures mean that within the short compass of one and one-half human generations, we had a people from a folk culture in the rural slum South suddenly transplanted into metropolitan living in Metropolis USA. . . . In the case of the Negro, we have a rather peculiar situation. He has been an American for a longer period than the average white person, but it is only in the last generation and a half that for the first time in his American citizenship, he has been thrown into the unique aspect of American civilization which is urbanism as a way of life. The adjustment process for him, therefore, is not "Americanization," but one of urbanization.[2]

[2] Hauser, Philip M.: "Implications of Population Trends for Urban Communities." Paper presented at Institute on Metropolitan Problems, Milwaukee, University of Wisconsin, February 1, 1958.

Long-existing patterns in political and economic power have been upset in some of our cities. There is an atmosphere of social revolution, certainly of social conflict, arising from these conditions in our big cities.

Pragmatic realism should persuade the police to be knowledgeable about these sociopolitical developments. It is clear that the best program in police-community relations will not, in and of itself, make much difference with respect to critical problems of housing, employment, education, recreation, health and sanitation, etc., that are the main issues in the social malignancy of our cities. It is for this reason that police-community relations must be viewed in the larger social context. It is also for this reason that the police should be eager participants in community-wide efforts to help solve problems that are not, in the direct and explicit sense, police problems.

In some municipalities, police-minority relations means the Puerto Rican, the Spanish-American or perhaps the Indian. But in almost all of our major cities, it means the Negro. Negro civil rights efforts have reached proportions and a militancy unheard of until recent years.[3] In the past, issues of racial equality have been mainly the concern of a handful of white liberals and progressives, and the bulk of the white community was largely untouched by their appeals. In particular, racial discrimination was viewed largely as a geographic problem belonging to the South, while the northern white remained rather smug about the somewhat wider opportunities presented by his cities to the Negro migrant. The struggle for Negro rights was seen by northern white liberals as an effort to persuade southern white bourbons to relinquish their discriminatory practices, and in that way to win more freedom for the Negro. The passivity of the Negro, in his own behalf, was implied.

Beginning gradually in 1954, and with much greater impact with the Montgomery bus boycott a few years later, there

[3] For the ensuing description of "The Movement" in civil rights, I rely heavily upon the remarks of Robert B. Mills, Chief Psychologist, Mental Health Division, Cincinnati Board of Health, in a speech to Institute on Police-Community Relations, Cincinnati, June 8, 1964.

has come to be widespread public recognition of the fact that the Negro has found a voice (a sense of identity) and a tactic destined to revolutionize the civil rights struggle. And there has been no little astonishment and consternation about this in white circles.

Subsequent events have covered the entire country and left the white northern middle-class citizen very little about which to be complacent. His suburban housing pattern has been challenged, his school system has been labelled as de facto segregated, his labor union has been branded as discriminatory, his employer accused of nonhiring or nonpromotion of Negroes and his recreation spots picketed for their exclusiveness.

From the viewpoint of the white-community resident, the revolution for Negro rights has turned from a rather abstract issue in some distant part of the country into a direct threat to his property, his job, the education of his children and the manner in which he spends his leisure time. In effect, the white resident is, for the first time in many cases, forced to express an attitude—to take a stand, if only by his silence.

Many previously unexamined feelings are now being forced into the limelight. While no monolithic description of either white or Negro feelings is valid, there surely is evidence suggesting that many whites are in a state of flux and uncertainty regarding the efforts in behalf of full rights and freedom for and by Negro citizens.

On the positive side, a substantial flow of good will and idealism which was previously latent has been activated. Increasing numbers of whites have participated in demonstrations, in raising funds, in offering jobs and housing, in creating scholarships and in speaking up, in one way or another, in support of the manifest cause. As might be expected, however, some vociferous opposition has also been triggered, both from individuals and in organized form. Yet, generally speaking, the prevalent mood among whites remained—until recently—one of hoping the whole thing would blow over.

The summers of 1966 and 1967, and the catastrophic assassination of Dr. Martin Luther King in the spring of 1968, following closely on the heels of publication of the report of the

National Advisory Commission on Civil Disorders, have changed the picture drastically. It should be clear now to all that America's racial crisis is, as the Commission says, "a picture of one nation divided."

What about the police? Of all the "minority groups" in the community, the police are perhaps the most misunderstood. They feel that they are not responsible for the conditions which have precipitated what Charles Silberman calls "the crisis in black and white," yet they feel that most of the solutions are somehow expected from them and that they are easy targets for abuse and criticism.

The police have the most continuous social contact with Negro people of any predominantly white organization. For numerous police officers in the big cities, it is daily, face-to-face contacts, often involving the adjudication of family disputes, personal counselling services, making arrests, setting ground rules for future behavior, or simply passing the time of day with many Negro citizens.

Conversely, for most Negroes, the white community is rather remote and inaccessible. But the white police officer is always around and may be perceived as the representative of "Whitey's Law," a visible symbol of a social system which is regarded as patently unjust. Thus, the police officer takes the brunt of the gripes, frustrations and anger felt by the Negro over his lot in life.

The apparent preoccupation of civil rights organizations with police conduct stems from the fact that the patrolman has such intimate contact with the Negro community. The police officer is an easy target of the Negro's displaced hostility. The criticism so frequently directed against the police by minority groups often is really directed against the larger white community power structure, but it is displaced to the nearest, most readily available target. No doubt this accounts for some of the irrational elements that occasionally appear in Negro complaints against police.

Since the police have been drafted, so to speak, for the frontline of the civil rights struggle, and they do not enjoy being targets, their reaction is understandable. However, the decisive factor which tends to warp the viewpoint of the big-city police officer, on questions of Negro rights, is the great amount of energy and effort required to carry out the difficult and dangerous job of containing what is incorrectly called "Negro crime."

There is, of course, no such thing as Negro crime. There are crime-breeding social conditions which happen to predominate in neighborhoods where Negroes and other minorities reside in high proportion. The elimination of these social cesspools is, in part, what the Negro protest is all about. The so-called Negro crime rate is only one of the numerous evidences of personal and social disorganization reflecting society's moral bankruptcy. For these conditions the police are no more (and no less) responsible than are other elements of the community, since we are dealing here with total community responsibility.

Thus suggested is the dual stereotyping process, in the image of the police officer by the Negro on the one side, and in the image of the Negro by the police officer on the other side.[4] These images are nurtured and cultivated by the tactics, on each side, of "firing darts at one another from twenty paces" as a substitute for developing meaningful channels of communication.

The stereotypes are mutually reinforcing. In this process, the characteristic epithets appear; for example, charges of "police brutality," with clamor for establishment of citizen review boards to handle citizen complaints against the police. And on the other side, often an exceedingly defensive police reaction, rooted in part in the reflexes of police who have too often been the objects of society's scapegoating for all manner of social ills. And there it is—the heart of the problem in law enforcement and race relations in our big cities.

A provocative question is whether nonviolent protest and peaceful integration will be displaced by "Black Power" as the rallying theme for the Negro's advance to full equality and

[4] *See* Preiss, Jack J. and Ehrlich, Howard J.: *An Examination of Role Theory: The Case of the State Police.* Lincoln, University of Nebraska Press, 1966, pp. 136–42. Also Baldwin, James *Nobody Knows My Name.* New York, Dell, 1962, pp. 65–67.

first-class citizenship. Numerous observers have said that the zenith of nonviolence passed before the death of Martin Luther King. The emphasis appears to be shifting toward a form of Black Racism—the idea that Negroes are *better* than whites —morally superior and more fit to lead blacks. Bordua states the issue as follows:

> The most fundamental of recent changes is the entrance of the Negro into civil society. Like most such events, the occasion is one of turmoil and violence. . . . Negroes are now legitimate claimants to protection by the police. [Moreover] like all citizens in a modern legal community, they are now entitled to protection from the police. The balance is hard to strike in any situation, but it points to the most fundamental, long-run issue in police-Negro relations.[5]

The most emotion-packed complaint directed against the police is that of "brutality"—technically, the use of undue or unreasonable physical force in making arrests. In practice, its meaning is broader and includes verbal or psychological brutality, e.g. the use of terms such as "boy," "nigger," "Ruby," or "Sambo." Some observers have referred to police brutality charges as one of the "symbolisms" of race relations, i.e. a term really meaning general harassment of the minority by the majority.

The complexities of the brutality issue are not widely appreciated. The vast majority of the complaints prove to be groundless upon investigation, so the police say. But there appear to be adequate grounds in sufficient cases to have prompted the United States Commission on Civil Rights to study the question and to report that ". . . while most police officers never resort to brutal practices, . . . police brutality is still a serious problem throughout the United States."[6]

Police officials insist that brutality charges have been exaggerated. They defend the relatively frequent use of force in arresting Negroes on the grounds that Negroes are more likely to

[5] Bordua, David J.: "Comments on Police-Community Relations." Unpublished manuscript, Urbana, Department of Sociology, University of Illinois, 1968.
[6] U.S. 1961 Commission on Civil Rights Report: *Justice*. Washington, D.C., U.S. Government Printing Office, 1961, vol. 5, p. 3.

resist arrest. The fact is that little work has been done within police circles to identify and sharpen the standards against which the "average" police officer makes his split-second judgment as to how much force is necessary to make an arrest or to control a suspect. The courts have much more time to review these judgments later. It should be added that whether brutality actually exists is less important than whether it is thought and believed to exist, in significant sectors of the community. Basically, the problem comes down to lack of trust in the police department.

A particularly thorny question for the police that has arisen in the general context of "The Movement" in race relations and civil rights is handling demonstrations.[7] Sometimes it is forgotten that the parade, the picket line, the mass meeting, the public rally and the written petition have been commonplace in this country for generations. Over the years, abolitionists, suffragettes, temperance propagandists, religionists, peace advocates, war advocates, trade unionists, political partisans and a host of others have engaged in public demonstration, seeking thereby to acquire popular support for their views and to enlist adherents. Marching throngs and noisy assemblies have proclaimed free silver, the single tax, federalism, greenbacks, "54–40 or fight" and the alien and sedition laws.

Contemporary racial demonstrations, however, appear to be quite different. For one thing, they *are* racial. The thousands of marching faces, mostly black, worry white Americans. Negroes are behaving as they are not "supposed" to behave. As Charles Silberman has put it:

> For a hundred years, white Americans have clung tenaciously to the illusion that if everyone would just sit still—if "agitators" would just stop agitating—time alone would solve the problem of race. . . . Myrdal (who believed white Americans were torn between their devotion to the American creed and their actual behavior toward Negroes and called this *An American Dilemma*) was wrong. White Americans are not torn and tortured . . . they are upset by the current state of race relations, to be sure. But what troubles them

[7] *See* Morsell, John A.: "A Rationale for Racial Demonstrations." Paper presented at 10th Annual National Institute on Police and Community Relations, East Lansing, Michigan State University, May, 1964.

is not that justice is being denied but that their peace is being shattered and their business interrupted.[8]

In such circumstances, the surging insistence of Negro demonstrators has introduced a new factor into the national life. The traditional image of the docile, passive Negro has been shattered. The core of the problem is the failure of most whites to see Negroes as people. This is why many Negroes are unmoved by the evidence that their demonstrations may be producing a backlash of resentment among otherwise neutral northern whites. After all, these Negroes say, it is better to be actively and positively disliked than to be overlooked or ignored.

Another feature of today's demonstrations that arouses concern, especially by the police, is the varied forms of protest. There have been picketing, marching, parading, rallies, mass assemblies, prayer vigils, fasting, sit-ins, kneel-ins, freedom rides and other activities as well that may be classified properly as civil disobedience.

The forms vary as the purposes vary. Not all the activities have been peaceful, legal and nonviolent. Bloodshed and death have become widespread. The police, and in some cases the National Guard and federal troops, have been hard put to control demonstrations within the framework of the Bill of Rights and due process of law.

What is civil disobedience? Some argue that it is any deliberate infraction of a civil law with intent to be arrested. Others argue that a restaurant sit-in, for example, is not civil disobedience. Such a sit-in is based on the premise that exclusion from a licensed public facility on account of race is a violation of a constitutional right. If such an act violates local law, it is the local law that is in defiance of the law of the land.

This is an example of the perceptual difficulties in the racial civil-rights situation which make the responsibilities of the law enforcement officer so demanding. It is complicated further by the fact that Negro demonstrations today implicitly assume lack of trust in traditional legal processes to secure redress of

[8] Silberman, Charles G.: *Crisis in Black and White.* New York, Random House, 1964.

injustice. The police officer is symbolically identified with this legal system; indeed, he is regarded as of its very metabolism. It is no overstatement, then, to state that our country is in the midst of the mightiest internal convulsion since the Civil War. There appear to be no signs of relaxation until the Negro has gained first-class citizenship everywhere.

It may be useful in concluding this analysis to identify more specifically some of the basic reasons for minority-group dissatisafction with the police. These reasons are evident in the following excerpt from a report of a public hearing by the United States Civil Rights Commission in Cleveland, Ohio, in April, 1966:

> The complaints of the Negro community against the police department are legion. But the most frequent complaint is that of permissive law enforcement and that policemen fail to provide adequate protection and services in areas occupied by Negroes. There is also the complaint of police brutality, and closely associated with it is the allegation that police officers are discourteous to Negro residents and frequently subject them to verbal abuse. In addition, Negro residents complain about arrest and detention practices of the police department. They also vigorously criticize the way some demonstrators were arrested and the failure of the police to protect civil rights demonstrators from unlawful violence. Finally, Negroes argue that the police department practices discrimination in its personnel policies.

Permissive law enforcement and "other discriminatory practices," then, seem to be the two major problems which are at the root of Negro antagonism toward the police. Verbal abuse and the discriminatory application of stop-and-frisk practices are ancillary charges. Part of the problem is that what might be regarded as discriminatory from one point of view is defended as good police work from another point of view.

In the "other discriminatory practices" category, the President's Commission on Crime in the District of Columbia identifies such matters as frequent instances of arrest under the "failure to move on" provision of a local statute, the employment of dogs, and the arrest of intoxicated Negroes while white persons simply are advised to "go home and sleep it off." The Commission also stresses complaints concerning the use of excessive force and "the manner in which officers question citizens on the street."[9]

As for the charge of discrimination in police personnel practices, a number of reasons may be cited. First, there is the basic distrust of minority group members toward the police, as discussed earlier. Few minority group members apply for police employment; those who do run the risk of being criticized or scorned in their own group. Second, the standards which have been established for entrance into police work are designed without appropriate recognition of certain minority group differences, e.g. written examinations, stress on verbal skills, height requirements, and others. Finally, character investigations and oral interviews often employ the standards of the white community and thus operate to the detriment of the minority applicant.[10]

With the exception of some whites from the lower socioeconomic groups who have the same general complaints against the police, and some whites who are, for want of a better description, of a "liberal bent," the vast majority of whites are either apathetic toward the entire problem or they support the police. They seldom see the police as perfect, but they do visualize steady improvement and are willing to wait for slow and steady change. Their feelings seem to be that as police salaries are improved, we will get better men, and in the meantime the police are doing a pretty good job under difficult conditions. The majority of their complaints seem to be in the area of service and technical competence.

Certain "backlash" signs can be detected, however. Certain individuals express dismay and fear as a result of what they classify as "the too-rapid pace of the civil rights revolution;" or, in more cases, they indicate serious concern over the specter of riots. In their anxiety, they tend to see the police as

[9] Report of the President's Commission on Crime in the District of Columbia. Washington, U.S. Government Printing Office, 1966, pp. 203–24.

[10] This portion of the analysis, relies significantly on *A National Survey of Police and Community Relations*, a report for the President's Commission on Law Enforcement and Administration of Justice, prepared by the National Center on Police and Community Relations, School of Police Administration and Public Safety, East Lansing, Michigan State University, January, 1967.

their sole protection against violent disorder. But there is serious question that local police can cope with the situation. They are too few in numbers, too thinly deployed, and too lacking in military command and control structure to be effective against large masses of rioters.

Chapter 13

THE NEGRO COMMUNITY

President's Commission on Law Enforcement and Administration of Justice

POLICE EFFECTIVENESS

The NORC survey shows that nonwhites, particularly Negroes, are significantly more negative than whites in evaluating police effectiveness in law enforcement. In describing whether police give protection to citizens, nonwhites give a rating of "very good" only half as often as whites and give a "not so good" rating twice as often. These differences are not merely a function of greater poverty among nonwhites; they exist at all income levels and for both men and women.

Other surveys indicate a similar disparity in views. The Louis Harris poll, for example, shows that 16 per cent fewer Negroes than whites—a bare majority of 51 per cent—believe that local law-enforcement agencies do a good or excellent job on law enforcement. A survey in Watts found that 47 per cent of the Negroes believed that the police did an "excellent or pretty good" job, while 41 per cent thought they were "not so good" or "poor."

In Washington, D.C., the BSSR survey found that Washington Negroes have decidedly different attitudes than whites as to how the police carry out their duties, as the responses to the following statement indicate: You would have to replace at least half the police force to get a really good police.

	Nonwhite Males	Nonwhite Females	White Males	White Females
	Per cent	Per cent	Per cent	Per cent
Agree	40	28	18	11
Disagree	40	52	60	62
Don't know, etc.	20	20	22	27

NOTE: From The President's Commission on Law Enforcement and Administration of Justice: *Task Force Report: The Police.* Washington, D.C., U.S. Government Printing Office, 1967, pp. 146–148.

About half the Negroes, in contrast to two thirds of the whites, believed that the police deserve more respect than people in the neighborhood give them. However, almost as many Negroes as whites believed that the police had a high reputation in the neighborhood (almost 60%), felt that they deserve more thanks than they got (over 85%) and thought that the police should get more pay (68%). A poll in Detroit in 1965 found that 58 per cent of Negroes did not believe that law enforcement was fair, and an earlier poll in 1951 found that 42 per cent of Negroes believed that it was "not good" or "definitely bad."

POLICE DISCOURTESY AND MISCONDUCT

Negroes show even greater attitude differences from whites with regard to police discourtesy. The NORC national survey found, as to respectfulness to "people like yourselves," the following differences between the attitudes of Negroes and whites:

	White Annual Income		Nonwhite Annual Income	
	$0 to $2,999	$6,000 to $9,000	$0 to $2,999	$6,000 to $9,000
Males:	Per cent	Per cent	Per cent	Per cent
Police very good	56	67	34	31
Police not so good	4	4	22	6
Females:				
Police very good	62	66	28	41
Police not so good	3	1	12	45

A 1965 Gallup poll showed that only 7 per cent of white males but 35 per cent of Negro males believed that there was police brutality in their area; 53 per cent of Negro males thought that there was none.

A survey of the Watts area of Los Angeles concerning opinions on the existence of "brutality" found:

Existence of Police Brutality	Total	Age 15 to 29	30 to 34	45 and Over
	Per cent	Per cent	Per cent	Per cent
A lot	22.2	24.4	25.0	17.1
A little	24.6	35.6	22.7	14.3
None at all	15.1	17.8	11.4	14.3

Thus, nearly 47 per cent of all respondents and 60 per cent of all those from 15 to 29 years of age believed that there was at least some police brutality. Of those who had answered "a lot" and "a little," approximately half claimed that they had witnessed it.

Another survey of Negroes in the general area of Watts by the University of California at Los Angeles found that a high percentage of those surveyed believed the police engaged in misconduct, said they had observed acts of misconduct or indicated that such an act had happened to someone they knew or to themselves:

Police	Happened in Area	Saw It Happen	Happened to Someone You Know	Happened to You
	Per cent	Per cent	Per cent	Per cent
Lack respect or use insulting language	85	49	52	28
Roust, frisk, or search people without good reason	85	52	48	25
Stop or search cars for no good reason	83	51	49	25
Search homes for no good reason	63	22	30	7
Use unnecessary force in making arrests	86	47	43	9
Beat up people in custody	85	27	46	5

This study also shows that males below the age of 35 were most critical of the police. For example, 53 per cent of young males reported they had been subjected to insulting language; 44 per cent to a roust, frisk or search without good reason; 22 per cent to unnecessary force in being arrested; and 10 per cent to being beaten up while in custody. Well over 90 per cent of young males believed that each of these kinds of incidents occurred in the area and 45 to 63 per cent claimed to have seen at least one of them. There were no substantial differences based on economic levels. Negroes with higher education reported more insults, searches without cause and stopping of cars without cause.

The BSSR survey of Washington, D.C., found that over half of the Negroes and only a quarter of whites thought that "many police enjoy giving people a hard time." Ten per cent of Negro men and 6 per cent of Negro women claimed to have seen unjustified police use of violence in contrast to no white men and 3 per cent of white women. The BSSR study also showed a clear difference between Negroes and whites in their beliefs concerning police discrimination between whites and Negroes. Sixty per cent of Negro males, as compared to 29 per cent of white males, said the police did discriminate. Of those who believed that Negroes were treated worse, the following differences existed as to the kind of discrimination:

	Rudeness	Picked on More	Brutality
	Per cent	Per cent	Per cent
Negro males	53	60	48
White males	25	38	—

Yet, as many Negroes as whites (almost 80 per cent) said that "there are just a few policemen who are responsible for the bad publicity."

A survey in Harlem in 1964 concerning police brutality showed that of the 63 per cent of the respondents with an opinion, 12 per cent thought that there was a lot of brutality, 31 per cent a little and only 20 per cent none at all.

A survey of junior high school students in Cincinnati found that only 41 per cent of the Negro boys and 58 per cent of the Negro girls disagreed with the statement that "the police are mean." The following figures show the difference between white and Negro teenagers:

	Police Accuse You of Things You Didn't Do	Police Try to Act Big Shot	Police Try to Get Smart With You If You Ask a Question
	Per cent	Per cent	Per cent
White girls	40	33	34
White boys	56	46	46
Negro girls	60	51	56
Negro boys	65	69	70

A study of teenagers in Kalamazoo, Michigan, in 1957, similarly found that "only 41 per cent of the Negroes (teenagers) gave favorable answers when questioned on the fairness of the police, while 79 per cent of the whites responded favorably."

Surveys may not accurately reflect the full extent of minority-group dissatisfaction with the police. In-depth interviews with members of minority groups frequently lead to strong statements of hostility, replacing the neutral or even favorable statements which began the interview. For example, a study of 50 boys from the slums of Washington concluded that as a result of real or perceived excessive force, humiliation and other police practices, they regarded the police as "the enemy." Attacks on police officers, interference with arrests, disturbances and riots starting with police incidents and verbal abuse by citizens offer abundant testimony to the strong hostility. The way in which such hostility can become an important factor in a riot is illustrated by the following statement of a resident of Watts to an interviewer: "Two white policemen was beating a pregnant colored lady like a damn dog. They need their heads knocked off. I agree 100 per cent for the Negroes going crazy—they should have killed those freaks. Yes, treating niggers like dirty dogs."

This incident, which was thought by many people in Watts to have been the cause of the 1965 Los Angeles riot, never occurred. But many Negroes apparently were prepared to believe that police officers act in such an improper manner.

A survey of Watt's residents by the University of California at Los Angeles showed that 21 per cent thought that police mistreatment was the cause of the riot. In contrast, only 2 per cent of whites considered police brutality as the cause. The study further found that those Negroes who believed that the police abused people (used excessive force, beat up persons in custody, were insulting, and engaged in other misconduct) or who claimed to have seen such abuse or to have been subjected to it, were more likely to have been active participants in the riots.

The Commission's studies of police-community relations in 11 localities throughout the country showed serious problems of Negro hostility to the police in virtually all medium and large cities. In short, as the Philadelphia Urban League's 1965 report states, "many Negroes see the police as their enemies; and they see them as protectors of white people, not as protectors of Negroes, as well."

POLICE HONESTY

The NORC survey disclosed that sharp differences exist as to how citizens view police honesty. About two thirds of whites but only one third of Negroes thought the police to be "almost all honest;" less than 2 per cent of whites thought that they were "almost all corrupt" in comparison to 10 per cent of nonwhites. A Louis Harris poll in 1966 found that approximately 15 per cent of Negroes (almost four times as many as whites) believed that many police officers in their communities took bribes. A survey in St. Louis found that 46 per cent of Negroes in contrast to 24 per cent of whites believed that "dishonesty is one of the characteristics of many of our city police."

NEED FOR POLICE PROTECTION

Although surveys disclose that Negroes are substantially more hostile to the police than whites, Negroes also feel strongly about the need for police protection. This is not surprising, since a much greater proportion of Negroes than whites are the victims, as well as perpetrators, of crime. For example, in Watts, of the 41 per cent of Negroes who believed that the police are doing a "not so good" or "poor" job (47% thought that the police were doing an "excellent or pretty good job"), many cited lack of adequate protection as the basis of their opinion rather than brutality, discourtesy or discrimination. The Cincinnati survey of junior high school students showed that 83 per cent of the Negro boys agreed that "without police there would be crime everywhere."

A survey of Harlem in 1964 showed that 39 per cent of the respondents considered "crime and criminals" as the biggest problem for Negroes in the area. This was the third highest category, following economic complaints and housing. Complaints about police misconduct were not one of the nine most frequently mentioned categories. A subsequent survey in Harlem found that 21 per cent of those interviewed believed that dope addiction was the area's biggest problem and 11 per cent thought crime and juvenile delinquency were the biggest problems; these were the first and third most frequently mentioned problems. As to problems in their block, those interviewed ranked them in the following order:

	Per cent
1. Crime in the streets	28
2. Dope addiction	20
3. Need for better police protection	15
4. Murders	3
5. Drunks in the hallways of buildings	3

A 1966 Louis Harris poll in Washington found that Negroes as well as whites considered crime and law enforcement the greatest community problem. The staff report of the United States Civil Rights Commission on "Police-Community Relations, Cleveland, Ohio" concluded that the "most frequent complaint [of Negroes] is that of permissive law enforcement and that policemen fail to provide adequate protection and services in areas occupied by Negroes." Neighborhood groups in the Bedford-Stuyvesant area of New York came to the same conclusion. And the Michigan State survey found that this was one of the two most frequent criticisms of the police by minority groups throughout the country.

Most Negroes, regardless of their feelings, do not physically or verbally react with hostility in routine situations. A Commission study which viewed thousands of police-citizen interactions in several cities found that 11 per cent of the citizens reacted deferentially, 76 per cent civilly, and only 6 per cent antagonistically. The differences between Negroes and whites were negligible. Negroes talk frequently about the "good cop" who, while fully enforcing the law, treats them as fellow human beings. And, as has been shown, Negroes greatly desire better police protection. Consequently, there is every reason to believe that relations between the police and Negroes can be substantially improved.

However, the problem may be aggravated unless immediate steps are being taken to improve police-community relations while America's cities are becoming more heavily populated by minority groups. For example, in Washington, D.C., Negroes now constitute a majority of the population; in 9 other cities, they constitute over 40 per cent of the population and in 17 more, over 30 per cent. By 1970, it is projected that Negroes will constitute half the population in 4 cities of over 100,000 population; 40 per cent or more in 10 additional cities including Baltimore, Detroit, Newark, St. Louis, New Orleans and Nashville; and 30 per cent or more in 23 more cities including Atlanta, Memphis, Chicago, Cleveland, Philadelphia and Cincinnati. The problems inherent in policing such cities by police forces comprised largely of white officers may become even worse if effective action is not taken.

Chapter 14

THE POLICE AND THE COMMUNITY

NATIONAL ADVISORY COMMISSION ON CIVIL DISORDERS

INTRODUCTION

We have cited deep hostility between police and ghetto communities as a primary cause of the disorders surveyed by the Commission. In Newark, in Detroit, in Watts, in Harlem—in practically every city that has experienced racial disruption since the summer of 1964—abrasive relationships between police and Negroes and other minority groups have been a major source of grievance, tension and, ultimately, disorder.

In a fundamental sense, however, it is wrong to define the problem solely as hostility to police. In many ways the policeman only symbolizes much deeper problems. The policeman in the ghetto is a symbol not only of law but of the entire system of law enforcement and criminal justice. As such, he becomes the tangible target for grievances against shortcomings throughout that system: against assembly-line justice in teeming lower courts; against wide disparities in sentences; against antiquated corrections facilities; against the basic inequities imposed by the system on the poor—to whom, for example, the option of bail means only jail.

The policeman in the ghetto is a symbol of increasingly bitter social debate over law enforcement. One side, disturbed and perplexed by sharp rises in crime and urban violence, exerts extreme pressure on police for tougher law enforcement. Another group, inflamed against police as agents of repression, tends toward defiance of what it regards as order maintained at the expense of justice.

NOTE: From the *Report of the National Advisory Commission on Civil Disorders.* Washington, D.C., U.S. Government Printing Office, 1968, pp. 299–307.

The policeman in the ghetto is a symbol, finally, of a society from which many ghetto Negroes are increasingly alienated.

At the same time, police responsibilities in the ghetto have grown as other institutions of social control have lost much of their authority: the schools, because so many are segregated, old and inferior; religion, which has become irrelevant to those who lost faith as they lost hope; career aspirations, which for many young Negroes are totally lacking; the family, because its bonds are so often snapped. It is the policeman who must fill this institutional vacuum and is then resented for the presence this effort demands.

Alone, the policeman in the ghetto cannot solve these problems. His role is already one of the most difficult in our society. He must deal daily with a range of problems and people that test his patience, ingenuity, character and courage in ways that few of us are ever tested. Without positive leadership, goals, operational guidance and public support, the individual policeman can only feel victimized. Nor are these problems the responsibility only of police administrators; they are deep enough to tax the courage, intelligence and leadership of mayors, city officials, and community leaders. As Dr. Kenneth B. Clark told the Commission:

> This society knows . . . that if human beings are confined in ghetto compounds of our cities, and are subjected to criminally inferior education, pervasive economic and job discrimination, committed to houses unfit for human habitation, subjected to unspeakable conditions of municipal services, such as sanitation, that such human beings are not likely to be responsive to appeals to be lawful, to be respectful, to be concerned with property of others.

And yet, precisely because the policeman in the ghetto is a symbol—precisely because he symbolizes so much—it is of critical importance that the police and society take every possible step to allay grievances that flow from a sense of injustice and increased tension and turmoil.

In this work, the police bear a major responsibility for making needed changes. In the first instance, they have the prime responsibility for safeguarding the minimum goal of any civilized society—security of life and property. To do so, they are given

The Police and the Community

society's maximum power—discretion in the use of force. Second, it is axiomatic that effective law enforcement requires the support of the community. Such support will not be present when a substantial segment of the community feels threatened by the police and regards the police as an occupying force.

At the same time, public officials also have a clear duty to help the police make any necessary changes to minimize so far as possible the risk of further disorders.

We see five basic problem areas:

1. The need for change in police operations in the ghetto to ensure proper individual conduct and to eliminate abrasive practices.
2. The need for more adequate police protection of ghetto residents to eliminate the present high sense of insecurity to person and property.
3. The need for effective mechanisms through which the citizen can have his grievances handled.
4. The need for policy guidelines to assist police in areas where police conduct can create tension.
5. The need to develop community support for law enforcement.

Our discussion of each of these problem areas is followed by specific recommendations which relate directly to more effective law enforcement and to the prevention and control of civil disorders.[1]

POLICE CONDUCT AND PATROL PRACTICES

In an earlier era, third-degree interrogations were widespread, indiscriminate arrests on suspicion were generally accepted and "alley justice" dispensed with the nightstick was common. Yet there were few riots, and the riots which did occur generally did not arise from a police incident.

[1] In performing this task we wish to acknowledge our indebtedness to and reliance upon the extensive work done by the President's Commission on Law Enforcement and Administration of Justice (The "Crime Commission"). The reports, studies, surveys, and analyses of the Crime Commission have contributed to many of our conclusions and recommendations.

Today, many disturbances studied by the Commission began with a police incident. But these incidents were not, for the most part, the crude acts of an earlier time. They were routine, proper police actions such as stopping a motorist or raiding an illegal business. Indeed, many of the serious disturbances took place in cities whose police are among the best led, best organized, best trained and most professional in the country.

Yet some activities of even the most professional police department may heighten tension and enhance the potential for civil disorder. An increase in complaints of police misconduct, for example, may in fact be a reflection of professionalism; the department may simply be using law-enforcement methods which increase the total volume of police contacts with the public. The number of charges of police misconduct may be greater simply because the volume of police-citizen contacts is higher.

Here we examine two aspects of police activities that have great tension-creating potential. Our objective is to provide recommendations to assist city and police officials in developing practices which can allay rather than contribute to tension.

Police Conduct

Negroes firmly believe that police brutality and harassment occur repeatedly in Negro neighborhoods. This belief is unquestionably one of the major reasons for intense Negro resentment against the police.

The extent of this belief is suggested by attitude surveys. In 1964, a *New York Times* study of Harlem showed that 43 per cent of those questioned believed in the existence of police "brutality."[2] In 1965, a nationwide Gallup Poll found that 35 per cent of Negro men believe there was police brutality in their areas; 7 per cent of white men thought so. In 1966, a survey conducted for the Senate Subcommittee on Executive Reorganization found that 60 per cent of Watts Negroes aged 15 to 19 believed there was some police brutality. Half said

[2] The "brutality" referred to in this and other surveys is often not precisely defined and covers conduct ranging from use of insulting language to excessive and unjustified use of force.

they had witnessed such conduct. A University of California at Los Angeles study of the Watts area found that 79 per cent of the Negro males believed police lack respect for or use insulting language to Negroes and 74 per cent believed police use unnecessary force in making arrests. In 1967, an Urban League study in Detroit found that 82 per cent believed there was some form of police brutality.

The true extent of excessive and unjustified use of force is difficult to determine. One survey done for the Crime Commission suggests that when police-citizen contacts are systematically observed, the vast majority are handled without antagonism or incident. Of 5,339 police-citizen contacts observed in slum precincts in three large cities, in the opinion of the observer, only 20—about three tenths of 1 per cent—involved excessive or unnecessary force. And although almost all of those subjected to such force were poor, more than half were white. Verbal discourtesy was more common—15 per cent of all such contacts began with a "brusque or nasty command" on the part of the officer. Again, however, the objects of such commands were more likely to be white than Negro.

Such "observer" surveys may not fully reflect the normal pattern of police conduct. The Crime Commission Task Force concluded that although the study gave "no basis for stating the extent to which police officers used force, it did confirm that such conduct still exists in the cities where observations were made."

Physical abuse is only one source of aggravation in the ghetto. In nearly every city surveyed, the Commission heard complaints of harassment of interracial couples, dispersal of social street gatherings and the stopping of Negroes on foot or in cars without obvious basis. These, together with contemptuous and degrading verbal abuse, have great impact in the ghetto. As one Commission witness said, these strip the Negro of the one thing that he may have left—his dignity, "the question of being a man."

Some conduct—breaking up of street groups, indiscriminate stops and searches—is frequently directed at youths, creating special tensions in the ghetto where the average age is generally under 21. Ghetto youths, often without work and with homes that may be nearly uninhabitable, particularly in the summer, commonly spend much time on the street. Characteristically, they are not only hostile to police but eager to demonstrate their own masculinity and courage. The police, therefore, are often subject to taunts and provocations, testing their self-control and, probably, for some, reinforcing their hostility to Negroes in general. Because youths commit a large and increasing proportion of crime, police are under growing pressure from their supervisors—and from the community—to deal with them forcefully. "Harassment of youths" may therefore be viewed by some police departments—and members even of the Negro community—as a proper crime-prevention technique.

In a number of cities, the Commission heard complaints of abuse from Negro adults of all social and economic classes. Particular resentment is aroused by harassing Negro men in the company of white women—often their light-skinned Negro wives.

"Harassment" or discourtesy may not be the result of malicious or discriminatory intent of police officers. Many officers simply fail to understand the effects of their actions because of their limited knowledge of the Negro community. Calling a Negro teenager by his first name may arouse resentment because many whites still refuse to extend to adult Negroes the courtesy of the title, "Mister." A patrolman may take the arm of a person he is leading to the police car. Negroes are more likely to resent this than whites because the action implies that they are on the verge of flight and may degrade them in the eyes of friends or onlookers.

In assessing the impact of police misconduct, we emphasize that the improper acts of a relatively few officers may create severe tensions between the department and the entire Negro community. Whatever the actual extent of such conduct, we concur in the Crime Commission's conclusion that ". . . all such behavior is obviously and totally reprehensible, and when it is directed against minority-group citizens it is particularly likely to lead, for quite obvious reasons, to bitterness in the community."

Police Patrol Practices

Although police administrators may take steps to attempt to eliminate misconduct by individual police officers, many departments have adopted patrol practices which in the words of one commentator, have ". . . replaced harassment by individual patrolmen with harassment by entire departments."

These practices, sometimes known as "aggressive preventive patrol," take a number of forms, but invariably they involve a large number of police-citizen contacts initiated by police rather than in response to a call for help or service. One such practice utilizes a roving task force which moves into high-crime districts without prior notice and conducts intensive, often indiscriminate, street stops and searches. A number of persons who might legitimately be described as suspicious are stopped. But so also are persons whom the beat patrolman would know are respected members of the community. Such task forces are often deliberately moved from place to place, making it impossible for its members to know the people with whom they come in contact.

In some cities, aggressive patrol is not limited to special task forces. The beat patrolman himself is expected to participate and to file a minimum number of stop-and-frisk or field interrogation reports for each tour of duty. This pressure to produce, or a lack of familiarity with the neighborhood and its people, may lead to widespread use of these techniques without adequate differentiation between genuinely suspicious behavior and behavior which is suspicious to a particular officer merely because it is unfamiliar.

Police administrators, pressed by public concern about crime, have instituted such patrol practices often without weighing their tension-creating effects and the resulting relationship to civil disorder.

Motorization of police is another aspect of patrol that has affected law enforcement in the ghetto. The patrolman comes to see the city through a windshield and hear about it over a police radio. To him, the area increasingly comes to consist only of lawbreakers. To the ghetto resident, the policeman comes increasingly to be only an enforcer.

Loss of contact between the police officer and the community he serves adversely affects law enforcement. If an officer has never met, does not know and cannot understand the language and habits of the people in the area he patrols, he cannot do an effective police job. His ability to detect truly suspicious behavior is impaired. He deprives himself of important sources of information. He fails to know those persons with an "equity" in the community—homeowners, small businessmen, professional men, persons who are anxious to support proper law enforcement—and thus sacrifices the contributions they can make to maintaining community order.

Recommendations

Police misconduct—whether described as brutality, harassment, verbal abuse, or discourtesy—cannot be tolerated, even if it is infrequent. It contributes directly to the risk of civil disorder. It is inconsistent with the basic responsibility and function of a police force in a democracy. Police departments must have rules prohibiting such misconduct and enforce them vigorously. Police commanders must be aware of what takes place in the field and take firm steps to correct abuses. We consider this matter further in the section on policy guidelines.

Elimination of misconduct also requires care in selecting police for ghetto areas, for there the police responsibility is particularly sensitive, demanding and often dangerous. The highest caliber of personnel is required if police are to overcome feelings within the ghetto community of inadequate protection and unfair, discriminatory treatment. Despite this need, data from Commission investigators and from the Crime Commission disclose that often a department's worst, not its best, are assigned to minority group neighborhoods. As Professor Albert Reiss, Director of the Center for Research on Social Organization, University of Michigan, testified before the Commission: ". . . I think we confront in modern urban police departments in large cities much of what we encounter in our schools, in these cities. The slum police precinct is like the slum school. It gets, with few exceptions, the worst in the system."

The Police and the Community 141

Referring to extensive studies in one city, Professor Reiss concluded:

> In predominantly Negro precincts, over three-fourths of the white policemen expressed prejudice or highly prejudiced attitudes towards Negroes. Only one per cent of the officers expressed attitudes which could be described as sympathetic towards Negroes. Indeed, close to one-half of all the police officers in predominantly Negro high crime rate areas showed extreme prejudice against Negroes. What do I mean by extreme racial prejudice? I mean that they describe Negroes in terms that are not people terms. They describe them in terms of the animal kingdom. . . .

Although some prejudice was displayed in only 8 per cent of police-citizen encounters, "The cost of such prejudiced behavior I suggest is much higher than my statistics suggest. Over a period of time, a substantial proportion of citizens, particularly in high crime rate areas, may experience at least one encounter with a police officer where prejudice is shown."

To ensure assignment of well-qualified police to ghetto areas, the Commission recommends:

1. Officers with bad reputations among residents in minority areas should be immediately reassigned to other areas. This will serve the interests of both the police and the community.
2. Screening procedures should be developed to ensure that officers with superior ability, sensitivity and the common sense necessary for enlightened law enforcement are assigned to minority-group areas. We believe that with proper training in ghetto problems and conditions and with proper standards for recruitment of new officers, in the long run, most policemen can meet these standards.
3. Incentives such as bonuses or credits for promotion should be developed wherever necessary to attract outstanding officers for ghetto positions.

The recommendations we have proposed are designed to help ensure proper police conduct in minority areas. Yet there is another facet of the problem: Negro perceptions of police misconduct. Even if those perceptions are exaggerated, they do exist. If outstanding officers are assigned to ghetto areas, if acts of misconduct, however infrequent, result in proper and visible disciplinary action, and if these corrective practices are made part of known policy, we believe the community will soon learn to reject unfounded claims of misconduct.

Problems stemming from police patrol cannot, perhaps, be so easily resolved. But there are two considerations which can help to allay such problems. The first consideration relates to law-enforcement philosophy behind the use of techniques like aggressive patrol. Many police officials believe strongly that there are law-enforcement gains from such techniques. However, these techniques can also have law-enforcement liabilities. Their employment, therefore, should not be merely automatic but the product of a deliberate balancing of pluses and minuses by command personnel.

We know that advice of this sort is easier to give than to act on. The factors involved are difficult to weigh. Gains cannot be measured solely in the number of arrests. Losses in police protection cannot be accepted solely because of some vague gain in diminished community tension. The kind of thorough, objective assessment of patrol practices and search for innovation we need will require the best efforts of research and development units within police departments, augmented if necessary by outside research assistance.

The second consideration concerning patrol is execution. There is more crime in the ghetto than in other areas. If the aggressive patrol clearly relates to the control of crime, the residents of the ghetto are likely to endorse the practice. What may arouse hostility is not the fact of aggressive patrol but its indiscriminate use so that it comes to be regarded not as crime control but as a new method of racial harassment. All patrol practices must be carefully reviewed to ensure they are properly carried out by individual officers.

New patrol practices must be designed to increase the patrolman's knowledge of the ghetto. They will require getting the patrolman out of the car and into the neighborhood and keeping him on the same beat long enough to get to know the people and understand the conditions. They will require training the patrolman to convince him of the desirability of such patrol. There must be continuing administrative supervision. In practice as well as theory, all aspects of patrol must be lawful and conform to policy guidelines. Unless carried out with courtesy and with some understanding of the community, even the most enlightened patrol practices may degenerate into what residents will come to regard as harassment. Finally, this concept of patrol should be publicly explained so that ghetto residents understand it and know what to expect.

Chapter 15

THE GHETTO, THE GHETTOIZED AND CRIME

STERLING TUCKER

Crime rates for most types of offenses are highest in America's big cities. And, within our big cities reside high concentrations of black Americans.

The most serious of all criminal offenses occur with greatest frequency in the slum areas of our largest cities. And, over 40 per cent of the population of inner-city slums is black.

Crime rates in United States cities are highest in the center of the city and decrease proportionately as distance from city center increases. Central city areas in most of America's metropolitan areas are predominantly black while other areas tend to remain white.

There are many who juxtapose facts and statistics in an effort to prove a relationship between race and the perpetuation of crime, between blackness and criminality. But such juxtapositions do little more than distort the facts and feed the prejudices of the bigoted. Neither race nor color—in and of itself—is a factor which bears any relation whatsoever to the Commission of Crime. Rather, "Numerous studies indicate that what matters is where in the city one is growing up, not religion or nationality or race."[1]

SOCIAL AND ECONOMIC DEPRIVATION AND LAWLESSNESS

Conditions in the inner city which today hurry blacks along the path to easy money and a special brand of self-respect,

NOTE: From *Federal Probation*, September, 1969, pp. 5–10. Reprinted with permission.

[1] President's Commission on Law Enforcement and Administration of Justice, *The Challenge of Crime in a Free Society.* Washington, U.S. Government Printing Office, 1967, p. 57.

yesterday hurried European immigrants residing in America's cities down similar roads. Just as social and economic deprivation today turn many inner-city blacks to lawlessness, similar conditions in the past encouraged large numbers of immigrants, crowded into small, inadequate, cold inner-city dwellings and frozen out of decent jobs, to make their own rules and rise—or eat—however they could. Many found crime an easy road to real comfort—the only way to acquire status. Traditional, conventional means of "making it" were unavailable to them.

> In the low-income areas, where there is the greatest deprivation and frustration, where, in the history of the city, immigrant and migrant groups have brought together the widest variety of divergent cultural traditions and institutions, and where there exists the greatest disparity between the social values to which the people aspire and the availability of facilities for acquiring these values in conventional ways, the development of crime as an organized way of life is most marked. Crime, in this situation, may be regarded as one of the means employed by people to acquire, or to attempt to acquire, the economic and social values generally idealized in our culture, which persons in other circumstances acquire by conventional means.[2]

Thus, ". . . The inner city has always been hard on whoever is living in it . . . it is in the inner city that delinquency rates have traditionally been highest, decade after decade and regardless of what population group is there."[3] Indeed, inner-city areas which reported high crime rates in 1920 ". . . had high rates in 1900, although the ethnic composition of the area had changed almost completely. The rates remained the same for the area whether it was occupied by Poles, Germans, Italians, or Swedes."[4] And juvenile crime rates follow the same pattern. "The official statistics over the 60-odd years of the juvenile

[2] Shaw, Clifford R. and McKay, Henry D.: *Juvenile Delinquency and Urban Areas: A Study of Rates of Delinquents in Relation to Differential Characteristics of Local Communities in American Cities*. Chicago, University of Chicago Press, 1942, p. 439.
[3] President's Commission on Law Enforcement and Administration of Justice, *op. cit.*, p. 59.
[4] Hunter, David R.: *The Slums: Challenge and Response*. New York, The Free Press of Glencoe, 1964, p. 70.

court's existence have largely reflected the waves of immigration from Ireland, Italy, Poland and, more recently, the migration from Mexico, Puerto Rico and that of non-whites from the South."[5]

It is no cliché that slums breed despair, hopelessness, degradation, disease of the body and disease of the mind. Slum areas are colorless, drab, monotonous. There is little of beauty, while examples of dilapidation and shabbiness abound. The slum dweller feels little pride as he looks around the outside or the inside of his home. Indeed, shame is the more common reaction; ". . . home has little holding power for the child—it is not physically pleasant or attractive; it is not a place to bring his friends; it is not even very much the reassuring gathering place of his own family."[6]

A lack of space also characterizes the slum environment; there is not enough room for privacy; there is but limited space for recreation and play. Space is always at a premium—inside or out; privacy and freedom are sought but in vain. Apartments or homes are shared with relatives or with friends. Rooms are shared with brothers, sisters, cousins, parents. "Now most scientists agree that among all vertebrates from mice to hippos to men, the one universal condition that produces uncontrolled aggression is overcrowding. Among humans, hostility erupts when people start intruding on each other's "personal space."[7]

Ghetto property, more often than not, is in a state of poor repair. Facilities are inadequate to meet the need and are taxed beyond their capability and often give way. Plumbing and heating frequently fail; appliances are old and rickety and highly erratic. There are no traces of stability or permanence durability to be found. Residents are forced to live with no assurances. The heating system may fail on the bitterest of winter evenings; rats may appear or reappear when the baby is born.

---

[5] Robison, Sophia M.: Juvenile delinquency. *Current History*, June, 1967, p. 342.

[6] President's Commission on Law Enforcement and Administration of Justice, *op. cit.*, p. 62.

[7] Poppy, John: Violence: we can end it. Look, June 10, 1969, p. 22.

Slum neighborhoods teem with criminal activity that is apparent to even the youngest pair of eyes. Dope pushers, numbers runners, prostitutes, pimps and drunks are on the streets when the children leave for school in the morning; they are on the streets when children pass by again after class or after work. Bars are everywhere. Violence is part of the landscape.

A sense of frustration and failure is in the air. Residents' lives seem circumscribed by forces which will not allow them to live. Indeed, holding ghetto dwellers back is not lack of will but lack of opportunity. By following conventional routes, they *cannot* get a good education, they *cannot* get decent employment, they *cannot* become upwardly mobile, they *cannot* get out. As Julius Horwitz phrased it, "A slum is a neighborhood where people infect one another with the virus of failure, and where children are infected long before the virus is detected."[8]

And there is the alienation—alienation caused by a governmental structure that is not present and does not seem to care, by white-faced policemen who harass as much as they protect, by social workers who sit in judgment, by landlords who come to collect but not to fix. There are shopkeepers who overcharge and merchants who not only cheat but get court backing when their unsavory practices are challenged. Protection is doled out in unequal quantities; the ghettoized black gets the least.

How can cynicism be avoided? How can men respect laws that mock and rape? How can men be men? What should astound America is not that so many have turned to crime, given the nature of slum life in the inner city, but that there have been so few.

LIFE FOR THE BLACK AMERICAN CAN BE SELF-DEFEATING

Life for the immigrant in the slum was bad enough; life for the American black man is even more difficult and is, in fact, reflected in the high crime rates. Unlike the immigrant, the black man cannot hide his mask of difference. The foreigner could, with but little effort, learn the ways of his new land,

[8] Horwitz, Julius: The arithmetic of delinquency. In The New Light on Juvenile Delinquency. New York, Wilson, 1967, p. 18.

brush up on his English and eke out a meager living. If times got rough enough and confidence waned, he could look with pride to his children to whom he was offering limitless opportunities. Because of *his* sacrifice, they would have a chance to make it. Their lives would count for something, so his life took on meaning. What with a few years of American schooling, his children could march out of the ghetto into jobs with futures. The discrimination he had faced would not plague his progeny. His stigmas—an accent, native customs, a different mode of dress, a long, "un-American" name—each could be eradicated by an act of will. Economic and social barriers could then be penetrated easily.

For the black man, discrimination has been a constant, a fact of life for generations, and he can expect more of the same for his children and grandchildren. His badge of difference—his skin color—is ineradicable; and it is precisely this badge which is responsible for his being walled in, far from the American bounty.

Job prospects for the unskilled slum dweller today are much dimmer than they were for the immigrant of the 1800's. The latter, it is true, was forced to take a low-paying, demeaning job, but such jobs existed, and they existed in quantity. Industry was booming and crying out for unskilled and semi-skilled labor. Factories needed more and more manpower. According to Robert Conot, "The immigrant was exploited, but he was seldom frozen out of a job."[9]

In today's job market, black inner-city residents *are* frozen out, for there is little room for the untrained. The number of blue-collar jobs has sharply declined, much as the number of white-collar jobs has multiplied. In 1900, 16 per cent of the labor force held white-collar jobs;[10] today, white-collar workers represent 47 per cent of the force.[11]

[9] Conot, Robert: *Rivers of Blood, Years of Darkness*. New York: Bantam Books, 1967, p. 438.
[10] U.S. Department of Commerce, Bureau of the Census: *Historical Statistics of the United States: Colonial Times to 1957*. Washington, D.C., Government Printing Office, 1961, p. 74.
[11] U.S. Department of Labor, Bureau of Labor Statistics: *Employment and Earnings: Monthly Report on the Labor Force*. XIV, 7 January 1968, p. 47.

As the society relies more on automation and mechanization and less on unskilled manpower in farming or other manual occupations heavy pressures are brought to bear on each individual to conform to certain educational and occupational specifications. In previous decades an unskilled, untrained person could find employment in various manual occupations or he could retain independence and provide for his family as a small farmer or farm laborer. His skills could be general, his competence acquired from practice rather than from formal training.

Today this era has largely passed and each individual is required to fit into a niche in the economy even though his background has not enabled him to make this kind of adjustment.[12]

Finally, it is harder to be poor today than it was in the past. The affluence that is supposed to be America is all too visible on the television screen. Affluence is *in* the living room but yet *of* another world. The comparison between what is seen and what is lived is stark and debilitating in itself. Then, there are very few year-round jobs, and fewer which offer promotional opportunities. Prices are spiralling and the occasional sometime job will not keep food on the table for a family of four. The immigrant could look to City Hall for help, or he could turn his sights westward and acquire free farming land under the Homestead Act. Or, he could get a job as long as he wasn't choosy. But the black man today is treated with indifference or disgust by most of his city's officials, farming is hardly a solution to his problems since agriculture has become big business, and within the city there are never enough jobs.

Little wonder that there is crime. Little wonder that crime is flourishing. Only the blind cannot see it being nurtured. Only the blind continue to advocate programs of individual rehabilitation to the exclusion of programs aimed at rebuilding impoverished neighborhoods, at enriching fetid soil. What James S. Plant concluded many years ago is just as relevant, just as prophetic, today.

> The folly of believing that happiness and goodness can be fabricated by machinery (agencies) will be exposed only when we

[12] Delinquency and its causes. In *Juvenile Delinquency*, a Report of the Committee on the Judiciary, United States Senate. In The New Light on Juvenile Delinquency, p. 11.

understand that the ills, corruptions, and hypocrisies of a cultural pattern flow into the child and man and "become a part of him for the day, for the year, or for stretching cycles of years." If it is true that the triumphs and tragedies of the street flow into and become a part of the child, then all programs of personality change must manage somehow to change the street.[13]

THE EMERGING CREATIVITY OF THE GHETTO

Much of the black world has stopped looking across the tracks for assistance, for the help that has been given has always had the wrong emphasis, the wrong target. Most blacks have finally come to realize that whites will not initiate any meaningful change in the system, that what is lacking over there is not the knowledge or the wherewithal but the will. Many, therefore, are working to overcome what the white world refuses to change. They are trying to rebuild their streets and their neighborhoods. They are making efforts to save those men society discarded when they were mere boys. And they are beginning with those already branded by society as "criminal." Together they are working to remake their world.

In Washington, D.C., alone, there are three large operations, all of which are ghetto-inspired and ghetto-led, which are keeping many from turning to crime out of sheer desperation. Bonabond, an organization dedicated to helping ex-convicts, was conceived in 1966 by four employment counselors in Washington's poverty agency who were continuously stymied in their efforts to find employment for ex-convicts. Employers pleaded "no-job-without-bonding-against-loss," and area insurance companies refused to bond men with records. The counselors quickly lost their patience and decided to establish their own bonding program which has been highly successful.

As it worked in the Washington community, Bonabond discovered only a dearth of jobs available to ex-convicts—unbonded *or* bonded. Thus, a job-development component was added to the operation. In addition, the organization is helping men seeking skill improvements enter training programs,

[13] Plant, James S.: *Personality and the Cultural Pattern.* New York, Commonwealth Fund, 1937, p. 18.

and it tutors those trying to get high school equivalency diplomas.

Bonabond has also realized that one of the major causes of recidivism is narcotics addiction and consequently has set up a narcotics anonymous group through which addicts receive individual therapy from staff members and group therapy along with other ex-convicts. A similar group has been organized inside the Women's House of Detention where addicted inmates are thus prepared for life on the outside and urged to seek continued support from Bonabond upon their release.

EFEC (Efforts from Ex-Convicts), a group similar in outlook and aim to Bonabond, was organized in 1966 by a group of people concerned about the lack of services available in the Washington area to men who had served time in prison and who were trying to "go straight." It did not take much research to discover that the city's poverty agency was passing over the needs of the ex-con.

At first, weekly meetings were the main thrust of the organization. Group therapy was offered, and men were given a chance to air their grievances against the system, against their employers. When group members considered a man's problem legitimate and it involved a work situation, a group of ex-convicts representing EFEC would seek out the employer in question and listen to his side of the story. Bargaining would follow, at which time the ex-convicts tried to educate the employer in the multifold problems of the man with a record. More often than not, the employer agreed to give the employee another chance.

EFEC, like Bonabond, helps its members find gainful employment. At first, the organization relied primarily on the poverty agency's employment services, but now, according to Chairman Rev. Griffin Smith, it uses ". . . everything available in the whole city that can help a man get a job or training."[14]

With its limited resources, EFEC realizes it will accomplish little if it concentrates all its efforts on meeting with individual employers and working with individual ex-convicts. Conse-

[14] Interview with Rev. Griffin Smith, chairman, Efforts From Ex-Convicts, Washington, D.C., May 28, 1969.

quently, members have tried to saturate the public with information to dispel the many illusions that persist about the ex-convict. EFEC representatives have appeared on numerous radio and television shows. They have addressed private and governmental organizations and have testified before congressional and investigative commissions. Perhaps EFEC's greatest successes are the policy changes it has effectuated as the result of negotiations with several governmental agencies and with the local Board of Trade. EFEC was instrumental in challenging and overturning a parole board ruling that ex-convicts would lose their parole if they associated with other ex-cons. The organization also pressured the Board of Trade until it passed a resolution urging all of its members to hire qualified ex-convicts. EFEC saw that a special office was established within the United States Employment Service to deal specifically and immediately with the employment problems of ex-convicts. And finally, EFEC pressured the federal government until it agreed to eliminate a question concerning past arrests on the application for government employment and until it agreed that applicants were not bound to list their criminal records acquired as juveniles.

Another operation indigenous to Washington is Pride, Inc. Initially formed to do summer clean-up work in Washington's dirtiest streets and alleys, Pride has stayed in business with subsequent contracts from the Labor Department. It has hired many of Washington's toughest youths and put them to work in a number of endeavors. Its alley-cleaning Neighborhood Service program employs about 700 "dudes," and according to former operating boss James E. Sanders, "For many of us guys it's the first time we tried to make it legal."[15] About 90 per cent of the men on the squad have police records; a third are on parole.

Pride officials have proved the assumption that there are "normal leadership roles" within seemingly "disordered" gangs of youth and that these leadership roles can ". . . be channeled into positive directions if the existing order within the groups

---

[15] Washington Post, March 23, 1969, p. D-3.

... is not disturbed."[16] By using the existing power relationships within existing youth groups to help device recruitment plans and techniques, program plans and ideas, Pride has become a viable organization that today keeps money in the pockets of over 800 "dudes."

And Pride is going even further. It is on the way to becoming economically self-sufficient; it is on the way to realizing its ultimate goal of establishing employee-owned, profit-making businesses that will employ and develop the talents and skills of hard core as well as educated blacks, businesses that will build up the ghetto economically. Pride's money-making arm, Pride Economic Enterprises, Inc., first set up the Pride Landscaping and Gardening Company which has paid and trained about 50 Pride men. In September, Pride opened a 24-hour service station which is providing employment and training for Pride workers while it makes money for Pride. The operation has been a great success. And on the drawing chart are even more ambitious plans, plans to establish a 2.5 million dollar modern automotive service center with a complete line of services available to the client.

Around the country, former gangs of youth which once spent their time fighting, robbing and killing are today refusing to let their environments defeat them. In Chicago, the once notorious Vice Lords became the Conservative Vice Lords, Inc., in 1964 and with a change in name came a change in philosophy and tactics. Instead of ruling the streets, the young men today are engaged in developing and running profit-making enterprises. Their first venture was the opening of an ice cream parlor; this was followed by the establishment of the African Lion, a store in which Afro-American jewelry, clothing and art were sold, and in which an art, teaching and exhibition center, "Art and Soul," was created. The Conservative Vice Lords will soon take over the management of two Tasty Freeze ghetto establishments; all employees will be hired from off the streets.

In Philadelphia, the Young Great Society is today brimming with programs and program ideas. Beginning with a modest

[16] Pride, Inc. "Interim Report," submitted to OMPER, U.S. Department of Labor, 1967, mimeographed, pp. 1–2.

sports program, the YGS today sponsors over 75 teams and is responsible for providing recreational activities for ghetto youths. The YGS provides other community services as well; it runs an Academy for boys whose family lives are falling to pieces, it operates a day-care center, a tutorial program, and a Narcotics and Alcoholic Center. Mantua Enterprises, the profit-making arm of the Young Great Society, is a holding company for incipient black businesses. It seeks out businesses available for sale, sets them up under experienced management and employs ghetto men who are involved in a management-training program and who will, within a specified amount of time, assume control of the business operation. Mantua presently operates an engraving plant, manufactures some small appliances, runs a pillow factory and operates a restaurant that serves hot lunches to nearby factory workers.

Similar one-time gangs are creating viable profit-making organizations in New York, New Orleans, Minneapolis, San Francisco and elsewhere around the country. All are still fighting—but today they are fighting to build and create a better environment, a better life for themselves and for others like them, for all those relegated to inner-city ghettos.

The success stories are out there. And more and more indigenous groups are organizing for action all the time. But most organizations are small and as yet have little operating capital; tens of thousands are, by necessity, left untouched. There are thousands of inner-city blacks in each of our major cities who still ". . . see success only through the window of their television sets, or in the sleek black convertibles piloted around the slums by pimps, pushers and numbers racketeers . . . [thousands] who have no reason to anticipate success through the traditional route of education and hard work."[17] Crime offers one of the few escape hatches; for many it is the only one. And as long as we on the outside keep the ghetto an isolated and desolate island, we will see desperation acted out; we will witness humanity in some of its most ugly moments; we will see chunks of our cities reduced to ash.

[17] Elliott, Osborn: A guest in ghetto America. *Newsweek*, June 9, 1969, p. 41.

Those with conscience and dedication and energy are doing their part from within. Those of us on the outside sit. Or we make the same motions we have been making for years. Or we jump on the "law and order" bandwagon.

There are other alternatives to consider; there are new, relevant, exciting approaches to be tried. If we can but focus for a moment on the creativity of the ghetto and not on the criminality and the destructiveness, we, too, may learn. *We* may learn to stop destroying. *We* may find that *we* have the power to change the gruesome statistics.

PART III

YOUTH AND THE POLICE

INTRODUCTION

There is a growing antagonism between young people and the police, a situation that is becoming even more critical in light of the country's drug abuse epidemic. Explanations of this problem are numerous; solutions, at least workable ones, are scarce.

In Chapter 16, Dr. G. Thomas Gitchoff deals with a single aspect of an 18-month study of suburban juvenile hostility. "Police Response to Juvenile Hostility in Suburbia" describes a program which attempted to engage a delinquent social structure in an effort to decrease violent activity and police conflicts in a small California community.

The remaining articles—"Schools vs. Cops," "The Court, The Police, and the School," "Cops on Campus," "Maryland State Police's Student Training Programs" and "Campus Confrontation-Northwestern Style"—view as imperative the necessity of communicating to school children the ramifications of unlawful conduct and the necessity of community responsibility.

Chapter 16

POLICE RESPONSE TO JUVENILE HOSTILITY IN SUBURBIA

G. THOMAS GITCHOFF

In an age of increasing juvenile irresponsibility, even middle-class suburban communities are being forced into the realization that their streets are not immune to delinquency. Police operating in this setting are discovering that traditional methods may not be appropriate or effective. The arrest of a juvenile in this milieu carries with it a vast assortment of considerations that are not present in the city slum. Because of these facts, suburban communities are actively seeking methods to counteract the lessening of social control without resorting to the stigmatizing use of the formal law-enforcement system. As a consequence, the police also must search for new alternatives in order to maintain their invulnerability and avoid offending the public they serve.

It was from such concerns that the City of Pleasant Hill, California, actively sought the aid of the University of California School of Criminology in developing a program that would provide a few answers to the question of suburban delinquency. In the fall of 1966, an 18-month demonstration project was initiated which was based on findings of a preliminary study done by the School of Criminology. The findings of this study[1] are believed to have universal relevance, since the community was selected for federal funding precisely because it represented a typical middle-class suburban area.

The two most significant findings of the study were that

NOTE: From *The Police Chief,* January, 1971, pp. 52–57. Reprinted with permission.

[1] Lohman, Joseph D., Carter, Robert M., et al.: *Middle Class Delinquency: An Experiment in Community Control.* Berkeley, University of California School of Criminology, April, 1968. See also, Gitchoff, G. Thomas: *Kids, Cops & Kilos: A Study of Contemporary Suburban Youth.* San Diego: Malter-Westerfield, 1969.

1. Delinquency in this suburban area was a group phenomenon requiring prevention, control and treatment approaches that utilize the social systems of youth if the problems of delinquency and deviance are to be addressed in a meaningful fashion.
2. The power of this community to absorb delinquency internally through unofficial means has been significantly lessened and without special efforts may soon completely disappear.

If, then, delinquency is related to the social systems of youth, these very social systems would have to be engaged if any effective gains are to be made. Given the fact that in this study 70 per cent of youthful crimes involved two or more participants, it can readily be seen that individual castigation may not achieve the results hoped for. On the other hand, the community was rapidly losing its ability to cope with delinquency without referral to official county agencies. The study showed that 70 per cent of the cases were handled unofficially in the field by law-enforcement agencies, reflecting the efforts of law enforcement to encourage the community's absorption of delinquency. Despite these efforts at community control, 50 per cent of those arrested have had prior experience with the police.

THE YOUTH COMMISSION

The research program which ensued in this city was instituted through the city's own youth commission, a unique city commission composed of eight adults and seven youths. Among the commission's goals was the reduction of delinquency through the recognition of the adolescent social system and its subsequent utilization to bring about the desired change. To be effective, programming would of necessity have to be planned and implemented by youth, to serve youth. Ultimately it was hoped such a program would increase the community's ability to absorb delinquency by acting as an unofficial mediator between youth and the agency structure, thus providing a needed source of referral and informal counseling. It soon became obvious that coordinated efforts would be needed to avoid duplication of effort and to magnify the effectiveness of any single program. After several joint meetings with agency personnel, it became the unofficial custom for police and probation officers to stop by for coffee and discuss any particular youth or delinquent activities with the staff of the Youth Commission. This arrangement made it possible for the commission to act in a remedial and preventive capacity. Ideally, the police could pinpoint potential problems for the commission which they themselves were not in a position to deter.

ANTAGONISM IN POLICE-YOUTH RELATIONS

The delinquent youth of this community were polarized around two drive-in hangouts corresponding to the city's high schools. Most of the youth who frequented these places had a continuing record of police involvement. The two centers of activity were the generating points for much of the juvenile violence, vandalism and drug dispersal. Drinking and drunkenness became an increasingly open activity in the parking lots of both hangouts. Simultaneously, juvenile violence soared to an unprecedented high. Much of the violence was based on a geographical distinction corresponding to the physical locations of the hangouts. This distinction was synonymous with the identity derived by participating in the youth culture of the hangout. For example, one fight was motivated by the following dialogue:

Fieldworker: What happened at Si's the other night?

Youth: We were just sittin' around when a couple of guys from the Happy Burger (their crosstown rivals) came in.

Fieldworker: So what happened then?

Youth: Well, they wouldn't of been there if they weren't looking for trouble, so we asked them what their problem was.

Fieldworker: What did they say?

Youth: I don't remember, but the way they said it wasn't too cool, so we thought we better set them straight.

At first glance, it is difficult to believe this conversation took place in a community which has an average income of over 12,000 dollars a year. Despite the overlapping of communities and lack of discontinuity in the geographic composition of the city, a segregation according to "turf" had taken place among the delinquent youth. This delineation served as a point of reference in justifying violent attacks and planning large rumbles. The police were, of course, aware of the intensity of this problem, but were plagued by increasingly poor relations with these distinctive youth subcultures. The situation climaxed when several boys were "jumped" and severely beaten for virtually no reason. Though the police had tried to cope with the current difficulties with a minimum of formal action, the activity of the two groups had become so aggressive and their manner so provocative that routine measures were rapidly becoming obsolete. As one officer remarked: "We got the word from the top that we've been too easy. We're getting pushed, and hard. We have to crack down from now on."

Several incidents had brought police-youth relations to an all time low. All of these involved the use of force by police in subduing their youthful adversaries. The question was whether the police used more than necessary force in handling the situation and naturally each side had to justify its viewpoints. Whatever the validity of the issues, they did serve to debilitate relations to an inoperable level. Informal persuasion gave way to coercive measures in the most trivial of situations.

NEED FOR NEW ALTERNATIVES

Traditional punitive measures served only to inflame and antagonize the youth. However, other channels of communication had weakened to the point of ineffectiveness. The police felt they had been "nice guys" long enough. The local probation officer also complained of having no methods of prevention at his disposal other than detention. The schools admitted their inability to work with such youth and felt the school could better do its job without them. The youth commission fieldworkers met with the entire caseload of the local probation officer and were successful in gaining considerable youth participation in commission programs. However, the problems seemed to continue unabated.

Due to the continuous contact between agencies dealing with youth, a cooperative recognition was reached which led to the initiation of interagency meetings. The goal of these meetings was to find vehicles for increasing the understanding of youth for police purposes and expectations.

The need for techniques to increase the absorbing power of the community through unofficial action was the principal concern. The police felt a responsibility to keep youth out of juvenile hall but also stressed they had a job to do. Therefore, they believed youth-police contact in a positive sense could only be increased through informal programming where all views could be aired freely without any sense of reprisal. Many of the officers felt the concept of informal social control had waned with the increased growth of the community and the subsequent need for greater police mobility. Contact on the neighborhood level had to be sacrificed for the efficiency derived from segmented superficial contact. As a result, the youth of the community had not received the opportunity to deal with policemen as total individuals, but instead, their only contact consisted of limited negative confrontations. Some method was needed to restore an expanded level of communication in order to reestablish the rapport necessary for informal control and the lessening of antipolice antagonism.

Several officers offered their off-duty time to any program that could begin to break down the barriers in police-youth understanding. The Youth Commission felt they could aid as a catalyst in recruiting youth and taking care of any administrative responsibilities. The recreation district was willing to aid with any of its resources, though it was at a loss for programming ideas that would appeal to "hard" youth.

The real dilemma was to contrive a program which could elicit voluntary participation from the delinquent subcultures and police and still maintain an atmosphere of reasoned discourse. The youth were approached by the commission fieldworkers in order to get some idea of the kind of program the youth would be interested in attending. The youth expressed a deep concern over their ignorance of the law, a deficiency which they felt made them vulnerable to exploitation by the police.

They requested that some arrangement be made with the police that would enable the youth to get an adequate explanation for police actions in specific incidents so that misunderstandings could be clarified before they were compounded. The commission fieldworkers relayed this information to the police, who were quite receptive to initiating a regular system of feedback to acquaint youth with the problems and perspectives on the other side of the fence.

POLICE-PROBATION-YOUTH DISCUSSION GROUP

In an effort to develop an informal program capable of being understood by both youth and authoritative agencies, the police-probation-youth discussion group (hereafter referred to as the discussion group) was designed to acheive the following goals:

1. Offer youth an arena to air their grievances.
2. Involve various official agencies cooperatively working to develop positive lines of communication with youth.
3. Develop mutual respect and understanding of each other's points of view.
4. Reestablish concepts of the informal personalized relationships of the "cop on the beat approach" to a contemporary suburban community.
5. Increase the community's ability to informally and unofficially absorb their own delinquency rates.

These goals are by no means exhaustive. In this regard, it could be said that the subtle measures utilized to mutually reeducate police, probation, and youth represents an innovative program addressing itself to one of the most critical needs for establishing communications not only in suburbia, but also in urban and rural high-crime areas.

It is important to note that in the early discussion groups, the police were typically defensive and somewhat skeptical as to the nature of such a program. Traditional police attitudes and philosophies were expounded to a point that the youthful participants became oblivious and, in a phrase, "tuned-out." In an effort to remedy this situation, the commission fieldworkers met intensively with the officers. During these informal sessions, various social problems were discussed from several points of view. As a result of this broader exposure and stress for greater objectivity, the officers adopted a more sophisticated attitude. This single effort on the part of the officers accounts significantly for the subsequent success in gaining the respect and understanding of the youths. In addition, the increased empathy derived from these positive exposures led to improved authority-adolescent relations.

DISCUSSION-GROUP TECHNIQUES

Certain devices and techniques were utilized to stimulate discussion and avoid hostile impasses. They consisted primarily of the use of actual cases which youth wished to discuss, as well as psychodrama and informal seminars. Cases were discussed and analyzed. Challenges, counter-challenges, shouting, and vulgarity comprised one portion of the session. Subsequently, this led to a fair level of sophisticated debate.

It was observed that the youths' tendency to act out and rebel could effectively be understood through psychodramatic techniques. The participants were highly interested in trying this new experience after it was carefully explained to them. Briefly, the technique consisted of seating all participants in a large circle, similar to that found in group-therapy sessions. Within this circle, two chairs were placed facing each other, one occupied by the authority figure (either policeman or probation officer) and the other occupied by the complaining youth. The audience was invited to interrupt either of the speakers at any time by simply standing and placing his hand on the speaker's shoulder. This gesture indicated a wish to supplement the speaker's dialogue and could be either accepted or rejected by him.

After the case has been explained by the complaining youth, the action is stopped and roles are immediately reversed. The authority figure, having heard the complete case, now assumes the role of the complaining youth. The youth in turn assumes the role of either police or probation officer.

Juvenile Hostility

The interaction and dialogue of these psychodramatic sessions vary according to the personalities involved and their ability to empathize. An example of the cathartic interaction was demonstrated in the following dialogue, which took place under conditions of considerable stress. Several incidents of hostile police-youth contact had preceded the discussion group, and a large number of youths were present to witness the "confrontation" between the arresting officer and the youth involved. In this particular session, the incident was briefly outlined by the youth as follows:

> I was on Charley's bike (motorcycle) makin' my way down Kirk Lane, when this cop comes out of nowhere to pull my ass over. Right off, he starts givin' me a bad time and keeps lookin' for somethin' wrong with my bike. He checked everything and couldn't find nothin' wrong. So he lets me go. So I take off and I'm just about home when he stops me again. Now, I can't figure why he stopped me again, because he just checked me out a minute ago. He tells me I didn't have a license plate, so I show him my temporary paper permit. Then he wants to see my driver's license and I told him I wasn't goin' to show it to him. Then he says, I better show it to him or I'll be sorry. So, I'm so p.o.'ed, that I'm not showin' him nothin'. By this time all my neighbors and my old man come out of the house to see what's happenin'. So I guess the cop got shook and went back to his car. So then he turns around and comes back and tells me that I have to go with him if I don't show him my license. Now, I wasn't about to go anywhere with him. So when he walked toward me, I ran into the garage and got a big two by four. When the cop tried to grab me, I dropped the two by four and climbed a tree. About that time another cop car got there and the two of them were waiting for me. I got scared, jumped down from the tree and ran, but the big cop caught me.

This represents the youth's side of the story to which the other youths present reacted quite sympathetically. However, even the youths detected several defects in the story as will be illustrated in the following dialogue, wherein, the role reversal finds the police officer acting as the youth and the youth assuming the role of the police officer. For purposes of brevity, the real police officer will be called Chuck and the youth involved will be called Freddie.

Freddie (acting as police officer): You were going a little too fast down Kirk Lane.

Chuck (acting as youth): So, I wasn't doing anything wrong.

Freddie: Don't you know you can get a ticket for speeding?

Chuck: Speeding? Who says I was speeding?

Freddie: It looked like you were going a little too fast.

Chuck: So why bug me by checkin' out my whole bike?

Freddie: Remains silent.

Jerry (real officer assumes role of Freddie's conscience): Do you know how many stolen police motorcycles we recover every year by stopping and checking them out?

Chuck: I didn't steal nobody's bike.

Jerry: How do I know till I've made a check?

Chuck: So why did you stop me the second time after you let me go?

Freddie: It didn't look like you had a license plate and I didn't notice it the first time I stopped you.

Chuck: I did have a permit, so what's the beef?

Freddie: So why didn't you just show me your license?

Chuck: Because you got me so damned mad, I wasn't goin' to show you nothin'.

(Writer's note: Several youths present remarked at the stupidity of the refusal to show the license.)

Ted (a high-status youth acting as Freddie's conscience): The law says you have to show identification anytime you're asked to do so by an officer.

Chuck: Well I didn't have none on me.

Ted: Don't you know it's against the law to drive without a license?

Chuck: Yes, but I lost it.

Ted: Well why didn't you tell me that in the first place instead of giving me all that crap?

Chuck: You're the one that's giving me all the crap!

Jerry: Is that why you had to call me a nigger?

(Writer's note: Audible silence in the room at this revelation.)

Chuck: Well I was p.o.'ed. But that didn't mean you had to go call more cops.

Jerry: How many people were out there already?
Chuck: A couple.
Jerry: Yes, about ten, including your dad, brothers and onlookers.
Chuck: They weren't goin' to do nothin'.
Jerry: How did I know?

The developmental pattern of the discussion is a classic example of the psychodramatic process. Several key points are illustrated by the police-youth interaction. Structurally, the police-youth discussion group proceeds through several identifiable stages which generally take form in the following series:

1. The youth tells his version of the incident, selectively avoiding indicting information. The other youths present are in sympathy with their peer and form a bloc against the police. This is the critical point at which the police are most vulnerable to responding aggressively to the threatening situation. But this would be the greatest pitfall. Instead, the police must move out of their role as law enforcers and empathize with the youth by becoming that very person. Hence, the officer is forced into a situation in which he must gain a better understanding of the youth's dilemma.

2. The youth takes the role of the policeman and continues to play this role to fit his description of the incident, selectively avoiding important elements. The counterbalancing mechanism comes into play when others present who have information about the incident become the youth's conscience when they feel he is not "telling it like it is." Other youths, probation or police officers can fulfill this function adequately, as our dialogue illustrates:

Chuck (policeman playing the youth): You're the one that's giving me all the crap.

Jerry (as the conscience of Freddie): Is that why you had to call me a nigger?

At this point, information was revealed that the youth had selectively avoided, both when telling his story, and when playing the policeman's role. This revelation shook the foundation of the youth's story and made the credibility questionable. However, as indicated, an outside agent was needed as the catalyst to put the incident into its proper context. This move had the effect of loosening the police-youth polarization. This reaction was further enhanced by the peer-group setting.

3. The dynamics of peer group interaction are rooted in group pressure. To take full advantage of this concept, vehicles must be found to neutralize the natural police-youth dichotomies. The most effective device for developing maximal advantage from peer-group pressure is the use of ridicule, in which the youths themselves feel their peer failed to succeed in selling his side of the story and they no longer care to identify with a figure who is losing status. For example:

Freddie (playing the police role): Then why didn't you simply show me your license?

Chuck: Because you got me so damned mad, I wasn't goin' to show you nothin'.

Ted (a high status youth): The law says you have to show identification anytime you're asked to do so by an officer.

Chuck: Well, I didn't have none on me.

Ted: Don't you know it's against the law to drive without a license?

Chuck: Yes, but I lost it.

Ted: Well, why didn't you tell me that in the first place instead of giving me all that crap?

This interaction found Freddie under the ridiculing attack of a high-status youth. The result was that the peer group naturally followed the viewpoint of the leader (Ted), leaving Freddie in a discredited position. This mechanism drew the youth into a middle ground of understanding with the police in which meaningful communication was now possible.

CONCLUSION

It would be presumptuous to suggest that a panacea or sure-fire delinquency prevention program has been developed that effectively transforms youthful offenders into law-abiding citizens. There are, however, certain facets of the program that meet and remedy basic shortcomings in the youth-authority relationship.

Basically, the greatest need requiring ratification is that of adequate communication between youth and authority figures. Communication alone or the paying of lip-service to this concept is useless. It is axiomatic that understanding of this communication or dialogue must flow both ways. Both adults and youth must not just talk *at* each other, but must talk *to* each other and be able to grasp the meaning of what is being said.

It should be apparent to those knowledgeable in the area of delinquency prevention and causation that youthful crime in suburbia represents a need for innovative and effective programming. The social-political structure of suburbia requires somewhat different approaches in delinquency prevention than those utilized in the urban or rural areas. It is evident that the custom in suburban communities is to seek methods of prevention and social control that do not stigmatize juveniles by involving them in the formal law-enforcement system.

Since the basis of this project was to approach the delinquency problem as a group phenomenon in order to utilize the social system of youth and to increase the community's power to internally absorb delinquency through unofficial means, the unique position of the Youth Commission and its police-youth program was effectively demonstrated.

The continued impact and success of the police-probation-youth discussion group has demonstrated the urgent need to address the problem of communication and understanding between authority figures and youth. In similar terms, the discussion group has afforded hostile youth an arena in which to air their verbal hostility. This unique position, in turn, offers the authority agencies, mainly police and probation, an opportunity to air their grievances, explain policies and seek meaningful communication and understanding with youth. Although both parties concerned are sometimes shaken to their foundations and their security threatened, the eventual result is one of rapport and camaraderie rarely found among police, probation and youth.

The implications of such a police-probation-youth discussion group could have a favorable and far-reaching impact in restoring respect for law and mutual understanding of the role and function of the authority structures and the youth culture. Efforts such as the discussion group could be implemented on a broader scale in our larger cities by establishing such discussion groups within each police district or precinct and dealing only with the most hostile and delinquent youth. The establishment of the traditional "cop on the beat" approach can and is being modernized effectively to re-establish the mutual lines of communication and understanding needed in a rapidly growing, highly mobile and impersonalized society.

The stress is on reaching that portion of hostile youth that currently is not being addressed and repeatedly continue to turn up on the police blotters or in juvenile hall. It is imperative that official agencies begin addressing these youths in order to regain the favorable image requisite for effective and equitable law enforcement and reduction of juvenile recidivism.

The onus is not only on society in general but more specifically on the official agencies who must search for new alternatives to maintain their invulnerability and avoid offending the public they serve.

Chapter 17

SCHOOLS VS. COPS

JAMES P. KELLEY

Two Massachusetts State Police officers entered the high school. They were invited to attend a driver-training lecture sponsored by the Registry of Motor Vehicles. The principal was not in the office to greet these uniformed officers and so they were directed to the classroom where the lecture was to take place. Unfortunately, they took the wrong turn and entered the cafeteria study hall in which at this period of the day there were over 100 high school girls and boys. Under normal circumstances, a large group of young people in a study hall is not a desirable situation. But to add two uniformed members of the State Police to the woes of the two study hall teachers was too much to contend with. The study hall erupted into talking and laughing, and several derogatory remarks were heard. One or two students uttered "oink, oink," "pig, pig."

The officers were appalled and made their displeasure known to the principal. One officer stated that he had been treated with more respect at Walpole State Prison than in that high school cafeteria study hall.

How could the school authorities explain to these two extremely angry officers that the tensions which normally exist in an authoritative situation with young high school students do explode with *any* interruption—and particularly so if uniformed police officers enter a classroom.

The police should become more familiar with the local school. They should try to understand the pressures on the administrators, which are not only political but also psychological. The children in the schools, with all their attributes and failures, are the product of our modern permissive and materialistic society. These children are from the homes of businessmen, po-

NOTE: From *The Police Chief*, April, 1971, pp. 40–41. Reprinted with permission.

lice officers, laborers and from every spectrum of American society.

Police authorities cannot afford the luxury of avoiding our schools until trouble brews. The police officer should become a familiar and friendly face to our students.

This gap of understanding between police and school authorities must be closed. For a number of years, law-enforcement agencies followed a "hands off" policy towards colleges and secondary schools. Recent events at our major colleges and in many of our high schools involve open revolutionary activities, selling and use of drugs, extortion and other criminal activities. This criminal behavior has brought a new area of concern to those interested in keeping the peace in the local community. Some of the large cities have patrolmen assigned to schools because of the crime and violence that often take place within that school. Smaller towns and cities are experiencing the same disruption within the walls of the local high schools.

Traditionally, in our democratic society common law, as derived from the English system of government, has been a prevailing factor in drawing a definite line of demarcation between the law-enforcement agencies and the academic community. Educationalists have condemned any efforts on the part of law-enforcement agencies to infringe upon the academic community. In many high schools, the police officer is not welcome if he appears in his uniform. School boards have established policy that the police officer is not to enter the premises of the school in uniform or to interrogate any students during the school day. However, the police officer (in plain clothes) may be given permission by the superintendent of schools to interrogate the student after school hours in the presence of a school representative. This policy prevails in many central Massachusetts school systems.

Drug addiction is not new in the major cities of the United States. In 1955, during a routine investigation by the author at the Belmont High School in West Los Angeles, the principal did not seem to be concerned about a student involved with stolen cars (Dyer Act violation). He advised that his major problem was drug addiction on the part of the students in his school.

In 1970, in Massachusetts, drug addiction is a factor in the larger towns and is beginning to reach the smaller communities. The psychiatric social worker at the drug clinic at East Gardner State Hospital advised that in the local drug scene, the pusher carries on his business at the water cooler in the high school in many cases. The police officer, as well as the educator, should be aware of this. If the problem of drug addiction and other related criminal activities have their start at the water cooler in the high school, then certainly the police authorities should realize that they must become involved in a preventive program in cooperation with the school board.

Lack of funds for additional police personnel in small communities plus the increasing demands of municipal employees for pay increases have limited the money available to police chiefs to add juvenile and safety officers to their departments. Juvenile officers have made significant progress in developing communication with young people.

The traditional "closed-door policy" of the school department to the police department has given rise to the question of how enforcement or prevention can be successfully achieved without this cooperation. The municipal leader of the community—whether it be the mayor, city manager, selectman, or alderman—must launch a campaign to obtain public understanding and support for programs that would involve the schools and police department in a joint cooperative effort to curb crime.

Chief Ernest Chiasson, of the Athol Police Department, has started an active campaign with the cooperation of the School Department in coping with the growing drug problem. This cooperation extends beyond the drugs to the sharing of information of mutual interest in criminal matters. The police should take the initiative and assure educators that they should not fear a takeover by police authorities if they will become involved in a preventive program.

The police cannot shove this problem of school relations aside or delegate it to those who may not realize its importance.

On the college campus, the president must provide forceful leadership if he expects the faculty to have any support with problems involving criminal activities on the campus. If the president does not support campus security officers, the college is heading for trouble. The police chief must be personally involved if he expects officers to have any support in curbing criminal activities in the public schools. And the school board or trustees must back the administrator and encourage cooperation with the police.

The day of intellectual aloofness and tolerance is long past. Those who would destroy our public institutions have found refuge in the ivy-covered academic communities. They should not have sanctuary in these institutions!

Police officers should be tolerant of a "cool" attitude by some educators or a poor reception by students. It should be remembered that the attitude of students reflects the public attitude toward police. Most of the students are friendly or apathetic. A few students will be openly hostile. The police should not let the public "braying" of a few individuals give them a false impression of the school.

Furthermore, the field of education has been the host to many young men who have entered the teaching profession in order to avoid the military draft. Their motivation in entering the field of education is not a valid one. When the Vietnam war is over, many of these "teachers" will depart for other professions. Meanwhile, their radical and antiestablishment attitudes are widely publicized and demonstrated. The police officer must seek out cooperation from individual school officials.

Beware of the so-called professional "association" with its claim that they control the thoughts of their membership. Friendly attitudes and cooperation start at the grass roots with individual teachers and students.

If anyone requires "a crutch to lean on" to justify cooperative action by police and school authorities, then let him remember the following from English common law: "The greater good of all must prevail." The greater good of our community, state and nation is at stake.

Chapter 18

THE COURT, THE POLICE AND THE SCHOOL

Louis W. McHardy

In our struggle today against juvenile delinquency, it is generally agreed that no community institution or agency can function effectively in a vacuum. Segments of the problem become the province of different agencies, but no one institution or agency has complete responsibility for coming to grips with the juvenile delinquent and his problems.

The remarks which follow are general statements about the importance of a cooperative relationship between three such agencies in the community—the court, the police and the school. They are based upon observations and discussions of a breakdown in the cooperative relationships of these three agencies that occur in many communities throughout the country. If ever a need existed for a positive relationship among agencies, it does so today with the juvenile court, the police, and the school. Never before have such demands and pressures been placed upon all three institutions.

The problems of troubled youth have mounted disturbingly each year and continue to challenge the court, the police and schools. Society not only puts greater demands upon each of them, but places the blame for increasing delinquency at the doorstep of each.

According to the President's Commission on Law Enforcement and Administration of Justice, ". . . one in every nine youths—one in every six male youths—will be referred to juvenile court in connection with a delinquent act (excluding traffic offenses) before his 18th birthday."[1] It further reports that the

NOTE: From *Federal Probation,* March, 1968, pp. 47–50. Reprinted with permission.

[1] *The Challenge of Crime in a Free Society.* A Report by the President's Commission on Law Enforcement and Administration of Justice. Washington; U.S. Government Printing Office, 1967, p. 53.

"11- to 17-year-old age group, representing 13.2 per cent of the population," was responsible for at least 50 per cent of all burglaries, larcenies, and motor vehicle thefts in 1965."[2] During the 5-year period from 1960 to 1965, "arrests of persons under 18 years of age jumped 52 per cent for willful homicide, rape, robbery, aggravated assault, larceny, burglary, and motor vehicle theft."[3]

Practically all of these young people pass through the portals of schools, police stations and the juvenile courts. Each of the three agencies aspires to have some alleviating effect on the trend or pattern of delinquency—to prevent or break the chain of misbehavior. Each is concerned about the vitality and importance of its role in delinquency prevention and control. In a sense, they are on the front lines of a battle being waged night and day against a numerically superior enemy with environmental resources of its own for ammunition and support. The war-scarred elements of these three agencies lack such logistical support.

Society has not provided the support these agencies need. Personnel, training, facilities, funds, organizations and equipment are found wanting. Trained and experienced teachers and school counselors leave for better-paying jobs and better living conditions, just as skilled police officers and probation officers do.

Under fire, waging a struggle against a common enemy, it would seem that these creations of government—the courts, police and schools—would be allies, supporting each other in their efforts. But unfortunately this often is not the case. The school principal may denounce the juvenile court for failure to detain and "send away" a schoolyard troublemaker. The probation officer may accuse the police of brutality. The police officer may be refused admission to the school to question a burglary suspect. The school-board member demands "toughness" from the court while the judge pleads to school authorities for special-education facilities. It goes on and on and is a feature in almost any newspaper.

[2] *Ibid.*, pp. 55–56.
[3] *Ibid.*, p. 56.

All would agree that a relationship nurtured by antagonism and criticism is most unfortunate at best. Instead of community *organization*, this often results in community *disorganization*. In place of a common front with mutual and similar objectives, a weakened and drained line of resistance results.

ELEMENTS IN A POSITIVE RELATIONSHIP

A positive relationship among these agencies requires knowledge, communication and respect.

Knowledge

Awareness of the other agency's location, organization, function, problems and capabilities is most important. Without this basic knowledge, there can be no appreciation nor understanding of the other's work.

A school teacher may be a highly skilled instructor of civics or social studies and know little about the operations of a juvenile court. His failure to understand why a vandal is not incarcerated in a state correctional institution immediately upon apprehension often serves to frustrate a court intake worker.

The refusal of a school district to transfer a child to another school at the whim of a probation officer, who knows nothing of what is offered at either school, can create difficulties.

The homicide detective who works long and weary hours to obtain a confession from a recalcitrant 16-year-old, only to have the judge throw it out as having been obtained in violation of his constitutional rights, is at a loss in understanding why it was necessary for the court to take the action it did.

Knowledge about each agency, then, is important. One agency must not only know what the other does and why, but it also must make every effort to give information about itself. Knowledge about the work of each agency must remain not only with the executive, the commander, the director or the principal but also must be communicated to each person at the working level.

Knowledge about the particular problem dealt with is vital.

The troublesome truant, for example, can mean one thing to the school, another to the police and another to the court. The meaning for each should be known to the other.

One excellent means of enhancing understanding of what one agency expects of the other is to have written agreements. Lawrence E. Higgins, in an article prepared for discussion at the 1960 White House Conference on Children and Youth, in March 1960, citing the importance of such agreements in eliminating misunderstanding, said:

> Although in general the law states the respective areas of responsibility, a statement delineating the function of the police department in rendering police services to juveniles is desirable. A statement of this kind, mutually agreed upon, would tend to eliminate many of the misunderstandings which occur between the police agency, the courts, and other agencies in the community.[4]

This is an especially good practice to follow and has worked well. Particularly where there is a turnover in agency personnel, it is helpful to have a guideline statement of mutual responsibilities and relationships which may be relied upon no matter who is at the helm.

Statutes and ordinances which govern the authority and procedure of courts, police and schools should be widely disseminated and interpreted by the responsible officials. It is distressing to discover that a school official has never read his state's juvenile court code. What is even more disturbing is to learn that an occasional court representative is not aware of its provisions!

Communication

Dialogue must precede agreement, knowledge or understanding. As Harold J. Leavitt noted in his text, *Managerial Psychology*, "People begin, modify, and end relationships by communicating with one another. Communication is their channel of influence, their mechanism of change."[5]

[4] Higgins, Lawrence E.: *Specialized Police Services for Juveniles*, 1960, p. 17.
[5] Leavitt, Harold J.: *Managerial Psychology*. Chicago, University of Chicago Press, 1964, p. 138.

At a national meeting a few years ago, the commander of the juvenile bureau of a police department in a large city boasted publicly that his men were not even talking to the staff of the juvenile court in his county. Juveniles apprehended during the work day of the court were placed after hours at the distant detention home, to be picked up by the court's intake worker the following day, in order that the police officer would not have to undergo the "red tape" of the court's intake procedure.

In this same city, it was court practice never to notify a school that one of its students was in difficulty, for fear the student would be expelled or suspended under the standing policy of the local school board. When the matter finally came to the attention of the school, as most serious situations inevitably do, it was not in a position to be of much help.

Communication is not the sole prerogative of the executive. Ideally, it should occur on every level, particularly the working level. This is not to imply that channels or administrative lines of authority should be ignored but rather that the probation officer should be able to discuss a case with the police officer and that the school counselor or social worker can exchange views with the probation officer.

Communication should be continual and involve all parties interested and concerned. Where there is a special department in the school system to handle problem children, the police and courts often overlook the respective schools of the children; the principal and teachers are left in the dark about the child. By the same token, police officials whose work is not directly related to juvenile matters may be out of touch with the courts and the schools if not brought into dialogue.

Respect

William H. Sheridan of the Children's Bureau, in *Standards for Juvenile and Family Courts,* points out:

> Since the common objective of the court and the agencies is to provide care or treatment for children, there must be mutual respect and willingness to work together. Mutual respect, in this case, is more than personal admiration. It involves regard for the

tenets of each other's profession and for the contribution each can make. A court cannot work effectively with an agency which does not recognize the rights of individuals assured by law and the court's function to protect these rights. An agency cannot work effectively with a court which believes the treatment of social processes used by the agency are only incidental to its ability to provide a child with a bed, or which believes it should direct each step of care and treatment.[6]

Respect also goes beyond a positive feeling for the other organization. It must reach out to include the persons who comprise that organization. It involves a willingness to comprehend how and in what ways the person performs his work, the skills he must call upon to carry them out, and the problems with which he is confronted. Further, it is most important that there be a realization of the complementary nature of the roles of the agencies—how their work dovetails into a total program. The court, police, and schools are part of a broad spectrum, including many agencies and institutions.

Promptness in responding to requests and inquiries, courtesy, and a willingness to cooperate are characteristics of respect. Irresponsible public criticism has no place in cultivating or maintaining a positive working relationship. Problems between agencies should be handled out of the public eye. Bitterness engendered by an irate public statement often requires a long time to heal. In the meantime, all programs can suffer.

Each agency must not only respect the other but also should attempt to win respect for itself. Humility often plays an important role. This comprises an ability to admit being in error or to acknowledge not having the solution to a problem. Expressed appreciation for the work of a cooperating agency helps win respect. But one of the best ways to attain respect is to respond to requests efficiently and with dispatch.

Confidence in the work and staff of each cooperating agency is an important factor in achieving mutual respect. Self-confidence is another.

Providing support in times of crisis is also helpful. Coming

[6] Sheridan, William H.: *Standards for Juvenile and Family Courts*. U.S. Children's Bureau Publication No. 437. Washington, U.S. Government Printing Office, 1966, p. 124.

to the defense of another agency when it is being attacked unfairly is seldom forgotten and paves the way for a pleasant and meaningful working relationship.

SUMMARY

Garrett and Rompler, in their recently published study of delinquency, *Community Resocialization: A New Perspective*, cite the "very practical necessity for interagency cooperation and coordination."[7] In commenting on agency relationships as they exist now throughout the Nation, they state rather alarmingly: ". . . if we look at the level of coordination of existing resources which could contribute to the treatment, control and prevention of delinquency, we see that it is so poor that an integrated attack on the problem is not possible."[8]

The community itself often is deeply disturbed by the lack of a cooperative relationship among institutions and agencies. Expressions of these frustrations often take the form of hurtful and digressive legislation. What society is saying when this occurs is "if you people cannot get together and work these things out, we will give you a way to do it," or "we will take it away from you and turn it over to someone in whom we have confidence." The community will stand only so much. Excuses mean little to the man on the street.

The courts, the police and the schools are directly accountable to the public. Often they are not the large bureaucracies in which one can become lost or where a matter can be referred to a state office or federal headquarters. So-called "buck passing" is much more difficult within a local agency.

As Garrett and Rompler point out, a variety of skills and resources are needed to cope with delinquency.[9] Delinquency prevention and control are not the exclusive province of the schools, the police or the courts. They are mutually dependent upon one another and must work cooperatively and meaningfully in their efforts to educate, protect and rehabilitate.

[7] Garrett, James E. and Rompler, Peter O.: *Community Resocialization: A New Perspective*. Washington, The Catholic University of America Press, 1966, p. 25.
[8] *Ibid.*
[9] *Ibid.*, p. 29.

Chapter 19

COP ON CAMPUS

Walter Varnes

Pioneering a new phase of police-community relationships, the Monterey Park Police Department has instituted a "Cop on Campus" program at the local high school. Just as its name implies, the project involves placing an officer on the school's campus on a regular basis, to meet with students, discuss questions they have about law enforcement and present the law-enforcement view of current social problems. It is hoped that the program will result in increased communication between the police and the young people who are just beginning to develop their adult attitudes toward society.

Today, many small but vocal groups are giving the public a distorted view of its responsibility in preserving law and order. The sole responsibility is seemingly placed with the policeman who, at the same time that he is given the responsibility, is also being accused of being unworthy to have it.

From these groups we hear that the policeman mistreats those he takes into custody; we hear that the policeman bases his treatment of a law violator on the race of the violator; we hear that the policeman is not properly trained in carrying out his sworn duties.

The fact is, however, that the policeman today is more self-controlled, more impartial in his enforcement of the law, and better trained and equipped than ever before.

What the policeman really needs to do, therefore, is to let the public know what his position is, what his feelings are, and why he does the things he does as he enforces the law.

This, then, is the basic idea behind "Cop on Campus." It is a person-to-person program which, in giving students an inside

Note: From *Police*, March-April, 1968, pp. 80-81.

look at law enforcement, aims at helping them grow into adulthood with a favorable view of the police and the law.

For a thorough explanation of the program, we should look at its history, its mechanics and its future.

"Cop on Campus" was conceived by the Police-Community Relations Subcommittee of the Monterey Park Community Relations Committee in the fall of 1966. After the idea was introduced, considered and organized into an actual program, it was presented to the City Council in January of 1967. At the same time "Cop on Campus" was moving through the echelons of city government, it was also being presented to the administration, faculty and students of the high school involved.

Police Chief Everett Holladay met with the school's principal and boy's dean, who scheduled the chief to present the idea to the school's student cabinet. The student leaders welcomed the program, as did the superintendent of the school district in which the high school is located. At an assembly on campus, the chief told members of the student body of the new program. Student response was surprisingly favorable. Less than two weeks after the Monterey Park City Council and school officials endorsed the program, a police officer made his first appearance on the school's campus.

The mechanics of "Cop on Campus" are simple: An officer appears on the campus two days each week, during student lunch hours. He circulates through the groups of young people, answering questions and discussing problems.

Only two guidelines were established as basic to the project: (a) that the assigned officer be strictly an information officer, not involving himself in any investigative police action on the campus and (b) that he make every possible attempt to communicate with student-body members, emphasizing the need for their support of law enforcement and answering their questions on law and law enforcement.

Presently, one sergeant is appearing on the campus fitting this duty into his regular departmental assignment.

With the "Cop on Campus" project only recently instituted, its future is still in the planning stage. City officials are currently evaluating the success of the project and are considering new phases of it, including expanding the number of hours an officer will be on the school grounds each week and increasing the number of officers assigned to this duty. Officials of the high school district in which the school is located are also considering construction of another high school which would, of course, call for still more manpower for the program.

Thus far, "Cop on Campus" has been well received by everyone involved. This is emphasized by the fact that when Sergeant Charles Carter (presently assigned) appears at the school, he is always surrounded by a group of students.

"Some of the students ask very good questions. Others ask questions which have very obvious answers. The important thing, though, is not the questions themselves but the interest in the policeman that the students show just by coming around to see me," the sergeant comments. An example of student interest was also noted by the school's principal: "We at first had the sergeant appear in civilian clothes but so many of our students asked that he appear in uniform that we relayed their request to the sergeant, who has since begun to wear his uniform. We were glad to see that the students were having a positive reaction to the sight of a uniformed officer on campus, he said.

In conclusion, it appears that "Cop on Campus" is moving into a real vacuum in the experiences of the school's young people. Of those who have had experiences with law-enforcement officers, most have been law violators, especially in the traffic area. Since a person waiting to sign a traffic citation is hardly in the mood to appreciate the way the officer fulfills his sworn duty, this program is especially valuable. It gives a young person a chance to approach an officer as an equal and ask why he was cited, why the officer acted the way he did, perhaps why a particluar law is enforced in the manner in which it is.

There are, of course, some areas in which "Cop on Campus" still has a long way to go. One of the prime areas is in contacting students who have really strong anti-social and anti-police attitudes—"campus rebels," so to speak.

The sergeant has begun an aggressive program of his own to break down the barriers that have arisen between these young citizens and the police. "When I see a group of these youngsters, I walk right up to them and begin a conversation on my own. Some of them are really surprised to see that a policeman is interested in them other than as an arrest statistic," he comments.

This, then, is "Cop on Campus." If law enforcement is to continue to be a virile social entity and if it is to continue to attract the intelligent, dedicated young men and women it needs to fill its ranks, law enforcement must come up with some solid programs to give some solid facts about crime, society and the police to young people who, in the not-so-distant future, will be the ones who will be making the decisions on what should and should not be the law, and what the police may and may not do in combating crime.

The need for a program like this can be readily seen by anyone who has been taking a careful look at current feelings in society regarding enforcement of laws. Because many prominent educators, clergymen and even public officials have begun to question some of our laws and law-enforcement practices, and because the courts in recent years have also radically changed their views on many law enforcement practices, it is only natural that young people should also ask questions. It appears that "Cop on Campus" has answers for young people's questions and that the program is in itself an answer to a real need.

Chapter 20

MARYLAND STATE POLICE'S STUDENT TRAINING PROGRAM

Lee E. Lawder

Ten young men, all honor students at their high schools, took one week's training at the Maryland State Police Academy in Pikesville, Maryland, during the month of August, 1970. These special young men were selected from schools throughout the state. In addition to high scholastic standings, each one had expressed a sincere desire to become a state trooper. The program was a joint cooperative effort of the American Legion and the Maryland State Police. The Legion picked up the check for all expenses incurred and the Troopers furnished the instruction and the facilities.

It was a two-way street. The Maryland State Police were on hand to greet the youthful newcomers to the Academy. The boys lived and studied in the Academy as the regular troopers do. The seminar consisted of fifty hours of police subjects.

The first class on Monday morning was, in a sense, an orientation for the new students. The work of the troopers and their responsibilities were accented. An outline of the week's training was presented and the Academy's rules and regulations were reviewed. The demerit system, notebooks and study habits were included in the first day's studies.

A briefing of the helicopter services and their importance to the citizens was given to the boys in the afternoon.

The subjects which were taught during the rest of the week were: police communications, Breathalyzer, radar operation, narcotics investigation, criminal law, firearms, causes of juvenile delinquency, first aid, public speaking and motor vehicle law. Interspersed during the week were sessions on physical training.

Note: From *Law & Order*, March, 1967, p. 34. Reprinted with permission.

Emphasis was placed on the necessity for discipline in a semi-military organization. The student cadets, through their contact and studies, gained a greater appreciation of the work of a state trooper.

The experiment with the high school youths was the first attempted by the Maryland State Police and it was regarded as a success.

The Maryland State Police Academy is one of the finest in the country. Over a thousand men have graduated since it opened its doors. In addition to training State Police, the Academy conducts other training programs for law-enforcement agencies throughout the state of Maryland. It also cooperates with the United States Department of State by conducting frequent tours for foreign students in the field of police criminal justice. The Academy is now under the direction of Captain Charles A. Kirkpatrick, Director, and Lieutenant Charles L. Andrew, Chief of Training.

Chapter 21

CAMPUS CONFRONTATION— NORTHWESTERN STYLE

Solomon Gross

The alienation of college students from the establishment, of which antagonism to the police is a by-product, has afflicted many areas of this country and indeed the world. This particular infection, although not of epidemic proportions, was present at Northwestern Connecticut Community College, a medium-sized institution tucked away in the foothills of the Berkshire Mountains in the town of Winsted, Connecticut.

The college image, because of the presence of long-haired students and an accompanying drug culture, has had negative reactions, particularly in the surrounding rural areas, but in Winsted the reaction of the townspeople and of the police in the neighboring towns does not seem that severe. Some of the credit for this is undoubtedly due to the firm policies of the President, Regina Duffy, and her administrative staff, as well as the fact that there is a continual opportunity for mingling of faculty and students in the college cafeteria. In addition, a required medical examination of students upon admission to the college has undoubtedly tended to filter out the hard-core drug addict.

However, hostility to the police does exist and was noticed especially in the law-enforcement classes, where there was a mixing of older police students and younger long-haired stuents. Some of the 19-year-olds were there because of a sincere interest in law enforcement as a future career. Others seemed concerned only with learning the "M.O." of the "Fuzz." The differences were most obvious when such topics as Supreme Court decisions, police civilian review board or the F.B.I. became subjects for class discussions.

Note: From *The Police Chief*, March, 1971, p. 42. Reprinted with permission.

The writer, who worked in a ghetto area in New York City for a number of years, had considerable exposure to the kind of hostility to police recognized in the classroom. In the ghetto, one met both people who had experienced arrests, had thrown bottles at police, demonstrated against police; and police officers who had been the recipient of these bottle-throwings, were against civilian review boards, and had permissive attitudes. A dialogue I arranged during my service in the ghetto, between these extremes, met with such success that it was recognized by the Ford Foundation, funded and expanded to other precincts in the city.

With this kind of background, the Law Enforcement Department, under Professor John McAllister, began approaching students, both long-haired and police, and teachers to initiate a similar dialogue. The police students were hesitant, for fear that their position as public figures would cause embarrassment to their departments for any rash statements they might make. But they finally consented and four police students volunteered.

The civilian student in the class also turned down the idea. But several instructors who were sympathetic to the students but anxious for the dialogue succeeded in obtaining other volunteers. There was some natural anxiety among the long-haired students about future harassment, but they were reassured and a date was set.

The Law Enforcement Department believed it was important to pursue the dialogue despite reluctance of some of the individuals involved. It was thought that if law enforcement was to become a profession and gain recruits who could bring to it a high intellectual level, the student community must be won over to support the police, join the police and do research in police problems.

To ease the fears of the students and give them the assurance to respond to sensitive discussions, it was decided to allow one member of their panel to be a youthful faculty member from a discipline other than police science.

In order to get the widest possible participation and points of view, the entire project was advertised to get maximum audience and it was held in the college auditorium. Our final proposal to the group was to videotape it. One reason was to see if the material could be used for future training or lecture sessions in the classrooms. The other was to get more college students interested in law enforcement, and we felt that the capability of future showings would enlarge the audience potential.

With the assistance of Mr. Herbert Granstein of the Audio-Visual Aids Department, the subsequent session was taped. The results were gratifying. In the formal discussion period, the students related many of their distasteful personal encounters with law-enforcement officers. The policemen, on the other hand, kept to the premise that they were bound by law to detect and prevent crime, and this implied some control of personal liberties in the area of necessary frisks and stoppings on dark roads under hazardous circumstances.

The police image on stage came over poised and calm, and despite some intensity on the part of the students, the police did not get ruffled. The students, highly articulate, were somewhat surprised by this and indicated that they believed the police were picked for this quality and were not those whom they were accustomed to meet on the highway.

The audience participation was more hostile; apparently both students and police in the audience had built up a "head of steam" and were anxious to get into the discussion. The writer suspects that this overt intensity would dissipate on stage where it would have a chance to vent. Many of the police students and other long-haired youngsters subsequently asked to be included in the next session.

An interesting dividend occurred after the official termination of the discussion. All members remained on stage in continuing discussion for at least fifteen minutes, milling about in the friendliest manner. It is likely that the students never had experienced this type of relaxed relationship with police. When questioned on this, two readily admitted this point.

Subsequently, this interaction was continued when several of the instructors and some of the police went to a local restaurant and spent two more hours in rehashing their points of view.

It is expected that further sessions will be recorded to develop this approach for the recruitment of college students into law enforcement and minimize campus differences. Other higher-educational institutions offering police science degree programs might benefit from a similar dialogue. The ever-increasing presence of police as students on college campuses makes it imperative to resolve areas of potential or actual conflict. A dialogue is one such means for resolution of the problem and is also an excellent police-community–relations approach.

PART IV

THE PRESS AND THE POLICE

INTRODUCTION

Contemporary social events—demonstrations, civil disorders, riots—have driven a wedge between policemen and the news media, two occupational groupings which had previously enjoyed excellent relations. During the civil rights demonstrations of the early 1960's, police-media relations began to deteriorate as electronic and print media representatives took a sympathetic view toward Negro demonstrators and a not-so-sympathetic view toward the police. Urban rioting exacerbated the conflict, rank-and-file police militancy escalated it, and the violence at the 1968 Democratic National Convention in Chicago, in which policemen and journalists came into physical confrontation, increased the break to an abyss.

It is essential to both groups—and society—that the police maintain good, even warm, relations with the press. Anything less would stifle the free exchange of information and thus be unacceptable. The press needs police support, and the police desperately require a sympathetic press to whom they can go with the truth and expect an accurate reflection of it in the media.

In Chapter 22, "Importance of the News Media," Raymond M. Momboisse stresses the point that journalists can become an asset to police administrators in the areas of crime prevention, criminal justice reform, professionalization and managerial efficiency. He recommends that police-press programs be established and guided by certain fundamental principles in order to insure mutual cooperation without disrupting the department's primary mission.

In "A Magna Carta for Police-Media Relations," Carter Barber, a journalist, describes the media policy of the Pasadena, California, Police Department. The Pasadena philosophy is fast becoming a model for other agencies desirous of upgrading their relationship with the press.

"Winning an Important Ally," by Jack Harpster, describes the strong support a local newspaper gave to its police department during National Police Week, while "Campus to Squad Room" tells the story of a university public relations director who acted as a volunteer press officer for the Memphis Police Department after Martin Luther King's assassination.

Chapter 22

IMPORTANCE OF THE NEWS MEDIA

RAYMOND M. MOMBOISSE

It is imperative that all news coverage be impartial, fair and complete. To accomplish this end, the police must not only maintain close and cordial relations with the press but must supply it with full and complete information whenever this can be done. Such conduct will convince the press of the integrity and honesty of the police. Such confidence is essential in the times of stress and confusion which result from a riot. At such times the press must have complete confidence in the police so that it can contribute to the overall effort of the police to establish and maintain order while at the same time performing its duty to fully inform the public of the events.

Our free press is one of the foundations of our form of government. An outstanding difference between life in this country and life in the dictator-ruled countries is the fact that our press has the right to print whatever it chooses, subject only to the abuse of that right. The press is free to criticize any phase of government, provided that all facts stated in the criticism be true. As a result, any attempt to interfere with the press or in any way to censor what it prints is a direct blow against our form of government.

The news media—press, television and radio—performs an extremely important function in our society. It supplies the public with the news, news of crime and police activity which the public has a right to know. The purpose is to help its audience to understand what is going on so that they can reach intelligent decisions about public affairs. Unfortunately, crime is one of the facts of community life, and if the public does not

NOTE: From Momboisse, Raymond M.: *Community Relations and Riot Prevention.* Springfield, Thomas, 1967, pp. 230–235.

understand it, it is unlikely that the situation will ever be improved.

It is the responsibility of the press to keep the processes of justice under constant public scrutiny. Full news coverage of agencies of justice provide assurance against discriminatory practices or corruption in office, both on the part of enforcement officials and of the courts. It is a protection to the good official. It is an assurance against the abuses of authority by bad officials. The omnipresence of reporters and cameras has had good effects not only in preventing police improprieties but also in recording public evidence of prudent police action.

Crime news is an important deterrent to crime because, either directly or inferentially, it carries the warning that crime does not pay. If there is any foundation in psychology for our assumption that repetition is effective, surely the press stories of arrest, conviction and sentencing, and execution appearing day after day must make some impression on the mind of the criminally inclined. Moreover, crime news aids in the apprehension of those who have committed offenses. It permits the widest dissemination of personal descriptions. It exposes the criminal to an army of volunteer intelligence sources and forces the criminal to show his movements if he is escaping.

Crime news puts the public on guard against the perpetrator of crime or against the perpetration of like offenses by other criminals. For many offenders, crime news provides a penalty more feared than the penalties of the law. Those who would laugh off offenses or even short imprisonment if they could pay the one or serve the other in obscurity near the penalties of public reproach. A short experience in dealing with those who try to keep their names out of crime news would presuade any press critic of the powerful influence upon many people of this deterrent. The confirmed criminal, the hardened law breaker, may be indifferent to this penalty, but thousands of persons who might otherwise proceed from minor to major crimes are influenced by it and avoid the repetition of offenses that have led to painful publicity.

The news media throughout the nation has consistently supported such things as the following:

1. Improved criminal procedures.
2. Better police facilities.
3. Improved police management techniques.
4. Better police equipment.
5. Increases in manpower.
6. Better selection and training procedures.
7. Increased pay for police officers.
8. Improvements in moving traffic.
9. Increased traffic enforcement that shows results in terms of accident reduction.
10. Intelligent, well-conceived enforcement policies.
11. More efficient criminal court systems and speedier justice.

These are just a few items. Each jurisdiction will undoubtedly have an equally long and more specialized list that will have significant local application. The end result is that the press supports good law enforcement, and certainly these press policies could find no reasonable objection to them from professional law-enforcement officers.

Certainly in the past, the news media has proved its responsibility or cooperation by voluntarily refraining from the publication of information which it knew would interfere with the successful apprehension of criminals and the rescue of kidnap victims. In recent times, when the ill effects of certain types of coverage of riots and demonstrations were called to its attention, steps were immediately and voluntarily taken to eliminate the undesirable practices.

POLICE-PRESS RELATIONS

Good press relations have not always existed in police circles, often because of the failure of the police to appreciate the position of the press. Some have not recognized, for instance, that the news media is probably the most potent force in American life. No great public reaction, nor even a moderate expression of democratic government, is possible without the public enlightenment that flows from a free and outspoken press.

In some instances, police departments have resented the

"nosiness" of the press, but even this resentment is not well founded. Newspapers live on news, and it must be timely news not cold statistics. Moreover, there is an urgency in newspaper work that requires the quoting of officers, another thing of which many policemen disapprove. Writers would be exposed to many libel suits were it not for the fact that they merely repeat what is told them by public officials. Furthermore, the public would not want to read what a newspaperman had to say about an incident since he was not in a position to know, whereas the policeman was. These are but some of the reasons reporters are sometimes unusually inquisitive about the details of a case.

Far from being a hindrance, the newspaperman often is a real asset to the police. Numerous crimes have been solved by the press receiving a "tip" and turning it over to the police. Even the recruit patrolman will admit he has been helped to overcome obstacles more than once by the seasoned and friendly newspaperman. Photographic and recording equipment possessed by the news media has been and may be made available to the police by previous agreement. Network television may make available the use of a helicopter with photographic equipment for reconnaissance purposes. Photographs and movies of the action have been made available to police for the evaluation of tactics employed or as a training media. Statements taken by reporters but not necessarily printed have been of value to police in planning. There is every reason to believe that in the future the police and the mass media can continue to cooperate fully; for the ultimate aim of both is the same, that is, the service to the community and attainment of justice for all.

The Press and Public Acceptance of the Police

Much of the acceptance or nonacceptance of the police by the people in the United States depends upon how the press, the radio and other mass media report or interpret the work of the police. The public will judge the adequacy and efficiency of the police department as reflected in reports of crime prevalence, police activity in crime detection and prevention, and misconduct and malfeasance on the part of the members of the force. Unfortunately, it should be recognized that normal police work is not publicized. Seldom does the public hear about the officer who carried out his assignments with a devotion to duty. This is not news. Malpractices make the headlines. Naturally, this tends to distort the image of the law enforcement officer in the thinking of the people.

Recognizing the function of the news media and its importance in our society and to the police is the first step toward better relations between the police and the press and, ultimately, between the police and the public. Next, a police department must have a positive goal in its press relations.

GOAL OF THE POLICE-PRESS PROGRAM

The goal of the police-press program is a maximum flow of information to the public through the press with a minimum disruption of the department's primary mission. It is impossible to lay out in detail a complete list of specifics of a press policy which would be applicable in all situations and in every organization. Each individual law-enforcement organization will have unique problems which will require it to evolve its own policy of press relations. What may be a satisfactory policy in one organization would not be in another, but certain general principles can be stated. They are as follows:

1. The police must recognize that cooperation with press, motion pictures, television, radio, publishers, writers, lecturers and educators is not only desirable but is essential.
2. The police must treat all representatives of news media impartially, including the minority representatives, showing favoritism to none.
3. At the scene of a serious crime, accident, emergency or other event, permissible information, when definitely established as fact, will be promptly released. Such releases should all be made through the officer in charge or an officer designated by him.
4. Every member of the force will be respectful in his con-

tact with others and give his name and badge number to anyone requesting it.
5. The police should not hesitate to make available to the local press newsworthy items which will tend to aid in forming a favorable public opinion of the police department. Such stories as transfers of key personnel, new recruits assigned to the division and retirements should not be overlooked as outlets. New divisional policies affecting the public, assignment of new equipment and station improvements should also be given to the press. The local press is usually interested in covering these stories in addition to crime news.

Chapter 23

A MAGNA CARTA FOR MEDIA-POLICE RELATIONS

CARTER BARBER

It is a fact of newspapering that most seasoned police reporters know more about the inner workings of law-enforcement agencies than the peace officers know about the principles of journalism. Accordingly, for many reporters of good will, educating the cops is an ongoing ambition. We want police to recognize the public's right to know about their operations. We want them to realize that it is news media's constitutional obligation to fulfill that right.

In any educating process, it takes two to tango. The police must be willing. If they are and the learning begins, the eyes of both "sides"—press and police, attempting in their own ways to serve a shared community—are likely to be opened wider. This was the experience, at least, in Pasadena, California.

Background to the mutual education includes another fact: that in the view of the press, the public's right-to-know has long been steadfastly resisted by most law-enforcement agencies in volatile southern California. It still is in most of the 22 police departments and sheriff's offices in the San Gabriel Valley (northeastern part of Los Angeles County) which I cover as senior police reporter for the Pasadena *Star-News* (circulation 70,000 daily).

Some recent, ripe examples of police suppression of news when I make my daily calls to the watch commander, the desk sergeant or the harried dispatcher include:

"Nothing of interest"—with a Superior Court judge in a cell 15 feet away, having been booked two hours previously on

NOTE: From *The Police Chief*, September, 1970, pp. 28–31. Reprinted with permission.

suspicion of the attempted murder of his wife with a carving knife.

"A routine suicide"—with a wealthy, naked executive found in the bed of his estranged wife, dead from two shotgun blasts.

"Get off my back"—a sheriff's captain's answer to press inquiries about a high school riot then in progress.

There are many other less stark examples and all have the common denominator that Chief Edward M. Davis, of the Los Angeles Police Department, recently admitted when, discussing "significant controversies between police and press," he told his agency: "Their biggest complaint was that we appeared to be covering up."

It used to be that way in Pasadena, too. Information to media was "granted" on the sufferance of the chiefs of police; usually it was "leaked" by a sergeant in his office. Individual reporters highly esteemed the chiefs and their sergeant; men from other media generally settled for what they did not know. Few really cared that sufferance did not equate with constitutional sanction of media's right to satisfy the public's right to know. Serenity and tranquility got everybody by in those comfortable days.

By 1967, however, Pasadena (population 126,000) stood on the brink of civic disaster. Problems of poverty, school woes and racial ferment threatened to overwhelm it. The old image of Pasadena as the stable home of a spectacular New Year's Day Tournament of Roses and Rose Bowl football game was near total eclipse. The crime rate was soaring to a point where, at the end of 1968, Part-I Offenses would be 20 per cent more numerous than during the previous year.

The old-line city establishment was out of touch with the "new" community. As a constituent agency, so was the police department, in large measure. Restoring communication between police and all citizens became an emergency imperative.

Accordingly, a long-simmering reorganization of the Pasadena Police Department (109 sworn officers, 57 civilian employees) was moved to the front burner. City government approved the reorganization early in 1968 and on November 15 installed one of its architects, Lieutenant Robert H. McGowan, as the new Chief of Police, succeeding H. Samuel Addis, retired.

One of the 41-year-old McGowan's first moves was to implement that part of the reorganization which set up a Staff Services Division, headed by a captain, whose sections included those for Internal Affairs and Public Affairs.

The Public Affairs Section, headed by a lieutenant, included the Community Relations and Public Information Units. The latter had slots for a sergeant, an agent (a rank between patrolman and sergeant in Pasadena) and a stenographer. The first openings were filled by fellows fresh from the complaint desk and patrol cars, who had little or no experience with news media. To guide them in their new roles (the sergeant who had handled the press for previous chiefs having been shunted to the Uniform Division's graveyard shift, despite news media protests), job specifications for the Public Information Unit were drafted. They came out in a "memorandum."

Dated December 5, 1968, and written by cops for cops, it was awful in the opinion of reporters—who happened to see it inadvertently. The draft charged the unit to build "a fair and positive impression of the police department" by "promoting public confidence, understanding and support . . ." It dwelled on things like a speakers' bureau and display of trophies won by police athletes and marksmen. It mentioned the term "news media" only once in its two-page entirety. In a casual, offhanded way, it permitted the unit "to prepare reports and coordinate the dissemination of information to the news media and the public."

All in all, the draft of Numbered Memorandum 172 was of a piece with the Public Information Unit's first entry into the new municipal telephone directory: "Publicity." It was strictly the glad-hand, speakers' bureau approach, confusing public relations with public information. The two are as different, of course, as advertising and journalism.

The draft was wholly self-serving in its guidelines. No policeman, confined within them, could have dealt with media demands to know about the inevitable unpleasantries of any department—rogue cops, bad arrests, unwarranted shootings at suspects, botched details and the like. All a member of the

Public Information Unit would be allowed to do was to glorify police, not serve the public via a free press.

Keenly disappointed because the draft did not protect the legitimate interests of a responsible newspaper and related media, the editors and I agreed to protest to Chief McGowan. We wanted to put the above objections before him.

There was no problem; I met with the chief at least once a week on a regularly scheduled basis. (The practice has raised eyebrows among his peers in Los Angeles County, Chief McGowan once told me. That is a pity. McGowan has good relations with news media, unlike many of the agencies which forego noncrisis meetings with the press.) Our objections were simply another item for the agenda. Would he hold up promulgation of the draft until the press had a chance to put an alternative before him?

Chief McGowan assented at once. Further, to facilitate the kind of parallelism we both wanted in the finished product of a public information code agreeable to both "sides," he assigned the commander of the Public Affairs Section to work with me. If Lieutenant John M. Marshall and I had troubles on the two-man ad hoc basis, we could call a plenary session of our respective superiors—editors and the chief's captains.

Making the most of the opportunity, I prepared a strong counterdraft:

> Police business is public business. The police work for the citizens. The public not only has a right to know about that work but also, through their elected representatives, has the ultimate say in it.
>
> Police records are public records, and their disclosure shall be full and free . . . News media, not police, shall determine what is newsworthy . . . Media reserve the right to go to any (police) individual at any time for any purpose . . . Disclosure shall be timely . . .

Purposes were to establish the public's right to know of police activities, both good and bad, and to preclude news "management" by a department. It was such a radically different approach to what the police originally had in mind with their first "publicity" draft of a public information policy that Marshall and I had to convene a plenary session almost right off the bat.

The meeting was held in February, 1969, at police headquarters. Sitting in with Chief McGowan and Lieutenant Marshall was Captain Thomas M. Winders, head of the Staff Services Division and, next to the deputy chief, third in command of the department (ahead of the commanders of the uniform, investigative and general services divisions' captains). From the newspaper were its editor, managing editor (a Pulitzer Prize winner in 1948), the assistant managing editor and myself.

We did not get very far at that first session. The police had come armed with numerous arguments about legal restraints upon them in the disclosure of information to media. This was the era of the trial of assassin Sirhan B. Sirhan (another Pasadenan) and a court-imposed "gag rule" on all concerned, especially police, was a towering, here-and-now example of restraints upon disclosure. Against this specific, we of the press could only offer the rather academic argument that the public had a right to know about what public servants were up to, in or out of uniform. We went away from that first meeting feeling that our premise should be better honed.

A surprise development helped immensely. At the end of April, a riot erupted at Pasadena High School in territory policed by the sheriff's department. The captain in charge mishandled the press and was summarily transferred. The lesson was not lost on the Pasadena Police Department, and in May, Lieutenant Marshall came up with breakthrough language on the issue of disclosure and cooperation with news media: "In our present day social turmoil, with the ranks of law enforcement directly faced with decisions and actions that affect the total community, we are obligated to keep that same community as well informed as possible . . . The police department recognizes the public's right to be fully and accurately informed on all matters involving the total police operation."

That was the premise in a nutshell. We turned to rearing a structure on that foundation. An early problem with the machinery of disclosure was the press' sought-for "unrestricted" access to all officers, at any time. Reporters don't want to be shunted to official spokesmen at the copshop; police don't want newsmen interfering on the scene. We settled the matter by altering unrestricted to "access to all employes (who) shall cooperate to the fullest extent with accredited members of the news media."

The police also wanted to require reporters to check out on-the-scene data with supervisors back at the station. We promptly pointed out that a departmental order for its own people could not bind the outside, civilian world. The police counterproposed, and the press accepted, language that "Media representatives will be expected (sic) to maintain close contact with supervising officers, whenever feasible."

There was no problem about whose nose for news would prevail. Police quickly agreed that "Media representatives shall be the judges of whether or not information is newsworthy."

Marshall and I left room, however, for police initiative. The so-called "Code 20" concept pioneered by the Los Angeles Police Department and the Los Angeles County Sheriff's Department was preserved, in Pasadena wording: "Personnel may volunteer information not specifically requested and shall make fair, impartial and prompt notification to appropriate media entities when incidents of obvious news importance occur."

That language stood to the end, as did an enlargement of the principle that Chief McGowan personally authored: "The department recognizes the mutual need for immediately available information in all cases of crimes or incidents of subtsantial importance or interest to media, especially those involving arrest and confinement . . . Members of the department shall take all necessary steps to insure prompt disclosure."

The question of how prompt and "timely" disclosure should be proved surprisingly difficult during the discussions and resulted in the calling of another plenary session. It turned out to be an eye-opener for the press delegates. The police were vehement that they could not disclose every development in an ongoing case, especially if it were "flaky," just to keep the press abreast of the total police operation. There were just not enough hours in the day or enough policemen to wet-nurse media or spoonfeed them on everything going on.

Chief McGowan, Captain Winders and Lieutenant Marshall were clearly taken aback when we of the newspaper replied, in effect, "Hell, just tell us what we want to know, when we ask you. We don't want to know about *everything*." And, for our part, we were deeply chagrined. We professional communicators had not been communicating on that vital point. A simple, two-word insert resolved the problem and the final language ran: "Subject to legal restraints upon the department, information shall be disclosed *on request* as it becomes available and in the fullest available scope."

An eye-opener for the police came when the press returned to the topic of restraints upon it. I had suggested language that the police "recognize legal restraints upon media and will not arrogate their application." (We later made the word "assume.") The point was, I contended, that the press has the right to run its own risks; police have no right to protect the press against itself by withholding information on the grounds that, "you're a family newspaper, you don't want to publish this . . ."

But what sort of restraints exist on media apart from the libel laws and gag orders a la Sirhan, the police inquired. It apparently was news to them that such strictures as laws against the invasion of a person's past life and present privacy are accompanied by the self-imposed restraints of taste and responsibility to the community.

Although they had been reading the *Star-News* literally for decades, the police had not realized, for example, that it does not name rape victims or specify suicides unless they are extraordinary and identification is integral. Otherwise the story confers anonymity or is skipped altogether. The police had not realized that the press does not publish everything it learns or needs to know—not by a long shot.

The police eventually acceded to our insistence that the press police itself. The language stood, with the added corollary that, "Conversely, the department will expect media to recognize legal restraints upon the police in the disclosure of information."

The department took hard to the idea that the policy we were evolving would benefit media men whom they disliked and distrusted just as much as it would facilitate those whom they did consider responsible. We settled that by stipulating that only accredited media men would have access to police records, and that "accreditation of media representatives shall be the province of the police and may be revoked for cause." An irresponsible newsman, abusing his contacts, could "burn" a case only once; his accreditation then could be yanked under the so-called veto provision.

Finally, as the public information policy neared completion, we added language which is unique, so far as I know. Its purpose was to codify the notions of good faith, common purpose, responsibility and other intangibles which amounted, in a word, to trust.

We established this with language declaring that the overriding purpose of the press-police code was "to facilitate their common objective of serving the community . . . (consequently) an atmosphere of trust, cooperation and mutual respect of the working needs of media and police is a vital goal of news media relations."

By November, 1969, Marshall and I felt we had made the code as pitfall-proof as humanly possible. Our two-man *ad hoc* committee convened a final plenary session and those attending agreed. By December, the policy had been blessed by all concerned. It was codified in the format of the department's policy and procedure manual, and promulgated January 13, 1970. It blossomed on bulletin boards in the police station and the newspaper. Letters of congratulation were exchanged.

HAS IT WORKED?

Then everybody waited to see how it would work in actual practice. Today, four months later, the consensus is that it has exceeded expectations. There have been, by actual count, only seven formal complaints by media men of frustration by officers of the Pasadena Police Department. There used to be that many during any fortnight.

As a direct result of the policy's disclosure provisions, media now receives the same Daily Report that is circulated among departmental supervisors, detailing felony arrests and Part-I Offenses during the previous 24 hours. It is an excerpt of salient cases among the literally hundreds recorded on the round-the-clock log.

A reporter wishing to develop a Daily Report or log entry now finds his access to officers involved to be unimpeded; there is very little buck-passing. Piecemeal disclosure has become the rarity rather than the rule.

There has been some backsliding (as mentioned, complaints by the press have not vanished totally), but it generally reflects the facts that the policy still is new—and cops remain humanly fallible. For example, a watch commander recently denied there had been anything of interest on his graveyard shift. It later turned out he had booked a woman on suspicion of murder in an adjacent city (which lacked a jail for females). "My God," the lieutenant said, when confronted with the suggestion the booking was of interest, "that's right. But we were holding her as an outside assist. She wasn't our case. I just forgot about it." He was believed.

The press is happy with the policy.

The police, for their part, appear entirely satisfied. They have not been betrayed in their increasing reliance on the press to live up to the "trust" aspects of the code, as well as the portions dealing with restraint, taste, responsibility and the determination of what is newsworthy. Two recent examples are typical.

The police volunteered, in living up to the code, that the son of a captain had been arrested on a minor narcotics violation. They hoped it was not all that newsworthy—but there it was. They expected the press would find out about it anyway and wanted to supply the facts straightforwardly. As it happened, the press already knew. The reporter concluded the arrest and offense were so routine and commonplace that even the subject's kinship to a captain did not make it newsworthy. He had passed it up.

In the other case, a reporter noted that two top detectives had been assigned to a "blind" entry in the daily log. Police flinched when the reporter, invoking the code, demanded to know its nature. "Purely an internal matter," officers said. The reporter insisted, his curiosity naturally honed. Further, it appeared this might be the acid test of the new policy. The police apparently sensed this also. Within hours, a top commander entered the press room at headquarters.

"This case involves a morals offense," he said. "It involves the spouse of an officer. There are sordid pictures. I suppose you want to see them. Here they are."

"Forget it," replied the reporter. "I don't even want to know the name."

That is the kind of atmosphere that has grown out of the policy enacted by police and press in Pasadena, and the public's right to know is assured (even if it is not always exercised).

The policy's influence already has spread beyond Pasadena to numerous southern California cities of like size. The Los Angeles Police Department has excerpted great chunks of the "Pasadena philosophy."

So have such groups as the California Bar Association and the California Newspaper Publishers Association, feeling that it has statewide application where police and press impinge.

Those of us who put the code together feel that it is a kind of Magna Carta for media-police relations in this era of misunderstanding, if not hostility and downright confrontation. We feel the policy has national validity.

Chapter 24

WINNING AN IMPORTANT ALLY

JACK HARPSTER

On May 17, while police officials all over the country were assessing the support their National Police Week activities had received in their local newspapers, the 13 law-enforcement agencies that divide responsibilities in the South Bay area of southern California sat back and contemplated their local press support. It amounted to over 1,300 column inches of space in the newspaper, or the equivalent of better than a full page for each day of the seven-day-observance; free posters to be used during open house ceremonies; and a strong editorial backing.

How did they accomplish it? *Quite simply, they asked for it. That's all!* There was no magic formula, no time-consuming drive to raise the 3,000 dollars it would have cost to buy the space. They simply asked for it; and to their amazement, their local daily newspaper, the South Bay *Daily Breeze,* not only met their request for help but voluntarily contributed seven times more space than requested.

The story of one newspaper's strong support for its police agencies during National Police Week dramatizes what can be accomplished in hundreds of communities throughout America if local police officials will actively seek a rapport with their newspapers.

The South Bay is a sprawling chunk of land that composes the southwestern corner of Los Angeles County. Within its confines lie fourteen incorporated cities and unincorporated parts of Los Angeles County. Torrance, the biggest of the area's cities, has a population of 140,000. The name South Bay is an unofficial one, and merely serves to identify the rough geographic boundaries of the area.

NOTE: From *Law and Order,* December, 1970, pp. 52–53, 66. Reprinted with permission.

Law-enforcement responsibilities for the area's near-million people are shared by the municipal police departments on nine of the cities, two substations of the Los Angeles County Sheriffs Department, one division of the Los Angeles city police department and one branch of the California Highway Patrol.

Obtaining newspaper coverage of worthy departmental events in the *Daily Breeze,* whose 60,000 circulation offers the only local daily coverage of the area, can often pose a problem because of the sheer number of police agencies vying for such coverage. For this reason, many of the municipal departments often turn to one or more of the area's ten independent weekly newspapers. By their very nature, however, these newspapers can only offer a once-a-week exposure for an event such as National Police Week. Too, due to their tight profit margins, they are usually unable to devote the large amount of free space needed to provide the shock-therapy impact obtained in the South Bay program.

This unique program began when Chief Charles Crumbly of the Manhattan Beach Police Department wrote for the Motorola "Police Image" advertising series described in the March, 1970, issue of *Law and Order.* The chief's original plan was to have the ads reproduced as posters and displayed in local stores during National Police Week. However, he discovered that the material was suitable only for newspaper reproduction, or convertible through an expensive process that no local print shop could handle. It was at this point and as a last resort, that Chief Crumbly dropped the ad mats off at the *Daily Breeze,* hoping that they would reproduce the wanted posters.

In two days, Chief Crumbly had his answer: the newspaper would not only print the posters and make them available to all thirteen agencies, but they also planned to run one of the full-page "Police Image" ads each day during the seven-day Police Week observance. In addition, Chief Crumbly was told, the *Daily Breeze* planned a strong "support your local police department" editorial at the first of the Week, and extensive news coverage of all the special activities planned by each of the thirteen agencies.

The reason the *Daily Breeze* took such a strong stand was summed up by Publisher Hubert L. Kaltenbach.

"We believe in what we're doing, and we feel the time for strong action has arrived," he said, "we can no longer just stick our big toe in the water to feel the temperature. If we have a strong conviction, and if it's sincere and in the best interest of our community, we feel we must dive in completely.

"At the *Daily Breeze*," he continued, "we feel that way about strict law enforcement. Therefore, it's our duty, as the conscience of our community, to speak out strongly, as we did on National Police Week."

This attitude has far-reaching implications for police officials nationwide because this conviction is not the sole property of any one newspaper. In today's language, "establishment" is a tainted word. But for lack of a more appropriate tag, it must be used to describe the majority of today's newspapers. They strongly support the tenets that form the foundation of our way of life. Foremost among these tenets is an orderly, due process of law. Thus, today, many newspapers from coast to coast—not all, but many—stand ready to take an extraordinarily strong stand behind their local police departments, such as the one taken by the *Daily Breeze*.

Unfortunately, however, newspapers, like policemen or merchants or barbers, or almost anyone else, are concerned first with their own immediate problems. So it becomes the job of the local police chief to actively solicit this support rather than sit back and wait for it to rise, phoenix-like, at his feet.

Or perhaps you are satisfied with the support your department is receiving from its local newspaper. They do an honest, impartial job of reporting the "hard" news of crimes, apprehensions, accidents, etc.; they always feature a mug shot of new additions to the force; their editorial slant is strongly pro-police. Fine, but there could be more. When was the last time they pictured one of your officers helping out at the Little League field; or the last time they gave you a free recruitment ad. (Do not feel skittish about it. The U.S. Treasury Department, the National Automobile Dealers Association, the Advertising Council of America, and hundreds of other organizations promoting worthy causes all ask for it—and quite often, they get it. Is not the cause of law and order equally worthy?) The point is, unless your department is a very unusual one, it is not receiving all the support it could from its newspaper. With a little work, you can probably improve the situation.

If you decide to take such a step in your community, who should you visit? Obviously, it is a case of finding that individual in the newspaper who is most personally involved in the broad spectrum of community service activities. On many medium and large newspapers this man is called the director of community relations, promotion manager, public relations director or community affairs director. Whatever his title, his responsibility generally includes reflecting his newspaper's image in the community. And assuming his paper is—as we have described it—a member of the establishment, then the image he wants to reflect is one of supporter of law and order. So you will find him an interested listener for any suggestions you may make regarding police support.

If your local newspaper has no one who fits the description above, then the publisher will probably be your best bet. He's the top man, vitally concerned with any problem that affects his community; and if he's behind you, you can't miss.

Or if you are unable to see the publisher, the editor is a good man to know. Remember, whomever you talk with, and on whatever executive level he sits, he is probably just as concerned over today's problems as you are. And generally he's eager to use his newspapers support wherever it will help better the community.

Many police chiefs leave the task of establishing a good press contact with their assistant or with one of their officers. However, the added prestige of a personal visit from the top man in the police department can add immeasurably to your success in winning this important ally.

Once you have the ear of your newspaper contact, let him know exactly how you feel his paper can help. If you have obtained the full-page "Police Image" ads and would like some of them published, tell him so. Most newspapers find themselves in the position of needing a quick "filler" from time to time when an ordered ad has not arrived on time, or when press combinations necessitate the addition of another page. When this happens, they are apt to use one of their own house ads to fill the space, or one of the hundreds of public service ads mentioned previously that regularly arrive through the mail. It's up to you to show him why the "Police Image" ad is more important from a local standpoint and should have preference over the others, at least occasionally.

If it is editorial coverage of a special event or activity you want, tell him that. If the event is news, he'll be glad to know about it. Often, the only contact your department may have with the newspaper is the reporter who covers the police beat. His primary concern is reporting hard news, and news of a special open house or awards ceremony you have planned will not interest him too much. So this type of news can often be disseminated more successfully through your special channels.

The primary thing to remember is that most newspapers do care. They care about your problems and the problems of the community, as well as their own. And if you will take the initiative and cultivate their concern—and do a little selling while you're at it—you will soon have a valuable and powerful ally working for you.

Chapter 25

CAMPUS TO SQUAD ROOM

Heber Taylor

Public relations textbooks recommend that practitioners be willing to help their communities or worthy organizations in time of need. This is the story of a public relations man who, putting this theory into practice, helped his city during a major crisis.

Charles F. Holmes is director of public relations at Memphis State University. A 1957 journalism graduate of the school, he worked five years for the Memphis *Commercial Appeal* before returning to his alma mater in 1962.

When Dr. Martin Luther King was assassinated in a Memphis motel on Thursday, April 4, Holmes called the Memphis Police Department to offer his assistance. The man he talked to was Frank Holloman, director of police and firemen in the city. The two had been acquaintances since the time, a few years earlier, when Holloman had worked for Memphis State as director of development.

Holmes had anticipated that the police would need help in press relations, so he was not surprised when Director Holloman asked him to serve as press officer for the Police Department during the crisis.

"I knew that after such a tragic and newsworthy event," Holmes recalls, "a worldwide representation of the press could be expected. I had been a police reporter my last two years with the *Commercial Appeal,* and I knew that the Police Department was not equipped to cope with an army of reporters in such a situation."

With the blessing of Memphis State University's president, Dr. C.C. Humphreys, Holmes reported to the Police Depart-

Note: From *Public Relations Journal,* June, 1968, pp. 13–15. Reprinted with permission.

ment on the morning following the assassination. He was assigned Assistant Chief Henry Lux's office—Lux would be too busy with outside duties to use it.

Holmes received a briefing from Director Holloman at the outset. He was scheduled to begin work with the press immediately, answering their questions personally or by telephone.

By the time he got to his office after the briefing, the calls were piling up. That was the way it was to be until midnight that night—in fact, through the four days that he helped the police. (He was not needed after April 8 because the news spotlight shifted from Memphis to Atlanta for Dr. King's funeral on April 9.)

By helping with press relations, Holmes felt that his efforts would allow the police to proceed with the work at hand.

"The police had three major assignments—the restoration of order to the city, the search for the murderer and the planning necessary for the mass march that was scheduled for Monday, April 8," he says.

THE EX-REPORTER KNOWS

Because of his experience as a reporter, Holmes felt that he knew the problems that newsmen faced, too. "I sought to provide them with whatever they needed, especially with sufficient investigative data."

Holmes found that there were many requests for information that could not be answered because providing such information would have hampered the arrest and conviction of the person or persons responsible for the murder.

As Holmes had expected, media requests took most of his time. He would take reporters' questions about the murder investigation, looting, rioting, fires, etc., and every hour and a half to two hours would get the answers from Director Holloman.

When several newsmen were interested in the same information, he released it in duplicated form. He arranged for press conferences during the first two days so that newsmen could ask the police director their own questions. The conferences, however, ran too long, and that approach was dropped.

Holmes estimates that some 150 to 200 newsmen converged on Memphis after the assassination. He dealt directly with about 75 to 100 of them. He worked with reporters form England, Australia, Sweden, France, and Yugoslavia. American reporters that he personally helped represent the networks, the news magazines, the wire services and many individual papers and stations.

INQUIRIES BY PHONE

In addition to the media personally represented in Memphis, press representatives from around the world were calling to see what information they could get by phone. (A Dallas journalist called to inquire if there were any indication that the assassin was from Dallas. Holmes was able to say no.)

Most of the calls were in good faith. Holmes, however, doubted the value of a call from a Hartford, Conn., man who seemed more than a little drunk and who insisted that the assassin was a Hartford bartender whom he obviously disliked.

Another important part of Holmes' duties was working with the television network pool as the networks prepared to cover the memorial march of April 8. (This was the march that Dr. King had planned to lead in behalf of striking sanitation workers in spite of a city injunction forbidding it.) Even after the city agreed to the march after the assassination, the police objected to it because of the safety factor.

Holmes found himself in the position of a go-between, first between police and march leaders, and then between the networks and the police. The route of the march had to be determined, and when it was, Holmes released it in duplicated form to all interested media.

THE NETWORKS' PROBLEMS

There was a special problem involved in network plans for covering the march because no one was to be on the rooftops—a person there might be mistaken for a sniper. After this was worked out and camera stations were assigned to the networks, one network was unable to get permission from the owners of buildings to use any of its three assigned spots. Renegotiations were then necessary.

Perhaps the low point in Holmes' four days of work for the city came when he gave out the rules governing the conduct of the media during the march. One rule agreed upon by march leaders and police was that newsmen had to join the march at its originating point, Clayborn Temple, or they could not march. On hearing about this provision, a New York broadcast newsman told Holmes:

"No - - - redneck Tennessee cop is going to tell me what to do!" (Holmes' desk sign read, "Assistant Chief Lux.")

Another rule that the march leaders had insisted upon ran into unexpected difficulty. No one was supposed to interview Mrs. King except at a press conference before the march. Because of flight difficulties in coming from Atlanta, Mrs. King arrived too late for the conference. When she joined the march, already in progress, reporters rushed to her in spite of the rule. The rush was so spontaneous nothing could be done to stop it.

There were several other problems to be faced during the crisis. For example, the Police Department did not have curfew credentials to issue to media representatives. Holmes could only notify reporters that proper press credentials would be honored. The yellow press cards given to reporters by the New York City police worked best.

The police had some difficulty in adjusting to him, a writer, working for them instead of against them. There was no problem in working with the director, however, and Holmes considers the hesitancy that he ran into easy to explain.

Rumors were an especially serious problem. They had explosive power in a super-charged city, and had to be carefully investigated and corrected when found to be false.

One rumor concerned an 18-year-old Negro youth said to have been shot by police. It turned out that the "youth" was a 48-year-old former convict who fired upon police when he was spotted carrying a rifle. A small arsenal of ammunition found on him indicated that he had planned to do some sniping that night. This case was an example of the rumors that were carefully checked out and handled well by the press when it got full information.

Another rumor of a "cab driver shot" turned out to have stemmed from a radio report by a cab driver who said that he had "heard a shot."

Some of his old acquaintances, Holmes says, wanted special favors from him—interviews with police officials, tips and confirmation of speculation. "I gave them sympathy, but I could only give out the information I knew," he says.

The Police Department did not have enough secretarial help to answer the barrage of calls coming in or enough money to put out as many information bulletins as Holmes would have liked to release. "The secretaries assigned also answered telephones for four other people, and did their paper work, and took reports and complaints over the telephone. They were tremendous."

He says that he does not know how successful he was in helping the Police Department and Memphis with the tremendous public relations problem it inherited with the firing of an assassin's bullet. He has not had a chance to make a complete study of how the media handled the situation. He has seen, however, stories written by several reporters who were in Memphis. He says that one newspaper, *The Wall Street Journal,* gave Memphis kind treatment; that one magazine was unkind; and that the rest of the media that he knows about (*Newsweek, U.S. News & World Report, Life* and the networks) were objective.

His impression of the coverage of the city in the foreign press—as reflected by his conversations with the foreign correspondents—was "positive."

Love for his city was a motivating force in causing Holmes to volunteer to help in the crisis. When he heard the news of Dr. King's death, he thought of Birmingham, Selma, Dallas, and small towns in Mississippi where civic images were badly damaged. He wanted to help newsmen to get the facts of the situation. He also wanted the chance to tell them some of the good things about the city, including its history of racial harmony and the successful integration of Memphis State University. In brief, he wanted to do what he could to get Memphis fair treatment.

He concedes that fairness can be elusive during a crisis. "There were violent reactions—both ways. Some people wanted to condemn the city completely. Others sent money to help the assassin escape or to defend him."

The newsmen who came to Memphis were a part of a panic situation, he believes. "They were afraid that someone was going to get some facts that they didn't have. The work of our public relations outpost in the Police Department was to reassure them as well as to help them get all the news that could be released."

PRESS AND POLICE THANKS

The stories that were written that commended the police and the thanks of the reporters he helped were very gratifying to Holmes.

A letter from Director Holloman to Holmes' boss, President Humphreys, was also extremely pleasing to Holmes. It spoke of "the tremendous service that Charles Holmes performed during the critical emergency. . . . I do not know what I would have done without his assistance. He handled the press in a superb manner. . . . I will never be able to express to Charles Holmes or to you how deeply grateful I am. . . ."

Overtime for the Police Department during the period of unrest cost Memphis over 500,000 dollars. When asked about payment for his four days of work for the city, Holmes' response was: "A turkey sandwich and a dill pickle."

PART V

THE FOREIGN EXPERIENCE

INTRODUCTION

The American police are facing a time of crisis and there are those who say that policemen in this country could go a long way toward solving their problems if they would just emulate their foreign counterparts—especially the English bobby. But as anyone who consistently watches network television news programs can see, foreign policemen have their share of troubles, too. These include drug abuse, massive demonstrations, skyrocketing rates of crime, racial and religious disruptions, age-grade conflict and community hostility.

Some of those who feel that American law officers could clear up the nagging community relations problems that face them by just copying foreign police innovations are displaying a degree of naivete, for one simply cannot transplant, intact, cultural elements to one shore that took centuries to develop on another. The classic argument that advocates of police reform here use to disarm the police is an excellent example of faulty reasoning based on a kind of reverse ethnocentrism. The English police, they say, do not carry firearms, so why should the American police patrol armed. They fail to recognize that we have a frontier heritage, one based on extreme individual action, the use of problem-solving violence and a gun-carrying tradition. In short—the English people are not armed, so it is not necessary for the bobby to be armed, with the reverse holding true in this country.

Yet, this is not to say that we cannot learn from the foreign police and adopt some of their innovations, as long as the procedures are compatible with our culture. Some universal principles exist regarding professionalization that can be implemented here.

In Chapter 26, George Berkley offers a broad overview of and perspective on the European police. Discussed are lateral entry, firearms policies, certain administrative and social processes related to policing and a surprising emphasis on education and training.

Chapter 27, "Law Enforcement in Great Britain," by David A. Booth, gives a basic description of English policing, with an emphasis on post-1962 developments. One of the most interesting themes involves three paradoxes common to the United States and Great Britain: (a) the constant clamor for crime detection and prevention, with an accompanying obstruction of it on the part of politicians and bureaucrats; (b) the expectation that the police simultaneously serve society and be its master; and (c) the universally recognized need for the police to professionalize but the lack of meaningful effort in that direction.

Chapter 28, L.G. Tyler's "The Police and Social Tensions," is a discourse on the role of the English police in the handling of emerging social issues. Reverend Tyler's recommendations for abating the crisis are not unlike those offered by American police scholars.

In Chapter 29, "The Royal Ulster Constabulary: its Function and Changing Role," Henry Kennedy explains the organization and administration of the police of the now famous Northern Ireland Province, in addition to providing an incisive analysis into the problem of assigning to a civil police force a paramilitary defense role. The article reveals the inadequate training accorded this particular force and points out the basic weakness in such a policy. Much of the criticism aimed at the force will be familiar to American police watchers.

Roy A. Wilson's "Police Administration in Australia" gives as clear and concise a description of the organization and management of Australian police services that has yet been published. Chapter 31, "The Danish Police: Function, Organization and Administration" gives basically the same type of introductory perspective.

"The Police of Tokyo," by T.T. Winant, recounts the unusual and distinguished police record of the Metropolitan police agency of Japan, while Robert Y. Thornton's "The Kidotai" describes Japan's elite mobile police task force unit, a special component charged with the responsibility of controlling civil disturbances.

Chapter 26

THE EUROPEAN POLICE: CHALLENGE AND CHANGE

GEORGE BERKLEY

Like their American colleagues, European policemen are having their problems. Modernization, urbanization and affluence have hit Western Europe with full force. In Germany, the once-prized virtue of order is suddenly not so prized any more. French police are seeing their prime source of information, the once-ubiquitous concierge, disappear with the growth of modern apartment houses; English police find the swelling tide of traffic is forcing them into increasing conflict with normally law-abiding citizens. Even race and ethnic relations are posing problems. Britain's troubles in this sphere are well known. Other European countries must contend with numbers of migrant workers from Eastern Europe and Turkey. Last year, a Swedish policeman was disciplined for having told a factory worker from Budapest, "I hate all Hungarians."

These problems have produced concern and this concern has produced action. European police departments are moving ahead on a variety of fronts to grapple with the police problems of their urban, affluent societies.

POLICE EDUCATION

One striking area of advancement has been education. Germany is perhaps outstanding in this regard. The German police recruit must complete a school and training program which lasts between three and four years before becoming a full-fledged member of the force. In the past, Sweden has given

NOTE: From *Public Administration Review,* September-October, 1968, pp. 424–430. Reprinted with permission.

ten months' training to its policemen. This year, the country increased police schooling to a full 12 months. Italy educates its policemen for over two years. France provides for six months' training. England, with a four-months' school program, is near the bottom of the list, although this is still a good deal more education than that offered by almost all American police systems.

Quantity is not the only distinguishing aspect of European police education. There have also been some interesting changes in content. Here again, the Germans may well be the trailblazers. Nearly 25 per cent of the German recruit's class hours during the first year is devoted to such subjects as psychology, history and government. The history texts vigorously point up all the injustices of the Nazi era. The political texts make good use of quotes from Aristotle, George Bernard Shaw and John F. Kennedy in stressing democratic values. The psychology texts emphasize the need for human understanding and a sense of humor. At the same time, they warn of the dangers of prejudice and group stereotyping. The recruit is carefully instructed to allow for the frustrations which such modern phenomena as traffic jams and increasing bureaucratization create for the average citizen.

Courtesy and friendliness are continually emphasized. The Berlin police academy distributes to its recruits mimeographed copies of complaints that have been made against policemen in the past and which, upon investigation were found to be justified. The policeman-to-be is to use these reports as study materials in learning how not to behave when on the beat. The enterprising Berlin police school even offers dancing instruction to its fledging patrolmen to help them acquire social grace.

Sweden also focuses a good deal of its recruit's time and effort on the mastery of non-police subjects. Police trainees spend 25 per cent of their class time on law and 15 per cent on social studies, including psychology. Their civics text opens with Lincoln's famous quotation of democracy as government of, by and for the people, and then goes on to hammer away at such concepts as civil liberties and minority rights.

The book's first picture shows a man addressing a crowd at London's famous gathering place for dissenters, Speaker's Commons at Hyde Park.

The more abbreviated schooling given French patrolmen does not permit such extensive attention to nontechnical aspects of police work. However, since 1964, the curriculum in the police school in Paris has included a full class-hour course entitled *Morale, instruction civique et education professionelle*. In this course the recruit learns, among other things, that he is "first a citizen, secondly a civil servant and thirdly a policeman."

TRAINING FOR SENIOR POSITIONS

The emphasis which many European police departments put upon education grows even more pronounced when it comes to grooming personnel for senior positions. Officer training usually runs from six months to one year, depending on the country and the grade. Customarily, such special training begins with promotion to the lieutenant level, although England has a one-year, college-level instruction program for sergeants. The instruction almost invariably includes courses in psychology and other human relations subjects. In Sweden, police officers in training are taken on tours of psychiatric clinics, prisons, alcoholism centers, etc. In France, a candidate for officer training must go before a jury consisting of high police officials, a judge and a university professor. The jury will present a subject of general social concern and the candidate must discuss it with the jurors in a satisfactory manner before he is allowed to sit for the lengthy written examinations. Candidates for detectives in almost all European countries must also pass examinations and, in virtually all cases, must take a special instructional program before achieving detective status.

LATERAL ENTRY

The importance attached to education makes European police departments reach out for more educated recruits, and most police systems on the continent make at least some provision for lateral entry. Since World War II, this feature has become highly developed in France. Half of the candidates for the French equivalent of a lieutenancy are chosen from among nonpolice candidates who hold a baccalaureate degree, while half the candidates for the *commissaire,* or inspector grade, are chosen from nonpolice applicants who hold a law degree. In both cases, the other half of the candidates are chosen from within the department. All groups receive the same schooling, six months for the lieutenants, one year for the inspectors. German police forces recruit 10 per cent of their detective forces directly from the legal profession, while the Swedish police recruit lawyers to fill some 300 of their top positions. England remains the only major democratic country in Western Europe without some provision for lateral entry.

POLICEWOMEN

In addition to reaching out for the more educated, European police departments in many instances are also reaching out for the distaff side. England has long been most notable in this respect, with nearly 5 per cent of all the country's constabulary positions held by women. Germany, Italy, and the Scandinavian countries also make substantial use of policewomen, utilizing them for specialized tasks such as interviewing female victims in auto accidents and assault cases, for youth work and for regular detective work. In Germany, all children under the age of 14 who come into conflict with the law are handled exclusively by policewomen. France remains an exception to this trend; except for a few female members of the Paris police, the French police forces are completely male.

POSITIVE WORK

The use of women and better-educated men in their operations, along with the stress put upon education for policemen generally, has helped many European police departments to make great strides in taking a social approach to police work. Swedish patrol cars, for example, carry extra gasoline, spark plugs and other materials designed to aid motorists. Swedish policemen give instruction to third- and eighth-graders on the law, run detective clubs for teenagers, and carry on intensive crime-prevention programs throughout the community. The postwar German police adopted the motto "The policeman— your friend and helper." In fulfilling this role, they stage puppet shows for young children, warning them of traffic hazards and child molesters, and operate traffic kindergartens for older children, who gleefully drive model vehicles while learning the rudiments of traffic safety. Rescue operations, bicycle clinics, full-scale crime prevention programs and a host of similar activities for the members of the community are enthusiastically carried out by the post-Nazi German police as they seek to achieve a new rapport with their citizenry.

The French police, though far behind many of their continental counterparts, have also started to undertake positive work. Since 1965, the *Sûreté* has been operating summer camps for young people from the ages of 15 to 21. It now has 22 such camps in operation, staffed almost exclusively by policemen. Across the channel, the English are lagging behind other countries in terms of an organized effort in preventive work, but because of their tradition and their unarmed status, the bobbies have long stressed a positive approach in their duties. A British patrolman who notices an elderly woman crossing the street and who fails to come to her aid is likely to receive an official reprimand if a superior officer observes his inaction.

It should be noted that positive work is viewed by many European police departments as an integral part of police work itself. It is not something to be done by a special community-relations division. Furthermore, European policemen, at least in England, Germany, and Scandinavia, do not rebel at being called social workers. As a matter of fact, a poll of Swedish recruits, taken by a psychology teacher at the Swedish police school in Stockholm, showed that social worker was their favorite alternative profession.

Positive work ties in closely with public relations work, and here, too, many European police departments have been making great efforts. The Swedish police staged a series of joint press-police seminars around the country during 1967 in order to discuss mutual problems. As a follow-up, certain policemen were assigned to work for short periods of time on various Swedish newspapers in order to gain understanding of newspaper problems. German police departments issue daily roundups of police activities to the press. They also hold annual open-house days at their police stations and stage biannual police shows. The Paris police have begun publishing a regular bulletin called *Liaisons* to explain their work to the public. The English police are staging frequent crime-prevention exhibits, and in 1966, the London police hired a professional public relations man.

USE OF FIREARMS

Despite all these efforts in creating a positive relationship with their clientele, European policemen, like policemen everywhere, also have to use coercion and force in the performance of their duties. However, here, too, they often show a high regard for human life and dignity. All continental policemen carry guns and clubs, but the clubs are usually of hard rubber, while the guns are invariably the 7.65 mm caliber which are similar to our .32 automatic. They are much lighter than the .38 specials, which are standard for American police departments. They are even lighter than the .32 regulars carried by New York City policewomen. Policewomen in Europe are almost always unarmed.

The restrictions on the use of firearms are quite stringent. In Scandinavia, France and Italy, a policeman may fire his gun only to save a life, his own or that of someone else. In Germany, he may, under certain circumstances, shoot at a fleeing suspect, but he must aim only at the arms or legs. German policemen must pass a test every other month showing that they are capable of aiming this well.

Once he has a suspect in custody, the European policeman must also respect the suspect's civil liberties, and these, in most countries, have become fairly extensive. The new French penal code promulgated in 1962 sets 48 hours as the maximum time for holding a prisoner before bringing him before a judge. In Germany, the police can hold a suspect only to the end of the day following his arrest. Since April, 1966, German police have been required to inform suspects of their rights and to provide them with counsel if they so desire. They cannot interrogate a suspect without his lawyer being present, unless the suspect expressly grants permission.

The European approach to interrogation is also worthy of note. Basic Swedish, German and French texts on this subject stress the need for treating the interrogatee in a dignified and humane manner. All forms of deception, as well as coercion, are strictly ruled out.

FUNDAMENTAL FEATURES

Underlying and fostering these aspects of European police work are several more fundamental features which characterize modern European police departments.

Centralization

European police systems are already highly centralized and are becoming more so. Sweden nationalized its police in 1965, reducing the number of police districts from over 500 to 119, all now firmly under the control of Stockholm. France, acting under a law passed in the summer of 1966, has amalgamated its two major police forces, the *Sûreté* and the Paris police. In Britain, the Home Office has been increasing its control over the local police departments. The Home Secretary now has the power to approve the appointment of all police chiefs and to hold them responsible for carrying out the various directives and regulations issuing from his office. Since the national government contributes 50 per cent of the budget of every police force, he has no trouble in securing ready compliance. In May, 1967, the Home Secretary ordered the country's 119 police departments to begin a series of amalgamations designed to reduce the total number of independent forces to 49. Such countries as Denmark, Norway and Belgium have long had a national police.

Germany's police operate under a federal system. There are 11 police forces for the 11 German states or *länder*, as they are called. However, the federal government supervises all police training and oversees police conditions generally. It supplies various subsidies to the state police systems and maintains a central detective bureau at Wiesbaden to give them aid. A few municipal police systems are still found in southern Germany, remnants of the American occupation which instituted them. However, they are diminishing in number every year.

Increased centralization has helped bring about some of the changes noted above. It permits the recruitment of high-quality personnel at the apex of the organizational pyramid. It facilitates the establishment of larger police schools with more complete training programs. It permits the marshalling of resources for a variety of positive-work programs and ensures that a social-service approach is emphasized throughout the country.

Civilian Control

Civilians do not just oversee, but actually run most European police departments. The Swedish police are under the direction of a former judge who in turn reports directly to a five-man board appointed by the Swedish Parliament. The recruitment of lawyers directly into the upper echelons of the system also increases the element of civilian control. A former teacher of French runs the main police school in the suburbs of Stockholm.

Germany's state police commissioners are invariably professional civil servants, usually with a doctorate in law. They are responsible to the state ministers of interior. The police departments they run are subdivided into various sections with all but one of them, that of the *Schutzpolizei,* or uniformed police, under the direction of a civilian. Even the detective force, or *Kriminalpolizei,* is presided over by a non-policeman, usually a former judge or prosecutor. Day-to-day control over the police forces in the districts is exercised by the civilian district administrators, except in those states which consist of one large city, such as Hamburg and West Berlin.

The newly unified French police are directed by a civilian secretary-general. Under him, civilians head up the *Sûreté* and the Paris *Préfecture.* The new chief of the *Sûreté,* for example, is a former chief of staff at the Ministry of Education. Civilians also occupy many other positions of command, and this has increased with unification of the forces. Half of the managerial positions (*postes dirigeantes*) in the police are now earmarked for civilian civil servants.

England also exhibits civilian control, although this is considered less of a necessity with a constabulary which does not carry arms, and which is, by long and firmly entrenched tradition, a civilian body. As noted above, the Home Secretary exercises fairly extensive control over all police work in the country. He also has a deputy who occupies himself more exclusively with police matters. In London, the present commissioner of the metropolitan police, Sir Joseph Simpson, is a professional policeman, but many of his predecessors were not. Under him, there are eight divisions, four of them headed by civilians.

The civilian presence is not simply felt at the top in some European departments but continues on downward into the working forces. Civilians make up nearly 25 per cent of the police employment rolls in Sweden and England. Equivalent figures for Germany are hard to obtain, but this is partly because the police are so interwoven with the general civil service. Secretaries and even civilian administrators transfer in and out of the police. Civilians are also frequently used as drivers, instructors, etc. France, however, still makes little use of civilians in police work below the managerial level.

The civilian influence also turns up in the design of the policeman's uniform. The modern German policeman, beltless and bootless, his gun and club hidden from public view, resembles an American bus driver. The French police are also issuing new uniforms which conceal the policeman's weapons. The English police uniform has long had a special pocket the hide the light truncheon which constitutes the only weapon of the British bobby.

This substantial degree of civilian control and influence in the police forces has probably assisted them in responding to present-day challenges. It appears, for example, to be one of the factors that has encouraged the increased emphasis on nonpolice subjects in the police school curriculum and that has stimulated the greater stress on social-service tasks.

Bureaucratization

Western European police departments tend to be highly bureaucratized: they tend to be governed by fairly formal and fixed standards of operation and behavior. Promotions up to the highest levels as well as to the detective branches are governed by set procedures, though this does not exclude weighing in work performance and oral interviews. Formal means of communication to the police rank and file are intensively used, including the publication of police magazines. Nearly all the national governments publish such magazines monthly, while three of the German states also issue them. Detailed disciplinary codes are common. The Police (Discipline) Regulations, 1965, of the British police cover over 60 pages of printed copy. There are also detailed procedures for policemen to follow when they wish to air a complaint, request a transfer, etc.

These bureaucratic police systems frequently feature a fairly high degree of employee participation. German police systems all have *personalräten*, which consists of three policemen, chosen by their fellow members of the force, who have offices within the main police administration building. There they receive and process complaints from their members. The French police have what are called round-table commissions (*commissions administratives paritaires*), half of whose membership is chosen by the members of the force through their unions. These commissions pass on all promotions and all disciplinary actions involving policemen. (The chairman, who has the deciding vote, is chosen by the administration.) British policemen elect members to the Police Council of Great Britain, which negotiates pay and pensions, and to the Police Advisory Board for England and Wales, which advises the Home Secretary "on general matters affecting the police."

Trade Unionism

Police unionism in most European democracies is highly developed. Virtually all policemen, including those at the officer level, in Scandinavia, Germany, France, and England belong to a union of one kind or another. In Sweden, the Police Union is a constituent unit of the Swedish White Collar Employees Union (*Svensk Tjänstmäns Förbundet*). In Germany, the Trade Union of Police (*Gewerkshaft der Polizei*) is an independent body, although negotiations with the German Trade Union League (*Deutsche Gewerkshaft Bund*) have been going on intermittently for several years. France has several police unions, although some of them are consolidating as a result of the unification of the police. They are affiliated with the *Confédération Générale du Travail*. The Police Federation of Britain is required by law to remain unaffiliated with the Trade Union Congress and is not called a union. However, its assistant secretary, Anthony Judge, says that for all practical purposes it is a trade union.

These unions seem to perform a valuable role in European police departments. They facilitate employee participation in decision-making, provide legitimate avenues for ventilating grievances and proposing ideas and strengthen professionalism. In many instances, the unions have favored increased education, stepped-up emphasis on positive work and tighter gun-control laws. They seem to have exerted little pressure for increased police power and have even encouraged restrictions on the use of force. The German police union lobbied successfully to permit its men in North Rhineland-Westfallen to carry lighter revolvers, and it has combatted any moves to equip the police with heavy weapons. Scottish patrolmen, at their 1967 convention, turned thumbs down on proposals to equip the police with chemical weapons. Previous suggestions to arm the British police with lethal weapons met stern rejection from the Police Federation. The Swedish police union chief, Gunnar Gunnarson, has told me he would like to see his members follow the British example and not carry guns. He said he would support such a step if certain conditions, including increased education for policemen, were met.

Police administrators in many of these countries often find the unions more of a help than a hindrance. Carl Perrson, who was head of the Swedish police when I visited that country in 1966, told me he would not be able to do his job effectively without a union. When I repeated the remark a month later to Roland

Fougere, deputy prefect of the Paris police, he indicated at least qualified agreement. "Their spokesmen frequently point out problems we don't know about and help us resolve them," he said.

The Political Process

Legislatures exert considerable control over the police in most European democracies. A near-classic example is the John Waters case which reverberated through Britain in the late 1950's. Waters was a teenage boy who was knocked down and given a nosebleed by two Scottish patrolmen after he had pestered them with complaints that they had torn his coat. Charges of police brutality arose in Parliament and the Macmillan Government was finally forced to set up a special commission to investigate the case.

Swedish parliamentarians are also quick to attack any suspected abuse of police power. When Stockholm policemen took pictures of some anti-Vietnam War demonstrators in July 1966 they touched off a furor in the Riksdag. The head of the police hastened to assure the legislators that it was the criminal police and not the security police who took the pictures. They did so, he said, only to have evidence in the event the marchers broke any law.

Demonstrations in Germany often produce parliamentary debates in the legislatures of those states in which they occur. Criticism of the police and close questioning of the minister of interior, who is accountable for them, frequently characterize such proceedings. Whenever a German policeman shoots and kills an unarmed person or a fleeing suspect, the parliamentary reaction is likely to be intense. In 1964, a customs official shot and killed a smuggler seeking to make a getaway on a bicycle. The North Rhineland-Westfallen state legislature reacted by staging a debate over police use of weapons which raged for several hours. They did this despite the fact that the man responsible for the particular incident was a federal official not subject to their control.

France's emasculated parliament is also a frequent critic of the police. Indeed, the famous Ben Barka case, in which two police officers were implicated in the kidnapping of a Moroccan leader several years ago, still produces occasional grumblings in the National Assembly and the Senate. Much criticism in recent years, however, has centered on the supposed unofficial police groups of the government known as the *polices parallelles*.

If European parliaments are quick to criticize their countries' police forces, the police often have representatives of their own to speak for them. In Scandinavia and Germany, policemen are allowed to hold political office, and many of them do. Several German policemen are members of the various state legislatures. Among them is the trade-union president Joseph Kuhlman. The Danish parliament customarily has four or five policemen on its benches. In Sweden, there is a small community in the southern part of the country which has elected all its policemen to its town council. In none of these countries has this police role in politics seemed to pose any problem or to cause any significant controversy.

CONCLUSION

Because of the nature of their work, as well as the uniforms they wear, the weapons they carry, and the hours they are forced to keep, policemen often tend to become a group apart from society. Many of the characteristics of the European police organizations examined above are helping to alleviate this long-standing and often troublesome problem of police isolation. For example, permitting policemen to participate openly in the political process through legitimate channels brings them directly into a critical sector of community life. It may help to deter them from nursing pent-up resentments against the society they serve and from feeling victimized through deprivation of one of the basic rights in any democracy.

Social integration of the police is also aided by lateral entry, which brings middle- and upper-class recruits as well as the better-educated into police work. Lateral entry may enhance ethnic and religious representativeness as well. One possible reason why there are German Jews in the German police, but virtually no British Jews in the British police (despite a much greater proportion of Jews in Britain than in Germany) is that the German police provide for the direct recruitment of lawyers. The use of women in police work also adds to this representative aspect.

Other features discussed above also further integration. These include civilian influence, positive work, public relations, and trade unionism. Unionism is particularly conducive to this end when the police union is affiliated with a larger union organization. However, even when the police union remains independent, it is able to provide policemen with recognized spokesmen, organs of communication, and a formal organization to facilitate contact with the larger society and to increase the latter's knowledge of, and awareness of, its police and their problems.

In summary, then, the European police departments cited in this article are moving, with varying degrees of speed and emphasis, toward the achievement of one of the basic goals of a police force in a democratic society. As the British Royal Commission on the Police put it: "It is no exaggeration to say that the police cannot successfully carry out their task of maintaining law and order without the support and confidence of the people. The police and the community are one."

BIBLIOGRAPHICAL NOTE

Much of the material in this article was collected by the author in interviews with European police officials and in inspecting their facilities and materials. However, he has also found various European police journals helpful. These include *Svensk Polis, Die Polizei, Die Streife, Dei Neue Polizei,* and the British *Police Journal.* All of them, except for *Die Streife,* are available at the New York City Public Library. A French magazine, entitled *La Nef,* which devoted its June-September 1963 issue to the French police, constitutes a valuable source of material. The *Final Report* of the British Royal Commission on the Police (1962) is also helpful. Especially useful books are: *The Police* by Ben Whitaker, Penguin; *The Policeman in the Community* by Michael Banton, Tavistock and Basic Books; and *Le Bras Seculier* by Casamayor, Editions de Seuil. The last-named work is, in the author's opinion, the best book on the police.

Chapter 27

LAW ENFORCEMENT IN GREAT BRITAIN

DAVID A. BOOTH

Societal conflicts present the British police with challenges not unlike those facing their American counterparts. If these challenges are to be met, the British police must overcome several shortcomings. They must ease their administrative inflexibility arising from a strong attachment to tradition, solve their interjurisdictional and intrajurisdictional problems, improve their personnel recruitment and end their racial discrimination.

Although some doubts are expressed about the transferability of police institutions and practices, several positive reactions to the societal challenges are noted, including the creation of specialized regional agencies, the consolidation of police forces, the application of computer technology for crime detection and data retrieval, the introduction of unit-beat policing and the relaxation of physical standards for personnel.

The conclusion mentions three paradoxes common to British and American police administration: (a) the legislative, executive, and judicial obstruction of police administration, (b) the role conflicts in the functions of the police and (c) the paucity of research efforts in police science.

Men so love their own world, someone has written, "that they do not know when it no longer exists." Institutions embody the values of the society that creates them. When they cease to keep pace with the changing values of society, as they often do, they no longer represent viable values and therefore tend to be ill-suited to the needs of the world they are supposed to serve.

NOTE: From *Crime and Delinquency*, July, 1969, pp. 407–414. Reprinted with permission.

In philosophy, in organization and in methods, the British police system, the result of over a century of steady growth, reflects many of the values of its pioneers. Today's world is not the world of Sir Robert Peel:[1] it has changed enormously, and all the changes make enormous demands upon the police, although some have also greatly facilitated the work of law enforcement authorities.

CONTEMPORARY SOCIETY

The society which the police are supposed to serve is radically different from the Victorian society in which the police systems were first established. It is characterized by a large number of conflicts and struggles—struggles between different generations, between black and white, between rich and poor, between core-city residents and suburbanites.

Although they are not all new, these struggles are important; each demands the attention of law-enforcement authorities. Riots, looting, arson and violence are all common and are symptomatic of a deep desire for change. Almost every major urban area in the United States has had a taste of terror, has felt the searing heat of anger and of fire. The police must cope with anarchistic elements who are obsessed with a desire to destroy not only the cities themselves but more especially the structures and institutions which they believe are standing in the way of participatory government.

Today's world is also much more mobile; the movement of people, goods and services continues to grow. In Britain, this extraordinary growth in mobility has not been matched by sufficient improvements in highways, in transportation facilities or in safety standards. The British police have had to expand their traffic control and have had to devote increased manpower to accident investigation and courtroom duty.[2] Extending the

---

[1] Sir Robert Peel, Home Secretary under Prime Minister Liverpool, established the first unified police force in London in 1829. *See* Chapman, Samuel G. (ed.): *The Police Heritage in England and America.* East Lansing, Mich., Institute for Community Development, Michigan State University, 1962, pp. 11–15.

[2] *The Times* (London), Jan. 12, 1967, pp. 1, 9. R.A. Cline states that "the number of police-hours spent in time-wasting activities which contribute neither to the enforcement of the law nor to the prevention of crime is disproportionately large." *See* The police under pressure. *The Spectator,* May 1, 1964, p. 580.

authority and responsibility of "traffic wardens" to permit them to make arrests for vehicular violations[3] and to man radar stations[4] has been suggested for lightening the constable's burden. But the situation still remains critical.

The United States and Britain are distressed by cultural, racial and ethnic animosities. Racial discord exists in Britain. An immigrant minority—poor, unacculturated and unadjusted to urban living—is beginning to protest against discrimination in housing and employment. Experience in both countries has shown that these problems are neither easily nor quickly solved.

Today's world is giving a bigger role to young people, but there is no evidence which suggests that those who make shambles of the world's great academic institutions are able to provide the judgment and the leadership that must accompany the bigger voice. On the contrary, available evidence suggests that young people now have a profound contempt for many of the cardinal institutions of western civilization.

Today's world evidences a strong sense of alienation—a strong distrust of authority—which is manifested by an expressed disdain for those who enforce the law. An even graver problem is that both the United States and Great Britain must cope with a new breed of criminal, who operates on an international scale and who thrives on violence. All of these changes impose new demands upon the police, and yet, as has been suggested, the police systems of both countries remain strongly shackled to the past. The attraction to tradition has contributed to some of the problems which confront British police today.

BRITISH POLICE PROBLEMS

British attraction to the past has not been without benefit. Some attachment is good; it ensures continuity. But it also tends to make the present a prisoner of the past. This condition is manifested in England in a variety of ways.

Many contemporary police practices are of Victorian origin.[5]

---
[3] *The Times* (London), Jan. 12, 1967, p. 9.
[4] *Ibid.*, p. 1.
[5] *Ibid.*, p. 9.

While they may be charming reminders of the past, their suitability to the last third of the twentieth century is doubtful. Some aspects of the system are retained because they are familiar, because they have been useful in the past and because they are comfortable. A classic example is the affection for the British constable, about whose origin, status and constitutional importance there is a gerat deal of historical sentimentality.[6] It is ironic that the key illustration in one of the newest books on British police administration[7] is that of an English bobby riding his bicycle along an English village street—as if this scene were typical of law enforcement in one of the world's most highly industrialized societies, which must cope with the problems endemic to a population density more than ten times greater than that of the United States.

Police personnel in Great Britain are also subject to a "host of . . . nineteenth century restrictions."[8] which severely limit their personal and social lives.[9] In recruiting personnel, British police forces emphasize physical requirements, such as height. The training of recruits still stresses drilling, saluting and allied paramilitaristic activities which were once believed to be essential parts of a police system.[10] Increasingly, questions are raised as to whether such practices prove highly utilitarian today and relevant to the problems that police face on British streets.

The number of police forces in existence in Great Britain seems extremely small when it is compared to the 40,000 police

[6] Goodhart, H.L.: Memorandum of dissent to the *Report of the Royal Commission on the Police.* Quoted in Rolph, C. H.: The best in the world. . . .*New Statesman,* June 8, 1962, p. 822.

[7] Hewitt, William H.: *British Police Administration.* Springfield, Thomas, 1965, p. 41.

[8] Hearn, C. V.: *A Duty to the Public: A Frank Assessment of Today's Police Force.* London, Frederick Muller, 1965, p. 27.

[9] Banton, Michael: *The Policeman in the Community.* New York, Basic Books, 1964, pp. 188–214.

[10] *Report of Her Majesty's Chief Inspector of Constabulary for the Year 1965.* London, Her Majesty's Stationery Office, 1966, p. 16; and Moriarty, Cecil C.H.: *Police Procedure and Administration,* 3rd ed. London, Butterworths, 1937, pp. 32–33. Also see *Royal Commission on the Police, 1960, Interim Report.* London, Her Majesty's Stationery Office, 1960, pp. 29–30; and Devlin, J. Daniel: *Police Procedure, Administration and Organisation.* London, Butterworths, 1966, pp. 251–52.

jurisdictions existing in the United States. Despite recent amalgamations, the country has an excessive number of units, many of whose jurisdictions and resources are still too small to benefit from economies of scale.[11] The multiplicity of police forces complicates interjurisdictional problems, whereas police organizations should analyze and improve the intrajurisdictional administration, the level and quality of law-enforcement activities and the responsiveness to the needs of their constituencies.

Another problem in British law enforcement lies in the difficulty in designing and achieving effective political supervision for jurisdictions which have been consolidated.[12] The typical solution is to set up *ad hoc* administrative political authorities, a generally unsatisfactory way to supervise the day-to-day operations of large police jurisdictions, because their administrations are neither notably efficient nor comprehensible to the people.[13]

British police systems suffer from a chronic shortage of manpower, now estimated to be 17,000. It has been aggravated by the Home Secretary's recent cutback in recruitment quotas, which was a part of the national austerity program.[14] Low pay (unadjusted for regional differences in the cost of living), long hours and poor fringe benefits contribute to the unattractiveness of police work.[15] What is more, the occupation of constable enjoys a rather low social status in Britain; yet "nothing has really been done to make the job more attractive to new entrants."[16] For these and other reasons, British police jurisdictions are failing to attract university graduates into their ranks.[17] Also, for those who are in the force, the "current opposition to specializa-

---

[11] Some of these arguments are developed in Whitaker, Ben: *The Police*. London, Penguin Books, 1964.

[12] Banton, *op. cit. supra* note 9, p. 106. See also No policy for police. *The Economist*, May 2, 1964, p. 466.

[13] No policy for police. *The Economist*, May 2, 1964, p. 465; Regional detectives. *The Economist*, June 20, 1964, p. 1344.

[14] *The Times* (London), May 6, 1968, p. 1.

[15] Hearn, *op. cit. supra* note 8, pp. 90–91. See also, *The Times* (London), January 9, 1967, p. 10.

[16] Hearn, *op. cit. supra* note 8, pp. 28, 94.

[17] *The Times* (London), April 7, 1967, p. 12. Some efforts have been made recently to send promising police recruits to college while they remain on the force. See Fighting crime. *The Economist*, Aug. 20, 1966, p. 711.

tion in police work" and the lack of interjurisdictional mobility make it very difficult for policemen who have developed special skills to transfer to other jurisdictions where their skills could be utilized more advantageously.[18]

British law-enforcement agencies also discriminate against nonwhites in at least two ways. First, they are said to be unnecessarily hostile in dealing with nonwhites.[19] Second, police jurisdictions have been slow to integrate. Few colored British subjects have applied for service in the police; even fewer have qualified. The publicity given to the employment of the first colored policeman a few years ago was disproportionate to its importance, but it did emphasize the lily-white quality of almost all British police forces.[20]

It is well known that the way in which the police perform their duties is of vital importance to the preservation of civil liberties. Recently, British police have been accused of using unnecessary force in handling large crowds engaged in various types of political demonstrations. They have also been accused of curtailing and impairing the civil rights of some of those whom they take into custody. Stuart Bowes notes in his recent book that these accusations, whether well founded or not, have caused some concern in England about the role of the police in contemporary society, and about the ability of the police to invade the privacy of the individual and to abuse his civil rights.[21] Phone tapping, spectography, letter-opening, secret photographing and television snooping have all occasionally been used by the British Police in carrying out their duties.[22]

British police jurisdictions have also shown themselves extremely reluctant to hire civilian auxiliaries to perform the administrative functions that are an essential part of effective law

---

[18] Banton, *op. cit. supra* note 9, pp. 7, 90.

[19] *The Times* (London), August 20, 1967, p. 3: November 23, 1967, p. 3; May 30, 1968, p. 3.

[20] *The Times* (London), March 16, 1966, p. 7. See also Hearn, *op. cit. supra* note 8, p. 28.

[21] Bowes, Stuart: *The Police and Civil Liberties*. London, Lawrence and Wishart, 1966, especially pp. 71–105 and 135–45.

[22] *Ibid.*, pp. 135–45. For the datum in spectography, See *The Times* (London), Nov. 25, 1967, p. 2.

enforcement.[23] This resistance to hiring civilians impels large numbers of British police personnel to perform tasks for which they are totally unsuited. It also means that the work quality is not as high as it would be if professional clerical personnel were assigned to the tasks.

DEVELOPMENTS SINCE 1962

This sketch of some of the problems provides an appropriate basis upon which one can discuss some recent developments in Britain that are more encouraging. These developments suggest that the British police are reacting positively to changes in contemporary society.

In 1964, nine regional crime squads were established in an experiment aimed at overcoming some of the interjurisdictional squabbles that had hampered crime detection in the past. These squads proved quite successful and have now become permanent.[24]

There has been a move toward amalgamation and consolidation. Under an Act of Parliament passed in 1964, the Home Secretary was given the authority to promote the consolidation of small forces. There will soon be only 41 forces in England and Wales, compared to the former total of 117.[25] It is anticipated that the creation of larger police jurisdictions will allow each police force to be more effective in preventing and detecting crime and will enable each force to adopt the most modern law-enforcement practices, to encourage the training and the retaining of specialists[26] and to obtain the costly equipment (e.g., helicopters)[27] that the smaller forces heretofore have been unable to finance.

A national electronic data retrieval system is being established and is expected to be fully operational by 1970. The system will

---

[23] Cline, *supra* note 2, states that the "secretarial facilities [of the police] are archaic."
[24] Lucas, Norman: *The C.I.D.* London, Arthur Barker, 1967, pp. 94–95.
[25] *The Times* (London), Nov. 30, 1967, p. 4. The number may be further reduced in the near future.
[26] Fighting crime. *The Economist*, Aug. 20, 1966, p. 711.
[27] *The Times* (London), March 7, 1967, p. 2.

make it possible for any police officer in any part of the United Kingdom to use his pocket radio to request and receive, within one or two minutes, the information that he needs to determine whether a car has been stolen and whether a suspect has a criminal record or is wanted by the police.[28] Also, a computer-designed fingerprint classification scheme is under study. If it proves effective, a national file of fingerprints for all British subjects over fourteen years may be established.[29] Another computer system has been programed to predict areas and times in which crimes are likely to occur.[30] Its application in patrol scheduling is obvious. It is well known that the police forces of some major American cities, such as New York and Chicago, are using computers for the same purposes, but these systems are municipal in scope. The importance of the British program is its national scope.

Another important development has been the introduction of a new type of patrol, known as the *unit-beat policing*. It was first tried experimentally in Accrington, Lancashire, and now will be introduced in many parts of the United Kingdom. Under this system, the local police officer lives in his district and operates out of his own house rather than out of the police station. This type of patrol is supposed to contribute to better community relations. Also, it allows the police officer to become thoroughly familiar with every detail of his beat.[31] However, as Banton suggests, familiarity of the police officer with the people on his beat may breed a sense of leniency in his treatment of some of them,[32] a paradox also noted by Robert Wood in his classic study of suburbia.[33] In the next few years, it is estimated that approximately two thirds of the population in Britain will be protected by this type of police patrol.[34]

[28] *The Times* (London), Nov. 30, 1967, p. 2.
[29] *The Times* (London), Jan. 7, 1966, p. 10; May 11, 1966, p. 1; Nov. 3, 1966, p. 8.
[30] *The Times* (London), Jan. 7, 1967, p. 7.
[31] *The Times* (London), Dec. 7, 1966, p. 10.
[32] Banton, *op. cit. supra* note 9, p. 82.
[33] Wood, Robert C.: *Suburbia: Its People and Their Politics*. Boston, Houghton-Mifflin, 1959, pp. 278–79.
[34] *The Times* (London), Nov. 30, 1967, p. 4.

Another important development has been the experimental use of television cameras established on the rooftops of large buildings to keep watch over the streets of some densely populated communities near London. The cameras have proven effective in detecting crime, have helped to lower the crime rate in the places where they have been used, and have also contributed to a higher incidence of arrests.[35]

One more development should be mentioned. Some police jurisdictions in Britain have recently lowered physical requirements for policemen and are making much greater use of women police.[36] It has now been established that several police functions can be effectively carried out by women, by men who are not towering giants and even by those who do not have 20-20 vision.[37]

What impact have these new practices and techniques had in British police administration? Have they helped the police to react effectively to the demands of contemporary society? One index that may be of use in assessing the efficiency of the police is the crime rate. In contrast to the American experience of recent years, the 1967 crime rate in England and Wales rose only 0.6 per cent.[38] In some areas, such as London, there was an absolute decline in known indictable offenses over the total for 1966.[39] But it is still too early to assess accurately the impact of these techniques in police administration. And, though some of the recent developments may be relevant to the American scene, one should not be overly optimistic about the transferability of police institutions and practices to this country.

THREE PARADOXES

Three paradoxes are common to both Great Britain and the United States. One is that there is a constant clamor for in-

[35] *The Times* (London), Jan. 4, 1968, p. 2.
[36] *The Times* (London), Dec. 17, 1966, p. 8.
[37] *The Times* (London), Jan. 12, 1967, p. 9. See also President's Commission on Law Enforcement and Administration of Justice: *Task Force Report: The Police*. Washington, D.C., U.S. Government Printing Office, 1967, p. 130.
[38] *The Times* (London), Feb. 17, 1968, p. 3.
[39] *The Times* (London), Jan. 31, 1968, p. 2.

creased detection and prevention of crime; yet the body politic appears to obstruct its achievement. In England, the police are hampered by the Home Office, by Parliament and by the courts. For example, the use of experimental nerve guns and tear-gas aerosols to immobilize criminal suspects was recently disallowed by the Defense Ministry, though these deterrents would seem to be as effective as Mace is proving to be in the United States.[40] A new bill to safeguard privacy has been introduced which will radically restrict the ability of the police to obtain evidence by wiretapping and by other secret devices.[41] Finally, court decisions in some recent cases have further restricted the admissibility in court of evidence obtained by the police[42] and also have severely limited the ability of the police to question suspects after they have been charged, although more recently some authorities have suggested a moderate relaxation of these restrictions.[43] Thus, it is interesting to note that the American policeman is not alone in having his hands tied behind his back.[44]

A second paradox of both the British and American police is that they are at once expected to serve society and to be its master. There may well be a basic incompatibility in the two roles,[45] the consequences of which have not yet been fully explored. Role incompatibility may have serious psychological effects: it may lower morale and the quality of performance at a time when the police are dealing with a public that is often subject to psychological stress.[46]

[40] *The Times* (London), Jan. 17, 1968, p. 2; May 18, 1967, p. 2; June 1, 1967, p. 2.

[41] *The Times* (London), March 12, 1968, p. 3.

[42] Evidence obtained by wiretapping by private individuals may be admissible evidence, but information from police wiretapping is not acceptable in court. (*The Times* (London), March 16, 1968, p. 5.)

[43] *The Times* (London), Feb. 21, 1968, p. 4.

[44] A recent decision by the U.S. Supreme Court suggests a loosening of the shackles that have lately hampered police work. See discussion of the "stop and frisk" cases in the *New York Times*, June 11, 1968, p. 1.

[45] Banton, *op. cit. supra* note 9, pp. 8, 243–60. *See also* Marshall, Geoffrey: *Police and Government*. London, Methuen, 1965, p. 16.

[46] President's Commission on Law Enforcement and Administration of Justice, *The Challenge of Crime in a Free Society*. Washington, D.C., U.S. Government Printing Office, 1967, pp. 91–92.

A third paradox stems from the desperate need in both countries for more professional law enforcement, yet neither country devotes much effort to the achievement of this goal. No major universities offer police degrees in Great Britain. In the United States, the number of institutions that have police programs is quite large, but the number of them that are carrying on serious research programs in this area is extremely limited. A recent survey of law-enforcement research being undertaken by institutes of police administration, bureaus of government research and other related agencies interested in urban affairs indicated that very few of them are actively engaged in research dealing with law enforcement.

What is the answer to these paradoxes, and can they be neatly resolved? The greatest need at the moment is more research. One of the recurring themes in *The Challenge of Crime in a Free Society* is the lack of empirical research upon which police decisions can be based. Only when social scientists begin to accumulate research studies in significant numbers will they be able to raise police administration to the high professional level where it belongs.

Chapter 28

THE POLICE AND SOCIAL TENSION

L.G. Tyler

For a number of years I have had the opportunity of being closely involved with police officers in many aspects of the study of police-community relationships. I was, therefore, very interested in the two articles by John Lambert and Chief Superintendent Johnson in the November 1970, issue of *Race Today*. The topic is of vital importance and many of the underlying issues such as police recruit and in-service training, pay, status, complaints procedure and, above all, the whole concept of the police role touch much more than just questions of race and color. The present issues of police-community relations, precipitated by the presence of immigrant groups, are classical ones in police history. Any distinctive social group brought into contact with the police presents the same potential sensitivity and reactions. Color is only a distinguishing and heightening factor in a particular case and ought not to be allowed to obscure some of the real police-community questions which have to be faced. In my own experience, groups of Teddy Boys, coffee bar teenagers, ton-up motor-cyclists, long-haired demonstrators, vagrants and work-shy inadequates have reiterated the same arguments about police harassment, brutality, misunderstanding and the unsatisfactory complaints procedure. The point to establish is that the problems of police and community relations ought never to be exclusively discussed on the basis of the color issue; nor should the debate be handled in such a way that the police and the public are polarized as having different interests in the total discussion. The dialogue must go on, but there is little good served by driving the police into a defensive position or by not acknowledging the wide variety of police opinion on many social matters and the liberal-mindedness of many police officers.

NOTE: From *The Police Journal*, April, 1971, pp. 175–178. Reprinted with permission.

In William Temple College, we have had considerable experience of running courses for police officers on these issues and we have felt it right to break down isolating attitudes by working under the title of "Police in the Community" rather than "Police *and* the Community." Police work, as traditionally understood, tends to isolate men in a special way, but most professionalism implies a measure of separation in today's world. Doctors, clergy, teachers, politicians, social workers and the industrial worker (not to mention academics) are all encapsulated in their own world. We feel more critical of the police group culture because their work impinges on society at so many points. A writer in a recent social-work review stated that there is no social issue which is not in theory at some point "a matter for the police." The result is that police officers possess a unique social experience, which unfortunately they are seldom allowed to sift and share with other agents working in overlapping fields. My experience has led me to hope that police might be involved at national and local level in much more cooperation, study and discussion with those who confront the same human and social problems and work the same areas. I have found that while the "law and order" approach gives a simplified rationale of the police function and is rooted in their historical origins, it only covers a section of actual police duties and represents only part of their interests. Of course, "law and order" are important concepts in any urban society, but they are not absolutes in the scale of human and social priorities. Many policemen get some of their deepest personal satisfactions out of the "social role" aspects of their work. A very experienced police officer said that "law is a blunt instrument to deal with our real problems," and Professor H.L.A. Hart made a similar point when he wrote: "Justice is a method of doing other things, not a substantive end. . . ."

What we primarily need today is to get rid of the legacy of nineteenth-century thinking which remains in society about the police and which is still not totally eradicated in the Police Service about themselves. The Police Service as we know it was brought reluctantly to birth in the nineteenth century. Constables were paid at the level of agricultural workers and recruitment was restricted to the lower social groups. No one would have conceded that the policeman was a professional man, and he would never have thought of claiming such a status. The fact is that today most professional groups have experienced a shake-up in their status certainties. During the last 20 years, social work and industrial management have acquired professional standing, albeit rather self-consciously. At the same time, police work has developed in sophistication, with much-improved resources for in-service and senior-officer–level training. Crime has been recognized as a permanent feature of advanced industrial communities while new legal and increasingly liberal views of personal and social patterns of behavior have raised many doubts about issues which once were regarded as settled. Protests and demonstrations are features of the age to which society has had to respond. For such reasons, the police role has become correspondingly complex. So frequently, our lack of knowledge on such questions as drugs and gaming has been prematurely recorded in legislative measures which had little chance of adequate enforcement. The police are left to supervise inadequate laws which, at best, would do no more than limit some of the symptoms of social disorders and uncertainties. My experience is that the police are reluctant to press for more laws but would, in general, welcome more rational, socially acceptable and unambiguous laws to supervise. Too many issues are passed to the police when there is no other agency to "carry the can." Colorado beetle, the registration of aliens and antiquated licensing laws are just parts of the variety of things which the police are expected to do. It is little wonder that they are selective, and with a chronic manpower shortage it is understandable that they will withdraw to a "narrow professionalism in law-enforcement terms."

The police function in a modern democratic state is a complex one. It demands proper status and recognition. Policemen need professional terms of reference, and there is urgent need for proper discussion about a professional code of ethics. For too long they have been overidentified with the law and too much police training aims at producing "mini-lawyers." They have been allied with one of the most conservative of all professional groups and it could well be argued that the law is the one traditional group which has been least touched by the spirit of the new world.

I agree with Lambert that it is unrealistic to regard the police as primarily agents of social change. That ought not to be their function. Their work should help to make necessary change possible and to ensure the social structures necessary to human dignity and development. We ought, therefore, as a community to see that the status of the policeman is high—as high as that of the politician, poet or priest through whom change comes. Many of the problems of the police are those of society itself, and their work focuses our tender spots and uncertainties. One of the encouraging features is that very few policemen want to be working against the best forces in the community. For the most part, they share our social idealism, and much would be gained if this great potential could be realized and both the policeman's experience and latent idealism more openly acknowledged.

When one considers what the police are expected to do—and law enforcement will always be liable to resentment, however justified—the surprising thing is not that we have so many complaints against the police, but so few. If society insists, for instance, that motor vehicles must display a current license, then those whose job it is to enforce the law are likely to encounter resistance from those who break it. If this simple incident is accompanied by the attitude: "You are only picking on me because I've got long hair or because I'm colored" then at once a complex problem of police-community relations is created, far greater than that occasioned by the initial illegality. Where incidents involve the use of physical force, then the situation is potentially more inflammatory still. Policemen are human beings forced to make on-the-spot decisions of the most sophisticated kind. They have to act immediately with no possibility of "a cooling-off period" and to take responsibility for what they do, be it right or wrong. Most of the rest of us can reflect on the case at leisure and our mistakes are more generously tolerated. One of the paradoxes of the British police tradition with its promotion system (which as a management structure is surely due for an overhaul) is that the most difficult street decisions are made and the tone of police-community relations established by the youngest and most inexperienced men in the service. I would like to see the status of the constable enhanced. Unfortunately, the present hierarchical police structures do little to help, and too many public attitudes still unconsciously maintain the old nineteenth-century position that the policeman was low in the social scale.

I would like to see the following suggestions implemented:

1. Much longer and more imaginative initial police training should be developed.
2. Some phases of police training should be carried out alongside the training of other professional groups.
3. The National Police College at Bramshill (where some excellent work is done for senior officers) should be incorporated within a university; especially one where there is a well-developed pattern of postexperience studies.
4. The police should be drawn into much closer contact with teachers, social workers, clergy and urban planners and their experience freely shared.

As the two articles in the November issue of *Race Today* indicated, the racial tensions in our society have highlighted the police function. There is no doubt that the police have taken the challenge most seriously, but this is a problem for the whole community and not them alone. It may be that the lessons we shall all learn in relation to the police and the immigrant problem will have something to teach other areas of social sensitivity.

Above all, we need to stimulate at local level the creative encounters between all those who care for justice and renewal in our urban society. Little good is done by academic criticism alone, but with goodwill and initiative we could tackle some of the complex problems of community stress and tension within which the police and the rest of us have to live and work.

Chapter 29

THE ROYAL ULSTER CONSTABULARY: ITS FUNCTION AND CHANGING ROLE

Henry Kennedy

The Royal Ulster Constabulary (RUC) is the civil police force of Northern Ireland. The force was founded in 1922 after the passage of the Constabulary Act (Northern Ireland), which was made necessary by the division of Ireland into two political entities: the Irish Free State (comprising 26 counties in the southern part of the island); and the state of Northern Ireland (an area of 6 counties in the northeast). These changes were brought about by the British government in order to solve the perennially troublesome question of Home Rule for Ireland.

Northern Ireland is a part of the political structure of Great Britain. However, it has a parliament of its own which has the power to legislate on internal affairs. But the British parliament retains control over external affairs, peace, war and succession to the throne.

One could be forgiven for assuming that the RUC would be a typically British police force, with unarmed "Bobbies" patrolling peaceful cities, and generally endearing themselves to a normally cooperative population. Nothing could be further from actuality! Northern Ireland has been for the last half century in a state of political and social agitation ranging from passive hostility between segments of the population to outright civil war. At the time of writing (September, 1971) there were 12,000 British troops supporting the RUC in defending key installations, and guarding streets, highways and bridges. Barbed wire barricades, euphemistically referred to as "peace lines," are stretched across streets in the slums of Belfast and Londonderry in order to separate warring sections of the community. Over 100 people have been killed in the disorders of the past two years, including seventeen soldiers and five members of the

RUC (in a state with a population of 1,500,000 and only two cities containing over 53,000 inhabitants). Indeed, so widespread was the rioting in the period 1968 to 1969 that one third of the RUC were casualties during that time.*

Complicating the policing of the area is the fact that the RUC is deeply distrusted by the Roman Catholic community. So deep is this feeling against the RUC that entire areas of Belfast and Londonderry, in the solidly Catholic ghetto areas, have been sealed off by the inhabitants and designated as "Free Bogside" or "Free Derry." These areas are classified by the RUC as "no-go" areas, and although the British army occasionally sends in a patrol, neither the army nor the RUC will venture there by night because of sniper fire.

How can such a situation exist in the United Kingdom, a nation characterized by moderation in its public stance, and by a tradition of police-public relations which is second to none? What exactly has been the experience of the RUC in handling the problems of Northern Ireland over the past fifty years? What was the role assigned to the RUC at its inception, and what has become of that role in the changing political climate of the state? To obtain answers to some of these questions requires an understanding of Irish history, of the effect of British control, and an appreciation of the significance of the very deep religious divisions which have plagued the political and social atmosphere of Ireland for over 300 years.

HISTORICAL BACKGROUND

At the source of Northern Ireland's recurring "troubles" is the question of whether or not Britain should have a presence in Ireland. After the Anglo-Normans conquered the island in the twelfth century, they and their successors discovered that the Irish were not easily pacified. And it can be correctly stated that few of the policies imposed on the native Irish were of a sort to win over a distrustful and resentful subject people.

One of the methods used by the British to create some degree

---

* Recent tumultuous events have considerably inflated casualty statistics.

of stability in Ireland was to establish "plantations." These plantations were colonies of English and Scottish Protestants who, it was reasoned, would be loyal to Great Britain and the Protestant throne, and whose presence would counter-balance the rebellious Irish. The plantation policy bore fruit, and it can be noted to this day that it is in precisely the areas of the old plantations that the Protestant faith and support for Britain is the strongest.

However, a policy of pacification by establishing garrisons can succeed only if the country in question is run on military lines and where democracy is absent. As Britain moved towards the creation of a democratic society in the eighteenth century so, too, did Ireland, and herein lay the seeds of radical change. Taken as a whole, Ireland was and is a predominantly Roman Catholic island, and as the British parliament granted successive franchise extension acts, it became quite clear that the Catholic segment of the Irish population was set on severing the British connection and establishing some form of Home Rule government.

In complete contrast, the Protestants, with very few exceptions, were unalterably opposed to any arrangement resembling Home Rule, because this would mean Catholic political control of Ireland. They reasoned that, to use the slogan of the time, "Home Rule is Rome rule."

Between 1868 and 1920, the battles over Home Rule were fought, sometimes through parliamentary means and sometimes by resort to open warfare. The concluding events of this period were the Anglo-Irish War, 1918 to 1921, and the passage through the British parliament of the Government of Ireland Act (1920), establishing two distinct subparliaments for Ireland, one in Dublin for the Free State and one in Belfast for Northern Ireland.

Northern Ireland has chosen to maintain its links with Britain, and the Free State evolved to complete independence as the Republic of Ireland. Of the Northern Ireland population, only 500,000 of the 1,500,000 are Roman Catholics. Almost all of the remainder are Protestant. Thus Northern Ireland has been a Protestant state since its founding.

The problems of Northern Ireland reached a new plateau

with the creation of the parliament in Belfast. The Roman Catholics were disgruntled, to say the least, to find themselves in that part of Ireland which did not attain Home Rule, and their annoyance was compounded by the somewhat devious manner in which the Unionist elements (those advocating continued union with Britain) had succeeded in establishing the partition of Ireland and creating a Protestant enclave. Consequently, a campaign of nonparticipation and noncooperation with the new government was mounted by Catholics. This campaign was supplemented by armed attacks on government installations by the Irish Republican Army (IRA), a clandestine, highly militant and mainly Roman Catholic organization which is dedicated to the principle of reunifying Ireland by force and eliminating all vestiges of British control. Although the IRA represents only a small segment of the Catholic male population, nevertheless they receive a considerable degree of support and comfort from Roman Catholic Ulstermen.[1]

The acts of the IRA tended to confirm in the minds of Protestants the belief the Catholics were disloyal to the Crown and to the Northern Ireland government. Therefore, the ruling group set out to create what the first prime minister of Northern Ireland called ". . . a Protestant parliament for a Protestant people." For fifty years, this has been the philosophy which has governed the actions of the Northern Ireland governments. Since 1921, when the first elections were held, the parliament has been controlled by the Ulster Unionist Party, a Protestant party which has had only one Roman Catholic member in fifty years (and he eventually resigned in frustration).

THE FORMATION OF THE ROYAL ULSTER CONSTABULARY

Prior to the division of Ireland, the policing of the country was done by the Royal Irish Constabulary. Upon the creation of the two new states, each founded a police force. The southern force eventually became the Garda Siochana (Civic Guards),

[1] In actual fact, Northern Ireland does not include all of the nine counties which make up the ancient Province of Ulster. However, among most of the population, the term "Ulster" is synonymous with Northern Ireland.

while the northern one became the Royal Ulster Constabulary (RUC).

As one can readily note from this brief historical account of the early years in Northern Ireland, a multitude of problems faced the police, many of which were quite different from anything facing the British police forces. Not only did the RUC face the challenges of ordinary crime, traffic etc., but it was also expected to defend the borders of the state from IRA hit-and-run commando-type raids into Northern Ireland. Furthermore, some of the IRA operated from within Northern Ireland and could strike at police stations or army barracks, then quickly disappear to find succor among the Roman Catholics of the community.

In its original conception then, the RUC was given the task of handling certain paramilitary duties and was organized accordingly. The RUC was the only British police force to carry sidearms. In its arsenals were to be found automatic weapons and armored cars. One of its branches, the Crime Special Branch, was created to collect intelligence on illegal arms and explosives and to suppress sabotage.

Perhaps the most controversial aspect of the RUC's organization was the Ulster Special Constabulary or, as it was commonly known, the "B" Specials. At the founding of the state, there was a civil war in the Free State which occasionally spilled over into Northern Ireland. As the authorized strength of the RUC was only 3,000 men, it was clear that this was quite insufficient to handle the situation. Furthermore, there were, among the Protestant population, plenty of men willing to defend the state and to assist the RUC in their duties. Consequently, Protestant "loyalists" were invited to join three categories of special constabulary, the most significant of which became the "B" Specials, a part-time uniformed and armed auxiliary of the RUC.

The men who formed the "B" Specials had existed as a group of armed Protestant irregulars before World War I under the name of the Ulster Volunteer Force (UVF). At the outbreak of the World War, they had joined the British Army, virtually en masse, as the 36th (Ulster) Division and fought with great courage in the European campaigns. The Specials began as an 8,285-man force and reached 10,780 in 1965.[2] The officially described duties of the Specials were ". . . to act in support of the Royal Ulster Constabulary in the protection of life and property and the maintenance of law and order." The Specials went on patrols of the border and defended installations. In the line of this duty, they became involved in some furious battles with the IRA and, like the RUC, suffered their share of casualties. It is generally conceded that without the "B" Specials, the state of Northern Ireland would have been hard put to survive its birth.

The very fact that the "B" Specials began as an all-Protestant group of irregulars (no Catholic has ever been a member) would indicate the depth of patriotic feeling to be found among its members. In the course of their duties, and partly because of bitter experiences, some Specials tended to regard all Roman Catholics as enemies, and as a result, the Specials became particularly detested by that religious group.

The Cameron Report, a document commissioned by the government to examine the disturbances in Northern Ireland, noted that it may well have been the case that ". . . among the groups of loyalists who from time to time were involved in clashes and conflict with Civil Rights demonstrators, there were identified members of the "B" Specials." The Report also noted that "B" Specials made "large use" of Orange halls for training purposes.[3] These halls are the local headquarters of the Orange Lodge, a militantly Protestant Northern-Ireland–based organization which does not permit Catholics to enter its ranks nor enter its halls. The basic tenet of the Order is "The Protestant Faith and the Crown of Great Britain."

Clearly, the social background of the "B" men, the scant training they received (one evening every two weeks), and the unbending Protestant attitude and composition of the group made them a rather blunt instrument for the complex civil and military duties assigned to them. They were not adapted to the sensitive role as an auxiliary police force.

[2] *Ulster Year Book 1963–1965.* Belfast, Her Majesty's Stationery Office, 1965, p. 266.
[3] *Ibid.*

THE ORGANIZATION OF THE ROYAL ULSTER CONSTABULARY

The RUC is a statewide police force. Its jurisdiction covers, from its headquarters in Belfast, all of the six counties of Northern Ireland. Each of the six counties is designated a police area, and in addition, the County Borough (City) of Belfast is also considered a police area, bringing the total to seven.

As of July, 1969, the strength of the RUC was 3,052, of a legally authorized complement of 3,500.[4] The Constabulary was deployed as noted in Table 29-1.

The ranks of the RUC are: Inspector-General, Deputy Inspector-General, Commissioner, County Inspector, District Inspector, Head Constable, Sergeant, and Constable. Each County, or police area, is under the command of a County Inspector. Belfast city is under the command of a Commissioner. These officers are directly responsible to the Inspector-General, who in turn answers to the Minister of Home Affairs in the Northern Ireland government.

Within each county are several Police Districts, under the command of a District Inspector who may, depending on the size of the District or the density of population, have the assistance of a number of Head Constables.

The Police District is divided into Subdistricts under the command of a Head Constable; however, in the less populated rural areas, these may be commanded by a Sergeant.

A rural RUC station can have a complement of as few as two Constables and in areas near to the border with the Republic of Ireland, may have as many as is deemed necessary, depending on IRA activities at the time. There are 70 RUC stations in Ulster and another 73 which may be opened on a part-time basis when necessary.

The branches of the RUC are as follows: Crime Ordinary Branch, Crime Special Branch, Traffic Branch, Security Branch, Special Constabulary Branch and Administration Branch. In addition, there is a Press Office which was created in 1969 to better inform the public of the RUC's activities.

[4] *Report of the Advisory Committee on Police in Northern Ireland.* Belfast, Her Majesty's Stationery Office, 1969, p. 14.

TABLE 29-1
DEPLOYMENT OF THE ROYAL ULSTER CONSTABULARY BY AREAS

County	I.G. D.I.G. Commr.	C.I.s	D.I.s	H.C.s	Men Sgts.	Cons.	Total	D.I.	H.C.	Women Sgts.	Cons.	Total
Antrim		1	7	10	67	267	352				6	6
Armagh		1	4	6	32	156	199				2	2
Belfast	3	6	16	47	207	906	1,185	1	1	5	23	30
Down		1	6	10	53	235	305				4	4
Fermanagh		1	3	3	22	81	110					
Londonderry City		1	2	6	22	92	123					
Londonderry County			3	3	23	101	130			1	4	5
Tyrone		1	5	6	40	156	208				2	2
Reserve Force			2	9	41	220	272				2	2
Depot			1	2	13	91	107					
Totals	3	12	49	102	520	2,305	2,991	1	1	6	53	61

From *Report of the Advisory Committee on Police in Northern Ireland.* Belfast, Her Majesty's Stationery Office, 1969, p. 47.

To join the RUC, a recruit must be a British national, 5 ft. 8 in. in height (5 ft. 4 in. for women), be between the ages of 18 and 27 years (20 to 35 for women), be physically fit, be of good moral character, and have passed a minimum of four subjects in the high school General Certificate of Education.

To determine the political reliability of candidates, a family screening is conducted by the RUC. This screening extends to first cousins of the applicant.

The training period of an RUC recruit consists of twenty weeks at the central RUC Depot in Enniskillen, County Fermanagh. The trainee then experiences 18 months' duty in a police station as a Probationary Constable. The training schedule is completed by a final eight weeks at the Depot. In-service training is held at all RUC stations on a weekly basis to familiarize all Constables with new laws.

In recognition of the importance of religion in Northern Ireland, and taking into account that one third of the population is Roman Catholic, the RUC has had a policy that one third of its force should be recruited from that religious group. For reasons which are obvious, this objective has not been attained. In 1969, Catholics in the RUC made up only 11 per cent of its complement.[5]

THE CIVIL RIGHTS AND IRA CAMPAIGNS OF 1968 TO 1971

For 47 years (1921–1968), the Ulster Unionist Party governed Northern Ireland and firmly adhered to the Policy of "A Protestant parliament for a Protestant people." Roman Catholics were distrusted, kept out of the mainstream of life, and were generally in a position of second-class citizenship. This was the practice even though, as time passed, most Catholics showed no inclination to overthrow the state or to join the "Bomb and bullet boys" of the IRA.

Catholics found difficulty in obtaining adequate housing for

[5] *Ibid.*, p. 29.

their families and were discriminated against in the employment market. Nevertheless, for Roman Catholics with large families, life was still economically more attractive in Northern Ireland, where the generous welfare provisions of the British system were available, than in the Republic of Ireland.

In 1968, after a series of particularly galling incidents, the Catholic community, joined by liberal Protestants and students from Queen's University of Belfast, began a campaign of sit-ins, marches and mass meetings. In any other region of the United Kingdom, such demonstrations would pass without much effect, and the police would have little more than a traffic problem to be concerned with. But in Northern Ireland, where the unity of the Protestants has been a key to political strength, where Catholic agitation has been synonymous with IRA gunmen and where critics of the political status quo have been automatically labelled disloyal to the Crown and the state, events took a different course.

The Civil Rights marchers were met by well-organized militant Protestant counter marchers, often under the leadership of the Orange Lodges of the Reverend Ian R.K. Paisley, the leader of his own Free Presbyterian Church. Street battles ensued, many of which became riots. The worst elements of both religious groups rose to the surface and the situation deteriorated. Buses were burned, shops looted and fire bombings of homes became commonplace. Threats, intimidation, assassination and criminal protection rackets were reported.

The RUC responded to these events and found itself in a position where it could not win. If police actions satisfied the Protestants, the Catholics claimed bias. If the Catholics were accommodated, the Protestants called it "mollycoddling" lawbreakers. Catholics and civil rights workers made accusations that in some confrontations where civil rights marchers faced Protestant militants, the RUC men would turn their backs on the Protestants and flail away at the Catholics with batons. In the Londonderry riots of October, 1968, and January, 1969, Catholics in the Bogside area of the town accused the RUC of malicious destruction of Catholic homes. The Cameron Report on the disturbances in Northern Ireland, stated:

We have to record with regret that our investigations have led us to the unhesitating conclusion that on the night of 4th/5th January, a number of policemen were guilty of misconduct which involved assault and battery, malicious damage to property in streets in the predominantly Catholic Bogside area, giving reasonable cause for apprehension of personal injury among other innocent inhabitants and the use of provocative sectarian and political slogans.

. . . we are afraid that not only do we find these allegations of misconduct are substantiated, but that for such conduct among members of a disciplined and well-led force, there can be no acceptable justification or excuse.

The RUC conducted its own investigation (the Baillie Report) and came to the same conclusions regarding the conduct of the Constables involved.

The situation in Northern Ireland had deteriorated so much by late 1969 that the IRA found conditions ripe for its peculiar brand of heroics. Bombings with fire-bombs and gelignite became more frequent. Banks, power stations, water supplies, border posts, police stations, bridges and public buildings became fair game for the IRA guerillas. In pursuit of their goal to remove British control from Ireland, the IRA have little compunction about the means used. Public buildings filled with office workers have been bombed, leaving as many as 40 (mostly young girls) injured by flying plate glass, and infants have been killed in the streets as IRA men indiscriminately fired bullets at British street patrols.

As conditions worsened, more troops were sent to bolster the normal contingent and to support the badly overstrained RUC. By August, 1971, 12,000 British soldiers were stationed in Ulster. By this time, the ostensibly peaceful civil rights campaign was long since passed and the gunmen of the IRA held center stage. Sniping on the army patrols became common, and off-duty British soldiers were murdered and left in ditches. No end to the situation, which was on the verge of civil war, was in sight.

THE HUNT REPORT

The serious nature of the 1968 riots during the civil rights campaign period of agitation forced the Northern Ireland government, under pressure from the British government, to appoint a commission (the Cameron Commission) to determine the causes of the disturbances. The report of the Cameron Commission revealed many social and political inequities toward Roman Catholics in Northern Ireland, as well as revealing some highly provocative behavior on the part of some supposedly peaceful civil rights marchers. In addition to this commission, the Government of Northern Ireland created, in August, 1969, an advisory board, which became known as the Hunt Commission, to examine the RUC in all its facets. The recommendations of the Hunt Commission, most of which have been carried out, were profound and far reaching.

First of all, the Report recognized that the RUC had a credibility and trust gap with at least the Roman Catholic one third of the population. It was recommended that the force become more accountable to the public for its actions and that a Police Authority, reflecting the proportions of the different groups in the population, be established. Also, it was noted that the force was well below its effective strength and that, as this was a serious drawback to effective and adequate performance of police duties, the RUC should be increased in size as soon as possible. In addition, it was stated that the military duties assigned the RUC and the "B" Specials were inappropriate for a civil force, and it was recommended that these duties be ended.

Other recommendations were that the Police Authority should be able to require chief officers to retire in the interests of efficiency; that the RUC should be inspected regularly by Her Majesty's Inspector of Constabulary; that the practice of carrying sidearms as a standard procedure should be ended; and that armored cars and certain other weapons should cease to be a part of the RUC arsenal. Furthermore, the report continued, the practice of reserving a specific portion of the force's strength for Roman Catholics should be ended, but "vigorous efforts" should be made to increase the number of Roman Catholic entrants into the force. The color of the uniform (black), it was suggested, should be changed.

One of the most controversial changes recommended was

that the "B" Specials should be phased out and that they should be replaced by two forces. The first replacement force would be a purely civil police volunteer reserve, and the second would be a purely military border guard force under the command of the British Army. This suggestion has been acted upon; the RUC auxiliary is known as the Royal Ulster Constabulary Reserve and the military force is known as the Ulster Defence Regiment.

Among the other recommendations of the commission were suggestions that cadet and high school programs be encouraged; that liaison with British police forces be established for in-service training purposes; that chief officers be made "vicariously liable" for wrongful conduct of Constables, that crowd-control training be given and that Sergeants and Constables should wear numbers on their uniforms (as the men in Belfast and Londonderry cities already do).

CONCLUSIONS

It is a truism that to be effective, a police force must reflect, and indeed be an expression of, the community it serves. It must be "armed" adequately, not only with control hardware but also with the knowledge and skill which is acquired by adequate training.

Clearly the RUC did not always meet these criteria. Organized as a civil force, it had military duties to perform. Armed mainly as a civil force, it often fought pitched battles against well-equipped adversaries. Operating in a religiously divided society, the RUC represented, with only a few exceptions, one group in the community. Faced with an upsurge of disorder, it did not have the manpower to meet demands. With the benefit of hindsight, it may be stated that it is not surprising that the surge of events swept over and sometimes engulfed the RUC.

The majority of the men in the RUC come from staunchly Protestant homes and are often members of the Orange Order. They have been brought up in an atmosphere of hostility and distrust towards Roman Catholics, upon whom the actions of the IRA are reflected. And as RUC men are killed and wounded by the IRA, as they have been for 50 years, a lifetime of anti-Catholic political socialization is reinforced in the minds of individual Constables.

Perhaps the changes wrought by the Hunt Commission will eliminate some of the weaknesses of the RUC in its dealings with the Roman Catholic minority and other political dissenters. Certainly, the removal of border duties, the addition of more Constables to the ranks, the new emphasis on crowd-control training and the closer contact with British police forces cannot help but be advantageous. Whether the change in uniform and the phasing out of sidearms and the "B" Specials will give the force a new image in the eyes of the minority remains to be seen. But it will be many years before any significant change in the Catholic attitude will be detected.

In the meantime, areas of Belfast and Londonderry are still beyond the effective jurisdiction of the RUC. In Belfast, groups of Catholic vigilantes have assumed the power to guard the populace from their own Catholic petty criminals, and a rash of tar and featherings have occured. Also, gunfights have broken out between rival factions of the IRA who dispute power, territory and philosophy in the Catholic districts. Their style is reminiscent of the Chicago gang wars of the Prohibition era.

It is quite likely that the success or failure of the changes made in the organization and role of the RUC will not be determined until peace comes to Northern Ireland, but the prospect of peace becomes more distant each day. In September, 1971, a mass meeting was held by former officers of the "B" Specials. This meeting was held behind closed doors. The reason for the meeting was to support a move to expand the Specials or to form an armed auxiliary force. Another rally of an estimated 23,000 Protestants was held on September 6th. As this meeting broke up, one police inspector was quoted as saying:

> They'll have to give us our guns back now, I'm convinced of it. Frankly I think it would be a terrible thing.
> We would lose a lot of our young officers to the IRA gunmen. But Faulkner (the Prime Minister of Northern Ireland) has to do something to cool his followers and in my view this is about the

only thing he can do. He can't and he won't give in to demands for a third force. It's guns for us, mark my words.[6]

To attempt to predict what the future holds for the RUC under the existing conditions would be foolish, and I decline to try.

[6] *The Guardian* (Manchester), September 11, 1971.

Chapter 30

POLICE ADMINISTRATION IN AUSTRALIA

Roy A. Wilson

The history of law enforcement in Australia shows a marked resemblance to the development in the United States. Both emerged from colonies of migrants who were virile, colorful and unrestrained in many ways, and were born of communities lacking a stable attitude to public safety and maintenance of order, although it was initially the responsibility of the army establishment to keep order. Although Australian police systems were to follow British types, they were influenced by the environment in which they were born.

The growth of the police forces in Australia commenced in the 1780's, in New South Wales, by the appointment of good behavior convicts who had been brought from England for the most trivial of offenses. They were called "Constables." The Magistrates were military officers. Then followed the English Parish System of the election of constables by local citizens. There was a limited use of Mounted Police—small patrols to combat outlaws who engaged in holding up gold escorts. The civil administration gradually replaced the military; police forces gradually adopted a uniform of a military type. The police themselves were a mixture of paroled convicts and discharged soldiers. The laws were an embodiment of English Common Law and Statute Law. Later, the gold discoveries in the 1850's gave birth to the State of Victoria—there was a rush of migrants from Europe and, with it, an influx of Chinese miners, the aftermath of which led to industrial strife, clashes between mounted police and armed miners, crime and violence. It was this riot in 1861 which forced the authorities to entirely reorganize the State Police Force along established lines of authority and responsibility. The government could

NOTE: From *Police*, May-June, 1971, pp. 44–50.

no longer ignore the need for a stable police force, for a trained, disciplined force and for state administrative control.

ORGANIZATION AND ADMINISTRATION TODAY

Eight state and territorial police forces, together with a federal force, maintain law and order in the Commonwealth. This means each force operates as an entirety within its own state boundaries. Each force is complete in its responsibility in terms of criminal investigation and traffic control, both in the cities, rural areas and arterial highways.

The chain of command in an Australian Police Force flows from the Commissioner through the Deputies and Superintendents, who are normally in charge of a region containing districts of which an Inspector (United States Captain) is in charge. Certain of the bigger forces have Assistant Commissioners (3). Their divided responsibilities are vested in crime, traffic and transport, and administration. These are operational, and are supported by the Public Service Ancillaries relating to the Secretariat, Finance and Budgeting.

The Commissioner's authority carries through all these channels, while he himself is responsible to the respective State or Federal Minister for Police. The tenure of the Commissioner's office is permanent, in that it is not affected by change in government or Minister, and he remains in office until the normal civil-service retiring age, which may be 60 or 65 years of age. The appointment of Inspectors (Lieutenants or Captains) are normally done with the consent of the Minister for Police, but other ranks are promoted by the Commissioner. There is practically no lateral movement between Police Forces, as the Police Federations closely watch the question of seniority in their respective services.

Police and Civil Service

All services employ civilians in those areas where possible; there is the use of females as police auxiliaries. They handle reports from the public in the Information Bureaus. They also type statements regarding accidents handled by patrolmen. Most of the forces have the members undertake a course in typewriting, and this aspect is used where a member is stationed at a location without female auxiliaries, such as rural or district police stations. The trend is towards a greater use of civilians and female assistants. Senior administrative posts in the Personnel and Financial Sections are filled by civilians. As you may be aware, in any service such as defense and police it is most important that the lines of authority and responsibility in the service be clearly defined as between the serviceman and his civilian colleague.

Legislation

Each state makes its own laws through its parliament. The criminal codes are similar in most respects, and currently there is being drafted a Uniform Criminal Code acceptable to all the states. There is also a Uniform Traffic Code, similar to the United States Code in many respects, and this has been accepted nearly in its entirety by State Governments. A Commonwealth Act provides for the procedure to be adopted in respect to the extradition of fugitives from a State back to the State where the crime was committed. This method is uncomplicated and very widely used. In the Commonwealth or Federal sphere, all laws are drafted by the staff of the Attorney-General, and then submitted to the Commonwealth Parliament which sits in Canberra, which in Australia is the equivalent of Washington, D.C. in the United States.

All state and territory forces maintain their own prosecution sections, staffed by police officers, who consider and lay appropriate charges and who also prosecute in the courts. In complex matters, and others which will inevitably go to a Superior or Supreme Court for hearing in the case of indictable offenses, then the police department may seek initial advice from the State Crown Prosecutor, who will eventually prosecute the matter in the higher court.

Generally speaking, the police forces do not have permanent legal officers and handle their own cases from arrest through to final adjudication by the court, with the exception, as stated, of the indictable offenses in the Supreme or Federal Court.

RECRUITMENT AND TRAINING

Recruitment and training demands an enlightened approach to obtain potential police officers from the scarce labor force. The police image and wage conditions reflect themselves in what the response is to the recruiting campaigns. My training school has an initial fourteen weeks' intensive training covering report writing, general knowledge, public speaking, discipline and physical training; also, training with the revolver is included on similar lines to the FBI and Los Angeles Police. In respect to law, the whole emphasis is on practical application of the law as it applies to the patrolman on the street or in the car. The instructors who have been experienced detectives or prosecutors conduct syndicate groups. I have discarded the system of cramming into initial training a wide spectrum of law covering ordinances or criminal law that the average patrolman only encounters once during his career. All examinations through the Officer (Inspector or Lieutenant) have basically the same practical approach. Even the examinations in respect to general orders, policy and administrative practice have questions centered about practical police situations.

The system of enlistment of recruits varies in the different states. With one exception, all the states rely on the enlistment of adults between 20 to 30 years of age, although most of them use the cadet system to a limited extent. The education standard is normally of four to five years in high school. The initial police training course averages 14 weeks, with the recalls to the classroom during the ensuing 12 months' probationary period. The emphasis during the initial training is on discipline, physical fitness, deportment on duty and in the court, report writing, public speaking and basic powers of arrest as face the ordinary patrol officer in the street. My courses have been evolved to meet the contingencies that the new patrolman meets in the field, and with an odd exception, they are the problems that every patrolman meets in every city of the world.

Training—Cadet System

This is highly developed in two or three of the states, but the systems vary. The South Australian one, which commenced in 1934, trains youths from 16 to 19 years of age along military academy lines. The training is phased to cover discipline, law and short lengths of service at Headquarters, and at district stations throughout the State. They are sworn into general police service at 20 years of age. At present, 300 would be in training, and batches of 20 or so graduate every three months. In some states they are educated by the Department to University-entry–level examinations. The taking of Degrees in Law is entirely at the initiative of the cadet; the result is that cadets who eventually graduate leave the police service.

Much of the training in police administration is based on Army Staff Colleges. However, police administrative training has still lagged years behind that of industry, and if we ignore the fields of production and marketing, we still find a common factor in cost control, the effective use of materials and men, and human relations.

The modern police officer must have the appropriate education, and by that I mean the development of his mind and personality and the qualities so requisite of a law-enforcement officer. These include integrity, adaptability and sound practical common sense. These can be developed in the Police College. The officer must be trained to think for himself, to develop an independence of mind, if he is to command any situation in the field or to direct subordinates.

All senior police training must be directed at developing an awareness in potential police executives of the changing political, economic, social and technological scenes and plan accordingly to meet the effects of these changes in a police department's practices and techniques.

This, then, means the administration must have the means of training that officer so that he has the ability to express himself with clearness, both verbally and in writing, to have the confidence to analyze problems and to make decisions and, importantly, to get the best out of his subordinates. Of course, supervising is not managing. One is concerned with making sure that a particular project is performed efficiently, but the managing involves the establishment of the objectives of a department or branch as such and organizing the men and materials which are available so that the optimum efficiency can be achieved.

Management must be responsible for not only maintaining a system of personnel rating but ensuring that it is used effectively and that the members know that it is not just another form filled in and then forgotten. The system must be such that the members know that the rating is a measure of job performance and attitude, and something which is a management tool used in the interests of the individual officer as well as being something to replace that old measurement stick, seniority.

The standard of success in any enterprise depends on its quality of management, and this applies with equal force to a police establishment as it does to industry. This term "management" means the collation of data on which decisions are made; the cost factor of operations; the scientific techniques understood and used; the selection and training of personnel for different levels of responsibility. The service that any police force renders reflects the personality, ability and leadership of the management core of the force. Opportunities and encouragement must come from top police management to the young officers with potential.

The development in recent years in the social sciences has brought home more closely to the police of the importance of human relations—not only outside the service but also within. It has become necessary to study leadership in a service, but leadership and management are often two different factors.

I would like to quote from Field Marshal Lord Slim who was Governor-General of Australia when he gave an address to the Australian Institute of Management in 1957:

> The leader and the men who follow him represent one of the oldest most natural and most effective of all human relationships.

The manager and those he manages are a later product, with neither so romantic nor so inspiring a history. Leadership is the spirit compounded of personality and vision; its practice is an art. Management is of the mind, more a matter of accurate calculation, of statistics, of methods, timetables and routine; its practice is a science. Managers are necessary; leaders are essential.

Police Executive Training

The Australian Police College located in Sydney, New South Wales, is sponsored by the Commonwealth, but each Commissioner from each of the States is a member of the Board of Control, and has a voice in the officer courses and the senior police executive courses conducted by the college. The college conducts courses for its own Federal police and associated agencies and an annual course for senior police executives from all parts of the Commonwealth.

The Police College has as its aims, the following:

1. To broaden the outlook of police officers to permit them to cope with increasing demands and constantly changing conditions in modern police forces.
2. To improve their professional knowledge, particularly in fields peculiar to officer rank.
3. To stimulate the mental energies of men who have reached or are reaching the higher ranks of the service.
4. To fit officers with a better understanding of the needs expected of officers in liaison and cooperation with responsible officers in other departments and service.
5. To prepare men to accept the responsibilities of leadership and executive action demanded of police officers.

The course covers two months, and the syllabus contains syndicate discussions, practical exercises on emergency situations and lectures on police administration, community relations, criminology, penology and sociology. Students are expected to study current books on these subjects. The following matters are discussed:

Police Administration: The selection of recruits; the use of intelligence quota tests, as used in the armed services; the promotion practice—merit and examinations versus seniority.

Operations: Patrol practices in the city, suburbs and rural areas; the use of the one-man as against the two-man patrol (police associations views on this).

Training: Initial and in-service, and preparation for examinations at different levels; examinations—the frequency and payment of increments for examinations passed but officer not yet promoted; training circulars, legal opinions and surveys; the importance of a driver-training program for police.

Criminal statistics: The value of a standard procedure and forms; a common definition of "crimes"; the need for a Central National Bureau to establish a national reference center for the government.

Emergency planning: This is an essential part of the training of a police administrator, or senior officer. He must be informed as to the resources and facilities in terms of equipment, vehicles, men and communications that are at his command on the occasion of a state emergency. This could take the form of a road, rail, or air disaster; floods or fires, or major political demonstrations.

The administrative practice to be followed invariably changes with the situation, the environment, the gravity of the emergency, and possibly the political climate prevailing. Guidelines can be laid down, but the Command Officer's experience, training and local knowledge will contribute to the success or otherwise of the operation. Example—abducted child. Students will be exercised in:

1. Situation assessment.
2. Operation planning.
3. Transport of men and materials.
4. Briefing.
5. Billeting arrangements.
6. Sustenance.
7. Communications.
8. Liaison with army in use of helicopters.
9. Military map and air-photo reading.

10. Establishing field headquarters.
11. Reconnaissance.
12. Debriefing.

The State Police Depatrment Contribution is to provide the following manpower and facilities:

1. Mobile field control caravan unit.
2. Mobile field radio unit.
3. Rescue Squad's mobile canteen unit, with staff.
4. Communications Branch two-way radio units, with staff.
5. Noncommissioned officer and twelve constables from Police Academy.

Human Relations: The important function of how to get along with colleagues, subordinates and others; the art of communicating.

Rostering of Staff: This must be influenced by the personnel available, the exigencies of the day and also the terms of the contract under which the personnel are employed. Here interpersonal relations can be adversely affected and the whole question of morale is exposed. The attitudes of individual officers towards their work varies and also changes with situations in their own domestic spheres daily. It is here that personnel rating and the value of counselling and determining attitudes to work come to the fore.

Criminal Investigation: The selection of suitable persons for this type of duty; supervision of detectives in field and office work; the need or otherwise for special squads; special courses for detectives.

Crime Prevention: The value of crime prevention, which displays something indefinable in terms of money or results; the wide use of marked and conspicuous police cars; extension of foot patrols, as against mobile units.

Vice Controls: Prostitution, narcotics, gambling, and liquor. These social vices will always be found in any city, large or small, in some degree. How should they be policed? By what officers—selected or general patrols? To what extent should the police extend tolerance to these operations, that is, prostitution, gambling or liquor?

Traffic: The extent of police involvement in traffic management; the value of being aware of the techniques involved in modern traffic engineering. Should detectives investigate the serious traffic crimes of hit and run and causing death, or should it be investigated by the trained traffic policeman?

Criminology and Penology: The senior police officer should have an understanding of the principles underlying these scenes. The administration of the law, its enforcement and its implementation in terms of the judiciary all have cause and effect within the teachings of the criminologist and the penologist. I suppose it can be said that for too long, the persons involved in the different activities concerned with law enforcement have remained within their own small functional areas and rather jealously rejected any intrusion by other disciplines into their jurisdictions.

Practical Precourse Exercises

Students attending the Senior Officers Course are required to prepare certain exercises for the Principal of the Police College. For example, in the 1970 course, candidates were required to study prescribed police textbooks and prepare essays on:

1. "The incidence of crime" (England and Wales). This was was to be submitted before the candidate reported to the College.
2. "Employment of civilians."
3. "Unit beat policing."

During a two-week break in the course, the students were attached to other police forces. This was of particular interest to police officers from Singapore, Malaya, New Zealand and other South Pacific Forces.

The preliminary studies, of course, cover how to study, how to research and logic and writing. A quick look at the textbooks prescribed show the preference for such writers as O.W. Wilson, William H. Hewitt and A.C. Germann.

Promotion

Promotion through the ranks in the different forces depends on the passing of the appropriate examinations, with medical fitness, and then seniority is considered. We have not yet reached the stage where members hold degrees or diplomas in police science, and so that factor is not one to be considered by police promotions committees. There is very little lateral movement because of police unions closely watching seniority within their own services.

Disciplinary Action

The States have Police Regulation Acts or Ordinances which empower the Commissioner to fine a member for a breach of discipline. However, generally, if a member is suspended, dismissed or reduced in rank, this is subject to Ministerial approval and the member has recourse to an Appeal Tribunal. If a member breaks a law in respect to dishonesty or a flagrant traffic breach, then he can expect to appear before a court, the same as a civilian. We have no Board of Inquiry constituted by civilians to investigate complaints against members. These are always done by an Inspector at the direction of the Commissioner, who finally decides what action will be taken.

CRIME

To remain dormant in today's society is to become extinct. There must be a continual appraisal of crime statistics and the effective deployment of personnel. Nothwithstanding the respect one has for the increasing use of scientific aids in crime detection, every experienced police officer knows that the art of being a good detective is wrapped up in his personal skill in handling suspects, either at the scene of a crime or soon after its commission.

The good detective must have an appreciation of just what science can do to aid him in his investigation and of the measures available to identify and preserve evidence at crime scenes. This, again, is the responsibility of a police administrator to provide his men with every opportunity to be trained in all aspects of the art of detection. A good investigator is a student of psychology—a graduate from the school of experience where he has rubbed shoulders as it were, with the hoodlum, the white-collar offender, the pervert and the sadist. The police administrator must, of necessity, strike a balance between knowledge gained from the school of practical experience and the academic standard required of the modern police-officer who has to meet in daily contest not only the criminal with sophisticated techniques but the erudite criminal lawyer or the spokesman for the Civil Liberties Group who has at his command all the legal and press media resources of the modern society.

Only three of the forces have graduates in science or chemistry in their scientific branches, and there is close collaboration with experts in various government departments. The general practice is to fingerprint every person arrested. The Breathalyzer has been accepted in Australia, and most States have laws supporting its use. The Commonwealth or Federal Police have a graduate in science who is available for neutron-activation analysis of samples, and who has access to the expensive equipment at the Lucas Heights Atomic Energy Research Plant near Sydney. This particular branch of science has not yet been deveolped to its optimum but has great potential. Most of the scientific sections have established ballistics libraries, a typewriter library, comparison microscopes and handwriting experts. There is a continual exchange of personnel and ideas between the forces, from Commissioner level to specialist units. The Lie Detector is not used in Australia.

Narcotics

Each State Police Force has its own narcotics or drug squad and is concerned with the possession and supply of prohibited drugs, or LSD as covered by their respective Health Acts. The Customs Department has a big organization and its Narcotics Bureau concentrates on the importation or smuggling of prohibited drugs into the country. They pay special attention to opium, marihuana and heroin. There has been increasing activity by this bureau due to the growing number of young persons attracted to the use of drugs, and arrests have increased threefold over the last two years. Courses for enforcement officers are currently being held on a national level in Austalia.

The principal drugs used in Australia are marihuana and LSD. The marihuana plant can be readily grown on the East Coast of the country but, of course, is illegal. Associated with the increase in drug use has been an increase also in thefts from pharmacist-shops (drug-stores), and these are amphetamines and barbiturates. Drugs in transit are also subject to theft. One consignment of morphine valued at 70,000 dollars was stolen from a commercial aircraft.

Sydney, a city of three million people in New South Wales, is the principal place for the distribution of all types of drugs.

Of a survey of drug users and sellers in Australia the age of 95 per cent of such offenders was 27 years, and 55 per cent of the sample was in the 18-to-25 years-of-age group. Two thirds were males. The majority was in the semiskilled labor force. Of drugs used, 39 per cent used marihuana, 24 per cent opium and its refinements, 16 per cent amphetamines and stimulants, and only 6 per cent LSD; of the drugs used, 22 per cent were smuggled into the country.

In 1969, there were more than 200 premises broken into from which drugs were stolen. The principal age group in New South Wales of persons described as "addicts" is 19 years and under. There has been a noticeable trend to graduate from cannabis to morphine and cocaine. Cannabis is no longer medically used in Australia, and its nonmedical use is prohibited, except for scientific purposes. Its use, however, has been doubling since 1966.

There has also been the disturbing use of opium in conjunction with marihuana. A number of United States Servicemen coming to Australia on R & R leave were detected in possession of marihuana. Action taken against some of them has resulted in an increase in the drug being sent by mail.

There is a United States-Australia Cooperation Agreement on Drugs of Dependence and, as a result a close cooperation between the Australian Customs Department Narcotics Bureau and the U.S. Bureau of Narcotics and Dangerous Drugs in respect to research and identification of drugs.

Australia is a member of the International Criminal Police Organization and has its National Central Bureau located at the Headquarters of the Victoria Police.

Central Crime Intelligence Bureau

This is a recently formed Bureau and part of the Commonwealth Attorney-General's Department. It is fed with information regarding narcotic addicts, counterfeiters, prohibited immigrants and political cranks who may commit crimes of violence against Heads of State or public dignitaries. Current investigation is being made into the use of computers by the Bureau, although the use of computers has been in vogue for some time by other large government and private enterprises. This Bureau is similar in concept to the FBI National Crime Information Center, or NCIC.

Central Fingerprint Records

These are maintained in Sydney, New South Wales. The present records number 1½ million and are supplied by all the State Police Forces of the Commonwealth. Each state makes a small contribution towards the administrative costs of the Records Section. Reference can be made at any hour of the day or night by radio or telex and the criminal's complete record obtained. The Bureau handles 220,000 inquiries a year for the State Police Forces. (See Part I, List of Crimes for 1968–69 period.)

POLICE AND THE COMMUNITY

The country has a population of twelve million and an area of three million square miles. Forty per cent of the total population is under 21 years of age. The largest age group is between 5 and 9 years of age.

In Australia, we do not have the concern with ethnic groups or communities of different nationalities. It can be said that the enforcement of the laws is not made difficult by the large migration of European migrants to Australia. There are dis-

AUSTRALIAN CRIME STATISTICS

Crime Classification of Offenses	1968	1969
Homicide	200	295
Murder		
Attempted murder		
Manslaughter		
Serious assault	2,508	2,204
Robbery	1,280	1,355
Rape	363	337
Breaking and entering	68,379	71,495
Dwellings, shops, office, and factory (all values)		
Motor vehicle thefts	29,280	30,922
Fraud	18,955	19,144
Forgery, false pretences, valueless checks		

tricts in which some nationalities, such as Italians, predominate, but it is not entirely exclusive, and newspapers or notices in foreign languages are on a very limited scale. The analysis of crime in Australia in terms of nationality has not been developed—authorities have considered that every effort should be made to assimilate migrants and not discriminate by nationality or selective study or fingerprinting. However, such studies are always of intense interest to the criminologist.

The average weekly earnings are 60 to 70 dollars for about 43 hours' work. Of the population of twelve million, nine million are Australian; United Kingdom, 900,000; Germany, 100,000; Greece, 140,000; and Italy, 300,000.

The past three years or so have seen the growth of the permissive society, the planned demonstrations and the sit-ins in public places, government departments and in Parliament House itself. The new techniques of protest by dissidents have called for special study by police management regarding the methods to be adopted to meet such challenging and changing social behavior. It has called for an entirely new concept in police attitudes and the exercise of tolerances that were unthinkable several years ago in terms of standards of public behavior in respect to conduct directed at property damage and infringement of personal liberties. Today, we have in Australia the full exercise of freedom of speech and action, but in some places there is the minority which does not recognize personal responsibilities nor has the wish to respect the rights or views of others.

The closing years of the 1960's gave a disturbing glimpse of the challenges to law enforcement everywhere that we must learn to meet in the 70's. The problems that confront police forces today are entirely outside the realm of vision of the most farsighted police administrator of 15 years ago. The whole maelstrom of sociological changes and changes in various forms that follow social unrest have thrust into the law-enforcement field tasks which at times appear insoluble and which a police force, because of the very nature of its responsibilities to government, cannot ignore. So the police, because of its basic function, becomes involved in physical conflict with groups protesting against national or local issues and on a wide spectrum of subjects. Quite apart from this area of police commitment, sometimes on the fringe, but always challenging society in the background, is crime in its many and varied forms, extending from minor white-collar offenses to the most sadistic of crimes.

In Australia, we also have our demonstrations and sit-ins supporting various causes—these all involve police personnel in times of increasing crime trends. One cannot deny the fact that crime is increasing, even in an era of economic affluence. You will also find that police problems everywhere are the same. Those of the New York patrolman and those of Sydney and Melbourne are similar basically, and the techniques are the same in fighting crime.

But the police administrator's responsibility to his government to maintain law and order must now, of necessity, encompass not only an educated police approach to rising crime rates but also a sociopolitical attitude to bitter community problems, and at the same time show an impartial, tolerant exercise of the laws, and interpret the legislation in an area of changing moods of the public. Is the possible to do this to the satisfaction of the law respecting sections of the community? The state of law and order in the communities of the world at the end of this present decade, will tell whether police administration has met the challenge of the 70's successfully or not.

Chapter 31

THE DANISH POLICE: FUNCTION, ORGANIZATION AND ADMINISTRATION[1]

THOMAS J. AARON

Denmark has a special problem not shared by other western European nations but not unique in other parts of the world. Its population is essentially agrarian and widely spread throughout the country. At the same time, Denmark has only one large and really important city—Copenhagen. The task of finding sufficient personnel to staff the nation's police systems and assuring even an approximation of efficiency and effectiveness among its rural elements would be an impossible one were it not for Denmark's decision to nationalize its police.

All police recruits are trained and serve their probation in the City of Copenhagen. Thus, the character of training and initial field experience of all Denmark's police are the same. When, after two years, these personnel leave Copenhagen for duty in smaller towns or rural areas, they carry with them the same knowledge of modern police techniques and skills as do their fellows who elect to remain in the city. Uniform police effectiveness and efficiency exists, therefore, throughout all Denmark. There are additional side benefits for the City of Copenhagen, too. The requirement that all policemen serve their first two years of duty in that city assures it of a constant flow of police personnel to meet its large, urban demands.

The Danish police are appointed by the State and their salaries are paid by the State. Until 1911, the police were municipal employees, but they served under chiefs of police appointed by the Crown. Usually these chiefs also acted as judges

NOTE: From Aaron, Thomas, J.: *The Control of Police Discretion.* Springfield, Thomas, 1966, pp. 11–23.

[1] Based upon field study and research at the Ministry of Justice, Copenhagen, Denmark, 1965.

and mayors. In 1919, the courts were placed under supervision of regular judges and most municipal affairs under popularly elected mayors. Thereafter, police chiefs restricted their activities to the prosecution of criminal defendants and tasks connected with police administration. From 1911 to 1938, first the Criminal Investigation Department and later the uniformed police were transferred to State control. This was done to achieve greater police effectiveness through unitary supervision, better co-operation between police districts, and standardization of recruiting, training and equipping the police.

When the police were transferred to State control in 1938, a central police administration was established under the direction of the Commissioner of Police ("Rigspolitichefen"), but certain characteristics of the former local organization of police still remain. For example, the local chief constables are still independent commanders of police personnel placed at their disposal by the central Commissioner of Police.

In Denmark, the police have more tasks to deal with than police have in many other countries. In addition to the maintenance of order and combating crime, the police are directly involved in the prosecution of criminal suspects, and they play a major role in national defense. Within its scope is also supervision of the Fire Brigade, health authorities, matters concerning the Law of Trade, conscription of young men for military service, alimony cases, registration and taxation of motor vehicles, and the control of public amusement. To a great extent, the police are used by other authorities to procure information in connection with matters of official interest.

Some functions of the Danish Police would, in many other countries, be considered nonpolice affairs. The larger police districts have special police sections handling cases involving health matters, sexual offenses, legal separations and divorces, alimony cases, paternity cases, illegitimate children, adoptions and change of names. Police personnel in these sections are called *civil-politiet* or civil policemen. After special training at the Police College, the Commissioner of Police may assign civil policemen to serve in these special sections. All members of the regular uniformed police are trained to handle these special cases, however, and in most districts these are regular duties of the uniformed police carried out under supervision of a civil policeman. The diverse tasks given the police mean that other authorities, as well as the population, find it a natural thing to ask the police for help in all kinds of matters.

Primarily, police have the task of maintaining order and the most important statutes regarding police activities are found in the Administration of Justice Act. In these statutes, the police figure as an administration organ coordinated with the criminal courts, the prosecution and police lawyers. The Danish Police operate within the Ministry of Justice, whereas police in other European countries operate within the Home Office.

Requirements for employment in the police are: Age of 21 to 26 years, good health, at least 5 ft., 6 in. in height, Danish citizenship, good character and a high school education. No written examination is required. Each applicant must have completed his military service with a good record. The applicant is interviewed by the local chief constable and orally examined by a screening commitee. He is examined by two physicians, and finally the Commissioner of Police makes the decision whether or not to appoint him.

Immediately after appointment, the new policeman undergoes ten weeks of training at the Police College in Copenhagen or its suburbs. Field instruction is given him in the basic police procedures of foot patrol, car patrol and traffic regulation. Two years after his appointment as a probationer, a permanent appointment is confirmed if the evaluations of the Police College and the police station commander where he served are satisfactory. Three years after his initial appointment he has usually experienced most of the duties of the uniformed police, and on application to the Commissioner of Police can normally request a transfer to a police station of his preference. After several more years of duty, he is required to attend additional classes at the Police College. After fourteen years service, he is, without application, promoted to police sergeant. Later, he may compete for promotion to Police Inspector 2nd class. Police Inspector 1st class, Police Superintendent, and Deputy Assistant Commissioner of Police. Promotions are actually decided by the Commissioner of Police, but formally through the Minister of Justice, based upon evaluation by superiors and a judgment of qualifications which include experience and seniority. No further training at the Police College is required before the next promotion. After promotion, however, personnel promoted to ranks above sergeant must attend an in-service training course in supervision.

After four to ten years in the uniformed police, a policeman may apply for transfer to the Criminal Investigation Department (C.I.D.). Normally, he will already have had six months' duty—a "rotation assignment"—in the C.I.D. because this duty is considered desirable experience in the training of all policemen. After being transferred permanently to the C.I.D., he attends a four-month special course at the Police College, and later regularly attends in-service courses. Comparatively, possibilities of promotion are better in the C.I.D. than in the uniformed police. The C.I.D. has more supervisory positions, and well-qualified personnel can advance to many police inspectorships within it. Other than this opportunity in the C.I.D., the same rules for promotion are used as for the uniformed police.

There are 20 to 30 women on duty with the C.I.D. and the civilian police. They are used for police duties for which women are more suitable than men.

The police procure information and statements in connection with divorce actions and legal separations supervised by the Ministry of Justice or the county governments, as well as cases regarding custody of children, approval of divorce settlements, exemptions from The Marriage Act provisions, etc. Consequently, the police employ a number of lawyers and a large administrative staff.

Personnel educated in law and employed by the police are the Commissioner of Police, the Commissioner of the Copenhagen Police, the 71 chief constables, 12 assistant commissioners of police to the Commissioner of Police and the Copenhagen Police, and about 180 assistant chief constables working jointly for both the police and the criminal prosecution. One hundred and fifty of the deputy chief constables work closely with the chief constables and act as deputies for them in police supervision, and the others are mainly occupied with prosecution duties (in Copenhagen called *advokater*, or police lawyers) or with administration. Usually, a deputy chief constable joins the police immediately after passing his examinations in law. He is appointed by the Ministry of Justice and is trained by serving in various offices of the police and the prosecution. Most chief constables are former deputy chief constables.

Approximately two thousand administrative personnel are distributed among police districts by the Commissioner of Police. Their work is mainly finance, clerical, registration, passport issuance and various other police administrative functions.

Retirement age for government personnel in Denmark is 70, but they may retire at 67. This is a rather high retirement age for policemen, but there are many things which can be done by older policemen. A few years ago, a regulation was introduced that if a policeman does not advance to Police Inspector 2nd class or higher before he is 63, he must retire, but he may also request retirement when 60. The pension of retired policemen may be as much as 75 per cent of terminal salary.

Denmark is divided into 72 police districts, each supervised by a chief constable (in Copenhagen, a *Politidirektor* or Police Commissioner, not to be confused with the Commissioner of Police). The municipality of Copenhagen is one district, and the suburbs of Copenhagen comprise seven other districts. All other districts contain one or more towns in the less-populated areas of Denmark. Apart from the biggest districts, the population figure for each police district is usually between 20,000 to 100,000 inhabitants. The Faroe Islands and Greenland each represent one district. The Chief Constable for the Faroe Islands comes within the sphere of the Ministry of Justice, whereas the Chief Constable for Greenland serves under the Minister for Greenland.

The chief constable in an area outside Copenhagen is the chief police executive of that district or locality. His immediate assistants are one or more deputy chief constables. In his office work a staff of clerks varying from 5 to 50, according to the size of the district. They are concerned with the administration of finance, registration, the collection of fines and alimony, issuing passports and drivers licenses, etc. These tasks are sometimes handled at the police stations by the uniformed police. A police district comprises one or more stations with both uniformed and C.I.D. police. In each district, one or more civil policemen are also assigned. The supervisors of these stations are police superintendents; C.I.D. police superintendents or police inspectors; and C.I.D. police inspectors, 1st or 2nd class, depending upon the size of the station. To take care of command responsibility, patrol leaders, section leaders or personnel required to handle cases demanding a specially qualified staff, the Commissioner of Police may assign a number of superior officers to these stations. Outside of the cities, the Country Police perform police functions covering areas with average populations of 6,000 to 7,000 inhabitants.

In rural Denmark, police work is carried out by the *landpolitiet* or country police. These policemen are independently capable of dealing with all police matters with the exception of criminal investigation. The country police are assigned residences and patrol cars. The State pays them a mileage allowance with a fixed amount per mile patrolled. They have two-way radios installed in their cars, enabling them to be in constant touch with the police station in town. They must usually be married—their wives attending to the office and the telephone when they are out on patrol.

There are three main groups of personnel in the Danish police: those graduated in law; the Criminal Investigation Department and uniformed police; and police administrative personnel. The police force, uniformed and C.I.D., has a strength of 6500 men—about 800 men short of desired strength. Uniformed police number 5250, and the C.I.D., 1250. Distribution of these personnel to police districts is done by the Commissioner of Police.

As a rule, the Commissioner of Police does not interfere with the administration of local police operations. In this, the local chief constable is responsible directly to the Minister of Justice. With the Commissioner of Police rests the responsibility for appointments to the police, police training, promotion of members of the police forces and police administration, and the distribution of personnel to the police districts. He supervises the distribution of police equipment and material and the keeping of accounts for expenses paid by the State to the police. He also supervises police organization in the districts and may give local police general directions for this purpose. Finally, certain police departments are organized directly under the Commissioner of Police.

Department A: Uniformed Police

Section 1: This is concerned with all matters pertaining to recruiting of uniformed police, the distribution of personnel to police districts, promotions, transfers, discharges and matters involving disciplinary or other action.

Section 2: This is concerned with technical operations of the uniformed police, among which are the use of dogs, radio communications, weapons, supervision of uniformed police in police districts and issuing of regulations for these activities.

Section 3: This is concerned with cooperation between police districts in operations carried out by the uniformed police when these operations affect other districts or exceed the authority of local districts. The Commissioner of Police supervises cooperation between police districts and other authorities, military and civil.

Section 4: This section includes traffic patrols in cars and motorcycles throughout the country which cross boundaries of police districts. The local chief constables may use these patrols to solve local traffic problems, and they make reports to guide the Ministry of Justice in traffic-control problems. The traffic section has a strength of approximately 150 men, and some of them are transferred from the police districts to traffic control for limited periods. The traffic staff is both police trained and technically trained. Personnel are stationed at suitable places in the country. All reports concerning traffic offenses are sent to the department in Copenhagen for statistical and coordination purposes, but the disposition of traffic cases is handled by the local chief constables.

Section 5: The Police Traffic Engineer works with complicated and technical traffic problems. He cooperates with the traffic police in these matters and others involving motor vehicle operation.

Section 6: This section is the police physician.

Department B: Criminal Investigation Division

Section 1: Personnel and equipment of the C.I.D. are supervised here.

Section 2: This is the "Interpol" liaison (international criminal intelligence cooperative).

Section 3: This is the travelling investigation section. About 30 experienced C.I.D. men assist the police districts when serious or comprehensive criminal cases arise.

Section 4: This is the National Criminal Record Office (*Rigsregistraturen*). A central file for the whole country regarding convicted and wanted persons, and stolen or missing property. This information is in both a general file and a special file. Descriptions, nicknames, *modus operandi,* etc., are all located here. The department has teletype communications with all police districts, and they are used for routine correspondence as well. The department edits the "Danish Police Information," which carries information of committed crimes, wanted persons, etc., to all police districts. The personnel totals about 20 C.I.D. men, 12 uniformed and civil policemen, and about 110 administrative personnel.

Section 5: This is the National Section for Identification. Fingerprints connected with criminal cases from the whole country are registered here, and laboratory examinations are made of evidence sent in from police districts. In Copenhagen and in Zealand, the section also investigates crime scenes. Arrested or detained persons are photographed by this section. In the files of this section are registered two hundred and fifty thousand persons. The personnel totals approximately 18 C.I.D. men and 6 administrative personnel.

Section 6: The Technical Section assists the C.I.D. when special skills or apparatus is required. The work is carried out by a main unit in Copenhagen and by four district units in Odense, Kolding, Aarhus and Aalborg. Personnel strength is about eighteen C.I.D. men in the main unit, and four to six men in each of the district units. C.I.D. personnel are not technically trained. If scientific analysis of evidence is required by the police, they are assisted by several universities and institutions possessing various technical experts.

Section 7: This is the missing persons section, which coordinates district searches for missing noncriminal persons. The police strength here is about 12 civil policemen.

Department C: The Administration Department

The administration department is occupied with various administrative tasks.

Section 1: This is the Secretariat. All general legal and financial matters concerning administration of the police as well as all administrative personnel in the police are supervised by the Secretariat. Administrative personnel are appointed, distributed to the districts and transferred through the Secretariat.

Section 2: The Accounts Section prepares the budget of the police and keeps account of expenses paid by the State to the police. It supervises the payroll of all employees of the police.

Section 3: The Management Section is divided into subsections dealing with the purchase and delivering of uniforms, equipment, weapons, motor vehicles, radio communications, office supplies, furniture, etc.

Department D: The Motor Vehicle Registration Department

This department was established in 1960 and registers all motor vehicles in the Copenhagen area, the district of Copenhagen and suburbs. It undertakes general planning and preparations in connection with motor vehicles registered by the police.

Department E: The Aliens Department

This department supervises the entire Kingdom with respect to applications from aliens for entry permits, residence permits and working permits. Here, the regulations and instructions for passport control are issued, and instructions are sent to the districts regarding aliens residing there. This control is directly carried out by the Aliens Department in Copenhagen and its suburbs. It also supervises passport control at the Copenhagen harbor and at the airport of Copenhagen in Kastrup.

Department F: The Police College

After training policies are established by the Ministry of Justice, the Police College trains police personnel in basic courses, in-service courses, promotion courses and special courses. Instructors are both a permanent staff of policemen attached to the college for a specific term of years and a number of policemen attached to the teaching staff temporarily while attending to their regular police duties.

Department G: The Intelligence Service

The Intelligence Service deals with matters of national security and the protection of government officials.

A Commissioner is in charge of the Copenhagen police. His closest assistants are six Assistant Commissioners—each in charge of a division—and one section chief in charge of the Secretariat, finance, statistics and other administrative tasks. The 1st Assistant Commissioner is in charge of all uniformed police in Copenhagen. He is assisted by a Deputy Assistant Commissioner of Police and 12 superintendents as section chiefs. The police personnel of Copenhagen total about 2000 men, with most of them stationed at nine police stations covering one district of Copenhagen. Centrally, the 1st Police Department consists of four sections:

1. The Secretariat Section, dealing with matters of procedure for police personnel, and information to the press and the public. Members of foreign police forces are given assistance through this section. It deals also with the licensing and regulation of restaurants, theatres and entertainment.
2. Personnel Section.

3. Civil Defence Section.
4. The Emergency Section. Personnel from district stations are assigned to this section for a period of one year. This section plans activities of the uniformed police for great events in the city, e.g. receptions of royalty, demonstrations, etc. It also acts as a reserve for the district police stations. The Communications Unit, the Police Dog Unit and the Mounted Police are organized in this section.

The 2nd Assistant Commissioner (2nd Police Department, C.I.D.) is chief of the Criminal Investigation Department and is assisted by one Deputy Assistant Commissioner, and six C.I.D. police superintendents. The department consists of about 325 C.I.D. men. Their tasks are carried out by personnel at Police Headquarters and by personnel serving at police stations in Copenhagen. Different types of crime are divided into four sections for operational purposes. There is an emergency section on duty 24 hours a day. Radio cars are on patrol throughout the Copenhagen area. The 2nd Assistant Commissioner is also in charge of the Criminological Museum (the Black Museum) on the premises of the Police College.

The 3rd Police Department consists of the Public Health Section, the Section For Sexual Offenses, and the Veterinary Section. The Assistant Commissioner is assisted by 1 police superintendent and 80 civil policemen.

The 4th Police Department deals with the cases concerning the Law of Trade, the Law of Domestic Relations, missing non-criminal persons and the issuing of passports. The Assistant Commissioner of Police is assisted by 1 police superintendent and approximately 80 civil policemen.

The 5th Police Department assists in the prosecution of criminal cases handled by the Copenhagen police. These cases are received from the 2nd Police Department when a suspect has been jailed or statements by the suspect and investigation have proved the case ready to bring before the court. The Department has 11 investigation sections, and each section is commanded by a prosecutor or police lawyer. The staff consists of C.I.D. men placed at its disposal by both the 2nd Police Department and the Office for the Prosecution of Criminal Cases. This office is also responsible for seeing to the disposition of sentenced criminals. One of the investigation sections deals with violations of currency, tax and customs laws.

The 6th Police Department deals with traffic control. The Assistant Commissioner of Police is assisted by three police superintendents and subordinate personnel—about 135 men from the 1st Police Department. While this department deals exclusively with traffic problems, it should be pointed out that uniformed police serving in local police stations spend much of their time with the regulation of traffic, accident investigation and violations of traffic laws. This department also cooperates with highway and street authorities regarding engineering questions, parking and traffic regulations, and control of taxicabs and buses. All reports concerning traffic accidents are forwarded to this department for examination. The department controls all driver-education schools, and driving tests are given by specially trained personnel of this department. Patrols are maintained for traffic-enforcement purposes. In cooperation with elementary and secondary schools, policemen instruct the school safety patrols in their duties. Safety patrols are organized from among older school children to help the younger children on their way to and from school at traffic crossings. Finally, there is a section which sees to the disposition of noncriminal sentences for traffic violations.

A number of agencies concerned with social welfare work closely with the Copenhagen Police. The Copenhagen Police have a welfare section for the relief of indigent persons with whom the police come in frequent contact. In Copenhagen, boys between 8 and 18 years of age may join the Police Youth Clubs. The C.I.D., as well as the *Police de Moeurs* or Vice Squad, cooperates with social agencies, giving help to persons who are objects of vice-suppression activity.

Thus, the Commissioner of Police and the chief constables are organized and directed on a national basis for administration, coordination, and mutual assistance; but initiative and independent responsibility to carry out police functions remains locally oriented.

Chapter 32

THE POLICE OF TOKYO

T.T. WINANT

Over the last few years, journals devoted to the policeman and his work have grown in number and sophistication. This cornucopia of riches on law enforcement has made today's lawman one of the best informed and professional of civil servants. There are, however, some gaps in the policeman's knowledge of his fellow policemen which have yet to be corrected. One of the major chasms is distance compounded by language. That is to say, the policeman of Europe or America is able to communicate with his counterparts only through a few international agencies which have been created to supplement the efforts of domestic police forces. Because of their proximity and similarity of background, it is only natural that the nations bordering the Atlantic keep the closest contact, often to the exclusion of other parts of the globe. These other areas, primarily non-Western, are even ignored altogether.

While it is true that many of the police forces of Africa and Asia have short traditions and histories, and a number are, in great measure, the products of nearly a century of European colonial control and manipulation, some police forces exist which, although influenced by European example, have maintained an older tradition and have a longer history. One of the most important of these is the Metropolitan Police Agency of Japan which has responsibility for keeping the peace and enforcing the laws of the capital of Japan—Tokyo.

The Metropolitan Police Agency, or the *Keishicho*, as it is called, is the oldest surviving police organization from the prewar period of Japanese history. The Agency was founded in 1874 to replace the bands of samurai (Armed Knights), serving

NOTE: From *The Police Journal*, April, 1971, pp. 167–172. Reprinted with permission.

as policemen, who had come from the leading feudal baronies which had overthrown the feudal Tokugawa military government in 1868. The Meiji government (the name Meiji is given to the period 1868–1912, the years of the reign of the Emperor Meiji) had decided that the retention of feudal warriors to protect the capital from disorder was not in keeping with the new image of modernity and westernization which the leaders hoped to project to the world.

At this early date, the Metropolitan Police were responsible for many more things than are their modern counterparts. These duties included supervision of hospitals, health regulations, fire prevention and control, supervision of traffic regulations, censorship of newspapers and other periodicals, monitoring of the movements of foreigners and other potential trouble-makers, control of building ordinances, economic matters which affected the well-being of society, the movements of temporary and permanent members of the labor force and any other matters which from time to time might be assigned to their jurisdiction.

Obviously this gave the police of Tokyo a rather large area of responsibility which could be carried out only if they actively intervened in the most intimate aspects of the lives of all the citizens in the capital area. Policemen were permitted to carry swords, which they continued to do until 1945, and had the authority to condemn to incarceration for violation of police ordinances any citizen without recourse to legal counsel or public trial. Because policemen were in charge of keeping a census of the local population, maintaining records of who lived where, with whom and how each person made his living, it was not unusual for citizens to come into frequent contact with their local law officer. Indeed, when a citizen had contact with his government for any reason at all, it was likely that it would be the policeman to whom he turned. If this were not enough, during the 1930's, when Japan was rapidly becoming a regimented and militarized state, there was instituted a system called the *goningumi*. This literally means "five person" or "family association" and was designed to make the members of five households responsible for each other's behavior. If one member of one family in the group were to commit a crime, the whole *goningumi* would be held liable for restitution. The local policeman was responsible for overseeing this system, and he felt free to interfere into intrafamily relations on a need-to-know basis. Small wonder that individualism has not been considered a characteristic of Japan, even today.

With their wide powers and energetic enforcement of regulations, the prewar Japanese police in Tokyo had a reputation for toughness and brutality which their successors still find hard to change. Police could, and did, slap or beat citizens who refused to comply with requests or directives. Incarceration for any period of time might actually mean death to those accused of crimes. It was not unknown to have those suspected of harboring dangerous thoughts tortured. A number are known to have died at the hands of their interrogators.

By and large, however, the Tokyo Metropolitan Police did perform their duties without excessive brutality. While some might disagree, there was in no sense a police state (operating) in Japan. The police could and did command the obedience of the citizenry. They did have the authority to act as both arresting officer and judge in many areas of citizen's behavior, far beyond that which the Anglo-American world would consider safe for essential human freedom and dignity. But there was no tradition of freedom as we know it in Japan, and the constitution adopted in 1889 was quite unclear on the subject of rights of citizens as opposed to their obligations. In the 70 years from 1874 to 1945, Japan underwent a staggering series of social, political and economic changes, from feudalism to the industrial age. She accomplished in that short span what it took western Europe 400 years to achieve. In the process there were no political revolutions, unlike in France or Russia, and only minor domestic unrest caused by social and economic dislocation. Efficient police work kept crime to a minimum and made Tokyo safer than New York or London throughout much of the late nineteenth and early twentieth centuries.

During the pre-World War II period, the Metropolitan Police attempted to combine their own tradition with the techniques employed by the most modern Western nations. The first manual of Western police work was completed in 1869 by Yukichi

Fukuzawa, the Edmund Burke of Japan. By 1872, the need for more information and experience with regard to modern police methods was recognized. The Inspector-General of the Tokyo Police Force, Toshiyoshi Kawaji, was sent to Europe and America, from where he returned in 1873 with the ideas which brought about the creation of the *Keishicho*. Known as the father of the Japanese police system, Kawaji created the framework of the national police organization which was to survive until after Japan's defeat in the 1941 to 1945 war.

As indicated earlier, the early modern Tokyo police were responsible for a multitude of activities which went beyond that which we would normally expect to be part of police work. The organization was large and somewhat unwieldy. The number of personnel actually employed in apprehending criminals, or work which we would recognize as falling into our own category of public safety (traffic control etc.), at any given time was actually quite small. It took a nearly complete reorganization of the Japanese government by the Allied occupation after 1945 to bring police work as we are familiar with it to a clearer definition of role in Japanese society.

When the Allies arrived in Japan in the fall of 1945, one of their first actions was to abolish those organs of government which they had come to identify with suppressive control over the civilian population. The Police Bureau of the Home Ministry, which had supervised all police outside of Tokyo, was abolished, its personnel purged from official life. Henceforth all police were to be placed under local control. Within the Metropolitan Police Agency, all departments and sections which had dealt with political or economic matters were abolished and their personnel purged. Thus ended the existences of such organs as the Thought Police; Censorship Department; Labor, Enterprise and Korean Departments, as well as the notorious Special Higher Police which had been responsible for the arrests of thousands in the 1920's and '30's and the investigation and intimidation of many others, including at least one former Prime Minister.

In the first years of the Occupation, the effort to reform the police system was mainly designed to prevent the recurrence of prewar abuses. The Occupation authorities brought in Lewis J. Valentine, former Police Commissioner in New York City, to survey the Metropolitan Police forces and offer suggestions on their reorganization. Not surprisingly, his proposals made the Tokyo Police resemble that of New York most closely. Those things which were essentially nonpolice functions were separated from the agency and a looser command set-up was instituted. Now completely independent of the central government (previously the Chief of the Metropolitan Police had reported directly to the Home Minister), it was possible for the police of Tokyo to devote their time to strictly police matters.

The initial reforms made between 1945 and 1949, however, were found inadequate to the demands of the time. Some social unrest and economic dislocation in the chaotic postwar period, compounded by the emergence of the ideological and political disputes of the Cold War, converged to bring about a more centralized and expanded police force than had been expected. While the police did not return completely to their prewar forms, a certain amount of regression did take place. The Metropolitan Police Agency today is still a far cry from its predecessors. They are not indeed, the democratic or "people's" police envisaged by the Allied Occupation.

To deal with public disturbances, mainly student demonstrations or riots, there is a highly mobile and efficient riot squad. This organization is made up of young and well-trained policemen who have learned how to carry on their duties without inflicting bodily injury, except in the most unusual circumstances, and then only accidentally. All of the men are expected to be proficient in the arts of weaponless defense, judo, etc.

Within Tokyo, there are a number of small cities in addition to the administrative districts of the central core of the Metropolis. For training and overall administrative purposes, the police of these cities are also united under the Metropolitan Police Agency whose director is responsible to the Governor of the Metropolis. Traditionally, the appointment of Inspector-General of the Metropolitan Police has been a political one, and this continues today. When a new governor takes office, a new Inspector-General, usually chosen from among the department heads of the Agency, is appointed. Policemen themselves come from all over Japan, and it is not at all unusual to find a large number of young men from rural areas throughout the Agency.

In the central part of the city, where traffic and human congestion is the heaviest, the Metropolitan Police use the most sophisticated of electronic and human resources to maintain safety and order. On street corners in the Ginza entertainment district, for example, there are television cameras placed on utility poles high above the intersections. These permit a central monitoring of vehicular and pedestrian traffic so that limited manpower can cope with the staggering traffic burden. This system has also been used to identify juvenile runaways and wanted criminals who tend to congregate around the places of entertainment.

Much like any other city with vast traffic problems, Tokyo suffers from serious air pollution crises. During the summer of 1970, pollution was blamed for the deaths of a score of school children during one unusually bad week-long period. Policemen, especially those assigned to traffic duty, have often been overcome by exhaust fumes. A few years ago, the police agency had oxygen tanks installed in those police boxes (*koban*) where this situation was most critical. The large number of respiratory and other pollution-related illnesses among policemen, however, continues to increase without much chance of early correction.

Ordinary patrolmen in Tokyo are assigned out of several district and city headquarters. These are located in the more populous areas, and are the centers for most mobile and communications units. From these central headquarters, patrolmen are assigned to police boxes scattered throughout the area. The number of men in each box is dependent upon need and facilities. Most men will work an 8-hour day for several days, and then take a 24-hour shift, during which they sleep on cots in the back rooms of the police boxes. Unmarried policemen generally live in dormitories attached to the headquarters or nearby. In the suburban city of Mitaka, for instance, there are two such structures housing approximately 20 to 25 men each.

Training and refresher courses for policemen are continuous. A certain number of hours each week must be devoted to physical training, mainly judo and similar sports. Every year each patrolman is given time off from his regular duties to attend classes at the police academy located in the Nakano district. For those selected by examination for promotion, the length of attendance is usually extended to include administrative and command techniques.

The normal period of assignment for policemen to one district is three years. Efforts are made to give everyone the opportunity to work in both the suburban areas, such as Mitaka or Hachioji, and in the more populous central districts, Shinijuku or Meguro. The lack of activity in the rural areas make some of the younger policemen yearn for assignment to either the riot squad or the high-crime entertainment districts. The former deal mainly with student disruptions and other large-scale public demonstrations, the latter with the professional criminal element. By far, the worst area in Tokyo with regard to crime and public disorder is the Shinijuku district. Here congregate the dissatisfied young, the socially disadvantaged, the poor, members of the Korean minority (having a similar status to the Pakistanis in England) and the degenerate. The Shinijuku railway stations, a center for intracity and long-distance trains and subways, has been stormed by students, laborers and hippies on several occasions. Pitched battles have been fought in the vicinity, with reinforcements being brought in by both police and demonstrators from outside the city. The unwillingness of the police to cause serious injury has not noticeably diminished the fierceness of these struggles. On the contrary, the students actually seem to court head-breaking. The remarkable restraint of the police in not accommodating them is a tribute to their training and discipline.

Perhaps the most eye-opening aspect of the achievements of the Tokyo Metropolitan Police is the crime statistics. During the spring of 1969, the International wire services carried a story which stated that the metropolis of Tokyo had gone for a period of 119 days without a major crime. That is, no murder, bank robbery, rape, etc. Even more impressive, however, is that this was the *third* time since 1960 that this number of days had passed without such crimes having been committed. There were also a score of periods exceeding one hundred days without major crime.

These statistics do not mean that crime is nonexistent in Tokyo. It just means that crimes involving bodily injury to others and major incidents involving property are scarce. Self-destruction, suicide, is the major human problem, while small property thefts are quite frequent. What keeps the policeman busy is the conciliatory role he plays in society. Because Japanese rarely resort to courts of law to settle business or family differences, they often take problems to the local policeman for his aid in settlement. In this process the policeman serves as a sounding board, an ameliorator, a listener, rarely an arbitrator. For the Japanese, who sets great store by peaceful conciliation, this duty of the policeman is most valuable. Whenever some minor conflict can be settled through the efforts of a police officer, it prevents aggravation of differences later. The maturity of police officers in handling this kind of problem and the trust with which their efforts are received by the population can be seen by the fact that even Junior patrolmen, some only in their late teens, are continuously dealing with persons of every age and social level.

The metropolis of Tokyo has indeed an unusual and distinguished record in the history of police work. Its achievements can match those of the best Western organizations, and these should certainly be better known to all who work in law enforcement.

Chapter 33

THE KIDOTAI

ROBERT Y. THORNTON

The Kidotai (also referred to as *Keisatsu Butai*) are the special police units charged with the responsibility of controlling civil disturbances in Japan. The term "KIDOTAI" may be translated as "Mobile Task Forces."

Often described as the world's most experienced anti-riot police, the KIDOTAI are divided into two separate categories.

First, there is the regular KIDOTAI. These are units established in Tokyo and certain prefectures after the violent May Day, 1952, rioting in front of the Imperial Palace. (A prefecture is roughly equivalent to a state in the United States.) The regular KIDOTAI has a present strength in Japan of 9,700 members. There are 5,300 regular KIDOTAI within the Tokyo Metropolitan Police Department (*Keishicho*). The latter are under the command of the Superintendent General of the Tokyo Metropolitan Police Department (MPD). The Director is, in turn, appointed by a civilian body, the National Public Safety Commission, with the consent of the Tokyo Public Safety Commission and the approval of the Prime Minister.

Second, there is the so-called *Kanku* or reigonal KIDOTAI. Regional KIDOTAI are assigned to a larger geographical area consisting of several prefectures and may be dispatched wherever their assistance is required. These units were established commencing in April, 1969, and have a total strength of 4,200 members.

In any major civil disturbance, the following types of police may be employed: (a) regular KIDOTAI, (b) *Kanku* KIDOTAI and (c) riot-trained regular police officers.

All of the foregoing types of units will serve under the command of a single anti-riot commander.

NOTE: From *The Police Chief*, July, 1971, pp. 65–73. Reprinted with permission.

RECRUITMENT AND SELECTION

All KIDOTAI are volunteers and are carefully selected from among those applicants who are successful in the KIDOTAI entrance examination. Usually there are twice as many applicants as there are positions to be filled.

The first requirement is that the applicant must be a duly qualified regular police officer who has completed the standard one-year training and orientation course for all police officers. In addition, he must have thereafter served a full year as a regular police officer. Applicants must be under 30 years of age, in good physical condition and of above-average intelligence.

Minimum physical requirements for entrance into Japan's national police force are 5 ft., 2½ in. in height and 110 pounds in weight. KIDOTAI police appear considerably taller, although they are not as large as most American police.

After service in KIDOTAI for two or three years, members usually return to their former units and continue their careers as law-enforcement officers. Service in the riot police usually leads to more rapid promotion. It is interesting to note that more than half of KIDOTAI members attend night classes to study for promotion examinations. One man in seven is already a college graduate.

PAY AND ALLOWANCES

KIDOTAI receive the same basic pay and allowances as other police with equivalent training and experience. This is approximately 120 dollars per month, after deductions. While this is only a fraction of the pay of United States police, it is comparable to pay scales in private employment in Japan.

KIDOTAI receive certain special allowances because of their duties, as do regular police officers of equivalent training and experience.

ORGANIZATION

The KIDOTAI is organized into what are termed "Mobile Units." (There are ten Mobile Units in the Tokyo Metropolitan Police Department.)

A Mobile Unit consists of four companies and a headquarters company. The strength of a regular company is 79 or 80 men. The headquarters company has a strength of 120 men.

A regular company is comprised of three platoons. The platoon consists of three squads plus the platoon leader (lieutenant). A squad consists of ten members plus the squad leader (sergeant).

PERSONAL EQUIPMENT

Personal equipment of riot police includes the following: a specially designed field uniform of gray twill (*shutsudo fuku*), navy blue plastic riot helmet, movable protective face mask (plexiglass), neck protector, body protector, specially designed gloves and elbow-length gauntlets, shin guards and protective shoes with metal toe caps. Most important is the convex duralumin body shield, approximately 4½ ft high and 2½ ft wide. Introduced in 1967, this shield has a slit at one end to allow for observation of the riot scene, and two sturdy perpendicular holding bars on the inside. The first bar is in the left-center, which the officer grasps with his left hand when carrying the shield. The second bar is smaller and is located at the top right of the shield. This is grasped with the right hand when required by the circumstances. In addition to the above, each officer carries, attached to his belt, a standard police nightstick, which is slightly longer but smaller in diameter than the United States model. It is not drawn or used except upon command.

Platoon and company commanders and certain others carry portable loudspeakers for issuing commands and also for incidental crowd control.

Japanese anti-riot police never carry or use sidearms.

SPECIAL VEHICLES

The KIDOTAI have some 25 different types of special vehicles. Most of these are assigned to and operated by the Special Mobile Unit in Tokyo (*Tokka Sharyo Tai*). This unit is the only one of its kind in the entire country. These special vehicles, all but one of which were designed and built in Japan to the specifications of the National Police Agency (NPA), include the following.

1. Reinforced personnel carrier (*Keibisha*), which carries 37 men. There are several types. One type can be used as a street barricade. Another has been designed with flat ends and doors front and rear so that the buses can be placed end to end to form a protective tunnel. Thus these vehicles may be driven in tandem up to the doors of a building in which rioters have barricaded themselves, and used as a tunnel to allow KIDOTAI to effect an entry to a building, even though demonstrators may be bombing them with rocks, Molotov cocktails and other missiles from above.

2. Water cannon-equipped trucks. There are actually several variations in use, with varying water-pressure capabilities. Both marking dye and tear gas may be used in the water.

Of importance is the snorkel water-cannon truck. This truck has a retractable "snorkel" which can be raised at the scene to permit delivery of powerful streams of water at high elevations and variable angles, then retracted for movement to another location or travel to and from the barracks. Special pumper trucks provide a resupply of water or specially prepared chemicals.

3. Special floodlighting trucks. These are specially designed to provide adequate floodlighting of a night riot scene. The lighting panel is affixed to the top of the vehicle and is fully screened and retractable while not needed or in transit. When raised, the light panel can be rotated easily to a full 360 degrees to assure complete lighting of any riot scene or part thereof.

4. Special identification vehicles. These are manned by personnel to take live TV pictures of the riot scene which are transmitted instantaneously to MPD and National Police Agency headquarters to enable higher headquarters to monitor, and if necessary direct, the progress of a particular operation. Personnel also take videotape motion pictures as well as still pictures for possible use as evidence in any subsequent prosecutions.

5. Mobile headquarters truck. This is a fully equipped, mobile command post, and serves as a field headquarters for the commanding officer at the scene.

In addition to the foregoing, the Special Mobile Unit has mobile wireless radio telephone trucks, barricade-removing scoopmobiles, mobile shield vehicles, small transportation cars (Jeeps), medium personnel cars, standard personnel transportation trucks (*Yusosha*), transportation and guard cars (diesel powered to avoid flammability of gasoline-powered vehicles, since a favorite device of rioters is to try to set fire to KIDOTAI vehicles). Others include foam-discharger trucks, high-powered public address trucks for crowd control, and special wrecker vehicles which are available to haul away any KIDOTAI or other vehicles that may become disabled or used by rioters as obstacles, barricades, etc.

The KIDOTAI do not have their own helicopters. When the occasion arises they borrow helicopters from the regular police.

The theory behind the specially designed vehicles is that the riot police feel that it is very important to get as close as possible to the demonstrators. Therefore, specially designed vehicles are required to accomplish this.

USE OF MOVIE FILM AND STILL PICTURES

KIDOTAI have found that 8 mm film is usually the best for their purposes; 16 mm is four times as expensive and it is more conspicuous when used by plainclothes officers filming the riot scene. It was pointed out that the Japanese were inveterate photographers, and it was not at all uncommon to see many private citizens taking films of the riot scene. Thus, if a plainclothesman uses 8 mm he is not so apt to attract the attention of vengeance-minded rioters. They find that plainclothesmen often have taken the best pictures of the riot scene.

STUDENT DISORDERS

KIDOTAI have standing orders not to intervene in campus disorders, no matter how severe the disturbance may be, without the request of university authorities.

Asked if there was anything different about operations in campus situations, Superintendent Nakamura of the Special Mobile Unit said that there were important differences in the tactics of dealing with a campus situation as compared with a street riot. He pointed out that a campus building very often is converted into a fort, with the dissident students holding possession of buildings several stories high. It is necessary to use special tactics and equipment (a specially designed mobile tunnel) to gain entry and evict these students. In some ways, this type of operation is considered easier than street demonstrations, where a major problem is always to separate and seal off the spectators from the rioters. He felt that campus sieges were really more easy to handle than street riots, because once you have gained entry to the building, evicting the rioting students is simply a matter of technique to avoid injuring any of the students who are about to be evicted.

KIDOTAI seldom, if ever, employ their nightsticks on student rioters. It has been their experience that such use produces a hostile response both from the students and the general public, the public then taking the side of the students, construing this as "police brutality." Another officer expressed the opinion that the Japanese public is quick to take the side of the underdog in such a situation.

Contrary to public attitudes in the United States, early student demonstrations enjoyed widespread public support in Japan. This has changed however, due to excessive violence and property destruction. (Nearly two thirds of the populace now favor tough measures to restore peace.) Oddly, when students fleeing police during one riot in front of a United States military hospital in Tokyo ran through private homes without first removing their shoes, this gross breach of traditional etiquette reportedly caused nearly as much loss of public sympathy as the rising level of violence.

Some foreign observers have stated that there is an unwritten "Code of Fairplay" between student rioters and the KIDOTAI to avoid killing one another. Asked whether he believed there was such a tacit gentlemen's agreement, one high officer told me he thought there might be. As he expressed it: "We are all

Japanese and we do not wish to kill one another." As a further example, he pointed out the fact that the rioters never attack the private homes or disturb the families of KIDOTAI. However, after seeing the savagery of the attacks on the riot police in the films of actual riot scenes, and viewing some of the homemade zip guns, bullets and other weapons and projectiles made and used by the students, I am not at all sure that there is such a gentlemen's agreement in force.

Student rioters have lost all of their recent skirmishes with the riot police. The latter feel that the militant students are now convinced that the KIDOTAI have the manpower, equipment and techniques necessary to maintain order. This, they feel, accounts for the recent noticeable tapering off in violent campus riots.

TACTICS OF MILITANT GROUPS

It is interesting to note that radical student groups have adopted many KIDOTAI tactics. They conduct secret training sessions and practice close-order drill and various riot formations. Almost all now wear plastic riot helmets to demonstrations. Each faction paints its helmets in a distinctive color, with the group's name painted in Chinese characters on the front of the helmets. During battles with police, they cover their faces with small bath towels, partly as a protection against possible tear gas and partly to hinder identification.

Weapons of rioters have gone through three phases: First, ordinary sticks; second, 4- to 6-foot long, squared staves (Gevalt poles), bamboo spears or lances; and third, pipes, iron rods, Molotov cocktails, bricks, paving stones, various acids and agricultural chemicals, sharp pieces of steel, homemade explosives and zip guns. (Government authorities have recently covered over many paving-stone streets, railroad tracks and sidewalks with asphalt so that rioters cannot pick them up to hurl at police.)

During the 1967–68 riot, students were first seen to commence the employment of Molotov cocktails and various homemade explosives.

Students and other militants have turned to multiple guerilla attacks at several points simultaneously, hoping to draw off the main body of KIDOTAI in these various diversionary attacks. For example, they will send small units against an embassy, the Diet building, the Prime Minister's residence, etc. Another tactic has been to create a sham disturbance in one location as a diversion, solely for the purpose of trying to draw off the KIDOTAI, while the main body of the rioters carries out its attack on the principal objective. These new tactics have resulted in the riot police discontinuing the use of large formations and substituting smaller squads. This is referred to as the *Yugekitai* system—meeting small-scale guerilla-type attacks.

Asked how he saw the progress of the struggles (*tosō*) between the demonstrators and the KIDOTAI, Superintendent Nakamura said that the January, 1969, violence at Tokyo University and the April 21, 1969, Okinawa Day demonstrations were the peak periods of violence. After this period, the actions of the dissident groups have become less violent. This was clearly indicated in the June 23, 1969, demonstrations, when the violence had definitely tapered off. He believes that while the demonstrators have not abandoned their plans for mass violence, they are beginning to realize that the police are capable of thwarting and containing any attempted violent overthrow of the government or any large-scale property destruction contemplated by the radical minorities.

USE OF PLAINCLOTHES OFFICERS

The Fifth Mobile Unit employs 20 plainclothes officers who gather evidence and other information at the scene of the disturbance. These officers may make arrests. There have been instances when these officers, as well as uniformed KIDOTAI, have been captured by demonstrators. On one or two occasions these officers have been stripped and beaten before they could be rescued by the uniformed officers. This is one of the reasons for the development of the "Flying Squad" rescue technique.

ANTIRIOT FORMATIONS

There are a great variety of tactical formations which are formed or changed at the command of the platoon leaders, company commander, etc., to meet the various types of riots and demonstrations, much in the same manner as the quarterback of a well-trained football team positions his team to move against the opposing team. For example, the platoon may be formed in a column of squads, with the three squads arranged in three columns, Indian file. The purpose of this formation is to move against the demonstration without injury to the demonstrators and using only the body shields. During my visit to the training area, the members were practicing various formations using the body shields, all showing how to protect their bodies from attacks from any quarter and against any type of missile.

Other examples are the *turtle back formation* (Kiko Taikei). This is a special formation employed when the unit is temporarily surrounded and no immediate retreat is possible. The squad or platoon huddles in a small compact group, placing their shields over their bodies to protect the group from rocks and other missiles.

Also employed on occasion is the *flying squad formation* (*Yugeki butai katsudo*). The flying squad formation is used to rescue a KIDOTAI member who has been captured by demonstrators. This is a pyramid-shaped formation of two squads, with the bottom of the pyramid open and pointed toward the demonstrators.

A special crowd-separating squad or platoon has the function of separating the rioters and bystanders. The tactics of this squad was clearly shown during a mock "riot" I observed on the parade ground of the 5th Mobile Unit. A group of "demonstrators" called "giraffes" because of the long flag-tipped bamboo poles which they carried, moved toward the KIDOTAI company. The riot police at first retreated. They then paused, and covered themselves on command, as if to invite the "giraffes" to pelt them with sand-filled socks intended to simulate rocks. After the "rock" barrage, which the KIDOTAI defended against by huddling behind a double-tiered row of shields, the riot police came roaring back at the "rioters" with a fearsome, guttural roar, much like an ancient Samurai cavalry charge one seen on Japanese television and started after the "demonstrators."

The special crowd-separating squad or platoon proceeded to seal off the "spectators" from the "demonstrators," preventing the "demonstrators" from escaping into the crowd. The remainder of the riot police charged out in pursuit of the fleeing rioters, capturing as many of their leaders as they could. It was explained that they were being arrested for interfering with police officers in the performance of their duties.

TEAR GAS

KIDOTAI use only tear gas (CN). The gas is delivered usually by tear gas gun or thrown in a canister. Tear gas is not used unless the demonstrators become violent, such as pelting the riot police with a barrage of rocks, Molotov cocktails, charging at them with their pike poles, etc. (Pike poles are referred to by KIDOTAI as Gevalt sticks, a German term.) In addition to firing tear gas from the guns, canisters are thrown into the rioters.

There are three kinds of tear gas used: tear liquid, which is mixed with water and used in either the water cannon or sprayed by helicopter; tear gas in powder form; and tear gas dispersed by means of smoke.

When tear gas is issued to individual riot police, it consists of five canisters which are strapped around the waist.

PARADE-CONTROL TECHNIQUES

Where the parade permit calls for a parade through a congested downtown area, the KIDOTAI will accompany the paraders along the route of march to make certain that they do not block traffic. (I witnessed such a demonstration involving 15,000 participants through the Akasaka district of Tokyo on the night of November 22, 1970.) This is accomplished by having a single column of riot police march directly alongside, with their body shields placed in such a manner as to confine the demonstrators to their side of the street. A parade may be composed of numerous separate factional elements. Paraders usually march four abreast in disciplined ranks like an army. They chant rhythmical slogans similar to those used in ancient festivals I have observed in various parts of Japan. Each rank of demonstrators usually carries a pole stretching across the column. If elements of the parade group have a previous record of breaking loose into the main traveled portion of the street for blocking traffic, vandalism, etc., there will be a double line of riot police accompanying that particular group or unit. In addition, other units of KIDOTAI in single file may accompany them along the parade route but across the street. If "snake dancers" seek to break out of formation, the accompanying riot police will assist them back into line by means of their body shields.

GUN CONTROL LAW

As do most European countries, Japan has a tight gun-control law which is strictly enforced. Ownership and possession of handguns by private citizens is absolutely prohibited. Hunting rifles and shotguns may be owned or purchased only after first securing a license from the police. Licenses are issued only to bona fide sportsmen. Maximum penalty for violation of the gun control law is five years' imprisonment.

SPECIFIC GROUNDS FOR ARREST OF RIOTERS

Depending on the facts, rioters may be arrested on any of the following grounds: unlawful assembly, unlawful assembly with a dangerous weapon, interfering with a police officer in the performance of his duties, unlawful entry or occupation of a building, trespass, blocking traffic, assault or causing bodily injury and interference with the rights of others.

Under Japanese law, police may hold a suspect for 48 hours without bail. Prosecutors have an additional 24 hours to file charges and may ask for a court order to detain the suspect an additional ten days to complete their investigation.

NONUSE OF FIREARMS

Every officer interviewed was strongly of the view that the policy of not using or even carrying guns was the right policy.

A slightly different reaction came from private citizens with whom the matter was discussed. As one 40-year-old business man, himself a college graduate, expressed it: "The fact that the students know that the KIDOTAI do not carry sidearms and know that they will not be shot at, no matter how serious may be their attacks on the police, is to my mind a bad thing. I think this leads the students to adopt the attitude that they can attack the police as violently as they wish and will not suffer any counterviolence. I think it would be a good thing if the police did carry sidearms."

OTHER DUTIES OF KIDOTAI

The advisability of using KIDOTAI for other police duties was a matter of considerable debate within the National Police Agency. After much study and discussion, the National Police Agency concluded that it would be proper to use the KIDOTAI for certain other duties. For example, on occasion they are employed as traffic police, rescue and disaster control police, and even in general police patrolling.

QUARTERS

Bachelor KIDOTAI members are quartered in their own special police barracks in certain prefectures. Married KIDOTAI live at home, except when on night shift every fourth day. There are four complete teams in each unit with one team always on duty. Every four days they have a day off, except in case of emergency.

COMMUNICATIONS AND FIRST AID

Both two-way radio communication and one-way short wave communication is employed. Individual KIDOTAI carry a tiny compact short-wave mobile transmitter with them in the performance of their duties. A special radio truck is employed in all field operations. This vehicle is also specially reinforced against rocks and missiles. KIDOTAI use the regular police radio frequency.

KIDOTAI do not employ a special first aid unit. They use the regular first aid services of the fire department.

FUNDAMENTAL PRINCIPLES AND THEORY OF RIOT CONTROL

The objectives of the KIDOTAI are as follows:

1. To protect human life on both sides of the conflict—both the persons provoking the disturbance and the police who are quelling the disturbance.
2. To move against the attacking formations quickly, using as many KIDOTAI as can be effectively used decisively in quelling the disturbance.
3. To carry out the mission in such a manner as to assure public acceptance and support.
4. To arrest all ringleaders of the attacking group as rapidly as possible.
5. To separate the bystanders from the militants as quickly as possible. (A special unit of KIDOTAI has the responsibility of separating the onlookers from the mob by loudspeaker and by special maneuver.)

Asked what he considered to be the most difficult problem in quelling a public disturbance, a senior officer of the National Police Agency (*Keisatsuoho*) stated that it was to maintain a proper degree of restraint without sacrificing the morale of the unit.

Mr. Hiroshi Yamaguchi, Director of the Security Bureau, National Police Agency, stated the theory and principles under which the KIDOTAI operates in these words:

> The KIDOTAI is a very unique organization. Because of national attitudes in Japan against the use of military force in domestic disturbances, KIDOTAI occupies a much different position than do the police of western countries.

(Japan's Self-Defense Force (*Jietai*) has not and can never be used unless the rioting is so great as to constitute "Indirect Invasion," as determined by the Prime Minister.)

> The policy and operations of the KIDOTAI must at all times be consistent with public opinion and national attitudes. The KIDOTAI must always be aware that their handling of a particular distur-

bance may have grave political consequences. For this reason, KIDOTAI equipment and tactics is always more defensive than offensive in nature.

Since the KIDOTAI is not a military-oriented organization, the attitude of the KIDOTAI toward the demonstrators is defensive in nature.

Even though the demonstrators may become excited and violent, the KIDOTAI must remain calm and cool at all times. Counterviolence is not considered the proper response to civil disorders. *Gaman*, self-control is the most important personal characteristic of the KIDOTAI.

The Japanese people have a deep appreciation and sensitivity in reference to individual rights, possibly more so than do the people of many other countries. This fact is responsible for the restraint practiced by KIDOTAI in their tactics and techniques: KIDOTAI members have unexcelled morale and esprit de corps—more so than the personnel of any other governmental agency in Japan, even the National Self-Defense Force.

INTELLIGENCE ACTIVITIES

KIDOTAI does not send plainclothes officers to infiltrate dissident groups in order to learn of their activities and plans.

The Communist Party of Japan and the JSP and JDSP are regular, ongoing political organizations. Information is usually obtainable as to their plans and other internal affairs.

The radical student organizations such as *Zengakuren* make no secret of their plans and future activities, but this is not true as to the hard-core leadership of these groups.

A more difficult intelligence problem is the so-called *Beheiren* (Peaceful Viet Nam Commission). This is a very new and loose-knit organization which includes many ordinary law-abiding citizens. It is sometimes very difficult to obtain hard intelligence on their plans.

MPD says that its intelligence unit has never failed to obtain accurate advance information of the exact date, time and place of any major demonstration or riot.

HANDLING OF CITIZEN COMPLAINTS

On rare occasions a citizen makes a complaint alleging excessive force or other asserted misconduct by a KIDOTAI member. These complaints are of two types: (a) direct complaint to

KIDOTAI Director and (b) complaint to Ministry of Justice (*Hōmusho*) or Public Prosecutor's office.

On one occasion at the disturbance in front of the United States Embassy this spring, a news cameraman complained that he was struck by a KIDOTAI member. After due investigation by the KIDOTAI Director, it was determined that the KIDOTAI had, in fact, struck the cameraman. The member was given a 10 per cent cut in pay for a period of one month.

TRAINING

KIDOTAI training is a daily activity and includes squad, platoon, company and unit drill in various antiriot formations and procedures. Training also includes special maneuvers to counter mock riots staged by other KIDOTAI members. Afternoons are devoted to class instruction and special athletics. Instructors make liberal use of films of actual riots, just as American football coaches use latest game films to spot flaws in team performance. *Kanku* KIDOTAI are trained for four months each in their own regional schools.

Discipline is rigid within KIDOTAI and drills are executed swiftly, precisely and without any milling around or chatter. Teamwork is highly developed, the men realizing that in a riot situation their own safety depends on the smooth functioning of the entire unit.

Great emphasis is placed on top physical fitness, with long periods being spent on the techniques of unarmed hand-to-hand combat. Each KIDOTAI mobile unit has its own *Judo* hall (*Kaikan*) where members work out daily in the defensive techniques of *Judo* (a type of Japanese wrestling). Also used in the physical training program is *Kendo*, another traditional Japanese form of physical combat. In *Kendo*, two participants duel with each other using two-handed swords. Trainees use bamboo swords and are protected with duelist's masks and body protectors. This is excellent training in how to defend against rioters armed with six-foot pike poles or Gevalt sticks.

Every police barracks has its trophy case to display trophies and awards won by unit members in regular *Judo* and *Kendo* competitions with other units.

The KIDOTAI has a detailed officer's manual of some 1,300 pages. It is printed only in Japanese and its dissemination is restricted to official use only. However, I was courteously permitted to view KIDOTAI training and one of the training films used by KIDOTAI. I found the films to be exceptionally well prepared and comparable in quality to our own Army training films.

The film showed squad training with the rock-catcher net. (A squad is comprised of ten men and a squad leader.) The front line of the formation consisted of a row of six officers carrying the large duralumin shields. Immediately in front of the row of shields, which were placed side by side and lengthwise, was a large mobile net about ten feet in height and supported by two poles at either side and carried by two bearers. The purpose of this net, it was explained, is to protect the members of the squad from rocks, Molotov cocktails and other missiles thrown by rioters. The remainder of the squad was positioned in rear of the shields and net in a semi-team drop formation. The squad leader positioned himself directly to the rear of the net carriers and in the middle of the other squad members. The squad members all carried the small personal shield (no longer in use) as well as the regular nightstick.

At a command from the squad leader, the net was raised quickly and the entire squad uttered a Samurai war cry and rushed forward.

(The rock-catcher net, while still used on occasion, is not used as often as formerly. Instead, they have developed a variety of formations in which the body shields are positioned in various ways to repel missiles.)

Second, an operations film showed many of the most violent demonstrations and the tactics and techniques of the police in controlling them.

STATISTICS ON RIOTS

Statistics on riots are king-sized, by American standards. Some major riots and demonstrations have involved over 100,000 participants. In 1968, radical students clashed with police on some 1,500 separate occasions. All in all, KIDOTAI arrested 2,737 rioters between October 1967 and July 1969.

In 1969, 3,000 were arrested in leftist-led student violence. In the April 28, 1969, Ginza riots, some 8,000 rampaging students ripped through Tokyo's finest shopping area, the Ginza, throwing gasoline bombs, smashing windows of department stores and battling riot police. The assigned reason for their conduct was the demand for the early return of Okinawa to Japan.

In the 1970 Anti-Mutual-Security Treaty demonstrations from June 1 to 23, the peak participation in all parts of Japan during this period was 1,347,801 man-days. There was a total of 3,536 separate incidents. The breakdown of participants was as follows: Socialists and trade union members and followers, 647,940; Communist Party members and supporters, 299,030; balance of participants were students and miscellaneous.

In the (October 21) demonstration in support of the Annual International Anti-Day May 4: 1968, 289,000 participants; 1969, 460,000 participants; 1970, 372,400 participants. During the June 27, 1970, demonstrations police arrested 1,798 demonstrators.

PENALTIES IMPOSED

For the most part, sentences imposed upon rioters by the courts have been fairly light. In some instances there has been public criticism of the light sentences imposed. Some citizens feel that students have been given the "kid glove" treatment and that if these same acts had been committed by workers, labor activists or others, they would have been treated with much greater severity. Maximum penalties have been as high as two years' confinement in some cases, but the majority have received no more than one or two months' confinement for their actions. Some critics assert that they have been released after only two or three days' confinement.

CASUALTY FIGURES

All of this violence has taken a heavy toll in police casualties. Between October, 1967, and July, 1968, some 6,000 police were injured in combatting these many disturbances. Yet in the last ten years, only two officers have been killed (in campus sieges), and 228 officers injured seriously enough to lose more than one month's time from duty. This is truly remarkable, considering the size and violence of the countless encounters.

Three students have been killed. According to unofficial reports, one girl student demonstrator was trampled to death by other demonstrators fleeing from street-clearing operations by riot police. A boy student died beneath the wheels of a police vehicle driven by another student who was attempting to steal it. A third student died as a result of burns from a Molotov cocktail thrown by himself or another student.

CAUSES OF RIOTS

Most large riots were reportedly leftist-inspired and were aimed at various political issues. These included, for example, the Prime Minister and his policies, the United States President and his policies, the United States-Japan Mutual Security Treaty, Okinawa, the Vietnam War, military activities in Japan, including both the Japan Self-Defense Force and the United States forces. In this same category were demonstrations against United States military bases and visits by American nuclear aircraft carriers and submarines.

Campus disorders in part reflected the enormous increase in university and college enrollments in Japan. For example, between 1958 and 1969, the number of universities in Japan increased from 234 to 379, and the number of colleges increased from 269 to 473. In terms of student enrollments, in the same period, university students increased from 578,060 to 1,354,927, and college students increased from 71,254 to 263,362. Thus it can be seen that university enrollments increased 2.34 times and college enrollments increased 3.69 times between 1958 and 1969.

Another factor was the effect of the democratization of Japan as a result of Occupation policies. With the Occupation, the old laws prohibiting unlawful assembly, etc., were repealed, and the citizenry was encouraged to achieve widespread participation in political events.

Student disorders appear to have been the result of a variety of asserted grievances, such as overcrowding, increased fees, large classes and the demand by some of the students for control of the administration of the universities and colleges. As has often been the case elsewhere, ultraradical elements exploited these grievances.

The only racial minority in Japan—approximately one half million Koreans—has not figured in any of the civil disorders.

RESEARCH AND DEVELOPMENT

Research and Development has been a constant and vital factor in the evolution of KIDOTAI techniques. The leadership in KIDOTAI has worked diligently to tailor their tactics, techniques and equipment to the needs of the situation. Two principles have been their guides: (a) continuous revision of tactics to achieve flexibility and (b) development of sophisticated techniques and equipment.

For example, they are now working on a community-relations technique. Another example is the development of a new foam generator for use against disorders at military bases. This vehicle will permit the KIDOTAI to employ a protective foam by means of a foam generator projector truck. Another new vehicle is the barricade-removing scoopmobile. Similarly, a mobile shield vehicle has been devised, a mobile multiple radio unit, a searchlight truck and a ladder truck. Of importance also is the designing of a mobile restroom or *benjo* truck, and a mobile kitchen to feed the members who may be required to remain at the scene for a considerable period of time and need to be fed. Other experimental vehicles include the evidence-gathering and identification truck. Recent developments have included the use of dye in water cannon trucks and also using tear gas in the water projected by water cannon.

The NPA staff are of the opinion that their tactics and techniques are adequate to handle all future disturbances and that they have the problem well under control.

Lastly, they feel that the guiding principle of *gaman* is the proper one, and that there is no need to adopt a "get tough" approach to the problem in Japan, as had been the case in the West.

SOME OBSERVATIONS ON KIDOTAI TACTICS

The following is a summary of my interview with a very experienced former KIDOTAI staff officer.

In keeping with the defensive philosophy of KIDOTAI, it is true that the KIDOTAI never strikes the first blow in any encounter. Generally, the KIDOTAI will allow the demonstrators to take the initiative, even at the risk of some injury to its members, before taking any affirmative action. If one were to liken KIDOTAI tactics to boxing, it could be said that KIDOTAI are basically counterpunchers. This is termed the "preventive offensive." Usually, if not invariably, in an encounter the KIDOTAI will allow the demonstrators to take the first offense (*Sen No Sen*). Following this, the KIDOTAI will launch a "preventive offensive" or counter-offensive. This is called *Go No Sen*. The basic reason behind this defensive posture is the familiar rule of *gaman* or restraint. There is always the basic concern of KIDOTAI for avoiding any action that would or could be construed as offensive. They do not wish to offend public opinion. It could be said, then, that the first principle of KIDOTAI tactics is the *preventive offensive*.

The second principle is to separate the spectators from the demonstrators or rioters. Under Japanese law, police authorities have no power to establish a curfew. As a result, the scene is usually clogged with spectators. This is directly opposite to the system in some western countries where a curfew is immediately proclaimed to clear the streets of spectators, e.g. British police curfews during Hong Kong riots. Although KIDOTAI always make an oral request for spectators to clear the area, this is seldom effective; so it is necessary to have a special unit of KIDOTAI take the next step, which is to clear the spectators and separate them from the demonstrators.

A third tactic is the pincers maneuver (*Kyōgeki*). This is

a maneuver familiar to every student of military tactics and consists of driving a wedge or two wedges from opposite sides into the flanks of the attacking group. The single and double envelopment tactic is also used. It can also be considered as a variation of this same maneuver, where one or two units of KIDOTAI will encircle or attack the rear of the rioting forces.

On occasion, the KIDOTAI have used a single weak central force (scarecrow battalion) which is assigned to guard a fixed installation such as the United States Embassy or the Prime Minister's residence as a holding unit, while keeping other units out of sight until called to perform the pincers or enveloping forces. This is sometimes referred to as the *Manaita* or cutting-board tactic. In essence, this means that the defensive or holding unit is acting as the cutting block to receive the brunt of the attack in front of the installation, while the pincers forces, having much greater strength, perform the decisive maneuver against the attacking force. There has been some difficulty in convincing the members of the defensive *manaita* unit that they should be the force assigned to bear the brunt of the vicious attack and even retreat in the face of overwhelming attack by the rioters, and then have the glory go to the pincers or flank attackers (*kyōgeki*) who deliver the *coup de grace*.

An important tactic is the capture as rapidly as possible of the leaders at the point of the attacking force. KIDOTAI has learned through years of experience that the strongest element of a riot group is the front line or point of the group and that the weakest is the rear. From this observation, and after suffering heavy casualties from launching frontal attacks on riot groups, they evolved the technique of the *kyōgeki*.

Tear gas should be used at medium to long ranges and after the stones have been thrown by the attacking group. This is a technique which they learned from the British antiriot police in Hong Kong.

RIOT-PREVENTION EDUCATION

Some time ago KIDOTAI asked the Crime Prevention section of the MPD to study and develop an educational program to try to dissuade students from rioting and committing acts of violence. As a result of these studies, KIDOTAI employs several prevention techniques. Taking advantage of the still-strong sense of family pride in Japan, the police send a personal letter to the parents of each arrested student, advising them of the arrest of their son or daughter and soliciting their cooperation in directing the youth to refrain from acts of violence.

They feel that their policy of treating the students kindly after arrest (offering the prisoners coffee and cigarettes) has been moderately successful. KIDOTAI have received many letters from students indicating that this approach has resulted in reforming some former campus radicals. Students who were causing these problems were mostly from rural prefectures—country boys and girls from fairly well-to-do middle-class families. KIDOTAI members are practically the same age as the students. They have tried to place themselves on the same level as the students in these various educational efforts.

One officer cited the instance of a burned student (both hands so badly burned by a Molotov cocktail that he could not bathe himself) who was given a bath by a fatherly jailer. As a result, the student became transformed almost overnight into a different person. Another example was cited wherein an understanding police matron had provided a young girl student radical with badly needed personal necessities, and had otherwise befriended her, again with good results.

In conclusion, the conviction was expressed that riot problems could not and would not be solved by police action alone. "The basic problem is one for the parents and professional educators to devise new ways of reaching and redirecting these few students who are involved in these violent demonstrations," the officer concluded.

Time did not permit an investigation and analysis of the student revolutionary movement. However, it may be noted here that this movement appears to be more leftist, much older and much better organized tactically than in the United States. Since July 1968, the leftist students have split up into at least five different factions and begun staging fierce and savage conflicts with each other in quest of sole leadership of the left wing movement. Their internal discipline is complete and they go to demonstrations in disciplined columns four abreast, like an army.

CONCLUSIONS AND RECOMMENDATIONS

Dr. S.I. Hayakawa, the famed President of San Francisco State College, who himself knows something about control of campus disorders, said recently on his return from a visit to Japan: "Japanese police are better trained for dealing with students than American police. They have simply had more experience."

It is the conclusion of this writer that the tactics, techniques, vehicles and equipment developed by Japan's antiriot police, and their handling of some of the largest and most violent civil disturbances anywhere in the world with remarkably low casualties, all without firearms, justify rating the KIDOTAI as among the most skillful anywhere.

I strongly recommend that the Law Enforcement Assistance Administration give consideration to taking the necessary steps to obtain permission from the government of Japan to enable interested police departments of every major city in our country, in due course, to send one of their best qualified antiriot officers to Japan on a federal training grant to study Japanese methods of controlling civil disturbances. It is my further recommendation that the grant should be sufficient to permit the officers selected to live with a tactical unit in the police barracks for at least three weeks and that the officers should participate in every aspect of KIDOTAI training and operations, except actual riot or police duty. At the latter, he should be present to observe at first hand the operating techniques of the Japanese antiriot police.

In order that the grantee can fully benefit from his training opportunity, the grant should be sufficient to provide the officer with a compulsory crash course in basic Japanese before he leaves the United States.

During this study I found that police from many parts of the world (except the United States) have come to Japan at the invitation of their government to study their police techniques. I think that it would be eminently desirable that we take advantage of their enormous experience and learn the highly sophisticated techniques and equipment they have so painstakingly developed during nearly 20 years of ·trial and error in dealing with some of the largest and most violent riots anywhere in the world. I view this as a must if we are to cope with this complicated, prickly and difficult social phenomenon which emerged in the 1960's and is continuing into the 1970's.

PART VI

AN INTRODUCTION TO THE POLICE-COMMUNITY RELATIONS CONCEPT

INTRODUCTION

The idea of formalized police-community relations programs is less than two decades old. But during the last ten years, especially in the post-1967 period, the concept has been almost universally adopted and implemented in various forms and degrees by the American police. This section offers an overview of the idea of formal P-CR from basically the same philosophical perspective.

"Police-Community Relations," by William Bopp and Donald Schultz, contains a brief introduction to the concept. "Typology," by Lee P. Brown, identifies and discusses the four general types of P-CR programs: (a) externally oriented, (b) youth oriented, (c) service oriented, and (d) internally oriented.

"Programming for Citizen Participation in Police-Action Programs" by Clement S. Mihanovich answers the questions "Whom do you wish to reach?" and "What do you wish to accomplish?" with your program. A discussion of operational techniques and procedures utilized to bring about citizen participation is also covered.

In "Community Relations," Harold Barney addresses himself to the three P-CR areas of "image," "attitudes" and "information," while Piet J. Van der Walt's "Police and Public" concentrates on the factors which determine and influence the attitude of the public toward the police.

Edgar Davis fears that too many human relations programs are directionless and in "A Method of Approach to the Tasks of a Human Relations Officer" presents a discourse on "how to" in that specialized field.

In Chapter 40, Donald Wrightington discusses "Public Relations for a Small Department" while in the last reading William Bopp chronicles a number of "Obstacles to Good Police-Community Relations."

Chapter 34

POLICE-COMMUNITY RELATIONS

WILLIAM J. BOPP and DONALD O. SCHULTZ

When in 1957 the St. Louis Police Department operationalized the nation's first formal community-relations division, there was evidence that most policemen, especially rank-and-file officers, viewed the concept as a frivolous nonessential undertaking at best, and at worst a dangerous experimentation during a period of critical manpower shortages. Over the years, however, this rather myopic view has changed and prevailing police opinion on the subject, pointed up by a recent survey conducted by the International Association of Chiefs of Police, now accepts the need for better police-community relationships and the formation of specialized police components to work toward that end. There is also evidence to indicate that many citizens also view the idea in a positive way, although similar opinion surveys show that a great deal of distrust and hostility still exists regarding the police, especially in minority communities.

Although police-community relations programs are aimed at the *entire* community, certain problems are unique to culturally deprived areas—i.e. language barriers, high unemployment, inaccessibility to government, escalating crime rates—and special attention must be given to them. Furthermore, racial rioting has motivated many police administrators to implement extraordinary programs. Not all of these programs have been successful, but what is important is that there now exists in law enforcement a genuine desire to improve relations between the police and the citizenry they have sworn to serve.

NOTE: From Bopp, William and Schultz, Donald: *Principles of American Law Enforcement and Criminal Justice.* Springfield, Thomas, 1972.

A SYSTEMS APPROACH TO COMMUNITY RELATIONS

Police departments that seek to promote respect for police goals and to improve their "image" will not be successful unless a systems approach is employed. Taking into consideration the nature of American social conditions, it is not unfair to state that most communities are not homogeneous groupings of likeminded persons but areas in which divergent racial, ethnic and social classes live, work and recreate. Therefore, a multifaceted approach to the issue is necessary. This is not to say that a police department should not emphasize a particular problem area but not to the exclusion of the rest of the community. It will not be sufficient to simply make officers available for speaking engagements, for this will create gaps in the overall program. Many individuals do not belong to civic associations and they will not be reached by policemen who only respond to requests to address these limited audiences. The Philadelphia Police Department has found that the formula, communication + courtesy + concern = good community relations is a workable one, but it must be applied to all the diverse *publics* in a community in order to be successful.

TYPES OF COMMUNITY-RELATIONS PROGRAMS

The International City Management Association (ICMA) has identified five broad types of police-community relations programs. The five are as follows:

1. *Educational programs* which are "issue related" in design and which have as their aim the bringing of community leaders together to discuss mutual problems and concerns.
2. *Police institutes on community relations* in which participants are brought together in a controlled environment to discuss selected issues. Guest speakers and consultants, experts in their field, are brought in to address the assemblage.
3. *Police training* which is a formulated course of study offered to both preservice and in-service officers as either specialized study in community relations or as an addition to a more comprehensive curriculum.

4. *Metropolitan police-community relations programs,* which are decentralized programs found in precincts or neighborhood city halls. A favorite device is the formation of police advisory committees made up of officers and citizens working together. A newer technique is the "community-relations trailer," a specially equipped house trailer which is towed to various neighborhoods and schools.
5. *Special theme programs,* which are essentially programs aimed at a specific area of interest—youth, blacks, Mexican-Americans, press relations. These types of programs are generally employed to lessen crisis situations, such as those that exist immediately following a massive civil disturbance.

OBSTACLES TO GOOD COMMUNITY RELATIONS

Law enforcement faces an uphill fight in its attempt to build a meaningful relationship with the community. Creating a favorable public attitude toward the police task is no easy undertaking, especially in light of the fact that many police-citizen contacts are punitive in nature. Harold Barney of the International Association of Chiefs of Police surveyed the field and found seven factors that consistently impede the development of community relations programs: (a) the traditional fear of the law and its agents, which is quite real and must be recognized; (b) errors in judgment on the part of individual officers, a problem that will continue to occur; (c) unpopular police actions in the form of enforcement of unpopular laws and ordinances; (d) refusing special privileges to people who fill important posts; (e) attacks in the press by columnists sympathetic with those who employ confrontationist tactics; (f) political pressure; and (g) the necessity of overcoming an unsavory police reputation. Add to Barney's factors an additional element, contemporary police labor militancy, and it becomes immediately apparent that police administrators have their hands full in fighting the problem of police isolation.

Chapter 35

TYPOLOGY

LEE P. BROWN

Since 1957, when the St. Louis Metropolitan Police Department established the nation's first formal police-community–relations division, almost every major city has initiated some form of police-community relations program. It is the purpose of this paper to establish a typology of police departments based upon their community-relations orientation.

A police department may orient its specialized comunity-relations program in one of four general approaches. Each approach represents the development of a group of programs which the department feels will better the relationship between the agency and the public. The distinction made here is an analytical one. Although four departments will be identified as being illustrative of the four types, probably no department is governed exclusively by the orientation described. In other words, one department may have, in addition to its primary orientation, characteristics of one or all of the other three types. It is important for the reader to understand that the typology only identifies an operating style of an agency and only suggests certain characteristics in an abstract form. The four types identified here are (a) externally oriented, (b) youth oriented, (c) service oriented, and (d) internally oriented.[1]

EXTERNALLY ORIENTED

Some police departments, in developing their community-relations program, have placed a heavy emphasis on implement-

NOTE: From *The Police Chief*, March, 1971, pp. 16–21. Reprinted with permission.

[1] Crime prevention programs are not listed as a specific type because each department considers crime prevention as an essential part of their police-community relations program.

ing a wide variety of programs which are operated under the title of police-community relations. Such programs are generally developed by a specialized police-community relations unit and are directed towards the general public or various enclaves within the community. This approach is called externally oriented.

The St. Louis Metropolitan Police Department is an example of an externally oriented department. St. Louis has a total population of about 720,000 people, 39 per cent of whom are black. Similar to all other large cities, St. Louis has large poverty areas which are characterized by tensions, frustrations and resentment toward police who apparently represent a tangible symbol against which poverty citizens can strike to relieve these frustrations. Also, in poverty areas, there is a high rate of crime considerably above the population proportion.[2]

The St. Louis Police Department has developed numerous programs which have served as prototypes for other cities. The basic objectives underlying the present St. Louis police-community relations program are to reduce and prevent crime in St. Louis through joint police-community cooperation and to improve intergroup relations in the community.[3]

To accomplish these objectives, the St. Louis Police Department has developed the following programs:[4]

Police-Community Relations Youth Council
Headstart Program
School Visitation Program
Say Hi Program
Youth Activities Program
Prenatal Program
Special Youth Program

---

[2] Police-Community Relations Planning and Development Program, a proposal for funding submitted by the St. Louis Police Department to the U.S. Department of Justice, Office of Law Enforcement Assistance, September 26, 1966, p. 5.

[3] "Police-Community Relations in St. Louis: Experience Report 103," a pamphlet prepared by the National Conference of Christians and Jews, January, 1966, p. 3.

[4] These are the titles of programs as listed by the St. Louis Police Department. A detailed description of each program may be obtained from that Department. Some programs listed here have been initiated and subsequently dropped.

Explorer Post Program
Police-Junior Aide Program
Cruiser Tours
Jaycee Award Program
Law Enforcement Assistant Award
Police-Community Relations Award
Police-Community Relations Training
Sergeants In-Service
Police-Community Relations Council
Tour Program
State Fair
Citizens Against Crime
Police-Community Relations Information Program
Clergy-Police Program
Brochures
Police-Community Relations Film
Visiting Officers Program
Police-Community Relations Store Front Centers
District Committees
Communications Program
St. Louis Council of Police-Community Relations
Mass Media Relations
Speaker's Bureau
Lock-Your-Car Campaign
Convention Letters
Businessmen's Meetings
Police-Community Relations Newsletter
Law Enforcement Day
Sanitation Project
Protection Project
Whom-to-Call Program
Police-Community Relations Committees on Housing Project
Block Watcher Program
Neighborhood Helper Program
Operation Little Sweep
Community Athletic League

As illustrated by the above list, the essential characteristic of an externally oriented department is its willingness to try various approaches to accomplish its goal. The structure of an etxernally oriented department is flexible and accommodates changes and experimentation in devising programs designed to achieve its goal. The variety of programs are, in general, operated external to the police department.

YOUTH ORIENTED

A youth-oriented department is characterized by police departments that direct the majority of their efforts toward the youth of the community. Here, reference is made to the efforts of the community-relations section and not the total police departments that direct tre majority of their efforts toward the munity relations unit are aimed primarily at the youth and the majority of the community-relations officers' time is spent working with youth.

The New Orleans Police Department is an example of a youth-oriented department. The City of New Orleans has a population of about 660,000, with 40 per cent of the number being black. "With ten federal housing projects, as well as other low income areas scattered throughout the city . . . policing presents certain problems."[5]

The Police-Community Relations Program in New Orleans was established in April, 1966. One of the major objectives of the program is: ". . . attempt to reach the youth of the community; where else would we start?"[6] With this objective in mind, the New Orleans Police Department has developed the following programs:[7]

Meetings	"Know Your Police Department"
Career Days	TV Series
Coloring Books	Air Flights
Saints Pro-Football Games	Employment Centers
Headquarters Tours	Summer Recreation
Special Sporting Events	Talent Contests
Movie Program	Send A Kid To Camp
Christmas Baskets	Officer Friendly Program
Self-Defense Program	Citizen Participation
Portable Swimming Pools	Special Programs
Swimming Program	Seminars
Police Buses	New Careers
Sprinkers	Additional Training
Amusement Park Program	Security Detail
Boxing	Investigations
Basketball Teams	

[5] New Orleans, Louisiana Police Community Relations Division, mimeo, no date, p. 3.
[6] *Ibid.*, p. 2.
[7] For a detailed description of these programs, *see* Cates, Sidney H. III: This Is

Out of the above list of 30 programs, 19 are designed primarily for youth. This illustrates the essential characteristics of a youth-oriented program: the primary emphasis is directed toward the youth of the community.

SERVICE ORIENTED

Some police departments, in developing their community-relations programs, have emphasized the alleviation of social problems as their basic objective. In such cases, the defining characteristic of the departments' community relations objective becomes the orientation of their specialized program. This type is called service oriented, using a term which describes what really should be the mission of the American Police System.

Illustrative of a service oriented department is the Winston-Salem Police Department. ". . . with a population of 143,000 . . . [Winston-Salem] has in miniature the big city problems of slums, crime and unemployment. In many ways a remarkable city—beautiful, historic, cultural, wealthy compared with some other places in the South—it has felt the mark of poverty; 15 per cent of the whites and 45 per cent of the non-whites fall below the official boundaries of deprivation."[8]

In 1966, the Winston-Salem Police Department established a Community Services Unit. The purpose of this Unit is threefold:[9]

1. To find people in need.
2. To direct them to those agencies or community resources where the need can be met.
3. To search out those things which are conducive to crime and see that they are rooted out of the community.

"The Police Community Service Unit is a service organization dedicated to the cause of helping citizens who, for many rea-

---

Our Story. A mimeographed publication of the New Orleans Police Department's Commun ty Relations Division.

[8] A New Approach to Crime Prevention and Community Service. Winston-Salem, North Carolina Police Department, mimeo, no date, p. 1.

[9] Background—Police Community Service Unit. Winston-Salem, North Carolina Police Department, mimeo, no date, no page.

sons, cannot, or lack the knowledge to, help themselves. In the day-to-day operations of the unit, its members act as "transmission belts" whereby those who have a particular problem are referred to an existing agency which is in a position to render the needed service."[10]

The above objectives have been carried out in the following ways:[11]

1. Upon discovering a specific case, or even in cases of apprehension, the first step for each officer is to ask the basic question, "Why?"
2. It will next be the duty of the police community services unit officers to investigate underlying causes and to assess all community resources available for said person and family, and to offer all possible means of protective service and aid, in order to give the citizen a new approach to his problems and a new outlook on life.
3. By working through the Experiment in Self Reliance, Inc., neighborhood service centers, and by becoming familiar with the entire area on a professional and friendly basis, the officers assigned to this unit have become closely related to and familiar with most of the neighborhood.
4. In many instances, this procedure has helped to prevent early criminal records for young offenders, and to give such young offenders a chance to solve their problems without going through court formalities.
5. One of the greatest services of the Community Services Unit is the giving to the community of a new image of the function of police regarding law and order, and instilling of new ideas in young people as regards to their respect for law and order.
6. Systematic case follow-up has been initiated to insure the effectiveness of the service rendered.

The essential characteristics of a service-oriented program is its concern and involvement in the socioeconomic problems of the community. Such a unit acts as a discovery and referral

[10] *Ibid.*
[11] *Ibid.*

agency for ridding the community of varied problems. Such a program, although primarily concerned with socioeconomic problems, also concerns itself with other activities. For example, the Winston-Salem Police Department is concerned with public relations, which is evident by its use of a Newsletter. It is concerned with crime prevention, which is evident in this statement:

"In view of our past experience, we must look for other means of preventing crime and decreasing the rate of recidivism. We must delve deeply into the 'Why' of crime."[12]

It is concerned with youth, which is evident by the fact that its Community Service officers follow up on all cases involving juveniles. They are concerned with community relations training, which is evident by the extensive training program they have developed.[13] Their primary focus, however, is on service.

INTERNALLY ORIENTED

Some police departments have not established a specialized community-relations unit but are still very community-relations–minded. Such departments operate on the premise that every officer is a police-community relations officer and attempt to involve all members of the agency in promoting good community relations. This type is called *internally oriented*. The essential characteristic of an internally oriented program is the realization that the officer on the beat creates community relations, be it good or bad.

The Covina, California, Police Department is an example of an internally oriented department. With a population of 30,000 people, Covina has only a small number of black families. Police-community relations for the Covina Police Department is designed to involve the total police department. It does not have a specialized police-community–relations unit, and if one is ever

---

[12] A Proposal for the Second Year Funding of the Community Services Unit. Winston-Salem Police Department, no date, p. 2.

[13] See for example, Curriculum for Police Community Service Unit Personnel. Conducted at Winston-Salem Police Training Academy, by The Institute of Government of The University of North Carolina, mimeo, no date.

created, "it will only serve in a staff capacity."[14] The philosophy of an internally oriented community relations program is articulated by Chief Fred Ferguson:

> We believe in Covina that it is possible to do a good job with fewer people if they are the right people with proper values, skills and equipment. Some communities facing the same type of problems have used another approach. They have trained several employees as experts in community relations. These few in turn meet with the various community groups and attempt to acquaint them with law enforcement problems and hopefully gain their support. In a community such as ours, it seems more logical to have all our personnel understand the people with whom they deal.[15]

In pursuing this philosophy, Chief Ferguson has implemented some novel programs within the Covina Police Department.

1. All of the police officers (including the chief) are attending college or are involved in some other continuing educational program. This endeavor is supported by both the police department and city government. The department supports it by rotating the work shifts around the school schedules and the city supports it by paying for the members' tuition and books.[16]
2. Chief Ferguson has initiated a program whereby a citizen who registers a complaint against the police department is invited to ride for one evening in a patrol car with officers to see the problems of those concerned with law enforcement.[17]
3. Members of the department underwent an extensive police-community relations training program designed ". . . to equip selected uniformed and non-uniformed members of the Covina Police Department with greater knowledge and skill essential to better understanding and dealing more effectively with members of the Covina Community and their own department.[18]

[14] Interview with Chief Ferguson.
[15] Price, Kendall O. and Lloyd, Kent: *Improving Police-Community Relations Through Leadership Training.* Inglewood, California, Creative Management Research and Development, 1967, p. 28.
[16] Interview with Chief Fred Ferguson.
[17] *Supra,* Note 15.
[18] *Ibid.,* p. 7.

The specific objectives of this police-community relations training program were the following:

   a. To obtain knowledge about the traditional Judaic-Christian Democratic view of man generally held in the United States and the application of the view to police-community relations.
   b. To acquire skills in interpersonal and intergroup relations.
   c. To gain information from the behavioral sources about the human individual, interpersonal and group relationships, complex organizations and the community as an environment.[19]
4. The department developed and implemented a program called Operation Empathy. This program is designed to give police officers a realistic, though brief, view of the world in which many of their "clientele" live. This is accomplished by "booking" Covina police officers into jail in a neighboring community for an evening.
5. The department operates a program entitled Coffee Klatch.
6. The department has implemented a program entitled Operation Empathy—Skid Row. Under this program, Covina police officers spend time in Los Angeles' skid row. Chief Ferguson explains this program:

> Our Covina officers, who were willing to become skid row inhabitants, were carefully selected and conditioned for the role they were about to play. Each man was given three dollars with which to purchase a complete outfit of pawn shop clothing. The only new articles of attire he was allowed was footwear—reject tennis shoes purchased for a few small coins. Among his other props were such items as a shopping bag filled with collected junk, and a wine bottle camouflaged by a brown paper sack.
>
> Conditioned and ready, our men, assigned in pairs, moved into the Los Angeles skid row district. They soon discovered that when they tried to leave the area, walking a few blocks into the legitimate retail sections, they were told, "Go back where you belong!" Our men knew in reality they were not "bums," but they found that other citizens quickly categorized them and treated them accordingly. Some women, when approached on the sidewalk and asked

[19] *Ibid.*, p. 8.

for a match, stepped out into the street rather than offer a reply, much less a light for a smoke.

During the skid row experiment, our men ate in the rescue missions and sat through the prayer services with other outcasts and derelicts. They roamed the streets and alleys, and discovered many leveling experiences. Some were anticipated, others were not.[20]

7. The Covina Police Department has proposed a new program, entitled Exploring Criminal Justice As a Total System. This program will be operated as follows:

The thrust of our proposal is to select two Captain rank police personnel and rotate them in a work experience training program with five different parts of the System which includes the District Attorney's Office, the Court, Corrections, Probation-Parole, and Mental Health-Welfare. While Mental Health and Welfare are not traditionally thought of as part of the system, current legislative trends would indicate that we should begin to consider them as such. For example, there is a desire on the part of some legislators to remove certain social problems, such as alcoholism and homosexual activities between consenting adults, from the criminal statutes. Obviously, some other referral will take place. Wherever possible, we hope to receive an exchange person from these agencies. The two Captains will alternate one month of work with the training agency and one month to relate back to the Police Department. Desirably, the exchange counterpart from the various agencies will move into a staff position during his month with us. His influence will undoubtedly have a positive impact which will be reinforced as each Captain returns. Relatively, the same impact is expected on the parent agency.[21]

A final example of Covina's police-community relations efforts can be seen in the appointment of a college professor as acting chief during Chief Ferguson's absence from the city. Under this experiment, Dr. Paul Whisenand, Associate Professor, Department of Criminology, California State College at Long Beach (a former Los Angeles police officer) served as chief of police for one month during Chief Ferguson's absence.[22]

The development of a program to improve every member of

[20] *Ibid.*, p. 22–28.
[21] Exploring Criminal Justice As a Total System. An Application for Grant for Law Enforcement Purposes, submitted to the State of California Council on Criminal Justice, April 29, 1969.
[22] Interview with Chief Fred Ferguson.

a police department thereby involving all officers in police-community relations is the essential characteristic of an internally oriented department. Such departments are willing to experiment and readily accept citizen input into changing or modifying the department's policies and procedures.

In conclusion, it appears that even though many police departments operate some form of police-community relations program, there exists a wide variation of opinion as to what orientation such programs should take. The paramount factor in determining where the allocation of police-community relations resources should be directed is the individual personalities involved in such programs.

Chapter 36

PROGRAMMING FOR CITIZEN PARTICIPATION IN POLICE ACTION PROGRAMS

CLEMENT S. MIHANOVICH

Whom do you wish to reach? What do you wish to accomplish? These are the first two questions you must ask yourself before you initiate any program to involve citizen participation in police action programs. After you have answered these two extremely difficult questions you must ask yourself another question: What techniques, procedures must I utilize in order to bring to fruition the citizens' participation in police action programs?

WHOM DO YOU WISH TO REACH?

Obviously, the ideal is to reach all. Obviously, this is not possible in most instances.

Whom, then, should you reach? The answer to this question depends on the characteristics of your population and the ecology of your community as well as upon the needs of your police department, needs that might change from time to time, depending upon circumstances and the vicissitudes of human events.

Despite the immediate needs produced by a particular crisis, you must always plan to reach as many as possible and to involve as many as possible in your program. Enumerated below are those individuals and groups who should be reached to achieve the best possible coverage:

NOTE: From *Police and the Changing Community*. Washington, International Association of Chiefs of Police, 1965, pp. 113-117. Reprinted with permission.

In general terms, you should reach the elementary school child, the high school and college student, the mother in the home, the church, the civic organizations, the neighborhood organizations, the social agencies, the minority groups and their special organizations, the businessman, and the senior citizen.

In terms of need, you should reach the potential delinquent, the actual delinquent, the dropout, the unemployed youth, the frightened housewife, the disturbed member of the minority group, the person with a grievance, the indifferent citizen, the chronic critic, the frustrated and bedeviled businessman, the problem-laden school principal, the worried minister or clergyman, the nervous senior citizen, the troublemaker, the ostrich with his head in the proverbial sands, the touchy propertyowner, the indignant prominent citizen, the police-baiter, the sarcastic youngster, the harassed social worker, the idealistically-motivated citizen, the young adult in an occupational twilight zone, the blasé inhabitant of the jungles of our slums, the comfortable middle-classer, and the citizen with his head in the clouds of self-righteousness.

In terms of immediate and lasting effectiveness, you should reach the natural leader of the neighborhood. He may be the postman, the tavern owner, the delicatessen operator or the small businessman. He or she is not too difficult to find if you know your neighborhood. They are not necessarily the educated or the professional but they are the ones that are in possession of a dynamic and magnetic personality who naturally exude confidence, trust and those elusive qualities of leadership. It is basically these upon whom you must build your foundation, for without them you are lost and your program will vanish into complete ineffectiveness.

WHAT DO YOU WISH TO ACCOMPLISH?

What are your general goals? What are your immediate and specific goals? These you must spell out according to your own individual needs and immediacy of the problems you face. However, it is obvious that any police-community–relations program must and does have a universally accepted set of general goals. They may be broad, overlapping and repetitive and at first glance they may appear to be utopian in scope and idealistic in purpose as well as all-encompassing. Your general goals and objectives may be similar to ours here in St. Louis, briefly stated as follows:

Maintain law and order;
1. Preserve peace.
2. Achieve highest cooperation with all citizens.
3. Establish friendly relations with the community through the neighborhood.
4. Reduce and/or eliminate crime, disorder and intergroup tensions.
5. Safeguard the accepted values and norms of the community.
6. Maintain open channels of communications.
7. Plan and implement programs to acquaint individual citizens with their responsibilities in the maintenance and preservation of law and order.
8. Plan and carry out programs to acquaint the general public with the growing professionalization of the police force.
9. Support the continued professionalization of the police department.
10. Secure increased and greater public cooperation with the police by educating citizens in the preservation and maintenance of law and order.
11. Promote increased cooperation between the police and other community agencies.
12. Assist in crime prevention.
13. Develop neighborhood consciousness and neighborhood responsibility.
14. Work toward the reduction of the crime rate.
15. Support the highest police standards and the highest police efficiency.
16. Conduct a continuing survey of community needs which affect enforcement of the law and maintenance of peace in the community.
17. Publicize these needs as they are discovered and trans-

mit them to the duly authorized person or agency for appropriate action.
18. Serve and act as liaison between representatives of the police department and the neighborhood.
19. Consult regularly on common problems of law enforcement and public safety with the police department, district commander, district police personnel, and the community.
20. Carry out, in cooperation with other existing organizations or agencies in the neighborhood, education programs designed to acquaint citizens in the neighborhood with the operation of their police department, and with individual citizens' responsibilities in the maintenance of law and order.
21. Promote sanitary and decent conditions in the neighborhood.
22. Study traffic controls for the safety of community residents.

These are our general goals and objectives. You will notice they are broad and, in some instances, repetitive and overlapping. This was done deliberately to give us the widest possible elbow-room.

However, these general goals and objectives can and should be refined into specifics, and spelled out in more detail. Some of the immediate and specific goals may well be any or all of the following:

Receive, process and answer citizen complaints concerning the police.

Review the crime situation in the neighborhood with the commanding officer.

    a. Support police in crime prevention.
    b. Assist in maintenance of law and order.
    c. Make the neighborhood crime-conscious.
    d. Make the neighborhood police-conscious.
    e. Support high police standards.
    f. Report and keep watch on crime breeding areas in the neighborhood.
    g. Inform citizens on all aspects of crime prevention.

Receive and process complaints of illegal and dangerous juvenile activities in the neighborhood and report on delinquency-prone activities and areas, such as:

    a. Pool rooms.
    b. Loitering.
    c. Corner gatherings.
    d. Liquor consumption.
    e. Sale of liquor to minors.
    f. Violation of curfew law.
    g. Truancy.
    h. Adults contributing to delinquency of children.

Auto theft prevention.

Report on traffic problems and violations, such as:

    a. Areas of high traffic violations.
    b. Abandoned autos.
    c. Illegally parked trucks and autos.
    d. Illegal use of restricted streets.
    e. Drag racing.
    f. Inoperative traffic lights.
    g. Damaged traffic signs.
    h. Unrepaired streets and alleys.

Unsanitary conditions.

    a. Littered streets and alleys.
    b. Uncovered rubbish or garbage containers.
    c. Defective sewers.
    d. Rat-infested areas, etc.

You may note that our specific goals are circumscribed within the boundaries of the smallest and most natural unit of the community—the neighborhood.

Another specific objective may be to inform the citizens of the powers and limitation of powers of the police; in other words, what the police can and may do and what they cannot or may not do.

These constitute only a small number of the specifics. A casual review of even this limited enumeration of specifics will reveal the ramifications, implications, and the potential involvement of citizens and how valuable their work can be to the police and, in turn, how much more effective the work of the police will be to the citizens.

Finally, these ramified ties, if properly maintained and adequately and continuously nurtured, will bind the police and the citizen into an ever-tighter bond of cooperation and mutual assistance.

WHAT TECHNIQUES?
WHAT PROCEDURES?

Once you have made your initial contacts in the neighborhood and you have selected the nucleus of your citizens' groups, you must continuously provide them with action-oriented programs that will involve them in the fulfillment of your general objectives and/or specifics. This action-oriented program must be so diverse as to include all of the members of the group. To form a group and then to permit it to remain idle is to destroy the group. Each member must have a clearly defined function that will occupy him continuously but not to the extent that it becomes onerous. It is therefore suggested that your groups be organized on a neighborhood basis, structured in a hierarchy supervised by you and by the chairman of your group. The key to the successful operation of any group is the involvement of the group in a series of clearly defined objectives most of which are achievable and therefore a source of gratification to the group.

Permit me now to give you some very concrete procedures, techniques and programs which may be utilized to realize the goals and purposes of the Police-Community Relations function in involving citizens.

First, it will be your duty to set up an action-program for them. Second, it will be your responsibility to thoroughly indoctrinate them in this program prior to its initiation. Third, it will be your responsibility to see to it that the task of carrying out the program is meted out in such a way as to spread the work more or less evenly among the members. Fourth, it will be your responsibility to see to it that you have a strong chairman who will carry out each phase of your program. Finally, it will be your responsibility to provide members with all the clerical help needed to carry out their work. Furthermore, you will have to be on their necks to see to it that everything functions smoothly and effectively.

Let me illustrate for you the structure of our committees which may help to clarify what I have just stated.

1. We have a police-community relations committee in each of our police districts with a membership of close to 3,000.
2. Each of these committees in each police district contains a number of sub-committees, eight in number.
3. Each of the sub-committees is headed by a chairman and five or more members.
4. Each subcommittee is assigned a clear set of ongoing functions that remain as a perpetual goal of the subcommittee. Thus we have:
    a. The Juvenile Committee to receive and process citizen complaints regarding juveniles.
    b. The Public Relations Committee to receive and process all complaints regarding the police and to publicize the activities of the District Committee.
    c. The Crime Committee to review with the District Commander the general and specific crime situation in the District and assist in crime prevention.
    d. The Auto Theft Committee to cooperate with the police in the prevention of auto thefts.
    e. The Traffic Committee to receive and process citizen complaints regarding traffic problems.
    f. The Sanitation Committee to receive and process citizens' complaints of unsanitary conditions.
    g. The Membership Committee to maintain and increase adequate membership in the group.
    h. The Program Committee to plan all programs for the District Committee meetings.

The chairman of each of these subcommittees is a member

of the Executive Committee. Each District Committee has a Chairman, Vice-Chairman, Treasurer, and Secretary. The officers and the Executive Committee constitute the guiding body in each police district.

The District Committees do not formulate policy. The policy is formulated by an independent body of prominent private citizens. This body is called the St. Louis Council on Police-Community Relations. Thus, although the Police Department of the City of St. Louis provides all the manpower, clerical and other help to erect and maintain the District Committees, the Police Department in the person of Mr. James Allman, the director of the Office of Police-Community Relations, is only one cooperative arm in the policy-making body. In other words, the St. Louis Council of Police-Community Relations is not a stooge or a tool of the St. Louis Police Department but in a very true sense of the word a citizens' group.

In order to coordinate the activities of each of the subcommittees on a city-wide basis, we have selected an executive secretary for each of the subcommittees. In other words, for example, we would have nine Juvenile Committees, one in each district, and these nine committees would meet periodically under the guidance of an Executive Secretary who is also a Chairman of the Juvenile Committee in his District. At these meetings they discuss their mutual needs and problems, and exchange information on a city-wide basis.

This, in outline, is the basic or fundamental structuring of our District Committees.

In addition to the ongoing functions of each of these subcommittees, each District is permitted to select a special project it feels fulfills a serious and immediate need in the District. Upon all of this, we superimpose an annual action-oriented program, which is parcelled out to the subcommittees. This action-oriented program, which differs from year to year, requires at least three months of planning, and it is done during the early summer months so that it is ready for operation in each district about September 1st.

You may recall that I have stated that all levels of the population must be reached in any program initiated by a Police-

Community Relations Office. This cannot be achieved except by a series of special programs carried on simultaneously in each District, area or neighborhood. A good illustration may be our current set of action-oriented projects.

Currently, each of our eight subcommittees in each District is assigned a specific clear-cut project, in addition to carrying out its stabilized or traditional functions which I have previously described.

The Juvenile Committee has been assigned what we call project "Operation Police Cruiser." Three high school students are selected once a month from each of the nine police districts and are taken on a night tour of the city in an unmarked police car in the company of a veteran, experienced officer. In addition, four times within the year we take a number of college students on the same tour. Here we involve the young adolescent and the young adult in the depths of police work.

The Membership Committee has been assigned the project of processing 40,000 to 50,000 elementary school children from the fourth to eighth grades in a specially designed program of touring the police headquarters.

The Public Relations Committee has the task of establishing a Law Enforcement Day in its District. This is designed to be an open house day in each District where the citizens can meet their local officers, study various crime-fighting equipment and discuss their mutual problems.

The Traffic Committee has been assigned an unusual project this year. I would like to present this project in detail, since it is unique in its approach and emphasis. Called "Social Science Project: Community Participation," this is open to and limited to juniors and seniors in the social science classes in all the high schools located within the city. It must be carried out by a team of not more than ten and not less than five juniors and/or seniors. Each high school may enter as many teams as it wishes, and there is no limit on the number of entries.

Each team, under supervision of a social science teacher, will select a program or a project which they will conduct in the community. The project can be in rehabilitation, neighborhood organization, social service or assistance to existing agencies. These are suggested examples:

1. Volunteering as workers in a settlement house, YMCA, YWCA, parish, church, etc.
2. Operating a week-end recreational program for elementary school children in the area.
3. Conducting a neighborhood clean-up project of some duration with a critical evaluation of the result.
4. Assisting the aged in the neighborhood or in a home for the aged.
5. Acting as big brothers or big sisters to a group of underprivileged children.
6. Assisting the juvenile officer in the Police District in a delinquency-prevention program under his supervision.
7. Conducting and supervising a teen-town in the neighborhood.
8. Planning and conducting a series of activities in the high school which would make students aware of the cost and consequences of crime.
9. Planning a uniquely special Thanksgiving and Christmas project to aid the needy in the neighborhood.

The projects are not limited to the above; a team may select any project in any area which involves them in any aspect of community or neighborhood work, reform, rehabilitation, assistance and participation. Community activity on a sustained, controlled basis and a report and evaluation of the project on a continuing basis is required. Each project must be in operation not less than three months. Each team selects a captain and a reporter or recorder who will keep a log of the program—when the project started, description of the activity, hours devoted to the activity, number of persons involved, and an evaluation of the success, problems, etc., encountered in carrying out the project. This project must be submitted to the Chairman of the Traffic Committee not later than April 1, 1965, and must contain or be accompanied by a written approval of the report by the social science teacher, giving the name of the school, the teacher supervisor, the class, title and location of the project, names, addresses and telephone numbers of every team member, name of the team captain, name of student writing the report, and name of the recorder.

These reports will be evaluated by a special panel of judges. In each District, three teams will be selected as winners. Each team will receive an award which will be presented to the school in the name of the winning teams. The three winning teams in each district will then compete for the city-wide awards. A panel of judges will then select the three best reports from all nine police districts. Every member of the winning team, including the teacher, winning the first prize will be given an all-expense-paid trip to East Lansing, Michigan, to attend the one-week Eleventh National Institute on Police and Community Relations at Michigan State University in May, 1965. The team winning the second city-wide prize will be asked to select three of its members (in addition to the teacher) who will also be sent on an all-expense-paid trip to East Lansing. The team winning the third city-wide prize will be asked to select two of its members (in addition to the teacher) who will be sent on the trip.

Entries will be judged on effectiveness, depth of involvement of the team, completeness of report, originality of the project, practicality of the project and contribution to the St. Louis community.

The Crime Committee's project is to establish at least two Police Explorer posts in each District and to hold a series of city-wide conferences on crime prevention.

The Program Committee is now working on improving the image of the policeman among our citizens by conducting a series of six lectures in each of the districts and involving, as speakers, members of all ranks in the Police Department.

The Sanitation Committee has been given the special task of organizing special meetings in each District with the local businessmen to discuss and analyze How the Businessman Can Assist in Preventing and Reducing Business Crimes.

The Auto Theft Committee has a novel project this year. Its special task is to assist in the organization, maintenance and use of what we call the St. Louis Police-Community-Relations Youth Council. This project also requires a more detailed explanation. Membership in this council is limited to high school students and further restricted to five representatives from each high school, comprised of the president of each class, the editor of the high school paper and three other students. The Auto Theft Committee determines the name of these representatives early in the school year and submits them to the Police-Community Relations Office; invites the class officers to each district meeting; involves the class officers in the functions and programs of the districts; gives the class officers an opportunity to express themselves at these meetings; and advises the Police-Community Relations Office on all matters dealing with the Youth Council.

SUMMARY

Through these programs and projects we have involved members of the District Committees, elementary school children, elementary school teachers and principals, high school students, high school teachers and principals, college students and professors in the behavioral sciences, the citizen in the neighborhood, the policeman on the street and the commander in the district, the local businessman and the young adult.

Thus, most of the major segments of the community are involved in action-oriented programs that are aimed at improving not only relations between police and citizen but also improving the neighborhood. This involvement will, we hope, contribute to the realization that a total commitment on the part of the community is needed to achieve universal order, safety and tranquility.

Our Police-Community–Relations Program, as you can readily surmise, has an underlying philosophy which is founded and embedded in scientifically demonstrated principles derived from the subject matter of the social-behavioral sciences.

The area of Police-Community Relations requires an interdisciplinary approach based on sound police-procedure principles coupled with known scientific facts and presented in terms of the needs of the community and the requirements of the police department.

All of this must be neatly wrapped up in a package that is labeled "the master key to better law enforcement and to the reduction of crime is in the hands of the citizens."

However, you must prepare the contents of the package and sell them to the citizen.

Chapter 37

COMMUNITY RELATIONS

Harold Barney

CREATING THE POLICE IMAGE

Police-public relations is the aggregate of the relationships of each officer to one or more private citizens. This definition is important because it separates the thinking that so many officers and police administrators have that public relations is the direct responsibility of the chief. Every contact an individual has with the police affects public relations. Something as simple as handling a citation for double parking, answering a phone complaint or giving directions serves to have some effect on the public relations of the department. The line officer then has the major role in creating this public reaction, for he has daily confrontation with the public.

Public support is essential to the successful accomplishment of the police purpose. It is difficult and sometimes nearly impossible to enforce laws that are not popular with the majority of the people. We should recognize that a public that observes police laws and complies with regulations relieves the police of a large share of their burden. Difficult programs can be carried out with strong public and community support, and preferred techniques can be used successfully in friendly communities.

Some departments have utilized a system of field interrogation whereby officers will interrogate persons found in strange areas at strange times and file a report which contains the citizen's name, description, time and place. Many communities have used this with great success, but in others it has caused

Note: From *Police Management.* Chapel Hill, University of North Carolina Press, 1969, pp. 69–73.

a great deal of internal conflict as it pertains to minority groups.

What is the difference between a community that can utilize this method successfully and one in which it causes conflict? Generally, it has a great deal to do with the community's concept of its police department and its knowledge of what the police are trying to do with the system. The utilization of a technique and the utilization of tools can be affected directly by the lack of good public relations or lack of recognition of what the law-enforcement agency is attempting to achieve in the community. One of the things we tend to overlook about the complaints of police brutality or the complaints of police discourtesy is not that in 99 per cent of the cases they are unjustified but that in 100 per cent of the cases the people had some belief that their charges could be supported. This is not a very settling condition!

Another situation that occurs conversely in regard to poor public relations is that sound and progressive programs are impeded. Nothing is as upsetting as having a good, sound, progressive program to put into effect for the good of the community—I'm thinking of the one-way street system—and having the community come down on your back about it.

Lack of public support has a definite effect on police administration. Morale is damaged when the activities of the police are misunderstood, and it becomes difficult to maintain the esprit de corps. The public's attitude is molded and shaped by the police who, in turn, reflect the public attitude. The action of each party is determined by his attitude and influences the conduct and attitudes of the others.

The police themselves may be the most important factor in the creating of public attitude about the police, but obviously there are other factors in constant play. People are inclined to reflect the attitude of the press and in particular to reflect the attitude of the editorial page. Motion pictures and television have a great effect on the public's conception of the police officer's role in society. In many communities there are strong influences in the form of personalities, leaders of groups or the goals of groups that tend to destroy public confidence and prevent proper rapport between police and public.

POLICE ATTITUDES

Police are in service to, not servants of, the community. The essence of correct police attitude is a willingness to serve but at the same time maintaining the difference between service and servility and between courtesy and softness. The officer should be firm but not rude, friendly and unbiased, pleasant and personal in nonrestrictive situations and firm and impersonal in situations calling for control. Prevention of violations rather than making arrests is the primary police purpose. One formula for this primary purpose contians the three "e's"—efficiency, effectiveness and economy.

We are concerned with many objectives in the law enforcement: the need to measure the effectiveness of various programs and the need to measure the productivity of all officers. We are actually in personnel management doing everything we can to search out the individuals who have much to offer the department and to see that they are placed in the areas in which they can be the most effective to the goals of the department. Merit rating is one of the devices that can be used to determine the qualities of an individual.

Members of the police department must know that their primary function is prevention and that their secondary function is to arrest people. This concept is important. Officers should recognize the line of demarcation between the police and the court function. Many times, officers in squad cars or officers on foot tend to moralize too much when they come into a situation or a complaint with a citizen.

CREATING THE POLICE-PUBLIC ATTITUDE

In spite of the fact that the most important public relations officer is the man on the street or the uniformed officer who is answering the calls for police service, the police administrator is confronted with the task of creating and maintaining the police-public attitude. Its development is affected and many times impeded by several factors: (a) the traditional fear of the law, which is very real and must be recognized, (b) errors in judgment on the part of individual officers, (c) unpopular police actions in the form of enforcement of laws and ordinances that offend individuals, (d) refusing special privileges to people who fill important posts, (e) press attacks, (f) political pressure and (g) the necessity of overcoming an unsavory police reputation.

The problems dealt with are not unique to law enforcement alone. These problems of public relations and public attitude are dealt with daily in business and industry. The businessman advertises and perhaps we should be doing a bit of advertising as to the quality of the service we are giving our community. Good will is as essential to success in police operations as it is to commercial enterprises. Public good will is developed by positive action. A department guilty of bad practices towards citizens' needs will meet impenetrable resistance when unwholesome changes break it down. But the greater the resistance, the greater the need to break it down.

Charles Reith states in *A Short History of the British Police* that the police have kindly words and helpful advice for anyone in doubt or trouble who comes to them. They fulfill an immensely beneficial social function in finding relief for the destitute, tracing lost persons and smoothing out family quarrels, misunderstandings and estrangements of every kind. It may be argued warmly in some quarters that the rendering of such service is not part of the duties and functions of the police. The answer, Reith continues, is that the friendliness, the confidence, the respect, trust and affection they receive from the people are almost the sole basis of the power and efficiency of the police of Britain. Whatever tends to strengthen this relationship strengthens and maintains the vitality of true democracy in Britain. Whatever tends to loosen the bonds of the public's relationship with the police must lessen also the power which the police derive from the public's appreciation of them. Any material decrease of this power will quickly lead to their increased dependence on the use of physical force, to the need by central authority of endowing them with despotic powers to enable them to fulfill their tasks, to police dependence not on being liked by the people but on being feared by them and to the opening of a short road for the transference of their organization into the only alternative form of police which is available, the article concludes.

The police should examine critically their own conduct in public contact and remodel it to avoid situations unnecessarily unpleasant to citizens. If the police attitude is unfair and unreasonable and if they unnecessarily embarrass, humiliate and annoy the public, that public will certainly withdraw its friendship and will justifiably resent ruthless campaigns that grow out of futile attempts by the police to meet their own inefficiencies. In terms of practices and procedures, we need to look for abrasive tactics and attitudes which might be misunderstood by citizens.

PUBLIC INFORMATION FUNCTION

Public reporting is an important administrative duty with which the heads of some departments may need some assistance in the form of a public information officer under the direct control of the chief. The need for a separate officer depends on the size of the department and not so much on the ability of the chief but whether or not he has the time to give to press relations, formal periodic reports, department publications and the many other devices used to keep the public informed of the police mission.

Two common misconceptions held by police administrators are that passing out material on police activities is unethical and that the public will misconstrue the information as an effort to build up the prestige of the department. There is nothing unethical about informing the public and it is the responsibility of each public official to maintain an informed citizenry.

The best means of demonstrating the kind of police department you have is through police service. The main purpose served by public information is to remind the people of the type of service you are giving and intend to give. These two should flow side by side, complementing each other.

Chapter 38

POLICE AND PUBLIC

Piet J. van der Walt

AIMS

The police undoubtedly occupy a strategic position in the administration of criminal law, and police operations are matters of direct interest to all sections of the community. As the trusted policeman carries out his duties, he becomes the symbol of justice.

In most democratic countries, the word "police" embraces that branch of the executive power responsible for the preservation of the internal security of the country, the maintenance of law and order, the prevention and investigation of crime and the tracking down of criminals.

The police are therefore responsible for order, peace, security and the safety of every man, woman and child entrusted to their care. This entails enormous responsibilities and obligations in times of social unrest when violence, lawlessness, crime and civil disorder have intruded into our daily lives and are threatening our personal safety and well-being and that of the community. It requires sacrifices and loyalty! The police form the first line of a country's protective and security services. They have a duty, a calling and a task as protectors of the public welfare and as the primary means of exercising social control.

These aims color and give real meaning to the life of a policeman. They bring him into contact with the people of a community and place him unquestionably at their disposal. It is only too true that the policeman is continually under the critical eye of the public and that a vivid spotlight is turned on him.

Note: From *Police*, May-June, 1970, pp. 28–31.

His behavior, his actions, his word, his comings and goings are continually in the spotlight. To carry out their duties successfully, it is imperative that the police command the respect of the public in order to establish sound cooperation. It is also imperative to find out what people really expect of their police and how respect and cooperation can be commanded. Only by being of service as respected leaders and protectors and by establishing healthy human relationships can a proper image be created and maintained in the interests of the police.

HUMAN RELATIONS

It is lamentable that the police cannot in all circumstances depend on the wholehearted cooperation of the public. But it is equally lamentable that members of the public cannot at all times be certain of the support, help, advice and friendliness of the police. This state of affairs forces us to turn our attention to one of the most burning questions confronting a modern police force, namely the relationship which exists, or should exist, between the police on the one hand and the public on the other hand. The importance and value of a sound relationship cannot be overestimated. If the relationship between the police and the public is not what it should be and if it is not characterized by mutual trust, respect, cooperation and help, no law, regulation or rule, however well formulated, framed and confirmed, will ensure the maintenance of law and order. This leads us into the field of human relations—in other words, how do human beings treat one another?

Every person and every police officer continually faces the problem of human relations. They meet it on the personal level, in their marital and home life, on educational, communal, labor, church, recreational and political levels. Indeed, daily the police officer is faced with one or more of these human relationships and he must act summarily with due regard to prevailing circumstances and his responsibilities as law officer. He has a duty and loyalty towards his own profession as well as towards the public he serves; even more! He must secure order, peace, satisfaction, protection and help. He must prevent crime, combat it and apprehend the wrongdoer. His conduct must ensure and guarantee it. His actions must not be calculated to frustrate these ideals or to sow dissent among the citizens or stir up unrest or revolutions. In his community, he therefore has to be the servant of the public as well as the symbol and upholder of law and order. He must serve the public and through his services become leader and confidant of that community.

The police officer must be a human among humans but must have a leader's personality. He has to deal with people and human behavior, and for that reason he must have an insight into human nature. He must know the human being with all his virtues, abilities, possibilities, ideals, faith, hope and love. But the police officer must also recognize man's vices, sins, envy, hate, jealousy, beastiality, sensuality, pride, cunning, immorality, baseness and deceitfulness. If there is one profession which demands that its practitioners arm themselves with a knowledge of human nature, it is surely that of the police. The policeman must have a knowledge of human nature so that he may serve, lead and protect man but also when necessary so that he can hunt him down and deliver him into the hands of the law.

Very few businesses, institutions and professions today have a greater need of sound human relationships—and I especially include race relations—than the police.

The relation between the police and the public may be either good (sound) or bad (disturbing, aloof). It is essential that it should be sound, and very sound at that. For this reason, serious efforts should be made to study this relationship problem and to employ every means to keep the relations on a sound basis. In this connection, the following question is, to my mind, extremely important and basic to any police organization.

WHICH FACTORS DETERMINE AND INFLUENCE THE ATTITUDE OF THE PUBLIC TOWARDS THE POLICE?

This is a difficult question to answer, as it will differ from country to country and from civilization to civilization. It appears to me, however, that certain basic factors outlined in the following paragraphs should receive attention.

Public Opinion

Public opinion is a binding and directive force in the life of a community and has great meaning to man and society. Questions therefore are What does the public say and think of police officers in their communities? Is their judgment favorable or unfavorable? Do they believe the policeman entrusted with their safety is a hard-working, honest, impartial and conscientious man? Or do they believe the opposite and ignore and despise him?

If opinion is unfavorable, efforts must be made and ways and means found to change public opinion so that a closer contact and cooperation can be established between the public and the police. Positive steps must be taken to obtain and retain the interest and active support of the public. This entails a task for the police as well as the public. This public opinion is influenced, among other things, by several factors.

The Press

The crucial question here is How does the press represent the police to the public? The press may make or break a police force! It is therefore essential to establish and maintain a sound relationship with the press in order that public opinion may be influenced to the good. In our time this is an urgent need which will in future become even more essential. In order to establish such a relationship the following should be considered, *inter alia.*

The police authorities should provide for special procedures and set up effective channels for closer contact with the press.

As far as possible, the chief of police and different commanding officers should maintain personal contacts with press reporters. They should ensure that police officers continually bring their activities, achievements, problems, etc., to the notice of the press. There should be clear and concise instructions as to the attitude of the police toward members of the press and their newspapers. Moreover, regular press reports concerning matters of general public interest should be issued by the police. By this means, the police obtain sound publicity, and public opinion can be influenced favorably and lastingly in the interests of the police.

With the aid of the press, a so-called "Police Week" can be organized annually to provide sound publicity for the police force and police activities. Such a "Know Your Police Week" or "Work With Your Police Week" may become an annual event. During such a week, the public can be invited to pay visits to police stations so that they may become acquainted with police activities. Furthermore, visits to institutions such as the flying squad, the police colleges, the dog kennels where police dogs are trained, the bureau of criminal investigation and performances of the police orchestra or police gymnastics which are open to the public may play an important part in awakening the public to a realization of the role played by the police in the community. It may also serve to make the public conscious of its own responsibilities and obligations to the police.

More use should also be made of apt slogans, etc., which should be placed and exhibited in conspicuous public places.

Regular pamphlets and brochures may be published and distributed. Talks and lectures should be given at universities, teachers' training colleges, schools and other organizations and associations. Documentary films should be produced and shown to the public. The possibilities in this area to establish a closer contact and cooperation with the public are infinite. In this connection, a police magazine directed to the public could play a leading role.

Radio, Television and Other Mass Media

The radio, television, theatres and other mass media which are important sources of information and publicity today, may also be enlisted to further a healthy relationship between the police and the public. This should be exploited to full advantage.

Personal Contact Between Police and Public

A more desirable attitude toward police could be established with the public if more personal contact between police and all members of the community were to occur. This applies to the police officer in his official capacity, that is, when he is on duty as well as when he is off duty. For 24 hours out of 24 hours, the eyes of the public are focused on the police officer, and when he misbehaves he discredits the whole force. Police officers must be integrated with the community on a large scale. They must join different organizations, associations and sports bodies, and must play a bigger part in public life. In this connection I have in mind the contribution of the police in juvenile care and other welfare services. If they are efficiently engaged in youth clubs, youth associations, youth organizations and so forth, they will be able to obtain the goodwill of these children and youths and foster a better relationship. It is on this level that they can prevent and fight crime and prove of great service to the country.

Treatment Accorded by the Police to Members of the Public "for the Sake of the Law"

How does the police officer act, for example, when members of the public lodge a complaint, give evidence or are detained for an alleged misdemeanor? The police have to serve the public and must treat any member of all races and groups with friendliness, integrity, impartiality, respect and deference. The police officer must bear in mind that whenever a member of the public lodges a complaint or seeks the aid of the police on any matter, it is of great importance to that particular member of the public. It may be a routine matter to the police officer—just one of the many types of routine matters he handles regularly—and therein lies the dangerous possibility of handling the matter in a thoughtless, unfriendly, and disinterested way, to the great dismay and annoyance of that member of the public concerned. The public must be able to put their trust in the integrity, honesty, justness, conscientiousness, responsibleness and kindness of every individual policeman. It is imperative, therefore, to raise the standard of the police force. To establish and maintain sound human relationships, it is further essential that the police authorities pay attention to the following basic requirements with respect to its own staff:

A systematic and efficient program of staff selection must be evolved, and the personal, social and moral aspects of each recruit's character must be stressed.

There must be a thorough, effective and sustained training program in keeping with the present demands of modern society. This includes the basic training given to recruits, as well as the progressive training of police officers in the service. Stress should be laid on the problem of human relationships in these training programs. A healthy attitude toward police work and to the public must be instilled. If this cannot be ensured, it may easily lead to friction which sometimes results in unfriendly, tactless, stupid, and ill-mannered treatment of members of the public to the detriment of the police image.

The police staff and their work must be thoroughly inspected at regular intervals as an integral part of the police organization.

Neat and practical uniforms with easily distinguishable badges are a necessity. This immediately rouses public interest. The appearance of a police officer very often influences his image in the public eye.

The police uniform is the symbol of law and order—of courage, perseverance, honesty and helpfulness—and therefore every police officer must take pride in his uniform. The uniform is the visible and inalienable testimonial enabling the police officer to act in the community and to fulfill his indispensable duty. Each police officer must bear in mind that every day he is contributing to the reputation of the entire police force. He is earning a good or a bad reputation. Remember that each police officer is both an architect and an engineer of the reputation of the professional status which is still in the developing stage and which needs a solid foundation. Therefore, each police officer should design, build and serve the police force in such a way that it will be an asset, a credit and a pride to a country and its people. And this he can only achieve by being of service—by showing kindness to those with whom he comes into contact, whether their skins are white, black, brown or yellow, and whether they are rich or poor, male or female.

Every police force has its "problem children" who cannot or will not cooperate! These persons are unfit for police work and it is best to get rid of their services—the sooner the better, as they cast a slur on the entire police force.

CONCLUSION

To establish sound relationships with the public and to improve the police image, law-enforcement authorities should pay special attention to the foregoing basic factors. The times and circumstances have made it necessary for the commanding officers of police departments to investigate these aspects thoroughly and to inform the public of the various duties, responsibilities, functions and activities of the police agency. The public should also be informed of their own role in maintaining law and order, because upon every citizen rests a responsibility to preserve the internal security of his country and, by all the means at his disposal, to prevent and fight crime and its henchmen at all times.

These aspects should have the same attention as other police activities. They must not be ignored, neglected or belittled. They must penetrate the everyday activities of the police in such a way that they become a main principle in the way of life for each individual police officer. Each man's success and happiness in life—and this applies equally to the life and work of a police officer—depends largely on his relationships with his fellow men, that is, the community with its rich variety of race, nationality, religious persuasions, political beliefs, family, economic and social levels and so forth. That is why police authorities must work toward sound human relationships both within the force between the individual officers and between the police and the public. A definite and planned program, based on psychological, educational, sociological, criminological and moral principles must be evolved to permeate the whole police force. The doctrine of excellent human relationships must become a characteristic of every policeman, and he must apply it daily. To do this, the policeman must have faith—he must have faith in God who gave him the opportunity and enabled him to undertake his responsible and difficult task; he must also have faith in himself, in his profession, in his superiors and in his inferiors, as well as in his fellow men outside the force. The police officer is lost without faith in these things, and without faith he cannot act in the most effective way to the benefit of every member of the public or national jury.

A police organization which has achieved success in the prevention of and fight against crime, in tracing the criminal, in protecting and safeguarding life and property, cannot be indifferent, cold, inhuman and hostile towards the community and those served by it. In the life of a community and a nation, there is nothing more certain to do irreparable harm to national unity, national existence, peace, order and security than the actions of an indifferent, inefficient, unfriendly and hostile police force which has no positive, purposeful and practical program to maintain sound human relationships.

A primary task is to establish and maintain sound police-community relations, thereby establishing the police agency as a helpful and protective service to the public.

Chapter 39

A METHOD OF APPROACH TO THE TASKS OF A HUMAN RELATIONS OFFICER

EDGAR DAVIS

ABSTRACT

It is the purpose in writing this discourse to present a method of "how to" in the field of human relations. It is by no means the last word of "how to" perform the tasks but, we believe, an initial effort, since all of the research we were able to make in the field failed to reveal any such procedure. It is an effort to vocalize the ideas and the work of many people who have vastly more experience in the field than the author.

As in all controversial spheres, this discourse is not expected to meet, nor will it meet, the approval or acceptance of all elements. It is, however, a sincere attempt to bring forth an objective, analytical and comprehensive study of the "how" involved in the duties and responsibilities of police officers working in the field of human relations as an assignment.

Above all, we are aware that any set rule, no matter how fluid it might seem, will not supply all of the answers when dealing with problems of human behavior. We do believe the newcomer in the field of human relations is in need of direction and the experienced human relations officer must sometimes be reminded of the direction of thrust for his effort, for as surely as it happens in other fields, the human relations officer, too, is sometimes afflicted with a desire to perform his task for the sake of perpetuation rather than the avowed purpose. To the aforementioned purpose this effort is dedicated.

NOTE: From *Police*, January-February, 1971, pp. 61–64.

HUMAN RELATIONS DEFINED

Human relations and its point of view is not concerned with sugar coating harsh reality. It is not to be equated with police management *in toto;* lives must be protected, criminals caught; the opportunity to commit crime lessened, and the public served. Yet this cannot be done without the human aspect of cooperation between all units of the police and all segments of the society.

Recent developments in the law-enforcement field have led to a search for a fresh approach to police administration and considerable interest has developed in human relations. This interest has brought a wider understanding of why people act in a certain manner, how they get along together in a group setting and the characteristics of each group. The psychological aspects of communication and perception, especially, have received much emphasis. There is no doubt that this understanding can and does tell us more about the human problem of participation in the whole of society. But the observer of large organizations, for example a police department, in an attempt to see them as a whole, is left with a sense of inadequacy and/or frustration. He feels a need to look beyond personal relations to the larger patterns of institutional development. Yet he knows, or must be made aware, that no social process can be understood and dealt with unless it is located in the behavior of individuals and especially in their perceptions of themselves and each other. The human relations officer is concerned with aiding line and staff officers of police and community organizations in linking the larger view to the more limited one, so they are awakened to how organizational change is produced by, and in turn shapes, the interaction of individuals in day-to-day situations. The larger the area of decision the farther the reach of its influence and the greater is the need for deeper and more comprehensive understanding of social (community) organizations and its main component—the human element.

Because the vast majority of the real or imagined problems between the police and the community appear to be rooted in bias—racial, religious, economic, etc.—it becomes a duty of the "human relations expert" to aid both the department and the community in developing tolerance and respect for each other.

Objective

The objective is to establish sound, reasonable, and mutually respectful rapport between the community and the police so that society's purpose, in this sphere, can be served; in point, its Police Department "serve and protect—indiscriminately."

Purpose

The general purpose for which the units exist can best be described in the following terms, though not mutually exclusive or all-inclusive.

The first task is to explore procedures, actions and attitudes of both the police and the community, currently in practice and planned, if available, that appear to be a source of friction between them. To attempt to work out mutually acceptable alternatives to such procedures. To present, in the form of recommendations, such solutions to the hierarchy of the police department and to the responsible community organizations and/or individual citizen.[1]

The second is to establish and maintain reasonable rapport with all organizations and ethnic groupings and with the leadership of all enclaves, in the overall society. To analyze, record and pass on (through proper channels) any pertinent information, obtained through such rapport, which may be utilized by the department to further its avowed objectives.

THE HUMAN RELATIONS OFFICER

In addition to his inherent duties as a police officer, the Human Relations officer must develop a clinical approach to the

[1] It is not intended or implied by anything contained herein that this unit's investigations will supplant or supercede the investigations into the conduct of police officers by either the Internal Inspections Division or direct command personnel but rather as an aid to those concerned through the utilization of the expertise of the Human Relations Section.

following duties and responsibilities. The items listed are, of necessity, oversimplified and not all inclusive. The human relations officer should attempt to understand other people, which involves a high degree of acceptance of people as they are. The above statement could be considered the cornerstone of human relations. It implies respect, tolerance, acceptance of human frailty and recognition of the uniqueness of each human personality. It also takes into consideration the understanding of how people see themselves, for there are no moral absolutes in human relations.

He should have an awareness of, and a sensitivity to, differences between his outlook and that of another man, coupled with an ability to maintain his own individual point of view in the face of such differences. He should realize that the individual's values, aims, aspirations and reactions are, in some measure, unique and he should not expect other people to be exactly like him.

He should have an ability to respond to and understand not only the logical content of what other people say but also the feelings and sentiments implied in their words and their behavior.

He should have some awareness of himself and the result of his behavior on other people. (The use of the word "some" is deliberate and is intended to designate degree.) Generally speaking, a distinguishing characteristic of the clinically oriented human-relations expert is an intuitive understanding of himself and the way he acts, which squares roughly with the way he looks to others.

The human relations officer should have an effective way of understanding the nature of the social structure or social system of which he is a part. He identifies or has a feeling for basic elements of the social organization isolated by human relations experts, such as the informal organization, status relationships, traditions or customs.

He must be realistic about the existence of a hierarchy of authority, responsibility, status and position in an organization and be alert to the way this hierarchy affects people's behavior, his own included.

In anticipating action in an organizational situation and even, to a greater degree, in an individual setting, he should instinctively be able to predict (within limits) how the individual or organization will respond. Such predictions should be exemplified by an analytical approach of "If I do this, what will happen?", weighing each alternative and producing the most probable answer to his self-framed question. Thus this approach is in opposition to saying "If I do this, I hope this will be the reaction."

In making recommendations for action, he makes intuitive, judicious use of those generalizations about social phenomena which he has constructed and tested by his own experience, and at the same time he continually watches for the unique elements in every concrete situation.

The human relations officer must not allow *laissez faire* to be the dominant approach to human relations. He should not be afraid or refuse to tinker with social processes, in particular, programs and approaches dealing with individual involvement.

He should be as competent in dealing with people as he is in dealing with things. No matter how much, how new and how sophisticated equipment becomes, the main element in police work is and will always be human beings and their behavior.

He must know what motivates people to act. He must know how people are likely to react in various situations and be prepared to utilize this knowledge for leverage and predictions.

He must never lose sight of the fact that the police agency is an important agency of the government, which is dedicated to the preservation of human dignity and individual rights and to the concept of government by laws. The police are the visible arm of government and are often recipients of the outward manifestations of the hostility, frustrations and expressed desires for change of the society and of the individual. The human relations officer must be mindful of that fact and govern his actions, his decisions and his recommendations with that fact in mind.

The human relations officer is, at the same time, both a human relations officer and a minority relations officer, since many of the problems he must face stem from the relationships between the police and minority groups.

He should attempt to foster close and intimate cooperation between the community and the disciplinary machinery of the department. He should be able to openly solicit inquiry by interested, responsible citizens (leaders of the community) to indicate the acceptance of the legitimacy of public scrutiny.

Finally, he should attempt to perform the role of mediator, communicator, catalyst, etc., at the scene of an incident. However, in doing so, he must be mindful of the fact that his recommendations and suggestions are viewed as a compromise by each group involved and must be sold with the same degree of fortitude and honesty to all factors.

The Liaison Officer must sell his solution to a problem as vigorously to the Police Department as a whole as he does to the community groups.

Qualifications

The basic qualifications of the human relations officer are the following.

He must possess an expressed desire to work with and for people in the most intimate manner.

He should possess an exceptionally high degree of intelligence.

He should have an increasing degree of exposure to the behavioral sciences.

He should be relatively free of personal bias.

He should be able to meet controversy.

He should not be timid in approach.

He should not be abrasive in manner.

He should be thick-skinned in the face of adverse opinions and actions.

He should be willing and able to perform any reasonable act in order to accomplish his assigned task.

He should not expect to always see tangible and immediate improvement, even for his best effort.

He should be able and willing to admit when his efforts cannot effect an outcome.

He must have a self-determination relative to the value of human relations projects in the face of venomous opposing opinion from any sources with whom he works.

He should approach his task as a person of action rather than of reaction.

Human relations officers should not adopt an automatic defensive attitude toward those who criticize and are hostile to them but should attempt to explore the problem openly; for many people most hostile to police are acting out of a misguided belief of right and/or law.

He must always bear in mind that many public services are an integral and important part of police work. Proper performance of such tasks adds as much to the professionalization of police work as does the suppression of crime and the apprehension of criminals in the most sophisticated manner.

In investigations and observations the liaison office *must* under the most trying circumstances, remain objective in outlook, control his personal bias and act professionally.

Duties

The administrative duties of a human relations officer are the following.

Administratively, a city is usually divided into a number of parts and two officers are assigned and held responsible for the activity in each area. Each team is assigned an unmarked vehicle. The teams are held responsible for its condition and maintenance, etc.

Morning roll call is conducted at a stipulated hour by a supervising sergeant. Information gathered, work done and analysis made since the last roll call is discussed. New assignments are made on the order of the commanding officer.

Liaison officers are then dispatched to the field to cultivate old contacts, make new ones and cover current events. During the course of the tour of duty, the field officers will interview all persons involved in any assigned case and gather any other pertinent information. The interview must be of sufficient depth to generate a valid and rational conclusion.

Reports on assigned cases are due no later than one week, seven days after assignment. When the investigation cannot be completed within the prescribed time, a progress report in the form of a To...... From...... will be submitted on or before the due date.

Periodic contact must be made with the office, during the tour of duty, so that the coordinator is constantly updated on what is occurring in the field. (A monthly expense account is available to cover phone calls, etc., by liaison officers.)

Except under the rarest circumstances, all requests and/or suggestions for change of conduct on the part of police officers should be made through the coordinator. Follow-up of such suggestions must be made so that the effectiveness of the unit and its program can be clearly ascertained.

It is not possible to list all methods (if they were known to one person or group) on how a line of communications can or should be established, but it is elementary that an introduction to leaders, supposed leaders or apparent leaders must be the first step. Whether this introduction is initiated by direct action on the part of the liaison officer or through an intermediary, *it must be immediate.*

Direct confrontations in which the police are or are not likely to become involved could be the subject of a request for the presence of the supervising sergeant or, if of sufficient magnitude, the presence of the coordinator.

Unless the immediacy of the existing situation demands otherwise, all liaison officers will present themselves at the unit headquarters or other designated place at a certain hour for a joint debriefing session, at which time the coordinator will determine if any information presented needs further discussion and/or his personal attention.

The reason for a joint debriefing session is so that the exchange of ideas and techniques can be shared, thus creating an on-the-job training session and the development of a high *esprit de corps.*

SUMMARY

The human relations officer cannot by oath or inclination ignore the commission of a crime in his presence; however, the essence of his assigned task is that his imagination is stirred by the process of group interaction and the vision of an harmonious team consisting of community and police trying to attain a better society through the proper performance of their respective duties.

Chapter 40

PUBLIC RELATIONS FOR A SMALL DEPARTMENT

Donald Wrightington

One of the biggest stumbling blocks in police work, especially in modern America, is poor public relations or no public relations. It is particularly important in this day and age when the police profession is coming more and more under the critical eye of a concerned citizenry for every police department to have a public relations program. If your department is located in a small, or even middle-sized community, some of the following suggestions may be worth examining. The entire list may be utilized as a public relations program or appropriate portions added to an existing program.

THE PUBLIC INFORMATION OFFICER

First, it is a wise move to assign a publicity-conscious, knowledgeable officer to the duty of handling a public relations program. In a medium-sized department, this could be his only task or at least a major one for him. In a small town, it might blend well with the duties of a juvenile officer or court prosecutor.

Once the assignment is made, and made carefully, guidelines must be established. All men on the department must be informed of what is being done, the aims of the program and how it will be conducted. That it is for their own good and the image of the department should be emphasized to insure their cooperation and help.

Note: From *Law and Order,* June, 1968, pp. 76–78. Reprinted with permission.

The next phase of establishing a program is to size up the needs of both the community and the department. If the public relations of a department are good, a program should aim at keeping them good by expanding whatever is working for them and adding new functions that may be equally successful. If, however, as in many cases, the public image of a police force is low, a slow, steady type of progress must be made, with great attention to details. An accurate record of each and every step contributing to the creation of the new image should be kept.

I will list specific suggestions, with the low–public-image department in mind. Other departments may find suggestions to adapt to their needs.

The public information officer must first discover all media available through which he can work. This includes newspapers (daily, Sunday and weekly). It also means radio stations, television stations, departmental or governmental newsletters and other types of local publications. In addition, he must become thoroughly acquainted with them, their style, content, personnel, publication and deadline dates. Then he must go to them, introduce himself, meet the people with whom he should establish personal contact and tell them of his program. He must find out from them what they expect from him and what they will accept and use.

WORKING WITH THE NEWS MEDIA

Now that he has investigated available news media, he is ready to begin a limited portion of his program. This should be done before moving into less direct, more subtle areas of public relations. The way to get started is to begin fulfilling what the media stated they could and would use. If it is actual news they are after, supply them with it. With the Chief's permission, the officer should seek the cooperation of the sergeants of the shifts, the desk or control men. He should ask them to inform him, either at a set time or whenever he calls, of the details of any incident that is of interest to the public. Using the style suggested or required by the media and the rules of propriety and common sense, he can begin funneling stories to them.

VARIETY IN NEWS

The public information officer should not restrict news to accidents, fires, investigations, and the like but should also include promotions, personnel changes, town-meeting proposals or requests made to police commissioners and city councils. When step one is in full operation, your public will be aware of your department.

SPEAKER'S BUREAU

Once a smooth communications flow has been accomplished, which can only enhance your public image and aid your public relations program, it is time to move into the more indirect methods of the program. The next step might be to take a look around the community to see what a police department speakers bureau could do. Then the public information officer can make the proper contacts to set up such an undertaking by calling school officials to arrange for safety and law assemblies; approaching civic, fraternal and social organizations with offers of speaker and demonstration services; and working through the community's churches to present programs for church-based organizations. He will find that he will experience little difficulty. As a matter of fact, his suggestions and programs will be welcomed.

TOURS OF POLICE STATION

Moving further into the realm of the indirect approach to public relations, the officer ought to explore the possibility of providing department-based activities for various segments of the community. This could start on a minor level with tours of police facilities for Boy Scout and Girl Scout groups, classes for youths and adults alike in such things as gun safety, judo and other forms of self defense, law classes and sponsorship of a driver-education program.

IN-SERVICE PUBLIC RELATIONS

One final but important phase of a public relations program for a police department has been purposely saved until last. Once the officer in charge of the program has reached a certain peak of success with his attempts (which will take time), he should be given authority to reorient the entire department regarding public relations. Having already attained some success, he will not have to talk with department members on a speculative basis. After receiving full backing from the head of the department, he must either through departmental meetings or an actual classroom program, sit down with department personnel and explain to them what is being done. Then, building upon the success already attained, he should outline suggestions for personal contributions by each man to the program. This final phase is very necessary but often neglected. Officers must be told that in-station and on-patrol confrontations with people are as important as anything a formal program can accomplish.

The point must be stressed, for example, that the use of tact and patience are absolutely necessary to the good public image of the department. Courtesy in telephone and personal contact with the public, proper use of department motor vehicles, great propriety in dealing with women and children—all of these must be adhered to.

If these suggestions are put into use, your department will find itself with a new image and a new relationship with the public. The importance of good public relations cannot be overstressed, for it is the public upon whom the police department depends for its upgrading in salary, equipment, and facilities. Be realistic. Work at this type of program, give it continuity, make it known, and you will help insure a successful future for your police department.

Chapter 41

OBSTACLES TO GOOD POLICE-COMMUNITY RELATIONS

WILLIAM J. BOPP

A police department may create a formal community relations unit which does its job with a high degree of proficiency, while at the same time the relationship between officers and citizens steadily deteriorates because of the agency's failure to recognize that human relations is the job of every man on the agency, not just a handful of specialists assigned exclusively to the P-CR task. It is, in fact, not the community relations officer who will have the most dramatic impact upon a department's battle to win the confidence of its citizenry but the line officer whose daily contacts with individuals will make the difference between exhilarating success and abject failure.

If one is to believe the volumes of material produced about the police by private individuals, foundations and public commissions, then the major weakness of most major police departments is in the component that most often contacts citizens—the uniform patrol force. Studies of the causes of racial disturbances have revealed that all too often it was a police incident which triggered many of the urban riots, a factor which cannot be offset by the glib talking of police-community relations officers. In all fairness to the police, however, it must be stated that they are continuously thrust into impossible situations, damned if they do and damned if they don't, more the victims of prejudice than practitioners of it. They neither *cause*, nor are they responsible for, the social conditions which motivate men to violate the law. And a good bit of the attack that is directed at the American policeman is not aimed at him personally or professionally but at whom he appears to represent—the "establishment," government, the "man," white middle-class values, etc. He is visible, the man in the middle, a fall guy for beefs of all shapes, sizes, colors and varieties. He is, generally speaking, the only man immediately available representing government, so it is he who takes the heat for failures at all levels of government.

Yet the fact that the police do not by themselves *cause* riots does not relieve them of the responsibility for taking whatever reasonable action they can to improve their relationships with the community, for as public employees performing a critical service and as fledgling professionals, anything less would be unacceptable. Those police departments desirous of engaging in the brand of law enforcement so desperately needed during troubled times will undertake a continuing system of self-evaluation to determine which of its policies should be modified or eliminated in light of the changing American social scene. Some of the areas which most often lead to police-citizen conflicts include authoritarian attitudes, traffic enforcement, the handling of citizen complaints, abrasive field practices and police rank-and-file "job actions."

AUTHORITARIAN ATTITUDES

Some sociologists have decried the authoritarian attitudes of policemen, stating that it stems partly from the social backgrounds of a police rank-and-file which takes its roots from the blue-collar working classes, and partly from the semimilitary stance of urban police agencies. Whatever the cause of a frame of mind which manifests itself in authoritarian traits and cynicism, it is clear that this type of conduct must be eliminated when encountered by police managers, a fact which is easy to write about but incredibly difficult to combat due to the nature of a craft which values coolness, requires a suspicious nature, legitimizes toughness and demands impartiality in each citizen contact. No simple answers to this problem are available; however, the march toward advanced education for the police may provide *an* answer, for broadened perspectives and a heightened sensibility toward the plight of the less fortunate and can result in a bridge to community understanding.

TRAFFIC ENFORCEMENT

The most frequent punitive citizen contact a policeman makes is with the traffic violator. Though most policemen tend to view this encounter as "routine," it is anything but "routine" to the average citizen, whose very livelihood may be at stake. A good deal of the heat generated by energetic traffic enforcement has been the result of revenue-producing quotas set by city officials and police administrators who apply an inordinate amount of pressure on line officers to write tickets. Offenses which, under other circumstances would have resulted in a warning often lead to the issuance of a summons under the quota system, and an abrasive police-citizen encounter.

THE HANDLING OF CITIZEN COMPLAINTS

Few factors have so driven policemen and citizens apart as has the issue of law enforcement's handling of citizen complaints of police misconduct. Police administrators generally feel that they are in the best position to act upon citizen grievances, while private individuals, especially racial minorities and civil libertarians, counter with the argument that only an independent external authority can conduct an independent and unbiased investigation. There have been three general types of grievance handling devices utilized by police departments:

1. Internal investigation, conducted either by a formal unit formed for that express purpose, an administrative officer assigned to an individual case or a line supervisor in the course of his regular duties.
2. Police review board, a board of lay citizens empaneled to investigate citizen complaints and conduct public hearings.
3. Ombudsman, an executive officer who is empowered to investigate complaints against the police and other com-

ponents of government. This method has been used infrequently.

The police have violently opposed the implementation of review boards, while many citizens simply distrust the police too intensely to accept as fair internal review, even though a number of agencies have proven that they *can* be trusted to investigate personnel complaints. However, too little attention has been focused on the ombudsman concept, which may ultimately prove to be the answer to a lingering issue.

ABRASIVE FIELD PRACTICES

Certain field practices by officers offend the sensibilities of citizens (i.e. field interrogation, stop and frisk). The fact that citizens are rankled by police action does not, in and of itself, mean that corrective administrative action should be initiated to stop reasonable police tactics. But a thorough and continuing observation should be conducted by police managers to determine (a) what action appears to be abrasive, (b) if the practice should be eliminated, modified or continued, (c) if policy should be drafted or revised in order to communicate to personnel their duties and responsibilities to citizens or (d) if a program of citizen education should be initiated.

POLICE RANK-AND-FILE "JOB ACTIONS"

The last half decade has seen the rise of police labor militancy, the manifestations of which have been more than a little harmful to good community relationships. Policemen who strike and engage in work speedups, stoppages and slowdowns, with no apparent regard for public safety, can undo in a night what has taken years of work on the part of reform-minded police executives. There is a good deal of irony attached to this problem, for in some cases, strong community relations programs have themselves had a radicalizing effect on line officers who, because of a lack of internal communication, were not apprised of the scope, direction, purpose and limitations of such schemes. Furthermore, urban racial difficulties have led to two collateral consequences: (a) the clamor for police chiefs to begin to relate more fully to the community, to be, in effect, externally oriented and (b) the push for more social science education for fledgling police executives, to the exclusion of technical coursework. The result is that police administrators realize too late that they have an internal problem and once it explodes, find themselves ill-equipped to cope with the situation. The time has come for public officials to demand that their chiefs be complete men, possessing the social awareness and administrative competence to deal rationally with militancy wherever it appears, either within or outside police ranks. Police administration is an art that is becoming *situational,* a factor which dictates that practitioners utilize such devices as *manipulation* (as opposed to command), shared decision-making, and effective two-way communications. There are many diverse communities within a city's limits, one of which is the police rank-and-file community. After six months to a year of addressing civic groups, police chiefs may find it profitable to attend a roll call or two.

PART VII

OPERATIONALIZING THE POLICE-COMMUNITY RELATIONS CONCEPT

INTRODUCTION

All the sociological tenets and abstract human relations principles in the world will be utterly useless to police administrators and community relations specialists if these ideas cannot be molded into a workable program of benefit to both police and community. Superior police departments are those with the courage to experiment and emulate successful programs initiated by other agencies. On this latter point, a good deal of credit must be given to the many fine police periodicals—*Police, The Police Chief, Law and Order* and *The Journal of Criminal Law, Criminology and Police Science,* to mention a few—who present a medium in which theorists and practitioners of the art of community relations can transmit their ideas to the law enforcement community. This section presents a number of P-CR concepts which have been successfully operationalized.

Glen D. King explains the successes and failures of "Storefront Centers," a device used to bring the police physically closer to the community without resorting to costly precinct operations.

Keith Kellog's "Uniforms and the Department Image" discusses an experiment which police administrators seem to either love or hate—the donning of blazers by line officers. A number of police departments have found that assaults on police officers have decreased when officers were issued blazers, a factor they attribute to a softened citizen attitude toward policemen. An alternate theory is that it is the *policeman's* attitude that is softened as he sheds the traditional police garb. In any event, the experiment has not as yet been evaluated fully enough to arrive at a reasonable conclusion regarding its success.

As the argument rages on about patrol cars vs. walking officers as a means of crime prevention, many police departments have arrived at a happy medium which also has community relations value. In "Detroit's New Community-Oriented Patrol," J. Morche and J. Colling chronicle the Detroit Police Department's increasing emphasis on motor scooter patrols.

A highly personalized approach to human relations was developed in the city of Covina, California, in which informal police-citizen get-togethers over coffee resulted in better communications. This program is discussed by one of its innovators in "Police-Community Relations Coffee Klatch Program."

"Footbridges for Law Enforcement" by Monterey Park, California, Police Chief Everett F. Holladay relates the total community relations program of a progressive small department, whose most fascinating idea is a "new arrivals" plan in which within two months of the date a new resident moves into town a police officer is dispatched to extend a welcome and provide information about the community.

Seeking answers to the nagging problem of racial prejudice, men of New York City Police Department's 106th precinct implemented a human relations workshop for a group of policemen of varying backgrounds, cultures and experience. A report on the workshop's procedures and an evaluation of its results are found in William McGarry, Edward Doyle and George Olivet's "An Invitation To Understanding."

The essence of good P-CR is *communication*. In those communities wherein large numbers of non-English speaking people reside, a natural stumbling block to communication—language—exists. In one community, San Jose, California, enlightened police administrators did something about the problem, a story that is recounted in "Eliminating the Language Barrier."

In Racine, Wisconsin, the uninitiated passerby may mistake the City's new 2.3 million dollar, three-story building for a public library, an error that brings smiles to the faces of police administrators, for the structure is in reality a public safety headquarters housing police, fire and civil defense operations. In Leroy C. Jenkins "It Doesn't Look Like a Police Station" the image-changing community relations value of constructing a functional, operationally integrated P.S.D. building, while not discussed in the article, is readily apparent from the discourse.

Chapter 42

STOREFRONT CENTERS

GLEN D. KING

In the short period since the first police storefront center was established, a considerable division of opinion has developed regarding the actual impact of this type of police activity.

Storefront centers have been enthusiastically acclaimed by some police administrators and citizens alike as a new, fresh and innovative effort by law enforcement to establish a better working relationship with the public. They conversely have been condemned by some police executives as an indefensive fragmentation of police manpower and by some citizens as a meaningless facade erected to shield from public examination the actual failure of law enforcement to develop programs demanded by the times. Storefronts have been called both the best hope for improved police-community relations and tired police-public relations propaganda with a new face.

A critical evaluation of storefront operations in a number of cities substantiates both the critics and supporters. Storefronts can be either a valuable new police effort or a useless front—depending on the basic philosophy with which they are approached and the methods by which they are implemented.

Basic to the implementation of any storefront program must be a determination of the objectives the program is designed to meet. Two objectives, either expressed or latent, will almost certainly predicate failure. If the police administrator hopes to overcome improper police activities in daily operations through utilization of storefronts, he has little chance for success. The storefronts must rather be an indication of the basic desire on the part of the entire police department to provide for the public as broad a spectrum of service as is possible.

NOTE: From *The Police Chief*, March, 1971, pp. 30–32. Reprinted with permission.

Of perhaps equal danger is the tendency to place too much hope in the program. While experiences in some cities indicate that considerable benefit can be derived from storefronts, they cannot be viewed as the solution to all of the problems in police-citizen relations. Expecting too much from storefront centers can cause both the police and the public to become quickly disenchanted and can result in the abandonment of the program. The problems which exist that result in strained relationships between the police and the public are not created by one circumstance or policy activity and cannot be solved by one activity. The problems confronting the police in their efforts to establish a better working relationship with the public served are complex, and a total solution is not to be found in any one type of activity.

Viewing police-community relations, and particularly the storefront operation, as basically a public relations activity will also likely doom it to failure. The police administrator must clearly distinguish between public relations programs, which are designed to interpret law-enforcement programs and practices to the public, and community relations programs, which must be designed to provide an improved level of service.

It is unquestionably necessary for a police department to seek public support for its activities. It must at the same time look for new ways in which it can expand and improve the service it provides.

While the basic attitudes with which a department approaches the establishment of storefronts are of critical importance in determining probable success, attitude is perhaps no more important than is method. Many police departments with the right kind of basic attitude have doomed their storefront programs very simply because of their failure to properly implement. While the methods followed by the individual police department must necessarily take into account the conditions that exist in the individual city, there are certain factors which no police chief who is planning to establish storefront centers can ignore. Failure to adequately consider any of these can seriously diminish the chances of success.

Although a basic chronology is necessary, the categories of necessary activity are not mutually exclusive and many must be carried on at the same time. For example, it is possible for the police administrator to consider the locations of the centers, the type of personnel which will be used to man them and the training to be given, concurrently. Certain steps must be taken before others become possible, but the police administrator would be wise not to place too much emphasis on firm establishment of a chronology.

Of major importance is the determination of location. Obviously, the centers should be located in the areas of greatest need, but care should be exercised that the determination of need is made on a valid basis. Some departments merely examine its calls for service and place the centers in those areas where the greatest number of calls originate. While the number of calls is a vital factor, it is only one of many which should be included in a determination of locations.

In almost any metropolitan area, the downtown business district is likely to be that area in which the greatest number of calls occurs. It is also likely to be that area in which the least number of citizens live. Since the basic purpose of a store center is to provide enhanced service to the public, its location should obviously be residence oriented.

A decision on location should also take into consideration the ability of those who live in the immediate area to interpret services available and to make government work for themselves. Some people, because of greater education and experience, are likely to understand more clearly the basic functions of government and are more likely to be able to avail themselves of the services that government offers. Since one of the basic objectives of a storefront center should be to make *government*—not just police service—work more properly for the citizen, the first center should be located in the area where the greatest need in this respect is believed to exist.

Since many of the persons who will avail themselves of the services offered by the storefronts must rely on public transportation, the sites selected for the centers should keep this factor in mind. Within obvious limits imposed by each area, the centers should be located as near public transportation facilities as possible.

Because of sociological factors beyond the control of the police, a great probability exists that the areas which meet the criteria listed above will also be those in which there is the greatest concentration of minority-group population. This can, unless care is exercised, lead to the conclusion that storefront centers are totally minority-group oriented. While it is not practicably arguable that the greatest need perhaps exists in areas where the greatest number of minority-group citizens live, these two facts should be viewed as corollary truths and not necessarily directly related. In other words, they are both facts which derive from a set of social circumstances and their existence is dependent upon these circumstances, not upon each other. A properly developed storefront system should ultimately place a center in every section of the city and not just in lower-income areas.

Care should be given to the selection of the building used to house the center. The facility itself should be compatible with the surrounding area and should not call attention to itself either because it is superior in construction and design to other buildings in the area or because it is markedly inferior. Efforts should be made not to antagonize residents of the neighborhood by establishing the center in facilities beyond the reach of those of the residents, but equal care should be taken that the center itself does not appear to be in dire need of basic support.

Of perhaps greater importance than the location of the centers is the determination of personnel who will staff them. Within the limits of his ability to do so, the police executive should select personnel who are likely to be acceptable not only to the citizens but also to the other members of the police department. The successful operation of a center will demand the active involvement of the entire department.

Personnel records should be used extensively in determining the suitability of an employee for assignment to a storefront center. A person whose sensitivity to public response is demonstrated by a large number of commendations and a limited number of complaints is obviously indicated. Since the operations of the center should be separated from the normal enforcement efforts of the department, the assignment of personnel whose basic attitudes seem to be oriented toward arrest statistics should be avoided.

There should be a pronounced identification of the center with the police department. Some departments, fearing public rejection of the offerings of the storefront centers, have established no visible identification with the police agency. The total activity is carried out by persons recruited from the neighborhood and uniformed officers are discouraged from coming into the centers. Such an attitude must be viewed as shortsighted. If any real benefit in improved police-community relations is to be derived, that benefit must be through the establishment of the relationship on a conscious basis.

Consideration should be given to the assignment of police officers in uniform to the center. This uniform should be identical with that worn by other members of the police department. It is not sufficient merely to establish better relations between a specialized community service officer and the public. If any real benefit is to be derived, it must be through a better relationship between the regular enforcement officer and the public. Some departments have furnished distinctive uniforms to community service officers and by doing so have gained more rapid acceptance of those officers within the community served. However, it is believed likely that such an approach sacrifices long-range benefits for more rapid gains.

Staffing by regular departmental personnel should be complemented by the recruitment of community-service personnel from the neighborhoods served. While the employment of neighborhood persons will probably cause their rejection by the more militant, the benefit from the point of view of both the department and the neighborhood resident is obvious. There is value in the contention that persons who live in a neighborhood are more likely to understand its problems than those who live outside the area. Thus, while the identification of the community-service employee with the police department may cause his rejection by a part of the community he seeks to serve, it will broaden his utility to the majority of the neighborhood residents. The establishment of this position can be used by the department as a method of implementing the recommendation of the President's Commission on Law Enforcement and Administration of Justice that three levels of operational police personnel be employed.

The police chief cannot assume that a proper attitude, determined by adequate selection procedures, will guarantee the success of those assigned to neighborhood centers. While a proper attitude must be present, there also must be present specific information relating to the area of assignment. This simply means that persons with a proper attitude must be assigned, but prior to their assignment they must be furnished with specific training. It is unbelievable but true that some police administrators have shown a willingness to assign a sizeable number of employees over a long period of time to storefront centers but have been unwilling to invest a few man-days in the kind of training which would increase the likelihood of success of the centers once established.

Certain basic areas should be included in the training program. Since it will be the responsibility of the community-service officer to assist the citizen in making government work for him, the employee himself must understand clearly what services are available through government. During the training program, representatives of each governmental department with a direct relationship with the public should be asked to explain in detail the services his component makes available. In other words, a fireman should describe the services available through the fire department; a representative of public works should describe services available through that department; a representative of the health department should describe activities performed by his component, etc. A tendency of the police shown in the past, to view themselves as separate and apart from other branches of government, makes this particularly necessary.

Representatives of other official and quasiofficial agencies should also be requested to explain their programs to the prospective storefront officers. Particularly, agencies involved in the administration of welfare and education programs should be invited because it is in this area that the greatest need is likely to exist. Many agencies of this nature exist and ordinarily are anxious to explain their programs and to explore with the police department areas in which mutual assistance can be provided. In brief, the officer should be provided with as much specific knowledge as is possible on services available from all sources, so that he may make these known to those with whom he comes in contact in his daily operation of the center.

The officer should also be given instruction in the nondirective method of interviewing. Most police officers have considerable experience in interrogation, but methods of interrogation are not likely to provide any real benefit in the operation of a storefront center. While the officer will frequently need to assist the citizen in the development of the interview, he should never assume the initiative to the degree that he removes from the citizen actual direction of the contact. The officer should remember that each contact between himself and the citizen should identify a method by which he can best help the citizen and this can be done only if he is effective in determining the citizen's actual problem.

Instruction should also be sought from a person who can and will candidly interpret the attitudes and beliefs of the community to the police officer. The best-intentioned person, provided with extensive training, can still be a harmful influence rather than a benefit to the program if he fails to take into consideration those things which are important to the people he seeks to serve. The employee must have access to specific information concerning the group with which he will most closely work if he is to provide for that group the greatest assistance possible.

A procedure must be developed by which problems brought to the attention of police are communicated to those agencies and departments capable of solving them. Rather than accepting only complaints involving police activities, storefront personnel should seek information regarding any troublesome area, regardless of its nature.

One department transmits to the city's chief administrator a form upon which details of each problem has been recorded. An employee of the administrator's office transfers this information to another form, which is then sent—over the administrator's signature—to the department with jurisdiction. While there is minor time loss involved in this procedure, it has the distinct advantage that requests for service are directed to each department by the chief administrator rather than by the police department.

A follow-up system, to insure that appropriate action has been taken, is also necessary. The citizen who calls to police attention a problem, then hears nothing further about his complaint, is not likely to be a repeat customer. After a problem has been solved, or reasons why it cannot be solved identified, the officer who originally made the contact should recontact the citizen and explain the action taken.

If careful attention is given to the factors described above, the probability of success of a storefront operation can be greatly improved. Perhaps the jury is still out on the question of whether the storefront concept provides a real benefit or is merely a fad. But undeniably, careful attention to basic attitude and methodology by the police can improve the probability the verdict will, in this case, be favorable.

Chapter 43

UNIFORMS AND THE DEPARTMENT IMAGE

KEITH KELLOG

Since June of 1969, each of the 16 public safety officers of the Burnsville (Minnesota) Department of Public Safety has been wearing a stylish navy blue blazer, light blue trousers, deep blue uniform shirt, and black tie. The officers wear no hats but still carry a large-frame revolver. Some wear their badges on their shirts; others carry them in their ID wallets. Some officers wear an even more informal uniform, with a "civilian" shirt and tie and a small-frame revolver.

Although a few other communities in the United States have allowed some of their officers to wear blazers, Burnsville, a village with a population of 20,000 located ten miles south of Minneapolis, is the only one in the nation whose entire force—even those riding in squad cars—are clad in blazers, according to Public Safety Supervisor Jules Butler.

The switch to the new uniform is one of three changes undertaken in the Burnsville Department of Public Safety to improve service and to improve the relationship between the police and the public. The other two changes were raising the educational requirement for an officer from a high school diploma to a four-year college diploma and establishment of a community-service officer program under which college students work part-time at the department.

Initiator of the innovations is 31-year-old David Couper, holder of a Master's degree in sociology, who was appointed director of the department in March, 1969. A soft-spoken man who keeps a portable FM radio playing symphonic music in his office. Chief Couper is a former Minneapolis Police De-

NOTE: From *Police*, January-February, 1971, pp. 69–70.

partment detective. He states that initially, some criticism from other police departments greeted Burnsville's changes, but no problems have arisen within the community or department because of them.

For about two years, public safety officers (PSO's) in Burnsville have handled both fire and law-enforcement duties. Chief Couper now also emphasizes a third duty, community work. "The PSO is a generalist," he said. "The community work might best be illustrated by the Youth Relations Officer—our response to the youth revolution. This officer's primary orientation is to work on problems without using enforcement. He can bring in psychiatrists, counselors, welfare people."

For performing three jobs, the college-educated PSOs receive salaries in one of the highest brackets for departments of the metropolitan Twin Cities.

Mr. Butler, second in command to Chief Couper, explained the twofold purpose of the new uniform. "One is to soften the image of police to the public," he said. "The other is to soften the policeman in his dealings with the public. For instance, suppose you are a private citizen driving down the road and you are stopped by a police officer. When you see the officer you develop anxieties, and when he stops you, they turn to frustrations. An officer's paramilitary clothing adds to the confrontation. A subdued unifrom also helps an officer subdue his own aggressiveness. In addition, the new uniform, including the nameplate worn on the blazer pocket instead of a badge, identifies an officer as an individual rather than just one anonymous member of a group. Before departments began using nameplates along with badges—about ten years ago—if you asked a policeman his name, he'd say, 'I'm badge number. . . .'"

Mr. Butler reports no adverse response from Burnsville residents on the uniform change. "Probably the greatest criticism has come from people in our own profession," he said.

Has anyone refused to cooperate with the informally clad officers? "So far, no," he said. "The other night we had trouble with prowlers. The situation dictated that we go door to door interviewing homeowners at 10 P.M. We just said we were public safety officers. We didn't do the Joe Friday routine or the Efrem Zimbalist approach. No one asked to see our badges."

Mr. Butler mentioned that one argument against blazers is the question of what happens on such occasions as when you have to go into a bar to arrest someone fighting? "The person who would pose this question is depending on officers' identification as policemen to get them out of this situation," Butler said. "If you're wearing a blazer, you've got to rely on yourself—your ability to deal with another human being—to handle the situation. . . . In some cases, too, a uniform has a tendency to raise a man's ire."

According to Couper, the four-year degree requirement follows a suggestion of the President's Commission on Law Enforcement and Administration of Justice. The Task Force Report on the Police, issued in 1967, stated: "The failure to establish high professional standards for the police service has been a costly one, both for the police and for society. . . . The quality of police service will not significantly improve until higher educational standards are established for its personnel."

The main reasons for the four-year requirement, according to Mr. Butler, are to equip an officer to handle the 90 per cent of his work that is unrelated to crime and, simply but significantly, to broaden an officer's horizons, to insure "the ability to be viable; to adjust; to be able to change." Butler noted the tendency, because of the demands of integrity and because of the working conditions, for an officer to develop "tunnel vision" and to become part of a police subculture in which almost all of a policeman's friends are other policemen, and involvement with police work detaches him from much of the rest of his community. "Some of the resentment we have received from other departments results from this rigidity," he observed. He then noted another uncommon characteristic of Burnsville's force: its youth. At 41, a veteran of a dozen years of police work, Mr. Butler is the oldest man on the force.

Under the third innovation—the community-service officer (CSO) program—half a dozen college students from the Twin Cities area have worked an average of 24 hours a week since June of 1969 in such duties as dispatching, telephone answering, clerical work, booking of prisoners and cleaning guns. Not very glamorous perhaps, but for their time, the students, whose majors range from sociology to business administration, receive three dollars an hour.

In addition, Mr. Butler said in explaining the purposes of the program, the students, who wear uniform shirts and badges but no weapons, receive "insight into problems of a public safety department—law enforcement, fire and community service. In turn, public safety officers get a chance to communicate with young people. Hopefully, they will understand one another's thinking—bridge the generation gap. A secondary goal is interesting young people in pursuing law enforcement as a career." A community-service officer program is another suggestion of the Task Force Report on the Police.

Chief Couper hopes for another major innovation in the near future: use of a computer to cut clerical work and to allocate police efficiently over the 28-square-mile community. On the basis of past records of location, date and time of crimes, a computer could recommend where best to locate officers to be most useful in preventing or detecting crimes. "Burnsville's crime rate," said Mr. Butler, "is about on a par with most suburban areas."

Chief Couper's recruiting literature reflects his eagerness to change the image of law enforcement. One flyer invites one to "Join the Domestic Peace Corps. . . ." Emphasizing the word "professionalism," the flyer advertises the department's need for "our 'new breed,'"—that is, "gentle men [sic] who are humanitarian, ethical, knowledgeable, and have a commitment to making our system of justice all that it should be. . ., the kind of man that can handle responsibility and authority, make important decisions, and (most important) the kind of man who likes people. . . ."

Chapter 44

DETROIT'S NEW "COMMUNITY-ORIENTED PATROL"

J. Morche and J. Colling

The motor scooters of Police Commissioner Johannes F. Spreen made their working debut in Detroit on September 28, 1968. Ten patrolmen and one sergeant were assigned to scooter patrols in the Mack-Gratiot Precinct—one of the three in which the scooters were used on a trial basis. The Police Department now has 34 motor scooters.

Two of the "rangers," which is the code name for the scooter patrolmen, are assigned to each scout-car territory. The scooter patrols will each work in liaison with a scout car, in contact via PREP (Personalized Radio-Equipped Police[1]) radio. Each territory is approximately eight by ten blocks in size.

In the beginning, the rangers will work a 9 A.M. to 5 P.M. shift. The Mack-Gratiot contingent worked through Thursday, October 3, when they were assigned to special World Series' duty. They have now returned to the Mack-Gratiot Precinct and the other rangers have begun work in the other two precincts.

The primary emphasis of the new project, called Community-Oriented Patrol (COP), is crime prevention. There is also to be a concerted effort to gain additional community support for the police force.

The 11 officers who started the scooter patrol on September 28 are part of the 36 men selected and screened for this duty. Heading the COP program are District Inspector Bernard G.

NOTE: From *Police*, November-December, 1968, pp. 93-94.

[1] See Computers—Sherlock Holmes Style, *POLICE*, Vol. 11, No. 6, July-August, 1967, pp. 7-13.

Winckowski, of the Inspectional Services Division, Lieutenants Alan Eichman and Richard Boutin, and Sergeants Billie Bishop, Alexander Harris and Art Howison. The patrolmen range in experience with the department from one year to sixteen years.

All applicants for the COP project underwent psychological as well as physical training. They next attended four half-day sessions at Wayne State University. The first session dealt with an analysis of police objectives, community orientation, current police operations and methods, and the specific function of the scooter patrols. The second session revolved around the community, the law, and the attitudes and history of minority and poverty groups. The third dealt with the community and the police department and their perceptions of each other and ways of making these views more positive. The final day involved "the professional police office," the implications of police professionalization and new programs.

Among those participating in the WSU training were Commissioner Spreen; WSU Director of Religious Affairs and former Detroit police aide, Hubert Locke; Former Second Deputy Commissioner to the Detroit Police Department and now Associate Director of the WSU School of Police Administration, Robert Lothian; and Associate Director of the Neighborhood Services Organization, Harold Johnson.

They then spent three full days at the Police Academy undergoing special training in community relations, sociology and psychology, as well as a review of their previous first-aid classes.

All 36 of the rangers also took five days of scooter training under Sergeant George Stanbury. Their final orientation session was held September 27 at police headquarters.

Spreen, who introduced the scooter concept in New York when he was Chief of Operations there in 1964, said, "The scooter is not a gimmick. I believe this is a new approach to solving the perennial problem of extending the range of activity with available police personnel and at a minimum expense."

He also cited the importance of patrolmen being seen by the

community rather than being insulated by a patrol car. This, he believes, will bring back the image of the beat patrolman while at the same time removing the disadvantages of foot patrol.

Scooters are used by the police departments in New York City, Cleveland and Nassau County, New York.

Spreen said that the scooter patrolman is able to cover an extended area "embracing several posts, and he may put aside his scooter when necessary to patrol on foot. The scooter patrolman thus is not a specialist but remains the all-around, all-purpose police officer covering a neighborhood area in the tradition of 'the cop on the beat.'"

As far as the personnel factor, Spreen stated: "Foot patrol is costly and perhaps somewhat archaic. Coupled with a two-way radio, this machine offers a considerable increase in police coverage with the same available manpower at minimum expense."

As to cost, Spreen indicated the scooters were a bargain, costing about 365 dollars. Six scooters can be purchased for the same price as one radio-equipped scout car. A four-door police car costs 2,162 dollars.

When the program was begun in New York, it was restricted to patrolling Central and Prospect Parks. With favorable reports on hand, the scooter patrols were expanded to seventeen precincts, although still restricted primarily to park work. One of the more gratifying results of the scooter program in New York, according to Commissioner Spreen, was the public enthusiasm which was evidenced. In reviewing the advantages of the scooters as experienced in New York, Spreen stressed the following:

1. Greatly extended patrol coverage over the foot patrolman—At least five times that of a foot patrolman.
2. Better police observation. Officer can survey 360 degrees, unrestricted by the car.
3. Ease of movement in congested areas.
4. Freeing of patrol cars for constant patrol and response to emergency situations.
5. Economy of operation. The scooter gets 50 miles to the gallon.

6. Reduction of patrol fatigue experienced by foot patrolman.
7. Increased morale and stimulation of recruiting.
8. Preventative and deterrent effect. While the foot patrolman may go unseen and unnoticed, the scooter patrolman is seen, and the sound of the scooter offers comfort to the residents and serves as a deterrent to would-be lawbreakers.
9. A new communication bridge with young people. The patrolman with his parked scooter acts like a magnet, drawing interested youngsters and helping to create a new rapport between them and the officer.
10. Interprecinct support. Spread to all precincts, the teams can provide a citywide operating network of instantly available personnel.
11. Inclement weather experience. Spreen indicated the scooters should be able to operate about three hundred days out of the year in Detroit.

Chapter 45

POLICE-COMMUNITY RELATIONS COFFEE KLATCH PROGRAM

JEAN ANDERTON and FRED FERGUSON

To Mr. Average Citizen, a police patrol car weaving through traffic under siren and red light is just another common, everyday occurrence. Mr. Citizen notes only that the police unit is intent on reaching a scene of emergency somewhere in the community. He gives no thought to the helmeted, uniformed man behind the wheel. He does not know the officer's name and would not be likely to recognize him in a meeting on the street. He is not particularly interested in the officer's problems, for he has his own to contend with. So until he needs help or breaks a law, Mr. Citizen will remain detached and aloof from the uniformed man who safeguards his community. Why?

In most cases it is because communications between policeman and citizen have been lost in the shuffle of progress. Gone is the once familiar, friendly "cop on the beat." Officers who once walked neighborhood streets now patrol their beats in high-powered, radio-dispatched patrol cars. And they must, for today in most communities law enforcement is spread thin and patrol beats are measured by miles rather than by blocks. In modern communities, populated with individuals from all walks of life and all ethnic groups, the police officer must not only perform his traditional policing duties, he must also be trained and prepared to handle diverse situations. He may be called upon to act as a mediator in family disagreements; as a counselor in juvenile problems or as a referee in neighborhood disputes. Yet, even though he becomes involved in the

NOTE: From *Police*, May-June, 1968, pp. 19–22.

intimate problems of the citizens he protects, the policeman remains a stranger in his community, for people tend to recognize the uniform, not the man.

"Crime," society says, "is a police problem." True. Yet crime is also a community problem, and if a police department is to be totally effective it must have the help of interested citizens who are willing to become involved and ready to accept their own role of responsibility in maintaining law and order. But how do you involve citizens? How do you reach them to let them know they are needed and that they can help provide extra eyes and ears for the uniformed men who patrol their neighborhood streets?

Some police departments have attempted to solve this problem by employing one or two men to act as community-relations officers. Highly trained, they are specialists in the field of public relations. Serving as the communications link between citizens and police, these experts handle the questions and complaints of the citizens. They investigate, correlate and report back to the inquiring citizen. Sometimes, by necessity or lack of first-hand information, they reply with stock answers that may or may not correctly apply to a particular situation.

In their public relations role these special officers tend to become disoriented from the man on the beat. Often important feedback—both positive and negative—is received through their community efforts, yet, unfortunately, little of this information filters back to the beat officer.

In the course of their work, these community relations officers often appear before large groups of citizens in neighborhood schools or before smaller groups at civic luncheons to outline law-enforcement problems of their departments. They ask at these meetings for citizen cooperation and assistance. Sometimes they get their message through—a few citizens respond. But in most cases the citizen quickly forgets the problems, the officer's name and even what he looks like. And this is understandable, for it is difficult to remember someone with whom you have had no personal contact.

For the Covina Police Department, faced with its own community-relations problems, personal contact appeared to be the important key for reopening communication lines between its own officers and its citizens. Based upon this premise, Jack Adams, Covina Police Captain, was assigned the responsibility of finding out if the key would fit.

Captain Adams studied the community-relations program initiated by Police Chief Everett Holladay of nearby Monterey Park, a neighboring Los Angeles suburb. Using his findings as a guideline, a program was adapted that would be conceivable and feasible for the Covina Police Department. From this planning evolved the idea of the neighborhood "coffee klatch."

Basically, the idea itself was simple. Invite a few couples from a given neighborhood to an informal evening get-together for coffee and conversation. Bring into the group the police officer responsible for patrolling their particular neighborhood and afford him the opportunity to present his department's viewpoints on law enforcement in the community. Over a friendly cup of coffee give the assembled couples an opportunity to ask questions, make known their personal expectations regarding efficient law enforcement and allow them to air their own gripes about the service. The idea was conceivable and it was feasible.

Turning the coffee klatch idea into workable reality consumed innumerable hours of planning and training. If the program was to be fully effective, each beat officer would have to become, in effect, a community-relations officer. Each man would have to be trained in special skills. He would have to be armed with adequate information that would allow him to successfully communicate in a different way with the public. To accomplish this, Captain Adams worked with each man, helping him develop individually in the all-important community-relations skills. With the training program established, it became necessary to next find individuals who would be receptive to the coffee klatch idea and would agree to host the sessions.

Getting couples to open their homes and invite neighbors in for the informal coffee klatches proved to be no great obstacle. Members of the Covina Woman's Club Juniors, enthused over the program's possibilities, volunteered their assistance. Acting as hostesses, they made preliminary arrangements for the initial get-togethers in their own neighborhoods patrolled by Covina officers.

When apprised of a scheduled meeting, the Police Department arranges for advance delivery of coffee, cookies, and movie projection equipment to the host home by a police aide (a nonsworn college student). Everything is in readiness when at an appointed time the beat officer, on duty and in uniform, arrives for his coffee klatch session. Parking his patrol car in the driveway, he clears radio contact with his dispatcher, then enters his host's home.

His host introduces him to each individual present, and in turn, the officer distributes attractive personal business cards bearing his name and other pertinent information. He encourages each member of the group to call him by his first name, pointing out that it is imprinted on his card.

Following introductions, the officer, armed with up-to-date police information developed for this specific neighborhood, speaks to the guests about the problems and events that are occurring on "their street." Through friendly, informal discussion he encourages response from the group.

Next, he presents a short movie, "The Door Was Locked," produced by the International Association of Chiefs of Police, which portrays typical home burglaries. He follows it with a discussion on crime prevention in the neighborhood, pointing out how each citizen can become personally involved in crime prevention.

The officer talks about his own role in the community. He encourages questions and attempts to answer each one intelligently and sincerely, carefully avoiding negative overtones that might indicate any form of defensiveness on his part.

Offering himself as a personal contact between law enforcement and citizen, the officer invites each individual to call him personally if any future questions or problems arise in which he can assist. He invites comments, including complaints, and makes it clear that he will welcome any opportunity to discuss them. He lets it be known that he is personally concerned about establishing a mutual relationship that will strengthen the sometimes critical feedback procedure, and he promises prompt and correct answers to all future questions, assuring that his replies will be fed back no later than the following day.

Before leaving the coffee klatch, the officer assures each couple that he will be continuously interested in hearing their suggestions, or their doubts, about his own job performance or that of a fellow officer on the beat. He reiterates that "their street" is also "his street," and that their concerns are his concerns.

Basically then, this is the coffee klatch—the personal contact—the key which the Covina Police Department is using to open the lines of communication between each police officer and the citizens on his beat.

Each officer of the Covina Police Department is expected to conduct at least one coffee klatch a month in his assigned beat area. If the meeting is his first, Captain Adams will accompany him, and through prearrangement the meeting will be videotaped. Using this technique, the officer is given the opportunity to see and hear for himself how he and the group reacted to various questions and problems that arose. The tape playback provides an excellent training device in which the officer can criticize himself.

One inherent law-enforcement problem is the tendency of many officers to become defensive when negative police-citizen contacts are related. Even worse, the officer often finds himself defending the actions of other officers when he has absolutely no personal knowledge of the situation being described. Such defensive attitudes cannot be overlooked, for they remain a constant hazard to successful communication between the police officer and the citizen. It is not inconceivable that the Covina officer conducting his first coffee klatch might find himself facing an insistent couple who repeatedly inject negative statements concerning police conduct in specific or generalized situations. The couple might add subtle or even open pressure in an effort to break the officer's composure, and the officer invariably finds himself taking a defensive stand in behalf of a fellow officer's involvement, even though sufficient facts are lacking. Under these circumstances, the dismayed officer finds that he has suddenly cut himself off from the group. The relaxed atmosphere becomes tense. The other couples tend to sympathize with the problems of their peers and begin to insert their own negative comments, often forcing the officer deeper into his defensive position.

At this point Captain Adams steps in and takes over the discussion. Gradually he brings the group back. When, finally, he introduces the "anti-police" couple as members of a little theater group planted to act out situations that any officer might find himself facing at a coffee klatch, the relaxed atmosphere returns almost immediately. The relief of every individual in the group is openly apparent—a new, closer relationship is evident. And if the officer readily admits that he erred in his handling of the situation, he strengthens the new relationship, for he proves that he, too, is a human being.

This planting of agitators in coffee klatch sessions has proven to be a realistic, convincing method for teaching each officer that he must, above all, eliminate every trace of personal defensiveness. Although this method of training may seem somewhat unusual, perhaps even unfair, the Covina policemen have accepted it, for they are accustomed to role-playing experiments and are well aware of the need for continual self-appraisal that can add strength to their relationship with members of the community.

Because each coffee klatch session lasts at least two hours, the time investment is naturally considerable, but the returns from the investment are equally great. Even the newest officer on the force is being given a chance to meet the citizens he serves in an unusual, yet positive manner. Each officer participating in the coffee klatches is provided a unique opportunity to get "into the action" along with the residents of the neighborhood he patrols, and he becomes the personal contact link between law-enforcement programming and the citizens on his beat.

Although still in infancy stages the coffee klatch program is finding its place with the role-playing techniques employed by the Covina Police Department in its in-serve police training.

Because it was an imaginative and experimental program, it was normal to expect resistance from the officers when the coffee klatch idea was first introduced. They, like most policemen, enjoy doing "police work" and tend to avoid nonpolice tasks. In addition, many of the men were not trained, polished public speakers and it was felt that this alone might develop anxieties in the beat officers who were to be involved. But the anticipated resistance never materialized. Instead, the officers accepted the program with surprising enthusiasm, and morale in the department has never been higher. Each man feels that he is personally helping to build a new bridge of understanding across the gap that had been steadily widening between himself and the citizens in his community. Each man has accepted his additional role as a community-relations officer and he takes pride in doing his job well. The problem has not become one of forcing the men to meet their once-a-month quota, as might be expected. Instead, the problem has become one of holding the men down to a reasonable number of monthly coffee klatch sessions.

The coffee klatch program continually provides new insight into police-community relations for the Covina officers. Over a cup of coffee the men are able to engage in healthy diversified dialogue that has little to do with the routine, investigative conversation usually conducted between policeman and citizen. The officers now are offered opportunities to conduct different conversations with different people in an atmsophere that is congenial and friendly, and they are discovering that they have many mutual interests with the citizens on their beats.

Perhaps the most important lesson that has evolved from the coffee klatches is the lesson in personal attitudes. Covina officers are learning the value of eliminating defensiveness when they are on the receiving end of negative feedbacks from disgruntled citizens, and equally important, they are learning to turn negative feedback into positive action.

Feedback from citizens who have already been involved in the coffee klatches indicates that Covina officers are again being thought of as individuals in the community they serve. Enlightened citizens no longer see them as mere pieces of expensive, uniformed machinery needed for community protection. Instead, these citizens are beginning to recognize the man as well as the uniform.

As the coffee klatch program gains momentum and spreads through the community, it is a predictable certainty that Covina's Mr. Citizen will give some thought to the uniformed man behind the wheel whenever he sees a police unit on neighborhood patrol. Mr. Citizen will know the officer's name and he will recognize him as an individual, perhaps even as a friend. Yet even more important, Mr. Citizen will be interested in the officer's law enforcement problems. He will know what they are and he will be aware that these same problems belong to him and to his community, for he has already discussed them with the officer—over a friendly cup of coffee.

Chapter 46

FOOTBRIDGES FOR LAW ENFORCEMENT

Everett F. Holladay

Since he walked the beat some twenty-five years ago when he was judged as an individual, the policeman has been motorized, mechanized and dehumanized. Science and technology have been a boon to his capabilities but his removal from personal contact with the citizen has plagued him to the point that traditional approaches to the need for enlisting citizen support to prevent crime have been about as effective as a bandage on a boil.

Crime prevention has been recognized as a prime purpose for our existence since the first police agencies were organized. And yet, since World War II, we have been waging a so-called war on crime, obviously losing battle after battle as evidenced by the increasing crime rates. And the cost of the administration of criminal justice is now reaching 30 billion dollars annually, while concern for personal safety in the minds of the citizenry approaches the level which existed when the West was first settled.

Any progressive police administrator will admit that simply increasing the manpower and the equipment is not the answer. Instead, what is needed is a true viable working relationship between the police officer and the citizen whom he serves. Yet never has it been more popular to question the policeman's activities nor the constituted authority which he represents. And, all too often, the attitude of the entire force is judged by the momentary unfavorable contact of an officer with an individual.

All kinds of proposals are being made to improve the image

Note: From *Law & Order*, January, 1971, p. 18. Reprinted with permission.

of the policeman: putting him back on walking beats (the crook would not like that!); putting him in blazer jackets to informalize his authoritarian symbolism; hiring special community-relations officers to "trouble shoot" the rough areas; and carrying on meaningful dialogue with critics.

We feel these are little more than symptomatic relief for the real need to reacquaint the officer with his community, and vice versa. To do this, we have devised a number of innovations which I call "Footbridges for Law Enforcement." These innovations require our patrolman to regularly get out of his patrol car and make contact with people on his beat under friendly and favorable circumstances. This personal contact extends from the kindergarten-aged child to the senior citizen.

P.A.C.E. (PUBLIC ANTI-CRIME EFFORT)

The organization of this group early in 1966 formed the basis for an active working citizen-police partnership. Responsible individuals throughout the city were recruited through the churches and service clubs to serve as crime-prevention chairmen. They regularly hold coffee klatches in their neighborhoods to which the beat officer is invited to discuss special problems and become better acquainted.

COP ON CAMPUS

A part of the regular duties of each beat officer is to visit the schools (including elementary) in his beat each week while the children are on their lunch break, not in an authoritarian capacity, but to communicate and answer questions which they may have. This program was also initiated in 1966.

NEW ARRIVALS

When an individual moves to our city, within sixty days, another "footbridge" is utilized. The uniformed beat officer will arrive at the door with a smile on his face, officially welcome the new citizens to our community, provide them with information about the city, its services, supply them with emergency telephone numbers and specifically discuss with them our crime-prevention programs and seek their assistance to make our city more secure from the intruder and thief.

RIDE ALONG

Our "Ride Along" program was initiated in 1964 when we invited students to "see it like it was" from the inside of a police car. We have now expanded this "footbridge" to include representative citizens from all groups.

COMMUNITY RADIO WATCH PROGRAM

Operators of citizen-band radios constitute an additional unit of the team under this program, and are utilized as additional "eyes and ears" of the Department through their capability of immediate reporting while they traverse the community.

SENIOR CITIZEN PATROL

The most recent such "footbridge" is to identify in each beat the senior citizen who lives alone and to personally acquaint each officer on that beat with that individual in order to make certain that he or she will feel a greater sense of security through this knowledge that they are receiving special patrol attention.

These concepts and others similar, constitute the "footbridges" of communication which bring the officer out of the patrol car—rehumanize him—and generate not only understanding and friendly relationships but a vast reservoir of citizen strength to our efforts, the result of which has reduced major crimes committed in our city from 814 in 1968 to 767 in 1969. Truly, the proof of the pudding is in the eating, and in this instance, it is palatable indeed!

Chapter 47

AN INVITATION TO UNDERSTANDING

WILLIAM MCGARRY, EDWARD DOYLE and GEORGE D. OLIVET

Many indications of polarization existed within police departments throughout the nation in June, 1970. These reports indicated that both black and white officers had refused to cooperate with each other in the enforcement of law. In Jackson, Mississippi, white police officers were accused of firing on black civilians implicitly because they were black. In other areas, black officers were accused of not supporting their white brother officers. There were widespread reports that black and white police were not acting as police officers but primarily as members of their ethnic group. Throughout the nation, police departments were experiencing the divisiveness just at the time when the increase in crime demanded otherwise.

To neutralize these countercohesive tendencies, a fresh experimental approach was needed. Under the title of a "human-relations workshop," an empirical program was instituted in the 106th Precinct to explore the need and apply such remedies as might be required.

SELECTING PARTICIPANTS

Manpower requirements for policing the precinct necessitated close programming. To obtain a racial and ethnic balance, 12 officers were selected from 26 volunteers to whom the purpose of the workshop had been explained.

Six of the selected officers were black and six were white. Insofar as possible, they represented a cross-section of age,

NOTE: From *The Police Chief*, June, 1971, pp. 20-27. Reprinted with permission.

length of service, squad assignment, social background, previous employment, education, religion, and political commitments—from militant to conservative.

It was considered most feasible to schedule 8 two-hour, open-ended sessions (which were the first and last hours of the second and third platoon), and for continuity, two sessions per week were planned. More sessions would have been beneficial, but summer demands for manpower precluded this.

The authors comprised a three-man team to structure the human-relations–sensitivity-training program. Approval of the program was secured from superior officers and the first session of "Invitation to Understanding" was held June 11, 1970 in the Unit Training Room of the 106th Precinct station house.

The brief synopsis of the eight sessions given below may be helpful to other departments planning similar programs.

THE FIRST SESSION

The 12 members of the workshop, in civilian clothes, were seated in a circle. Captain McGarry explained that it was their job to find out if there was an attitude of prejudice as great as some said and whether there was divisiveness between black and white policemen that was impossible to overcome. If this was the case, he asked, what could each one do to improve his attitude and be more sensitive to those around him as well as to members of the community. He explained the structure of the workshop and stressed meaningful participation as of great importance to the group. He emphasized that no one need fear embarrassment or repercussions from anything that they might say and that what was being striven for collectively was greater than the individual. He then turned the workshop over to the moderators, Sergeant Doyle and Officer Olivet, and participants so that his presence as a commanding officer would not inhibit full participation.

The moderators defined and stated the group rules for workshop participation: we must listen, we must be utterly frank, we will only get out of the time what we are willing to put into it, we should not scream at anyone, we should not attack any member of the group personally but rather learn to disagree, to discuss, and to listen, even if we do not agree. The ground rules for this type of workshop are many, and time was taken to make certain that all understood and could agree to them at the outset. At this time, the participants were told that if they were not present for a session there was no other person to take their place, hence it was important to start, continue and finish together as a group.

The moderators asked the group to pair off for each man to prepare a biographical sketch of his partner. It was explained that it was important to know more about the individual than he would be willing to divulge and therefore it would take good interrogation to determine a man's feelings about politics, education, emotional outlook, family background, philosophy, etc. Both partners were to have ten minutes in which to prepare a report on the other. When this had been done they were asked to introduce their partners and tell everything that they had learned about him. One after the other did so until all had reported. This revealed the obvious—there was a great difference in the group's structure. There were Catholics, Jews and Protestants; Democrats and Republicans; Liberals and Conservatives, with overtones of radical feelings on both sides of the political spectrum. This reporting broke down some of the barriers.

The second phase dealt with one-way versus two-way communication. The point of this exercise is to show that for successful communication, there must be two-way communication where questions and answers are involved, where one can define what one means and others can ask what they want to know. One-way communication is not constructive. The procedure called for one participant to seek to describe, without the benefit of questions from the other participants, the interpositions of four geometric figures which they then attempt to duplicate. This is one-way communication and usually ends in misunderstanding and failure. Then another participant attempted the same thing, but this time questions and answers were permitted. This resulted in better understanding and more accurate duplication of the geometric figures. This was a very apt illustration because the men could readily see its simplicity and obvious truth.

The last part of this session was given over to explaining and demonstrating that an optical illusion can distort truth. A subtle drawing shows the profile of two women, one old and the other young. A viewer at first look sees either one or the other but not both. When told that what he sees is not what someone else sees there is consternation. Everyone is certain that what he sees is the truth. Usually a class will split almost evenly on which profile it sees. After discussion, the participants were asked to show the opposing side of what they saw by outlining the face of the woman. The obvious result is that all men then see both faces. Discussion followed and the point was made that everyone believes what he sees is the absolue truth, and while in this drawing there are two truths that may be perceived, we see only one. The men themselves made other points which were pertinent to the session, breaking down preconceived ideas and feelings about the workshop and its aims. When the session ended the men were asked to write, at home, a short sentence on what they would do to reduce prejudice in the police department.

SECOND SESSION

Each man turned in his statement on ways to correct the problems of prejudice. Some of these comments were:

> If the department as a whole has the attitude of what it can give to the public instead of what can the public give to them, the larger portion of prejudice in the department would gradually be dissolved.
>
> We should institute a program to educate the new recruit in the past history of New York City and its citizens, problems they faced, conditions under which they had to live and the prejudices they had to overcome. With this knowledge, he will have a better understanding of the problems faced by today's minority groups.
>
> Policemen, on the whole, are practical and resourceful people, called upon to perform a fantastically diversified number of tasks. Policemen must be shown that by eliminating prejudice, their working conditions will be improved for there will be less tension in the streets from groups who feel that they are victims of prejudice.

> Segregation, discrimination and de facto segregation are the prime roots of the problem, and as long as they exist, we are plagued. The only thing that the police can do is to set the guidelines for men to follow . . .
>
> The word prejudice is overused and many times misunderstood. I am assuming we mean bigotry between different people. I'm prejudiced but I do not consider myself a bigot.
>
> It must become common knowledge, inside and outside the department, that prejudice or double standards will not be tolerated.
>
> The problem involved in remedying or eliminating prejudice within the department is one mainly concerned with leadership. Administrators and supervisors must become more deeply involved in carrying out their tasks.

After reading these statements, the men were given cards on which were printed the words, "I am," and asked to complete each I am statement with the first thoughts that came into their minds. The cards were then read back to the men without revealing their names. The majority of the men had completed the I am statement with a reference to their group attachment: "I am an American," "I am Catholic," "I am Black," etc. These statements show that each man sees legitimate group connections in his own life as important to him. The point then discussed was that each man sees his own group connections as part of his existence and is happy to greater or lesser degrees because of these connections. The moderators pointed out that the first line of prejudice extended to anyone is usually concerned with one's group connections and yet we all identify with groups. We see others as unlikeable because they are connected to groups such as white, black, Jewish, Catholic, Protestant, etc. We desire to be accepted with our group attachments, yet fail to extend this privilege to others. This prejudice can be eliminated to a great degree by practicing acceptance of individuals regardless of group connections. We must see people as individuals instead of group representatives.

The moderators asked the participants to tell everyone about the first time they had felt prejudice applied to them. This is an excellent technique. All the participants by their rapt attention evidenced their emotional involvement with the other men as each told of their experiences in their youth, military, school, and police department experiences when they were hurt by prejudice and became angry and disillusioned. There was such interaction from this subject and such a good, honest display of emotion that the entire time was devoted to this subject. A further breakdown of barriers became very obvious.

THIRD SESSION

At this session, some of the group members asked to discuss topics they wished to submit. A film, entitled "The Eye of the Beholder," was shown. The ensuing discussion brought out that emotional baggage weighs one down and prevents one from viewing things objectively. The members then shared their hang-ups on how projected attitudes into various situations can add to erroneous conclusions and deteriorations of good human relations. This is a rut that is easily fallen into unless one becomes part of the solution and not part of the problem.

The moderators took one man aside and told him a story about a woman who was going into the hospital for an operation and her husband was having a problem parking the car near the hospital. This officer was then asked to tell the story to the man next to him and so on until it had been passed on to the last man. This simple story traveling between just twelve men was ridiculous by the time it was ended. Distortion was almost complete. The discussion then centered upon the need for professionalization of attitudes and aims of policemen. It was indicated that part of this goal can be accomplished by disregarding rumors and dealing with realism where possible.

The subject of a person's sensitivity to being called names was introduced. The point was made that the recipient of name-calling feels both insulted and injured. One moderator stated he had seldom had his name pronounced properly and this was a source of aggravation to him. The other moderator expressed his sensitivity in similar areas and this stimulated others to do the same. It was agreed that all men feel they should be called, addressed and spoken to properly, thus not detracting from their humanity. This is a two-way street in communication and often a proper attitude can dispel a disagreement by the tone of speech. To have a friend, we must be one. To gain respect, we must give respect. We must yield to another the very right that we so very much demand for ourselves. Mutual respect expressed by simply saying "good morning" is appreciated by most men, yet this is often overlooked. All decided we must work on this problem and not shirk it as being someone else's job. A comical reaction resulted, during which everyone began to address each other with Sir, Mister, etc. The point had been made, however, and it became apparent from the men's reactions that this was an open nerve—all felt a need for being respected. It is not possible to review the many points discussed within the framework of the workshop; but in retrospect, the manner in which the participants expressed themselves openly, sharing their thoughts on what was important to them, will have lasting impact.

FOURTH SESSION

Each participant was given a list of subjects and asked to number them from 1 to 20 in the order of their relative importance. The list included career success, character, economic security, family, freedom, friendship, good disposition, health, honor, humor, knowledge, love, peace of mind, power, recognition, religious faith, respect, social acceptance, tranquil environment, and wealth. The results were reported to the group. It was apparent that race or other group connections had little to do with the order of rank given to the subjects. Color lines were crossed and recrossed as the individuality of each man was indicated by his choices. Discussion followed on why some men felt some topics should rank the way they had chosen them. Such comments as "Without health there is nothing" and "Peace of mind means everything" showed that the values of most policemen in the workshop were almost identical, with the first three choices centering upon family, health and peace of mind.

The moderators then prepared to hold an election. One "candidate" asked to be elected on a platform which denied there was prejudice in the department—and if it did exist it was not our job to do anything about it. The other platform was one which held there was indeed a problem of prejudice in the department and something should be done to eliminate it where possible—and it was everyone's job to work toward that goal. If elected, he said, he would put into effect a program of human relations whereby all members of the department could discuss and share their feelings and beliefs with others. In the ensuing voting, the workshoppers cast all twelve ballots for the positive, do-something candidate.

Several participants spoke on the history of minorities. The discussion ranged from the problems the Irish minority had in achieving recognition in this country to the problems of other minority groups facing similar situations. It was mentioned that often a minority will take an active role in a do-something program rather than remain involved in a do-nothing situation. There was good interaction in this discussion in which a wide difference of opinions was apparent on some points and very close agreement on others. In this no-holds-barred rap session, most white participants realized that all people desire change (even as their own forebears had) and that change is most desirable now. An excellent exchange of meaningful statements centered upon the need for an end to social injustice to help the affected minorities attain status in society.

FIFTH SESSION

The moderators asked the participants to form a circle after reflecting for a moment upon previous discussions in which they had shared experiences of prejudice or bigotry aimed at them. Then they were asked to think of those unwritten laws that are never enforced which state we must be fair to all and not injure another unnecessarily; that we must treat all men as we ourselves desire to be treated.

This led to the next step in the program. The men were asked to try to recall someone who had caused them to be embarrassed or insulted preliminary to conducting a sham trial in which one man would be the prosecutor and another the defendant. The prosecutor was to accuse someone in the room of being guilty of a crime. He was to specify the accusation and present his case to the jury (the ten other participants). The man who was chosen to be the defendant had to accept the invitation, sit and listen to the charges, and to the best of his ability defend himself with reasons and excuses for his actions. The moderators served as judges. This particular technique makes the prosecutor, even though he may share the feelings of the accused, defend the position that is forced upon him. The accused must think of all the reasons for a man to do what he was charged with doing and to present a defense sufficient to demand a not-guilty verdict. This thought process requires both the prosecutor and the defendant to defend a position regardless of his own personal feelings. The jury, of course, is intent upon the why's and wherefore's of the charges and just as intent upon the many excuses presented by the defendant.

Policemen are inventive under pressure. The success of this particular part of the workshop must be credited to these officers. Forgetting themselves, they became wrapped up in the situation before them. Some of the accused held particularly untenable positions; others fared better. The jury's verdict was to be delivered at the next session. The participants left, strangely silent.

This sham trial procedure, as well as the other techniques, was developed by one of the moderators to produce increased emotionally charged involvement. The results as measured by response of the workshoppers were most gratifying.

SIXTH SESSION

The participants took their positions for the continuation of the sham trial without being asked to do so. The men were then given a prepared list of questions to answer. The questions pertained to human relations and associated attitudes.[1]

[1] A photocopy of the questionnaire, which is too long to accompany this article, may be secured by interested police administrators from *The Police Chief*.

Each participant was asked to submit a short statement on "What I would do if I was a (black) (white) policeman." Each was to put himself into the place of an opposite member, i.e. a black officer would tell what he would do if he was white and vice versa, for the purpose of correcting attitudes observed in others that are injurious to human relations. There was some expression of disagreement with this. Many apparently thought there was a difference in what either black or white officers should do as policemen. It was further defined that we often feel the other guy is capable of doing more than we can to improve human relations. This technique, we believed, could do much to define what we think the other fellow could really accomplish by his actions. Still there was an undercurrent of feeling that there should be no difference in what either blacks or whites should do as policemen.

This consensus may be the most significant of the entire eight sessions.

SEVENTH SESSION

The short statements on "What I would do if I was a (black) (white) policeman" were returned. There was a constructive attitude evident in most of these statements. Others were objectively critical and made no referenec to black or white but rather what they would do under either situation.

The results of the questionnaire were also presented. The replies again indicated that black and white voted the same negatively and positively (as a general rule) on 95 per cent of the questions. In the following discussion, the participants tried to define what some of the questions really meant to them as policemen. There was an exchange of comments and further questions presented. Before the end of this session, the workshoppers developed critiques as basis for a paper to be approved for submission to the Police Commissioner. This 10-point Position Paper appears below.

The discussion took up the subject of the uniqueness of every man and woman. A poll was taken on how many blacks and whites tend to group all people of the opposite color into one group, believing that they act, feel, talk, vote, speak, think and dress alike. The poll indicated that the same perceptions exist in both groups.

The participants asked if Captain McGarry could attend the last session on an informal basis to answer questions they felt were important to them. Some said it was not fair to ask the Captain to come and sit under the gun, as it were, but they would like to report to him their feelings about the workshop.

For the remainder of this session, the discussion was open for any subject. Immediately twelve subjects were suggested. The men had reached the position of desiring to talk things out—to tell it like it is.

EIGHTH SESSION

The participants were asked to fill out a printed critique of the workshop with the same complete frankness that they had shown in the discussions. There remained one sham trial to complete, following which two additional topics were introduced for a good exchange of comments.

Captain McGarry addressed the final moments of the concluding session. He indicated he had been advised to the session-by-session progress and had gauged by individual conversation the reaction of most of the participants. He expressed gratification with results and promised to pursue the program in the interests of a more harmonious and efficient department. Individually, the workshop participants thanked the Captain for making the program possible, and their enthusiasm which had developed in the initial sessions was obvious.

The Position Paper was approved by all members. And there was a unanimous vote in favor of a follow-up workshop at a later date.

The reduction of divisive influences among the workshoppers became increasingly noticeable not only through observation and individual conversation, but from their own review of the data reflected in the questionnaires. It was best indicated, perhaps, during the final session when the subject of a proposed dinner for the group was raised. One workshopper said, "A month ago I would have said that possible embarrassment would have made a group dinner not worth the trouble, but now I say, let it start here." And everyone agreed.

TEN-POINT POSITION PAPER PREPARED BY PARTICIPANTS IN "INVITATION TO UNDERSTANDING"

1. Administrators in the police department play a prime role in being an example to policemen of ways to deal with men in an unprejudiced manner. The rank and file look to superiors for discussion, correction, or advice; and if not present, often causes a reaction of indifference to professional attitudes on the part of the members involved.

Point: Superiors are looked to for fair play and unprejudiced attitudes and actions in their decisions, and if not found, generate the same indifference they possess.

2. No prejudice should be shown against any member of the force trying to obtain an assignment in his own rank, i.e. clerical, harbor, aviation, emergency. The choice of men for these jobs should be made on associated skills and ability of the man chosen. This policy, though in effect at this time, should be examined continuously lest it become slack and therefore ineffective.

Point: Assignments within a rank must be absolutely without prejudice if the rank and file are to be satisfied with the decision.

3. At the scenes of riot and disorders where the black community is involved, assignments should not be made of black officers only, but rather on a black-white basis to show unity among the men, and to remove an unnecessary burden from the shoulder of the black officers. Heretofore some assignments at these riots have been of black officers with the thought that it would help to cool the situation if black confronted black. This is erroneous and it is far better to share the problem, black and white officers together. These assignments, if to be acceptable to all, must be made on a black-white basis regardless of whether the community is black or white.

Point: Black and white policemen should stand together in

these situations and there should be no assignments of black officers to the black problems or white officers to a white problem. All policemen are capable, and it must be made more obvious to the community, and to the rank and file.

4. The department should make it more obvious to all its members that assignment of black officers to narcotics, detective division, special services, etc., is made on the basis that these men work well in that capacity and that it is not just a soft position.

Point: It is thought by some that preferential treatment is accorded to black officers in certain assignments and the fact is that they are doing a good job; that is why they are assigned to that position.

5. A regular memo should be issued by the Police Commissioner and read at all roll calls to the effect that all members of the department need the cooperation of each other regardless of race or religion.

Point: The rank and file need reminding, as do all men, that we need each other to get a job done. This will also make it obvious that there is an interest in the problem from the top.

6. The Police Commissioner should respond to the charges recently made by one of the fraternal organizations within the department by stating that he would undertake to have police machinery investigate the charge and if it is found to be true, have measures taken to correct this condition. This statement should be made publicly.

Point: After this charge was made there was no answer but rather total silence, which inflamed the situation even further. A desire for good human relations in any police department is to be desired and an answer showing interest is expedient.

7. Guidelines should be issued for all policemen who respond to the scenes of riots and disorders. These guidelines, to be effective, must be instructive and inclusive and should set department policy for the aims and attitudes suggested for this current age.

Point: Policemen look to the top for certain orders and when they are not issued there is dismay and inaction. At these scenes of disorders it is necessary that a solid attitude be maintained and that the men be able to expect and know what that attitude is.

8. The Police Commissioner at certain times should call a panel of policemen together to discuss with him in an informal manner the problems that are present in the rank and file, the condition of human relations, ways to unite all policemen together for greater efficiency and to share with them his problems, etc.

Point: An informal meeting of the commissioner and policemen would show that cooperation is possible and he will seek any way to obtain it from the men who are patrol rank and file.

9. It should be made known to every man in the department that no crystallization of personal attitudes or politics are to affect the service of any member of the department. There is a job to be done, and it is to be done with maximum efficiency and skill.

Point: The department must define to all policemen where personal areas end and where police proficiency begins. The police service, to be effective, must be without political motivation or personal emotional problems.

10. A human-relations workshop program for policemen should be started in each precinct in this city, where policemen can be involved together on a voluntary basis, to search their attitudes and actions for possible correction. This will produce a nucleus of good attitudes and produce understanding within the department but mostly in the patrol force which is in direct contact with the community. Possible suggestions for consideration of such workshop programs are: (a) members of the force should volunteer to enter the workshop program; (b) members should be guaranteed anonymity in reports and feedback; (c) moderators should be members of the force who are uniquely qualified and trained for the job; (d) this human relations program should be attended on department time; (e) any suggestions forwarded to superiors should be considered and not rejected out of hand; and (f) comfortable facilities should be made available for housing the workshop such as good lighting, comfortable chairs, etc.

Chapter 48

ELIMINATING THE LANGUAGE BARRIER

J. Ross Donald and Louis Cobarruviaz

In our attempts to bridge the communication gap between the public and the police, and especially between minority groups and the police, we, as law-enforcement officers, should take the fullest advantage of every tool at our disposal. One such tool which is seldom utilized is the local radio broadcast. Radio broadcasts are usually available to even the smallest police departments in the nation.

We are aware, of course, that police agencies have long been using the short spot announcement or public-service announcement regarding a specific problem such as driving and drinking, bunco, etc. However, how many departments actually have regularly scheduled programs through which they inform the public about the law, about police procedures and about local law-enforcement problems?

In this article, the first emphasis will be on reaching minority communities (primarily Mexican-American communities). We must realize that there is a tremendous need for enlightenment of the non–Mexican-American middle class with regards to police procedures—particularly, the middle-class juvenile who increasingly does not understand why the police must do many of the things they do. This has been dramatically demonstrated time and time again by the questions asked throughout our city by the public in general.

It is this ignorance of the police functions, procedures and limitations that so often results in a bad police image and fear of the police. Regularly scheduled radio broadcasts can do a great deal to alleviate this problem with minimum cost and loss of man hours.

Note: From *The Police Chief*, June, 1971, p. 8. Reprinted with permission.

Radio stations can write off the time they contribute as a public service and thus are usually very willing to donate time to a well-organized program.

The City of San Jose has a large Mexican-American population, making up approximately 50,000 of the 450,000 total population. Many of these people do not speak English or speak English as a second language. To alleviate some of the friction between this segment of the community and the police, it was decided to begin a police Spanish-language information program. A local radio station, KAZA, was contacted and they agreed to donate, as a public service, a 15-minute broadcast segment every Saturday morning at 10:30 A.M. The purpose was to explain to this portion of the population as much as possible about the police function, about the law and about legal procedures in general. It was the opinion of our Police Chief J.R. Blackmore that much of the friction with the Mexican-American community has been caused by a lack of understanding of established police procedures and the nonrealization of the magnitude of problems faced in the field of law enforcement.

Under direction of the Deputy Chief in charge of the Prevention and Control Division, two community-relations officers developed the basic format. It was decided that in addition to information about the police, guest speakers from various service agencies in the community would be invited to present information which would be of interest to the Mexican-American community. This would include people from probation, parole, legal aid, the District Attorney's office and state employment. In doing so, the police department indicated that it was seriously concerned about the social problems in the community. However, the primary emphasis has been on the most visible aspect of the police—the patrol function. Although the broadcasts are in Spanish, quite often when interviewing a non-Spanish speaking officer regarding his work, one officer would ask the question in English and in Spanish while the other officer would translate the reply.

In the Southwest, where such programs would be extremely beneficial, Spanish-speaking officers should be called upon to handle this task. We have found that these men are sometimes hesitant because they feel that their Spanish, not being perfect, would not be adequate. It has been found that the public will overlook the minor linguistic errors because of their interest in the material presented. In San Jose, the fact that the police department would take such a step to reach the people has in itself changed many attitudes. The Mexican-American community thus begins to realize that we care about them. The officers have done a fine job of putting across our very honest concern.

In the entire San Francisco Bay Area, there are only two Spanish speaking AM radio stations, Radio KAZA and Radio KOFY. The polls for Radio KAZA indicate that its listening audience throughout Santa Clara County just prior to our broadcast is approximately 20,000 to 25,000. This is due to the long-standing popularity of the Mexican-American radio announcer who introduces our program. The majority of these listeners turn the radio on to KAZA and leave it there most of the day.

In our community-relations contacts, we have not received a single negative comment regarding the program, but time and time again positive remarks have been made by members of the Mexican-American community.

The radio station has also allowed us to use their prime time and announcers to cover numerous events such as the Fiesta de las Rosas Parade, the County Fair police display, and Police Day activities. While we were broadcasting at the fairgrounds, numerous Spanish-speaking people came to us to thank us for our program and to offer their compliments.

The success of this program leads me to encourage police agencies to enable capable officers of minority backgrounds to establish regularly scheduled radio programs for their non-English speaking communities. Through this program they can communicate with the people in their own language as to what the laws are, what the local policies are and how the police serve all segments of the population.

Chapter 49

"IT DOESN'T LOOK LIKE A POLICE STATION"

LeRoy C. Jenkins

Racine, Wis., recently dedicated a new 2.3 million dollar Public Safety Building. And at the opening-day ceremonies, one of the most frequently overheard remarks was "It doesn't look like a police station."

These off-the-cuff comments made us extremely proud of our modern three-level building that serves as headquarters for our police, fire and civil defense operations. For we had this exact thought in mind throughout the four years of investigation and study that went into the design of the structure. Yet, in spite of its attractive facade, the building contains some of the latest equipment available for safeguarding our city's 90,000 people.

We achieved the pleasing exterior appearance through the design of an extremely functional interior which segregates the public administrative areas from the work and circulation areas. This vitally important feature provides safe traffic flow for both fire and police vehicles, safety and security in the entry and exit of prisoner traffic and proper and efficient traffic movement for public and departmental personnel.

The distinctive main office wing, enclosed by bronze anodized aluminum wall panels, contains in a compact area all police functions to which the public commonly needs access. We even provided a drive-up window for the convenience of those citizens wishing to pay traffic or parking fines as quickly as possible. In a similar manner, the main entry to the Fire Department,

Note: From *The American City*, July, 1969, pp. 107–108. Reprinted with permission.

characterized by its lofty stairwell constructed of textured stone, gracefully leads to the areas of greatest public use.

Public access to the 50,000-square-foot police headquarters is off one of the city's major arteries. The east wing of the first floor contains offices for the court and traffic captains and the Police Community-Relations Division. This public section also has the drive-up window. In addition, the first floor has separate offices for shift captains, a sergeant's office, day room, roll-call and report area, lockers and a lounge.

The second floor, a beehive of activities, includes offices for the chief of police, inspectors, juvenile authorities, detectives and a conference room. All of these flank separate waiting rooms for the juvenile and detective bureaus. The floor also includes areas for writing investigation reports, juvenile interrogation, a massive record bureau, photography darkrooms, crime laboratory, show-up room and facilities for testing intoxicants.

LOCK-UP SECTION

A second-floor corridor leads to a 30-cell lock-up section. This area also houses our Communications Division. Here the operators have a view of all passageways leading to the tiers of cells. This eliminated the hiring of three regular and two relief jailers and saved us 35,000 dollars a year in salaries.

Use of an Ampex video tape system illustrates how up-to-date the building is. The system includes two recorders, two cameras (one with a zoom lens), and two monitors. We use the equipment for training, drunken driver examinations, criminal interrogation and for covering field work in major crimes. By taping lectures and classroom presentations, we can make certain every man gets a chance to view them. For criminal interrogations, we tape our officers advising a suspect of his rights, along with the subsequent questioning. We retain this for court use if requested.

Also, the department uses recording devices for all division reports. Officers call in these reports to one of three telephone recorders, while plainclothes personnel have their own units.

Department secretaries transcribe the reports from the tapes, reducing by hundreds of hours the time spent by officers who formerly had to fill out these reports by hand.

The new fire headquarters amply fulfills the threefold duty of preventing fires, fighting them and providing rescue service, according to Chief Russell C. Anderson. The building houses a 1,000-gallon triple combination Ward LaFrance cab-forward pumper, a 100-foot American LaFrance aerial ladder truck, two 500-gpm trailer pumps, a Dodge and a Ford panel service truck, an automobile for the Fire Prevention Bureau, and the chief's car.

NEW TESTING PRACTICES

In addition, the fire section has a 9,000-gallon pit for testing pumps. This eliminates the past practices of testing these units at the river. Also provided are hose-drying facilities, a graphic arts department and a technical library. A maintenance room allows not only lubrications and oil changing but the major repairs of all Fire Department vehicles. Moreover, the headquarters contains a 40-bed dormitory, kitchen and dining room facilities. The kitchen has a 23-cubic-foot freezer, refrigerator, broiler, griddle and deep fryer.

Simultaneous with moving into the new building, the Fire Department switched to a new telephone emergency reporting system. The emergency phones, located strategically throughout the city, connect directly with the central communications room at the headquarters building. The system also includes mobile phones that can be set up at beaches or public gathering places as needed. Once reported, fire alarms go out to the various fire stations over a telephone voice-amplification system. These are verified by the alarm dispatcher using a Teletype equipment system. Through this communication network, the department hopes to pinpoint the exact location of fires.

The building's 24,000-square-foot basement houses our Civil Defense Headquarters. Yet all but two of the rooms serve the day-to-day functions of the fire and police departments. These are the Civil Defense office and the emergency communications center.

The center provides both primary and backup communications utilizing radio, telephone and teletype services for all local departments as well as government agencies within Racine County. It also provides communication links with the Southeast Wisconsin Area Civil Defense Emergency Operations Center in Waukesha.

Also located in the basement area are a police pistol range, a school safety and bicycle patrol center, lockers, storage, a 550-seat auditorium, an exercise gymnasium and classrooms. A 170,000 dollar matching federal grant helped to pay for the double-use facilities.

As Mayor William H. Beyer so aptly worded it during the dedication, "The day of the big dumb patrolman and the grim station houses, the overfed fireman in long underwear and red suspenders is over. We are now equipped to cope with today and the future."